Theory of Demand

Real and Monetary

Theory of Demand
Real and Monetary

M. MORISHIMA and others

OXFORD
AT THE CLARENDON PRESS
1973

Oxford University Press, Ely House, London W. 1

GLASGOW NEW YORK TORONTO MELBOURNE WELLINGTON
CAPE TOWN IBADAN NAIROBI DAR ES SALAAM LUSAKA ADDIS ABABA
DELHI BOMBAY CALCUTTA MADRAS KARACHI LAHORE DACCA
KUALA LUMPUR SINGAPORE HONG KONG TOKYO

Printed in Great Britain
at the University Press, Oxford
by Vivian Ridler
Printer to the University

Preface

In this volume a number of papers concerning the theory of consumer's demand are combined with two survey articles on 'qualitative economics' and 'separable utilities' so as to make a unity which may be useful to final-year undergraduates and graduate students as well as research workers in the field.

In the theory of demand we often derive propositions (or laws) of the type, 'an increase in x_i diminishes y_j', by investigating a general equation system having xs as parameters and determining ys as solutions. Qualitative economics asks how rich a system can be in comparative statical laws without quantitative information concerning the coefficients of the equations; and thus it is logically prior to econometrics. In Chapter I all qualitative laws so far obtained are collected, which will be useful to econometricians as well as pure theorists.

Obviously, as is expected and is emphasized by Professor Archibald in Chapter II, purely qualitative results are meagre. However, there are some rather general conditions, such as the hypothesis that equilibrium positions are dynamically stable and the hypothesis that the system satisfies Walras's law, under which qualitative economics becomes more fruitful. Although these conditions are quantitative in the strict sense, they are acceptable in most systems, so that they may be considered to be as basic as purely qualitative information. We find, among other things, (i) that systems satisfying the Hicks–Morishima chain rules of substitutability and complementarity are the only non-trivial systems which obey definite qualitative comparative statical laws provided that the hypothesis of dynamic stability is imposed, and (ii) that gross-substitutes systems are the only non-trivial systems which obey definite qualitative comparative statical laws under the hypothesis that the system satisfies Walras's law or the homogeneity postulate. This explains to some extent why economic theorists are interested in these systems.

Also under the hypothesis that equilibrium positions correspond to the extrema of some function, it is found that an increase in the ith parameter results in a change in the ith variable in a definite direction. However, this theorem of conjugate pairs, though it seems at first sight, as it seemed to Professor Samuelson, that exceptions to it are hard to find in economic theory, is shown to be inapplicable to some economic problems. Archibald points out several exceptions in Chapter II, while in Chapter VI Mr. Martin finds another interesting exception in relation to durable consumption goods.

Chapter III surveys efforts in the other directions. Many authors have tried to specify the utility function so as to be able to derive demand functions in forms suitable for econometrical testing. Among such specifications separable utility functions are of major importance in current economic theory, as is shown by the number of articles that have appeared and are appearing on separability, additive separability, homogeneous separability, and so on. However, it seems to me that, because of the historical fact that the idea of separability was found independently in Japan, the U.S.A., and Scandinavia, research workers in this field are biased nationalistically and do not share common academic information with each other. The same things have been called by different names, and the same results have been obtained repeatedly by different persons. In such circumstances it is highly desirable to have a survey which will give a detailed bird's-eye view, and we hope that Chapter III, in which we have tried as far as possible to avoid bias, will do this job effectively. We hope also that Chapter IV will be useful as an example of the application of the idea of homogeneous separability to the demand theory.

Various theorems discussed in Chapters I and III are applied to problems of consumer's demand in the rest of the book. However, the main purposes there are (i) to remove unsatisfactory assumptions from the Tintner–Hicks multi-period theory of consumption and (ii) to revise the Slutsky theory of demand in such a way that demand functions of monetary goods (money and bonds) can be derived from it. Chapters V,

VI, VII, and X deal with the first problem. In spite of the fact that the Tintner–Hicks theory has been considered for a long time as the standard theory on consumer's choice over time, it is based on restrictive assumptions, such as that the consumer has precise expectations of future prices, that all commodities are perishable, and that a gap between the receipts and the expenditures in each period has to be filled by buying or selling bonds, but not by increasing or decreasing cash balances. We extend the theory so as to allow for uncertain price expectations in Chapter V, so as to be able to deal with durable consumption goods in Chapters VI and VII, and so as to admit substitutability between cash and bonds (as two means of transferring transaction balances in one period to another) in Chapter X. These extensions are partial in the sense that in each extension, only one of the Tintner–Hicks assumptions is removed, while the others are kept. But it is not difficult to synthesize them into a general theory, though it will be a very complicated one. A model presented by Mr. Gray and Professor Parkin in Chapter XII may be regarded as a kind of generalization of Chapter X, in spite of the fact that it is not multi-periodic; in fact, it treats cash requirements for transactions as being stochastic.

The second problem is the subject of Chapters VIII, IX, and XI. Chapter VIII reproduces a paper of mine published in 1952, which applies the idea of separability to the analysis of the demand for monetary goods. This paper still seems to me valid, but as it was written before many important articles on utility tree and portfolio selection appeared, it needs to be related to later contributions and reviewed in the light of more developed economic theory. This is done in Chapter IX, where it is shown that the general Slutsky effect can be split up into three effects: income, substitution, and want pattern effects. Want pattern effects, a new member of the Slutsky equation, are analysed in relation to the problems of ostentatious demand in Chapter IX and those of portfolio selection in Chapters IX and XI. Comparative statical laws of portfolio selection are derived there both with and without the assumption that the objective function depends on the expected return and the variance of return from asset holding only. In particular Chapter XI develops a revealed-preference-type analysis of portfolio selection, though it has to assume a mean–variance indifference map behind the scenes.

Three of the chapters in this book consist of papers that have previously been published elsewhere; they are

II: G. C. Archibald, 'The Qualitative Content of Maximising Models', *Journal of Political Economy*, vol. 73, 1965,

IV: M. Morishima, 'The Problem of Intrinsic Complementarity and Separability of Goods', *Metroeconomica*, vol. 11, 1959,

VIII: M. Morishima, 'Consumer's Behaviour and Liquidity Preference', *Econometrica*, vol. 20, 1952.

We owe thanks to the editors of these journals for permission to reproduce these articles. In the original version of his paper Professor Archibald acknowledged a long-term debt to his colleagues in the Staff Seminar on Methodology, Measurement, and Testing in Economics at the London School of Economics, and to Professor K. Lancaster. He was also grateful to Hugh W. Folk, Dipak Banerjee, Peter B. Kene, and Sidney Winter for comments he had received during the writing of this paper. I should like to repeat my expression of gratitude to Francis Seton for his help with the paper originally published in *Metroeconomica*. In revising the manuscript for publication we have been helped by the comments of Professor W. M. Gorman on Chapter II. We are also indebted to Ross Chapman, Herschel Grossman, and Leslie Robb for comments on earlier drafts of Chapter XII. Most of the work in this book was carried out with support from the Social Science Research Council, for which we give thanks. R. E. Bailey, M. E. Burns, and C. A. Pissarides worked for us as research assistants.

Most of the papers printed here were written while we were colleagues at the University of Essex.

We should like to make a particular mention of two other

former colleagues there, Professor R. G. Lipsey and Professor R. W. Clower, who are especially prominent in the subjects which are dealt with in this book, and who naturally had much influence on all of us. Although we have all (save one) left Essex, we shall never forget the exhilaration of helping to build a modern university in the oldest town of England.

M. M.

August 1972

Contents

Part III. Consumption

Part IV. Money

I. Qualitative Economics and Comparative Statics

M. G. ALLINGHAM *and* M. MORISHIMA

1. Introduction

1.1. *Qualitative economics*

QUALITATIVE economics is concerned with the derivation of meaningful theorems from economic systems that are specified only qualitatively, that is where only the signs of the elements in the Jacobian are known. In this chapter we investigate a general equation system in a number of variables with some locally unique equilibrium positions. Given the signs of the coefficients of the system we examine whether the variables converge to some new equilibrium levels when the parameters undergo some small specified change, and what predictions may be made concerning the direction of the change from the old to the new equilibrium positions. The problems examined thus constitute the qualitative side of local stability and comparative statics.

The relevance of the problem is essentially its generality, for there is a one-to-many correspondence between qualitative and quantitative specifications. This was first raised by Samuelson in the *Foundations*,(1) where he proposed three sources of meaningful theorems in economics: (i) 'qualitative economics', (ii) the hypothesis that equilibrium positions are stable, and (iii) the hypothesis that equilibrium positions correspond to the extrema of some function. We consider the first of these, first in isolation, then in conjunction with the others, and again in conjunction with other economic hypotheses. The investigation of the properties of purely qualitative systems (that is (i) alone) and of stable qualitative systems (that is (i) with (ii) or (iii)) is basically a mathematical problem, for the results are of sufficient

(1) Samuelson [1], chapter 3.

generality to apply to any type of system, though they are of particular interest in economics; once we introduce purely economic hypotheses we clearly restrict the applicability of the results.

It should be noted at the outset that qualitative economics is not a well-defined area, and we offer no formal definition at this stage. In a loose sense we may consider qualitative economics as economic theory based on the signs rather than magnitudes of certain entities. This, however, is somewhat arbitrary, for the information that an entity Z is in the interval $[0, \infty]$ is qualitative, but that Z is in the interval $[\alpha, \infty]$, or $[0, \beta]$, or $[\alpha, \beta]$ is not. A more basic problem, however, concerns the nature of Z, for the information that $Z > 0$ is qualitative for an unspecified entity Z, but if Z turns out to be the determinant of a 2×2 matrix (a_{ij}), then $Z > 0$ implies

$$a_{11}a_{22} > a_{12}a_{21}, \quad \text{or} \quad a_{11}a_{22} \in [a_{12}a_{21}, \infty],$$

which is quantitative. Because of this, at this stage we loosely consider qualitative economics as being only the qualitative band of the qualitative–quantitative spectrum along which we may move from purely qualitative systems through quasi-qualitative systems to the interface with quantitative systems. Since our interpretation of the subject-matter is to some extent arbitrary, the work surveyed is also to some extent arbitrary. We attempt to draw together the more important results explicitly concerned with the theory of qualitative economics, and only more briefly indicate the parts of 'standard' economic theory implicitly using qualitative methods and the region where the two merge. Indeed it is important to note that a large part of standard economic theory, including applications such as 'if x increases what happens to y?', is essentially qualitative, and could perhaps be investigated more efficiently through explicitly qualitative theory.

The remainder of this section (1) presents a brief historical review of the subject, followed by a formal statement of the basic model and definition of the problem. We then indicate some points of notation and give some established mathematical results which are used later; these concentrate on the theory of cycles in matrices, and on a particularly relevant class of matrix, the non-negative cycle or 'M'-class. (Such matrices where the Hicks–Morishima chain rule—see below—applies are here termed M-matrices, though they are termed $\tilde{M}$-matrices by Karlin [**1**] to distinguish them from Metzler matrices.) The section concludes with an indication of some applications of the theory of qualitative economics, and of some possible extensions.

The next section (2) investigates the solvability of purely qualitative systems, and gives the conditions for such systems to be solvable in terms of signs on the basis of the sign patterns of their coefficients alone. This is approached in three ways, firstly using the theory of cycles in matrices developed in section (1), secondly by constructing 'standard forms' based on determinantal conditions, and thirdly in the context of linear spaces. Having considered solvability we then turn to stability, and investigate the conditions for the system to be stable for all numerical values conforming to its sign pattern, and also for it to be stable for some such values.

Section (3) introduces the general quasi-qualitative information that the system is dynamically stable (the second of Samuelson's hypotheses), and investigates what difference this makes to its solvability; this is the qualitative side of the correspondence principle. Using static stability as a link this is then modified to the information that the equilibrium position corresponds to the extremum of some function (the third of Samuelson's hypotheses), and the new conditions for solvability are investigated. Clearly stability is not directly relevant in this section.

Section (4) introduces some specific quasi-qualitative information of an economic nature: that of Walras's law and of homogeneity, both separately and then together, under which restrictions conditions for solvability and stability are again investigated.

The final section (5) considers the relevance of the other three main sections for the derivation of theorems in comparative statics. It compares and extends such available theorems, and adds some new comparative statical laws.

1.2. *Historical review*

As has been mentioned above the relevance of qualitative economics was first emphasized in 1947 by Samuelson [**1**], who indicated the need for a 'qualitative calculus'. The first attempt at providing this was not, however, made until 1962, which marks the start of the subject in an explicit form. This start was made by Lancaster [**1**], who attempted to construct from determinantal conditions a 'standard form' into which all solvable systems could be manipulated, this giving the necessary and sufficient conditions for solvability. However, in 1964 Gorman [**1**] pointed out that many of the theorems in this original study were false because of confusion over weak and strong inequalities (i.e. between non-negativity and positivity and conversely), and also indicated the general case of which Lancaster's standard form was a particular example. This prompted a reply by Lancaster [**2**] synthesizing the two approaches and formulating Gorman's conditions in a new standard form.

The next attack on the problem was from a different angle. In 1965 Lancaster [**3**] formulated the problem more rigorously in the context of a linear space and its subspaces, with 'qualitative' being defined on orthants in the space or some subspace, thus differentiating between weak and strong inequalities; this was used to formulate a method for testing the solvability of a given system. This was followed a year later by the same author's extension simplifying the method, particularly that for deriving the actual solution, into a straightforward algorithm.(2)

We may distinguish two main movements in qualitative economics; the first, discussed above, investigating solvability alone through determinant and cone theory, the second investigating solvability and stability together mainly through cycle theory. The first work of the second movement was in 1965 when Quirk and Ruppert [**1**] (implicitly) used cycle theory to derive the necessary and sufficient conditions for stability of the system

(2) Lancaster [**4**].

(on the basis of its sign pattern alone). This was followed in 1967 by the examination by Bassett, Habibagahi, and Quirk [**1**] of the relation between qualitative economics and systems based on the M-class of matrices (defined below), particularly when stability is assumed. The implications of the stability hypothesis, and the conditions under which it may be applied non-vacuously, were further examined a year later by Quirk [**2**]. At the same time, Bassett, Maybee, and Quirk [**1**] also extended the results available under the stability hypothesis, as well as those on the M-class of matrix, and their study also developed a cycle approach as an alternative to the Gorman–Lancaster standard form approach for the conditions for solvability in purely qualitative systems. Again at the same time, Quirk and Ruppert [**3**] examined the conditions for solvability under the alternative general hypothesis that the equilibrium position corresponds to the maximum of some function, both unconstrained and constrained. Finally, in 1968 and 1969 Quirk [**1**, **3**] investigated solvability and stability under the more particular economic hypotheses that in a general equilibrium system Walras's law alone, or Walras's law and homogeneity, apply; more recently Hicksian stability under the Walras's law hypothesis has also been investigated in an unpublished paper by Habibagahi and Quirk [**1**].

The above summary is intended only as an indication of the historical development of the main ideas in the field. More specialized works which have not been mentioned include Archibald's analysis of the solvability of maximizing models when qualitative information is not available, and Witte's explanation of the so-called Patinkin paradox in terms of qualitative theory.[(3)] A brief survey of the subject is given by Quirk and Saposnik [**1**], and some of the more important mathematical results are collected together by Maybee and Quirk [**1**].

The studies mentioned here form the admittedly arbitrary basis of this survey, other works being considered mainly in their relation to these.

(3) See Archibald [**3**], contained, as Chapter II, in this volume, and Witte [**1**].

1.3. *Statement of the model and problem*

Our model consists of a system in n variables $y_1,\ldots, y_n$ and, without loss of generality, one parameter α, the equilibrium values of the variables $\tilde{y}_i$ being given by the n equations

$$F_i(\tilde{y}_1,\ldots,\tilde{y}_n,\alpha) = 0 \quad (i = 1,\ldots,n), \tag{1}$$

where the functions F_i are differentiable with respect to all their arguments. Differentiating (1) and evaluating all partial derivatives at their equilibrium values, we have the comparative statics system

$$\left[\frac{\partial F_i}{\partial y_j}\right]\left[\frac{\mathrm{d}\tilde{y}_j}{\mathrm{d}\alpha}\right] = -\left[\frac{\partial F_i}{\partial \alpha}\right] \quad (i, j = 1,\ldots, n),$$

which we may write as

$$Ax = b, \tag{2}$$

where $A \equiv [\partial F_i/\partial y_j]$ is an $n \times n$ matrix and $x \equiv [\mathrm{d}\tilde{y}_j/\mathrm{d}\alpha]$ and $b \equiv -[\partial F_i/\partial\alpha]$ are $n \times 1$ vectors. This is our basic model, which we examine for solvability.

To investigate the stability of this model we assume a dynamic tatonnement adjustment process of the form

$$\dot{y}_i = G_i[F_i(y_1,\ldots,y_n,\alpha)] \quad (i = 1,\ldots, n), \tag{3}$$

where the functions G_i are differentiable with $\mathrm{d}G_i/\mathrm{d}F_i > 0$ and $G_i(0) = 0$ for all i, and where $\dot{y}_i \equiv \mathrm{d}y_i/\mathrm{d}t$ is the time derivative of y_i. Approximating these in the neighbourhood of equilibrium by Taylor's series we have, omitting non-linear terms and again evaluating all partial derivatives at their equilibrium values,

$$[\dot{y}_j] = \left[\frac{\mathrm{d}G_i}{\mathrm{d}F_i}\right]\left[\frac{\partial F_i}{\partial y_j}\right]([y_j]-[\tilde{y}_j]) \quad (i, j = 1,\ldots, n),$$

which we may write as

$$\dot{y} = DA(y-\tilde{y}), \tag{4}$$

where D is a diagonal $n \times n$ matrix whose diagonal elements are $\mathrm{d}G_i/\mathrm{d}F_i > 0$, and $\dot{y}$, y, $\tilde{y}$ are $n \times 1$ vectors.

The solution of (4) is given by

$$y(t)-\tilde{y} = \sum_j \kappa_j \mathrm{e}^{\lambda_j t} V^j,$$

where λ_j is the jth characteristic root of the $n \times n$ matrix DA, with associated characteristic vector V^j, κ_j is a constant (provided that all roots are distinct; if λ_j is repeated r times, κ_j is a polynomial in t of degree at most $r-1$), and e is the base of natural logarithms. This converges in the sense that $\lim_{t\to\infty} y(t) = \tilde{y}$, or is stable, iff (if and only if) the real parts of all λ_j are negative. Thus the system (2) is stable (under a tatonnement process with speeds of adjustment given by the elements of a diagonal matrix D) if all characteristic roots of DA have negative real parts, or equivalently DA is a stable matrix.

We now define the sign of a scalar α as

$$s(\alpha) = + \text{ if } \alpha > 0; \quad s(\alpha) = 0 \text{ if } \alpha = 0; \quad s(\alpha) = - \text{ if } \alpha < 0,$$

α being of opposite sign to β if $s(\alpha) = s(-\beta) = -s(\beta)$. For real $n \times 1$ vectors and $n \times n$ matrices we have

$$s(x) = [s(x_j)], \qquad s(A) = [s(a_{ij})] \quad (i, j = 1,..., n),$$

and the sets of similarly signed vectors and matrices

$$\bar{x} = \{y \mid s(y) = s(x)\}, \qquad \bar{A} = \{B \mid s(B) = s(A)\}.$$

These sets are mutually exclusive, so $x \in \bar{x}$ and $x \in \bar{y}$ imply $\bar{x} = \bar{y}$. All y in a given $\bar{x}$ are similarly signed, as are all B in $\bar{A}$. $s(x)$ is termed a qualitative vector (Q-vector), and $s(A)$ a qualitative matrix (Q-matrix). If $s(x_j) \neq 0$ for all j, x lies in the interior of some orthant of R^n (real n-space), and $s(x)$ is an interior Q-vector; conversely, if $x_j = 0$ for some j, x lies on the boundary of some orthants in R^n and $s(x)$ is a boundary Q-vector. An equivalent notation is used for Q-matrices. Thus, for example, $[s(1)\,s(2)\,s(-1)]$ is an interior Q-vector $[+\,+\,-]$, but $[+\,0\,-]$ is a boundary Q-vector. Similarly

$$A = \begin{bmatrix} 1 & -2 \\ 3 & 0 \end{bmatrix} \text{ and } B = \begin{bmatrix} 3 & -1 \\ 2 & 0 \end{bmatrix}$$

belong to the same set,

$$\bar{A} = \begin{bmatrix} + & - \\ + & 0 \end{bmatrix}.$$

We may now define the system (1) as qualitatively solvable (Q-solvable), locally implied, if $s(\mathrm{d}\tilde{y}/\mathrm{d}\alpha)$ may be derived unambiguously from knowledge of $s(\partial F/\partial y)$ and $s(\partial F/\partial \alpha)$, or formally,

$$Ax = b \text{ is Q-solvable if } B \in \bar{A},\ c \in \bar{b},\ By = c \text{ imply } y \in \bar{x}.$$

Similarly we may define the system (4) as qualitatively stable

(Q-stable), again locally implied, if it may be shown to be stable from knowledge of $s(\partial F/\partial y)$ alone (note that

$$s(\mathrm{d}G/\mathrm{d}F \cdot \partial F/\partial y) = s(\partial F/\partial y)$$

since $\mathrm{d}G/\mathrm{d}F$ is a diagonal matrix with positive elements), or formally

$$Ax = \dot{x} \text{ is Q-stable if } B \in \bar{A} \text{ implies } By = \dot{y} \text{ is stable.}$$

We may now formulate our twin basic problems, which we emphasize are local, of (i) solvability and (ii) stability more formally as:

(i) characterize $\bar{A}$ and $\bar{b}$ such that $Ax = b$ is Q-solvable,

(ii) characterize $\bar{A}$ such that $Ax = \dot{x}$ is Q-stable.

Supplementary concepts and problems are defined in context.

1.4. *Mathematical preliminaries*

We now review some established mathematical results which we use below; as is to be expected these are predominantly concerned with matrix theory.

We first make clear the notational convention used. As far as possible scalars are represented by Greek letters, α, vectors by lower case letters, x, with typical elements x_j, and matrices by upper case letters, A, with typical elements a_{ij}, rows A_i, and columns A^j; a submatrix of A is written as A^{ij}, the cofactor of element a_{ij} as A_{ij}, and the jth principal minor of order i as $A_j^{(i)}$. To avoid repetition we make it clear now that all matrices have all elements real, and are square of order $n \times n$ unless it is indicated to the contrary; for clarity any non-square matrix, which will be of order $n \times (n+1)$, is underlined, $\underline{H}$ (this does not apply to submatrices, A^{ij}). A prime applied to a vector or a matrix denotes its transpose.

The basic mathematical theory used here but not generally in economics is that of cycles in matrices; this is discussed by Maybee [**1**], and summarized by Bassett, Maybee, and Quirk [**1**]. We define a cycle of length r in a matrix A as the product of the r terms

$$a_{il}\, a_{lm} \ldots a_{st}\, a_{ti},$$

so a cycle of length one is simply a diagonal element a_{ii}, of length two a product $a_{ij} a_{ji}$, and so on. We term a cycle of length greater than one a proper cycle, and of length greater than two a full cycle.

Two matrices A, B are said to be cyclically equal if every cycle of A has the same value as the corresponding cycle of B. A basic result obtained by Bassett, Maybee, and Quirk [**1**] is that if A and B are indecomposable (see below) they are cyclically equal iff there exists a non-singular diagonal matrix D such that $B = D^{-1}AD$.

A chain (of length r) from i to j in A, written $a(i \rightarrow j)$, is defined as the product of r terms

$$a_{il}\, a_{lm} \dots a_{st}\, a_{tj},$$

so a chain is a 'broken cycle', for $a(i \rightarrow j)a_{ji}$ is a cycle of length $r+1$; clearly a chain of length one is the single element a_{ij}, of length two the product $a_{ik}\, a_{kj}$, and so on.

An immediate application of the theory of cycles concerns decomposability. Note that a matrix A is decomposable if by identical row and column permutations it may be brought to the form

$$\begin{bmatrix} A^{11} & A^{12} \\ 0 & A^{22} \end{bmatrix},$$

where A^{11}, A^{22} are square; otherwise it is indecomposable. Clearly then A is indecomposable iff there is a non-zero chain $a(i \rightarrow j)$ of some length for each distinct pair of indices, i, j. In such a case there will exist a non-zero proper cycle $a(i \rightarrow j)a_{ji}$ for some non-zero a_{ji}, so we have the result that a matrix with all proper cycles zero is decomposable. Thus, for example, if A is of the pattern

$$s = \begin{bmatrix} - & + & + \\ 0 & - & 0 \\ 0 & + & - \end{bmatrix},$$

there are three cycles of length two, $a_{12}\, a_{21}$, $a_{13}\, a_{31}$, $a_{23}\, a_{32}$, and two of length three, $a_{12}\, a_{23}\, a_{31}$, $a_{13}\, a_{32}\, a_{21}$, all of which are zero, and A is decomposable. If, however, A is of the pattern

$$s = \begin{bmatrix} - & + & + \\ - & - & 0 \\ 0 & + & - \end{bmatrix},$$

we have $a_{12}\, a_{21} \neq 0$ and $a_{13}\, a_{32}\, a_{21} \neq 0$, so A is indecomposable.

More basically, however, we may use the theory of cycles in the calculation of determinants. This is developed by Bassett, Maybee, and Quirk [**1**]; here we consider an alternative explanation of this. Let $[p_1,...,p_n]$ be some permutation of the basic index vector $[1,...,n]$, and define $\delta[p_1,...,p_n] = 1$ if $[p_1,...,p_n]$ is obtained from this basic index vector by interchanging indices an even number of times, and $\delta[p_1,...,p_n] = -1$ if an odd number of changes is required. Then we may write the determinant of A as

$$|A| = \sum \delta[p_1,...,p_n]a_{1p_1}...a_{np_n},$$

where the summation is over all possible permutations $[p_1 ... p_n]$. Thus, for example, if $n = 2$,

$$|A| = \delta[1,2]a_{11}a_{22}+\delta[2,1]a_{12}a_{21}$$
$$= a_{11}a_{22}-a_{12}a_{21}.$$

This formulation gives an immediate explanation of the effects on $|A|$ of interchanging rows or columns, or of having a zero row or column, and similar operations. Now it is clear that each product

$$a_{1p_1}...a_{np_n}$$

constitutes, if $p_i \neq i$ for all i, either a cycle of length n in A or two or more cycles of lesser lengths; by taking account of this we may then express the determinant in terms of the cycles of the matrix. By considering the cofactor of an element in A as $\pm$the determinant of some $(n-1)\times(n-1)$ submatrix of A we may equivalently express it in terms of the cycles of this submatrix, or equivalently in terms of the chains in A.

Matrices may be classified on the basis of their cycles into those with non-negative cycles and those with non-positive cycles. The first class may be identified with the class of M-matrices; that is square matrices A which may be brought by identical row and column permutations to the form

$$\begin{bmatrix} A^{11} & A^{12} \\ A^{21} & A^{22} \end{bmatrix},$$

where the diagonal blocks are non-negative and square, and off-diagonal blocks are non-positive; if A^{11} is of order $k\times k$ and A^{22} of order $(n-k)\times(n-k)$, A is said to be partitioned at k. In the interior case (all elements non-zero) Morishima [**1**] shows that an equivalent definition is

$$s(a_{ii}) = +, \qquad \text{all } i, \tag{5}$$

$$s(a_{ij}) = s(a_{ik}\, a_{kj}), \quad \text{all distinct } i, j, k, \tag{5'}$$

which together imply that all cycles are positive.(4) Also important is the associated negative diagonal class of matrix obtained from an M-matrix, that is matrices of the form $A-\alpha I$ where A is an M-matrix and α exceeds all diagonal elements of A; such matrices are termed reduced M-matrices, the M-conditions (5′) clearly still applying. We should note that if a_{ij} represents the slope of the demand curve for commodity i in terms of the price of commodity j, these important conditions imply that, in the gross sense, substitutes of substitutes and complements of complements are substitutes whereas substitutes of complements and complements of substitutes are complements.

An indecomposable M-matrix A (partitioned at k) is similar to a Frobenius matrix A^* (a matrix with non-negative elements —so clearly its cycles are all non-negative), in the sense that A can be reduced to A^* by multiplying the first k rows and k columns of A by -1. Alternatively, A^* may be seen to be a special case of A partitioned at $k = 0$ or n. Bassett, Maybee, and Quirk [**1**] show that all indecomposable matrices with non-negative cycles are M-matrices, and conversely. This does not, however, apply in the decomposable case, as is apparent from considering the Q-matrix

$$\begin{bmatrix} + & + & 0 \\ + & + & 0 \\ - & + & + \end{bmatrix},$$

where all cycles of length one and one cycle of length two are positive and other cycles are zero, yet which is not an M-matrix.

The most relevant result concerning this class of matrix is immediately derived from the Perron–Frobenius theorems(5)

(4) (5′) implies $s(a_{ij}) = s(a_{ji})$ from $s(a_{kj}) = s(a_{ki}\, a_{ij})$ and $s(a_{ki}) = s(a_{kj}\, a_{ji})$; hence $a_{ik}\, a_{kj}\, a_{ji} > 0$. Similarly for longer cycles.

(5) Gantmacher [**1**].

because of the similarity between A and A^*. This is the Morishima theorem.(6)

THE MORISHIMA THEOREM. *If $A = M-\alpha I$ where M is an indecomposable M-matrix, then A is stable iff α exceeds the maximal characteristic root of M; in this case $-A^{-1}$ is an interior M-matrix (or A^{-1} is an interior anti-M matrix).*

We may note that when $k = n$ a reduced M-matrix becomes equivalent to a gross substitutes matrix, that is a matrix with all diagonal elements negative and off-diagonal elements positive; this is the particular case of the M-class of matrices investigated by Mosak [**1**], Arrow and Hurwicz [**1**], and others.

Finally we mention three basic theorems concerning the stability of general matrices. Here the principal minor of order i in A, $A^{(i)}$, is said to be *nested* in that of order $i+1$, $A^{(i+1)}$, if $A^{(i+1)}$ includes all the row and column indices of $A^{(i)}$; if A has a nested sequence of principal minors $A^{(i)}$ with $(-1)^i A^{(i)} > 0$ for all i, then A is Hicksian. Further, A has quasi-dominant diagonal if A is indecomposable and there exist some $d_j > 0$ such that

$$d_j|a_{jj}| \geqq \sum_{i \neq j} d_i|a_{ij}|$$

for all j, with strict inequality for at least one j.(7) The three theorems are as follows.

(i) THE ROUTH–HURWITZ THEOREM. *A is stable iff all*

$$k_i \equiv \sum_j (-1)^i A_j^{(i)} > 0$$

and

$$\begin{bmatrix} k_1 & k_3 \\ 1 & k_2 \end{bmatrix} > 0, \quad \begin{bmatrix} k_1 & k_3 & k_5 \\ 1 & k_2 & k_4 \\ 0 & k_1 & k_3 \end{bmatrix} > 0, \ldots, \quad \begin{bmatrix} k_1 & k_3 & \cdots & 0 \\ 1 & k_2 & \cdots & 0 \\ \cdot & \cdot & \cdots & \cdot \\ \cdot & \cdot & \cdots & \cdot \\ \cdot & \cdot & \cdots & \cdot \\ 0 & 0 & \cdots & k_n \end{bmatrix} > 0.$$

(ii) THE FISHER–FULLER THEOREM.(8) *If A is Hicksian then there exists a diagonal matrix D with positive diagonal such that DA is stable.*

(6) Morishima [**1**].

(7) The indecomposability requirement may be removed if each indecomposable subset of these inequalities has at least one strict inequality.

(8) Fisher and Fuller [**1**].

(iii) THE MCKENZIE THEOREM.[9] *A matrix with quasi-dominant negative diagonal is stable, and if it has all off-diagonal elements positive then all elements in its inverse are negative.*

Other general theorems are used less frequently, and are stated in the context.

1.5. *Applications and extensions*

It is not the main purpose of this survey to examine previous applications of qualitative economics, but we indicate here the general nature of these and where they may be found.

An indication of the relevance of purely qualitative economics may be found in the original work on qualitative economics by Lancaster [**1**]. Using two comparable five-equation models, this gives a qualitative explanation of one of the more important controversies in macro-economics, that between Keynes and 'the Classics'. All the differences between these models are differences in assumption of the sign pattern of the Jacobians (recalling that zero is a sign), and as qualitative economic theory indicates that the signs of certain elements in the Jacobian are irrelevant to the sign pattern of the solutions, it transpires that the only relevant difference between the Keynesian and Classical models is (respectively) the existence or absence of money illusion in the labour supply function. If this exists then the levels of employment and of real wages change when the quantity of money changes; if it does not exist there is the Classical dichotomy between real and monetary quantities.

A similar example in the case where stability is assumed is given by Quirk [**2**], where two Keynesian-type systems each with three equations are compared. Neither of these is Q-stable nor Q-solvable in the purely qualitative case, but when stability is assumed one system becomes (partially) Q-solvable, whereas the other is still not Q-solvable.

The importance of incorporating quasi-qualitative economic information is again illustrated in a macro-model by Witte [**1**], who investigates the so-called Patinkin paradox: an excess demand for commodities implies a decrease in the price of bonds,

(9) McKenzie [**1**].

but either an increase or decrease in the price of commodities. This paradox is shown to arise through ignoring the economic information implied by Walras's law, which provides restrictions on the numerical values of coefficients; thus although the purely qualitative system has no Q-solution, the quasi-qualitative economic system has a Q-solution. This solution is that as long as there is full employment and the rate of interest appears in the money function then the price of commodities rises.

These three examples illustrate the applications of each of our three main sections. A number of further applications have been given: for example under the maximizing assumption without qualitative information, Archibald [**3**] shows that the impossibility of piecemeal welfare economics is due solely to the absence of Q-solvability in the general case, while with qualitative information Quirk and Ruppert [**3**] derive some results on the theory of the firm for both unconstrained and constrained profit maximization. Examples of the actual techniques of solution are provided in many places; of particular interest is the solution of a five-equation macro-model by Lancaster [**4**].

These applications have been mentioned since they come from the more applied parts of economics, and thus are relatively indirect; clearly the immediate applications are in the more basic field of general equilibrium theory, and these are indicated in context.

Finally, we briefly consider some possible extensions of qualitative economics. Firstly, there are a number of particular gaps in the theory, which are indicated in context, and which mainly concern the extension of results from the interior case to the boundary, though this has received some attention from Habibagahi [**1**]. There is also the combination of various types of economic hypothesis, for example, the combination of the stability and 'economic information' (such as Walras's law and homogeneity) assumptions.

In a wider sense, since qualitative economics merges into general economic theory, more work on this interface may be valuable; this is essentially the introduction of quantitative information, which has received some attention by Lancaster

[**3**, **4**]. Another area which has hardly been entered in the explicitly qualitative literature is that of the global aspects of Q-solvability and Q-stability (we are here mainly concerned with the local problems); the extension of local to global Q-stability under economic constraints in the three-variable case has, however, been made by Quirk and Ruppert [**2**], and global results have been obtained in the related literature, for example those by Morishima [**3**, **4**] on the gross substitutes and M-cases. In the final section we consider some global extensions.

Two aspects which have received no attention but which might prove interesting are the relations between qualitative economics and the theory of separability of functions, and between qualitative economics and the theory of identification in econometric models, for these areas clearly have some ground in common.

The main purpose of this chapter, then, is to synthesize the various aspects of the subject, or to attempt to uncover what Bassett, Maybee, and Quirk [**1**, p. 561] have termed 'the chain that will someday tie together everything that has been done on qualitative economics'.

2. Purely Qualitative Systems

2.1. *Introduction*

In this section we consider the purely qualitative system $Ax = b$. We assume only knowledge of $s(A)$, $s(b)$, and commence by examining its Q-solvability; in other words we investigate under what conditions we may derive $s(x)$ or for what sign patterns of A, b we can determine the sign pattern of the solution, x. There are, however, degrees of Q-solvability: the system is *completely* Q-solvable if $s(x_j)$ may be determined for *all* j, and *partially* Q-solvable if $s(x_j)$ may be determined for *some* j. Now if A is non-singular we have $x = A^{-1}b$, so we first consider the conditions for A to have a signed inverse, or be qualitatively invertible (Q-invertible), or formally,

$$\text{characterize } \bar{A} \text{ such that } B \in \bar{A} \text{ implies } B^{-1} \in \bar{A}^{-1}.$$

We then consider the main problem of Q-solvability, since in general Q-invertibility is neither necessary nor sufficient for

Q-solvability. We may note, however, that if only one element of b, say b_j, is non-zero, Q-invertibility becomes sufficient, and in fact all that is necessary is that the jth column of A^{-1} be signed. This is Samuelson's 'conjugate pairs' case,(10) and since $b \equiv -[\partial F_i/\partial\alpha]$, this corresponds to the situation in which the shift parameter enters only one, the jth, equation; as Samuelson has shown, the assumption of conjugate pairs involves little loss of generality, and covers almost all models in economics.

We compare three approaches to the problem of Q-solvability, the first based on cyclical conditions, the second on standard forms (or explicit sign patterns) derived from determinantal conditions, and the third based on linear spaces. Finally, the problems of Q-stability and potential stability are discussed. The equilibrium should be at least potentially stable, because if it is Q-unstable it will never be established unless the economy is in the state of equilibrium at the outset by chance.

2.2. *Q-invertibility*

In considering Q-invertibility we first note that the (i,j) element in A^{-1} is the ratio of the cofactor A_{ji} to the determinant $|A|$, so for Q-invertibility of A we require that the signs of all cofactors and of the determinant of A be known, with, of course, the latter non-zero. This in turn requires that all terms in (the expansion of) each cofactor and the determinant should be weakly of the same sign, with some non-zero term in the determinant.

In view of our results on Q-stability below we consider the case where A has negative diagonal. In this case Bassett, Maybee, and Quirk [**1**] have shown that $s(|A|)$ is known iff all cycles of A are non-positive. If there is some positive cycle of A of length $r > 1$ (all cycles of length one are identically negative in the negative diagonal case) then without loss of generality let this be

$$a_{12} \dots a_{r-1r}\, a_{r1} > 0,$$

so there is in $|A|$ a term

$$\delta[2,\dots,r,1,r+1,\dots,n]a_{12} \dots a_{r-1}\, a_{r1}\, a_{r+1\,r+1} \dots a_{nn}$$

(10) Samuelson [**1**].

of sign $(-1)^{r-1}(-1)^{n-r} = (-1)^{n-1}$; there is also the diagonal term

$$\delta[1,\ldots,n]a_{11}\ldots a_{nn}$$

of sign $(-1)^n$, that is of opposite sign to the first term, so their sum and $|A|$ are not signed. Sufficiency follows since if there are h diagonal elements and k proper cycles in the term

$$\delta[p_1,\ldots,p_n]a_{1p_1}\ldots a_{np_n},$$

then

$$\delta[p_1,\ldots,p_n] = (-1)^{n-h-k},$$

and thus if all k proper cycles are non-positive

$$s(\delta[p_1,\ldots,p_n]a_{1p_1}\ldots a_{np_n}) = s(a_{11}\ldots a_{nn}) \quad \text{or } 0,$$

and all terms in $|A|$ are weakly of the same sign.

As all principal minors of order $n-1$ may be calculated similarly, an equivalent result applies to all diagonal cofactors. Using a similar argument to that for $|A|$ we may extend this to off-diagonal cofactors providing that all chains $a(j \to i)$ in the cofactor A_{ij} are weakly of the same sign.

Combining these results Bassett, Maybee, and Quirk [**1**] show

THEOREM 2.1. Q-invertibility. *If A has negative diagonal, it is Q-invertible iff all its cycles are non-positive and all chains $a(j \to i)$ in any off-diagonal cofactor A_{ij} are weakly of the same sign.*

This theorem may be illustrated by considering the negative diagonal Q-matrix

$$s(A) = \begin{bmatrix} - & + & + \\ - & - & 0 \\ 0 & + & - \end{bmatrix}.$$

Negative diagonality, of course, implies that all cycles of length one are non-positive, and we note that the remaining cycles,

$$a_{12}a_{21}, \quad a_{13}a_{31}, \quad a_{23}a_{32}, \quad a_{12}a_{23}a_{31}, \quad a_{13}a_{32}a_{21},$$

are also non-positive; further, all chains $a(j \to i)$ in each off-diagonal cofactor A_{ij} are weakly of the same sign, for example in A_{23}, the cofactor of a_{23}, the chains $a(3 \to 2)$ are a_{32}, $a_{31}\,a_{12}$, which are both non-negative. Thus the conditions of the theorem are satisfied, and A has a signed inverse. By direct calculation we have $s(|A|) = -$ and

$$s(A^{-1}) = \begin{bmatrix} - & - & - \\ + & - & + \\ + & - & - \end{bmatrix}.$$

If, however, we change $s(a_{31})$ from 0 to $-$ we have

$$s(A^*) = \begin{bmatrix} - & + & + \\ - & - & 0 \\ - & + & - \end{bmatrix},$$

and all cycles are still non-positive (so $|A^*|$ is signed), but now in A_{23} the chains $a(3 \to 2)$ are not weakly of the same sign, for

$$a_{32} > 0, \qquad a_{31}a_{12} < 0;$$

so A_{23}, and thus the (2, 3) element in the inverse, will not be signed. Direct calculation gives

$$s(A^{*-1}) = \begin{bmatrix} - & - & - \\ + & - & + \\ + & ? & - \end{bmatrix},$$

where ? indicates an unsigned element.

Theorem 2.1 provides an answer to the Q-invertibility problem in the negative diagonal case. Clearly if A is Q-invertible then the determinant and all diagonal cofactors are non-zero. Consider, however, the off-diagonal cofactor A_{ij}: if a_{ji} is non-zero then it forms together with diagonal elements a non-zero term in A_{ij}; if a_{ji} is zero and if A is indecomposable, then from the cyclic interpretation of decomposability discussed in section 1 there is some non-zero chain $a(j \to i)$, which cannot contain elements from the ith row or jth column of A, and so this chain forms, together with diagonal elements, a non-zero term in A_{ij}. We thus have the result of Maybee and Quirk [1] that if A has negative diagonal and is indecomposable and Q-invertible, then all elements of A^{-1} are non-zero. This does not apply in the decomposable case since some off-diagonal cofactor must then be zero.

Though, for stability reasons, we do not investigate M-matrices here, two results obtained by Maybee and Quirk [**1**] for these are worth noting. The first is that in the interior case such matrices are the only matrices leaving a Q-matrix invariant, that is $B \in \bar{A}$ implies $AB \in \bar{A}$ iff A is an M-matrix. Thus if all diagonal elements of A are less than unity the reduced M-matrix $A-I$ has an inverse which is the negative of an M-matrix since in

$$-(A-I)^{-1} = (I-A)^{-1} = I+A+A^2+...$$

all terms are M-matrices (providing the quantitative restrictions are such that this series converges). The second is that in the boundary case if B is an indecomposable M-matrix with all diagonal elements less than unity, then $-(B-I)^{-1}$ is an interior M-matrix. The first of these ties a result obtained by Krein and Rutman [**1**] that matrices leaving a Q-matrix invariant are similar to Frobenius matrices (and conversely) with the result that all M-matrices are similar to Frobenius matrices (and conversely), while the second provides a basis from which all the important results of the Perron–Frobenius theorem may be applied to M-matrices as well as to strict Frobenius matrices.

Related to the problem of matrices leaving a Q-matrix invariant is that of matrices leaving a Q-vector invariant, mentioned by Maybee and Quirk [**1**], that is the class of A such that $s(Ax) = s(x)$, for $s(x) \neq 0$. In the interior case $s(Ax) = s(x)$ iff the ith row of A, A_i, has the same sign pattern as x where $x_i > 0$, and the opposite pattern where $x_i < 0$; that is iff all $s(A_i) = s(x_i x')$. This may be generalized to the problem of characterizing the class A such that if $Ax = y$ any $u \in \bar{x}$ is mapped into some $v \in \bar{y}$, the condition in this case involving the sign of y_i rather than x_i, that is all $s(A_i) = s(y_i x')$. General results are not available in the boundary case, but equivalent conditions are available for monotonicity: $Ax > 0$ implies $x \geq 0$ iff A has positive diagonal and non-positive off-diagonal elements, with no non-zero proper cycles.

2.3. *Q-solvability: cycle approach*

We now turn to full Q-solvability. By the independent re-indexing or multiplying by -1 of rows or columns, the Q-solvable system,

$$Ax = b, \tag{1}$$

may be converted into

$$\tilde{A}\tilde{x} = \tilde{b}, \tag{2}$$

where $\tilde{A}$ has negative diagonal and $-\tilde{x}$, $\tilde{b}$ are non-negative. The procedure for this is shown by Bassett, Maybee, and Quirk [**1**]. Clearly the Q-solvability of (1) implies that of (2).

From this conversion procedure and the above Q-invertibility result we have the following results on Q-solvability. Firstly, all non-zero terms in $|\tilde{A}|$ must have sign $(-1)^n$, the necessary and sufficient conditions for which, in the negative diagonal case, are that all cycles should be non-positive, as shown above. Secondly, if $\tilde{b}_j > 0$ then, as $\tilde{x} \leq 0$, elements of the jth column of A^{-1} are negative, or cofactors of elements in the jth row of $\tilde{A}$ must have sign $(-1)^{n-1}$, which may be expressed in the chain form used above.

Bassett, Maybee, and Quirk thus obtain:

THEOREM 2.2. Q-solvability (cycle approach). *$Ax = b$ is Q-solvable iff, by the independent reindexing and/or multiplying by -1 of rows or columns, it may be brought to the form $\tilde{A}\tilde{x} = \tilde{b}$ where $-\tilde{x}$, $\tilde{b}$ are non-negative, $\tilde{A}$ has negative diagonal and all cycles non-positive, and if $\tilde{b}_i$ is positive, then all chains $\tilde{a}(j \to i)$ are non-negative.*

This theorem may be illustrated by considering (1) with A as the matrix used in the example of Theorem 2.1, and b of the sign pattern $s(b') = [0, 0, -]$:

$$\begin{bmatrix} - & + & + \\ - & - & 0 \\ 0 & + & - \end{bmatrix} \begin{bmatrix} s(x_1) \\ s(x_2) \\ s(x_3) \end{bmatrix} = \begin{bmatrix} 0 \\ 0 \\ - \end{bmatrix}.$$

We may convert this to (2) by writing $\tilde{A} = DAD^{-1}$, $\tilde{x} = Dx$, and $\tilde{b} = Db$, where

$$D = \begin{bmatrix} -1 & 0 & 0 \\ 0 & +1 & 0 \\ 0 & 0 & -1 \end{bmatrix}.$$

Then (2) becomes

$$\begin{bmatrix} - & - & + \\ + & - & 0 \\ 0 & - & - \end{bmatrix} \begin{bmatrix} -s(x_1) \\ s(x_2) \\ -s(x_3) \end{bmatrix} = \begin{bmatrix} 0 \\ 0 \\ + \end{bmatrix}.$$

Now $\tilde{A}$ has negative diagonal, and we may check that all its cycles are non-positive; further, $\tilde{b}$ is non-negative, and

$$b_1 = b_2 = 0.$$

We also have all chains $\tilde{a}(j \to 3) \geqq 0$; these are $\tilde{a}_{13}, \tilde{a}_{23}, \tilde{a}_{12}\tilde{a}_{23}, \tilde{a}_{21}\tilde{a}_{13}$. Thus the conditions of the theorem are satisfied, and $-\tilde{x}$ should have a positive solution, which implies that

$$s(x') = [+ - +].$$

Using the inverse of A calculated above we may immediately verify this by writing $x = A^{-1}b$, or

$$s(x) = \begin{bmatrix} - & - & - \\ + & - & + \\ + & - & - \end{bmatrix} \begin{bmatrix} 0 \\ 0 \\ - \end{bmatrix} = \begin{bmatrix} + \\ - \\ + \end{bmatrix}.$$

If, however, $s(b') = [- \; 0 \; -]$, we still have $\tilde{b}$ non-negative under the same conversion, and thus the same $\tilde{A}$ with negative diagonal and no positive cycles, but all chains $\tilde{a}(j \to 1)$ are not non-negative, for $\tilde{a}_{32}\tilde{a}_{21} < 0$. Thus the conditions of the theorem are not satisfied, and $\tilde{x}$ and x may not be signed. Here direct calculation clearly gives

$$s(x) = \begin{bmatrix} - & - & - \\ + & - & + \\ + & - & - \end{bmatrix} \begin{bmatrix} - \\ 0 \\ - \end{bmatrix} = \begin{bmatrix} + \\ - \\ ? \end{bmatrix}.$$

Note that in the conjugate pairs case where $\tilde{b}_i$ is the only non-zero element of $\tilde{b}$, the chain condition relates only to chains ending in the ith row of $\tilde{A}$.

2.4. *Q-solvability: standard form approach*

We next consider an alternative approach to the problem of Q-solvability based on standard forms, or explicitly on sign patterns. Here we treat the n variables $x_1, \ldots, x_n$ and parameter α symmetrically, and now write the system (1) in the form

$$\underline{H}y = 0, \tag{3}$$

where $\underline{H} \equiv [A, -b]$ is an $n \times (n+1)$ matrix and $y' \equiv [x', 1]$ is an $(n+1) \times 1$ vector.

As the illustration of Theorem 2.2 suggests, there is (except in the trivial case where $n = 1$) some positive number of zero elements in $\underline{H}$ required for Q-solvability of (3). There will then be a special case of the general system where $\underline{H}$ has exactly the minimum number of zero elements required for Q-solvability, or where there is maximum interdependence. We investigate this special case before proceeding to the general case.

The minimum number of zero elements is a necessary though not sufficient condition for Q-solvability. For the system to be completely Q-solvable, Lancaster [**1**] has shown that the matrix $\underline{H}$ must have at least $\frac{1}{2}n(n-1)$ zero elements, that is

$$N(0) \geqq \tfrac{1}{2}n(n-1).$$

However, for partial Q-solvability, this may be weakened to

$$N(0) \geqq \tfrac{1}{2}(n-1)(n-2),$$

provided that at least $n-1-(N(0)-\frac{1}{2}(n-1)(n-2))$ of the non-zero elements differ in sign from the remainder; this is illustrated by an example below.

This provides a simple counting rule for the necessary conditions for Q-solvability; sufficiency, however, depends on the arrangement of elements of different sign as well as their number. As in the cyclic approach we may independently reindex or multiply rows or columns of $\underline{H}$ by -1; then in this maximum interdependence case where $N(0) = \frac{1}{2}n(n-1)$, the system is completely Q-solvable iff $\underline{H}$ may be transformed by these operations to Lancaster's standard form $\underline{\tilde{H}}$, where

$$\tilde{h}_{ii} < 0, \quad \tilde{h}_{ij} = 0 \text{ for } i > j, \quad h_{ij} \geqq 0 \text{ for } i < j \;\; (i,j = 1,\ldots,n) \tag{4}$$

or where

$$S(\underline{\tilde{H}}) = \left[\begin{array}{cccc|c} - & & & & \oplus \\ & \cdot & \oplus & & \cdot \\ & & \cdot & & \cdot \\ 0 & & & \cdot & \cdot \\ & & & - & \oplus \end{array}\right], \tag{5}$$

$\oplus$ indicating $+$ or 0.[11]

If we write $s(\underline{\tilde{H}}) = s([\tilde{A}; -\tilde{b}])$ this implies that $\tilde{A}$ has negative diagonal with all cycles non-positive, and, as all off-diagonal

(11) Of course, in this particular case where $N(0) = \frac{1}{2}n(n-1)$, we must have $+$ in all places where we have $\oplus$ in (5), but we generalize from this below.

elements are non-negative, all chains $\tilde{a}(i \to j)$ are non-negative; this shows the equivalence with Theorem 2.2 in the case where all elements of $\tilde{b}$ are negative, or the maximum interdependence case.

If the system (3) has the above sign pattern of $\underline{\tilde{H}}$ (with $\tilde{b} < 0$) without any transformation, then $y > 0$, so that the system is completely Q-solvable. For partial Q-solvability, however, we may weaken the conditions of (5) to allow the first column of $\underline{\tilde{H}}$ to have any sign pattern.

We now examine the general case, where more independence than is necessary for Q-solvability is permitted. More elements are now assumed to be zero, so the conditions developed above remain sufficient, though not in general necessary. This may be seen from the example

$$\begin{aligned} h_{11}y_1+h_{12}y_2+h_{13}y_3+h_{14}y_4 &= 0 \\ h_{21}y_1+h_{22}y_2 \qquad\qquad\qquad &= 0 \\ h_{33}y_3+h_{34}y_4 &= 0, \end{aligned}$$

where

$$h_{11},\, h_{12},\, h_{21},\, h_{33} > 0; \qquad h_{13},\, h_{14},\, h_{22},\, h_{34} < 0,$$

that is, where

$$s(\underline{H}) = \begin{bmatrix} + & + & - & - \\ + & - & 0 & 0 \\ 0 & 0 & + & - \end{bmatrix}.$$

Here the number of zero elements, 4, exceeds the minimum number required, $\frac{1}{2}n(n-1) = 3$. This system cannot be brought to Lancaster's standard form (5); yet, for example, by considering an increase in y_1, it is clear that all y_i rise and fall together and the system is Q-solvable.

By considering the general case as a generalization of both the maximum interdependence case and this example, Gorman [**1**] has constructed general conditions for Q-solvability, which have been interpreted in terms of a new standard form by Lancaster [**2**]. A system is defined to be partitionable at k $(0 < k < n+1)$ if there is exactly one equation involving variables from both sets, $y^1 \equiv \{y_1,\ldots, y_k\}$ and $y^2 \equiv \{y_{k+1},\ldots, y_{n+1}\}$; each partition itself may be partitionable again, and so on. Clearly if the differentiated (linear) system in $n+1$ variables is to be determinate, it must contain n equations, assuming these to be linearly independent, and a partition of k variables must contain $k-1$ equations. Now if $\underline{H}y$ is partitionable at k we may write

$$\underline{H} = \begin{bmatrix} \overbrace{h^1}^{k} & \overbrace{h^2}^{n-k+1} \\ H^1 & 0 \\ 0 & H^2 \end{bmatrix} \begin{matrix} \}1 \\ \}k-1 \\ \}n-k, \end{matrix}$$

where we take the equation connecting the two blocks as the first. We have

$$\begin{aligned} h^1y^1 + h^2y^2 &= 0, \\ H^1y^1 \qquad &= 0, \\ H^2y^2 &= 0, \end{aligned}$$

where y is partitioned conformably. Now suppose that H^1, H^2 are such as to make their subsystems Q-solvable, giving, without loss of generality, $y^1, y^2 > 0$; then this solution satisfies the first equation, and thus the system is Q-solvable as a whole iff h^1, h^2 are of opposite sign, all elements in either vector being of common sign. The subsystems based on H^1, H^2 may be Q-solvable either because they conform to the maximum interdependence standard form or because they are themselves partitionable into systems satisfying these requirements. Since $s(\underline{H}) = s([A; -b])$, we have then a standard form version of Theorem 2.2, due to Gorman [**1**] and Lancaster [**2**]:

THEOREM 2.2′. Q-solvability (standard form approach). *$Ax = b$ is Q-solvable iff, by independent reindexing or multiplying by -1 of rows or columns, $\underline{H} \equiv [A; -b]$ may be brought either to* (i) *the form $\tilde{\underline{H}}$ where $\tilde{h}_{ii} < 0$, $\tilde{h}_{ij} = 0$ $(i > j)$, $\tilde{h}_{ij} \geqq 0$ $(i < j)$ or to* (ii) *the partitioned form*

$$\tilde{\underline{H}} = \begin{bmatrix} \tilde{h}^1 & \tilde{h}^2 \\ \tilde{H}^1 & 0 \\ 0 & \tilde{H}^2 \end{bmatrix} \begin{matrix} \}1 \\ \}k-1 \\ \}n-k \end{matrix}$$

with $\tilde{h}^1$, $-\tilde{h}^2$ non-negative and $\tilde{H}^1$, $\tilde{H}^2$ in the form of $\tilde{\underline{H}}$ in (i).

This theorem is illustrated by the system examined in connection with Theorem 2.2, where $Ax = b$ is

$$\begin{bmatrix} - & + & + \\ - & - & 0 \\ 0 & + & - \end{bmatrix} s(x) = \begin{bmatrix} 0 \\ 0 \\ - \end{bmatrix},$$

which when written in the form $\underline{H}y = 0$ becomes

$$\begin{bmatrix} - & + & + & 0 \\ - & - & 0 & 0 \\ 0 & + & - & + \end{bmatrix} \begin{bmatrix} s(x) \\ 1 \end{bmatrix} = 0.$$

We first examine the necessary conditions (implicit in the theorem) of the number of zero elements. It is clear that these are satisfied, for $\underline{H}$ has 4 zeros, exceeding the minimum of

$$\tfrac{1}{2}n(n-1) = 3.$$

We now note that this system is not partitionable, for there are at least two equations involving variables from both sets of variables of each possible partition. Thus $\underline{H}$, or $\tilde{\underline{H}}$, is already partitioned as far as possible, so we are only concerned with whether by independent reindexing or multiplying by -1 of rows and columns it may be brought to the form satisfying (4).

It is clear that this is possible, for if we reverse the order of the columns, place the last row first, and multiply columns 1, 2, and 4 by -1 we have

$$s(\tilde{\underline{H}}) = \begin{bmatrix} - & + & + & 0 \\ 0 & - & + & + \\ 0 & 0 & - & + \end{bmatrix}.$$

The conditions of the theorem are satisfied and the system is Q-solvable. Thus the theorem is consistent with Theorem 2.2.

The alternative system examined in connection with Theorem 2.2 has $s(b') = [-\ 0\ -]$, which implies

$$s(\underline{H}) = \begin{bmatrix} - & + & + & + \\ - & - & 0 & 0 \\ 0 & + & - & + \end{bmatrix}.$$

Here the necessary conditions remain satisfied, for the number of zero elements is equal to the minimum number, 3, yet $\underline{H}$

cannot be manipulated into the required standard form, so the system is not (completely) Q-solvable. If, however,

$$s(b') = [- \; - \; -],$$

then

$$s(H) = \begin{bmatrix} - & + & + & + \\ - & - & 0 & + \\ 0 & + & - & + \end{bmatrix},$$

and the necessary conditions for complete Q-solvability are not satisfied. However, those for partial Q-solvability are satisfied, for the minimum number of zero elements is now only

$$\tfrac{1}{2}(n-1)(n-2) = 1$$

provided that at least $n-1-(N(0)-\frac{1}{2}(n-1)(n-2))$, that is $n-1-1 = 1$, non-zero elements differ in sign from the remainder; this is clearly satisfied. By the same operations as used in the first example, $\underline{H}$ may be brought to a required standard form for partial Q-solvability. Direct calculation gives the partial solution $s(x') = |+ \; ? \; ? \,|$.

Adding the number of zeros in the null submatrices in the standard form of (ii) in the theorem and those required to make $\tilde{H}^1$, $\tilde{H}^2$ Q-solvable (as above) we obtain

$$N(0) = \tfrac{1}{2}(n^2-2k^2+2nk-3n+2k).$$

This is a maximum for $k = \frac{1}{2}(n+1)$ (or nearest integer), that is where the system is partitioned into two (approximately) equal subsystems, and a minimum where $k = 1$ or n (equivalent), that is the maximum interdependence case, where $N(0) = \frac{1}{2}n(n-1)$ as above.

2.5. *Q-solvability: linear spaces approach*

We next consider, more briefly, another approach to the problem of Q-solvability, suggested by Lancaster [**3**, **4**]. This considers Q-vectors to be specified on the interior of some given orthant of a given subspace of R^n, or of R^n itself, and Q-matrices as matrices whose columns, or rows, are Q-vectors in this sense. The underlying theory writes the system in the form (3) used in the preceding section and assumes this to have been normalized so that if the system is Q-solvable it gives the solution $y \geq 0$. We then use the basic result of linear algebra that either $\underline{H}y = 0$

has a solution $y \geq 0$ or $p\underline{H} < 0$ has a solution, and find for each column H^j of $\underline{H}$ the region of R^n where there is some p such that $pH^j < 0$. Then if the intersection of these regions over all columns is empty, $p\underline{H} < 0$ has no solution, and $\underline{H}y = 0$ has a solution $y \geq 0$.

This approach, however, requires the appropriate normalization. A simpler technique which does not is based on the fact that if we require a Q-solution for $\underline{H}y = 0$, we need all $H_i y = 0$, implying that all $s(H_i) \neq s(y')$, otherwise $H_i y > 0$, and that all $s(H_i) \neq s(-y')$, otherwise $H_i y < 0$ (unless $H_i = 0$). We may then list by sign pattern all 2^{n+1} orthants in R^{n+1}, and delete all those which have a sign pattern equal or opposite to that of any row of $\underline{H}$. Then if no orthant remains there is no Q-solution, if one remains there is a unique Q-solution, defined on that orthant, giving complete Q-solvability, and if more than one remain there are multiple solutions, defined on these orthants, giving possible partial Q-solvability. Finally, we may note the similarity between this approach and a suggestion made in Samuelson's original indication of the qualitative problem which is implicitly on these lines.

2.6. *Q-stability*

We now consider the Q-stability of the system, that is whether the solution to

$$\dot{x} = Ax \tag{6}$$

converges to the equilibrium position 0, given only the sign pattern of A. As noted in section 1.3, if A is Q-stable, then if D is a diagonal matrix with positive diagonal, DA is also Q-stable, i.e. A is stable for any positive speeds of adjustment d_{ii}. Further, if A is Q-stable with negative diagonal, then all principal submatrices of A are stable. The Routh–Hurwitz theorem indicates that the stability of A depends only on the values of its principal minors, and if A has negative diagonal these all involve a non-zero term involving only diagonal elements; so Q-stability implies that these are not cancelled out by other terms.

We may immediately note two necessary conditions for Q-stability which follow from the Routh–Hurwitz theorem. Firstly

A must have non-positive diagonal, for if $k_1 \equiv -\sum a_{ii}$ is to be positive independently of numerical values of a_{ii} we must have all a_{ii} non-positive (with some negative). Secondly A must be weakly qualitatively skew symmetric, that is, $a_{ij}a_{ji} \leqq 0$ for all i, j, which is similarly implied by the condition that

$$k_2 \equiv \sum_i \sum_{j>i} (a_{ii}a_{jj} - a_{ij}a_{ji})$$

be positive. Clearly these two conditions may be expressed as that all cycles of length one and two respectively are non-positive. A third necessary condition also follows from the Routh–Hurwitz theorem, as is illustrated in the case where $n = 3$; here the third order condition $k_3 > 0$, together with these two conditions, implies that all full cycles are non-positive. On the other hand the remaining Routh–Hurwitz condition,

$$\begin{vmatrix} k_1 & k_3 \\ 1 & k_2 \end{vmatrix} > 0, \quad \text{or } k_1 k_2 > k_3,$$

implies that all full cycles are non-negative. Thus all full cycles must be zero. In the case where $n = 3$, it is clear that these conditions are also sufficient, since they imply the Routh–Hurwitz conditions. We may note that the third condition provides a simple counting criterion for the minimum number of zero elements in a Q-stable matrix, this being $\frac{1}{2}n(n-2)$ for n even, $\frac{1}{2}(n-1)^2$ for n odd (which may be compared with the minimum number required for Q-solvability developed above, that is $\frac{1}{2}n(n-1)$).

Quirk and Ruppert [**1**] have extended these necessary and sufficient conditions to the general order case. Combining the results with the connection between Q-invertibility and Q-stability, noted by Bassett, Maybee, and Quirk [**1**], that if A is Q-invertible and has negative diagonal, then it is Q-stable iff it is boundary symmetric (that is $a_{ij} = 0$ implies $a_{ji} = 0$), we then have(12)

THEOREM 2.3. Q-stability. *If A is indecomposable,* (6) *is Q-stable:* (i) *iff A has all cycles of length one non-positive (with some negative), of length two non-positive, of length three or more*

(12) Quirk and Ruppert [**1**] and Bassett, Maybee, and Quirk [**1**].

zero, and non-zero term in its determinant; (ii) *in the case where all cycles of length one are negative, iff all cycles of length two are non-positive and of length three or more zero*; (iii) *in the case where A is Q-invertible and has negative diagonal, iff A is boundary symmetric.*

This theorem may be illustrated using the same Q-matrix as before, that is

$$s(A) = \begin{bmatrix} - & + & + \\ - & - & 0 \\ 0 & + & - \end{bmatrix}.$$

We first note that this is indecomposable, either in the standard way or, more simply, using the result that this is implied by the existence of non-zero chains $a(i \to j)$ for all distinct i, j. It is clear that A is not Q-stable, for the general conditions (i) are violated because there is a non-zero cycle of length three, that is $a_{13}a_{32}a_{21} < 0$; as all a_{ii} are negative, this of course follows from (ii) as well. As from the illustration of Theorem 2.1 we know that A is Q-invertible, the result also follows from (iii), for A is not boundary symmetric since $a_{13} > 0$, $a_{31} = 0$. It may be seen that the Routh–Hurwitz k_is are positive but we cannot ensure $k_1 k_2 > k_3$.

Consider, however, the Q-matrix

$$s(B) = \begin{bmatrix} - & + & 0 \\ - & - & - \\ 0 & + & - \end{bmatrix},$$

which again is indecomposable. Now all cycles of B of length one are negative, of length two negative, and of length three zero, and there is a non-zero term in its determinant, $b_{11}b_{22}b_{33}$. Thus B satisfies the conditions of (i) (or (ii)) of the theorem, and thus is Q-stable. It may be seen that all the Routh–Hurwitz conditions are satisfied. We may also note that B is boundary symmetric, since $b_{13} = 0$, $b_{31} = 0$, and $b_{ij} \neq 0$ otherwise, and thus as we already know from (i) (or (ii)) that B is Q-stable we may investigate whether B is Q-invertible. This may be checked by direct calculation, or more simply by noting that the conditions of Theorem 2.1 are satisfied (this last stage involves the second result noted below).

A connection between Q-invertibility and Q-stability has been used in Theorem 2.3 (iii); we may also note two interesting connections in the reverse direction, that is between Q-stability on the one hand and Q-invertibility and Q-solvability on the other, due to Quirk and Ruppert [**1**]. Firstly, any Q-stable system is partially Q-solvable for some appropriate choice of b, that is the conjugate pairs case. Secondly, if a Q-stable system is indecomposable with negative diagonal, then it is Q-invertible and therefore completely Q-solvable in the conjugate pairs case. This result does not, however, extend to the decomposable case as may be seen from the example

$$s(A) = \begin{bmatrix} - & - & + \\ + & - & + \\ 0 & 0 & - \end{bmatrix},$$

where A is Q-stable, yet the cofactor A_{31} and thus the inverse are unsigned. Thus decomposable Q-stable systems are not necessarily completely Q-solvable, but are partially Q-solvable if they have a negative diagonal. These results suggest a qualitative correspondence principle between Q-solvability and Q-stability.

Finally, consideration of Theorem 2.3 makes it clear that M-matrices are not Q-stable, though systems based on M-matrices may be shown to be stable under some quasi-qualitative constraints, discussed later.

2.7. *Potential stability*

We have so far examined conditions for the Q-stability of A, that is for A to be stable for *all* numerical values of the appropriate sign, or for *all* $B \in \bar{A}$ to be stable. We may also be concerned with the weaker property of potential stability (P-stability), that is for A to be stable for *some* numerical values of the appropriate sign, or for *some* $B \in \bar{A}$ to be stable. Clearly A may be P-stable if A is not Q-stable. Many systems which are not Q-stable may be interesting, but only if they are P-stable.

It is immediately clear from the McKenzie theorem that any negative diagonal matrix is P-stable, since the diagonal elements may be made sufficiently large in absolute value to be dominant without changing the sign pattern. This will not, however, apply if the diagonal is only non-positive, but Quirk [**2**] has shown that if a matrix with some zero diagonal elements is P-stable it remains so when these zero elements are made positive. Further, the Routh–Hurwitz theorem requires for A to be stable that all $k_i \equiv (-1)^i \sum_j A_j^{(i)} > 0$, so if all non-zero terms in all principal minors of order i have sign $-(-1)^i$ then $k_i \leqq 0$ and A is not stable. A necessary condition for P-stability is then that for each i some principal minor of order i should have sign $(-1)^i$. This and the previous result imply that a matrix with exactly one diagonal element negative is P-stable only if it has some cycle of length two negative, for otherwise we have $k_2 \leqq 0$.

We have then only partial results on P-stability; collecting these Quirk [**2**] shows

THEOREM 2.4. P-stability. (i) *A matrix is P-stable if it has negative diagonal*; (ii) *if A has some diagonal elements positive and B is of the same sign pattern as A except that the positive diagonal elements in A are replaced by zero elements in B, then A is P-stable iff B is P-stable*; (iii) *a matrix is P-stable only if for each i there is a term of sign* $(-1)^i$ *in the expansion of some principal minor of order i.*

This theorem then shows, for example, that the Q-matrix investigated above,

$$s(A) = \begin{bmatrix} - & + & + \\ - & - & 0 \\ 0 & + & - \end{bmatrix},$$

though not Q-stable, is P-stable, since it satisfies the conditions of (i) of the theorem.

Consider, however, the Q-matrix

$$s(B) = \begin{bmatrix} + & + & + \\ - & - & 0 \\ 0 & + & - \end{bmatrix};$$

this does not satisfy the conditions of (i), though it does satisfy those of (iii), since for example

$$a_{33} < 0, \qquad a_{22}a_{33} > 0, \qquad a_{13}a_{32}a_{21} < 0,$$

so we cannot on the basis of the theorem guarantee or rule out P-stability; (ii) only tells us that B is P-stable iff the Q-matrix

$$s(C) = \begin{bmatrix} 0 & + & + \\ - & - & 0 \\ 0 & + & - \end{bmatrix}$$

is P-stable, which is no more help. However, Quirk [**2**] has shown that in the case where $n = 3$ the Routh–Hurwitz theorem may be used to give necessary and sufficient conditions for P-stability; it turns out that the matrix $s(B)$ above is P-stable. On the other hand, we also have an example which satisfies the conditions of (iii) yet which is not P-stable, that is the Q-matrix

$$\begin{bmatrix} - & - & + \\ - & + & 0 \\ 0 & + & + \end{bmatrix};$$

this permits $k_i > 0$ $(i = 1, 2, 3)$, but does not allow $k_1 k_2 > k_3$. The theorem then indicates that we cannot in general be sure of P-stability except in the negative diagonal case, which, together with the importance of this case for Q-stability, is our justification for concentrating on this case in our discussion of Q-solvability. Finally we note that reduced M-matrices are clearly P-stable.

2.8. *Conclusions*

This ends our survey of purely qualitative systems. We may conclude that the scope for purely qualitative economics is small, for as indicated in Theorems 2.2 and 2.2′, solvability requires, apart from particular arrangements of signs, a large number of zero elements in the Jacobian of the system, that is substantial independence, whereas the problem in economics is essentially that of a general interdependent equilibrium.

When stability is required the conditions become much stronger, as Theorem 2.3 indicates; in particular, in the general case where the inverse of the Jacobian is not signed, the condition that all cycles of length two be non-positive implies that in a general equilibrium model no pair of commodities may be unambiguously labelled gross substitutes or complements, that is, that income effects must be strongly asymmetric. Further, the condition that all cycles of length three be zero precludes the Hicks–Morishima chain rule that, in the gross sense, substitutes of substitutes and complements of complements are substitutes while substitutes of complements and complements of substitutes are complements. These conditions are not compatible with most economic models.

Perhaps the most useful result is that connecting stability with the signing of the inverse. If the Jacobian (with negative diagonal) of the system is stable and indecomposable on the basis of its sign pattern, then a shift of demand from the numeraire to some commodity will lead to an increase in the equilibrium price of that commodity, the directions of changes in equilibrium price of all other commodities being unambiguously determined.

This qualitative correspondence, however, places strict restrictions on sign patterns. A possibly more helpful approach is the introduction of some general quantitative restrictions, which allows a weakening of the qualitative conditions. This is the second of Samuelson's sources of meaningful theorems: Samuelson's correspondence principle. Thus by assuming stability, which is necessary for meaningful comparative statics, we are able to impose such restrictions on the system as are useful in deriving some definite comparative statical results. Since we know that the conditions for potential stability are substantially weaker than those for qualitative stability, we restrict our attention to potentially stable systems and assume some safe, sufficiently general, quantitative restrictions, such as the column sums of a Leontief matrix not exceeding unity and capitalists' propensity to save being greater than workers' but less than one, to make the systems actually stable, and examine the conditions for qualitative solvability under the restrictions. This quasi-qualitative approach, which turns out to be more helpful than the purely qualitative approach, is examined in the next section.

3. Stable Qualitative Systems

3.1. *Introduction*

We now consider the imposition of some general quasi-qualitative restrictions on our qualitative system. Since the results derived from any system have no meaningful predictive content unless the system is stable, our basic restriction is that of stability. The main part of this section then investigates the conditions for the Q-solvability of the system $Ax = b$ on the assumption that the numerical values of the elements of A are such as to make it dynamically stable (DS). Formally we define:

$$Ax = b \tag{1}$$

is Q-solvable under DS if $B \in \bar{A}$, $c \in \bar{b}$, $By = c$, and the dynamic stability of A and B together imply $y \in \bar{x}$. Q-invertibility under DS is defined analogously.

Our main problem is then:

characterize $\bar{A}$ and $\bar{b}$ such that $Ax = b$ is Q-solvable under DS.

This then is a qualitative interpretation of Samuelson's correspondence principle. We may note at the start that for this to be non-vacuous A must be P-stable, and as only incomplete conditions for P-stability are available (section 2.7), our results will necessarily be limited.

Although dynamic stability is most relevant here, we also consider the related assumptions of 'static stability' and the maximization hypothesis, that the equilibrium position corresponds to the unconstrained or constrained maximum of some function. The latter constitutes an important case on its own, but is examined with the static stability hypothesis because of the strong mathematical similarity between these two restrictions.

3.2. *Q-invertibility under stability*

As in the purely qualitative case we start with the conditions for Q-stability. Because of our P-stability results we again concentrate on the negative diagonal case.

The immediate implications of the DS assumption on A are apparent from the Routh–Hurwitz conditions, which are of course satisfied here. These conditions include the inequalities

$$k_n \equiv (-1)^n |A| > 0, \qquad k_{n-1} \equiv -(-1)^n \sum_j A_j^{(n-1)} > 0,$$

which show that $|A|$ has sign $(-1)^n$, and at least one principal minor of order $n-1$ has sign $(-1)^{n-1}$; thus for some (unknown) j,

$A_{jj}/A < 0$. We also note that in the simplest case where $n = 2$ all cofactors are merely elements multiplied by a known sign and thus signed, as is $|A|$, so this is clearly Q-invertible.

In the general order case we investigate firstly matrices with non-negative cycles (M-matrices), then those with non-positive cycles. Within the first class we start with the interior case investigated by Bassett, Habibagahi, and Quirk [**1**], where all cycles are positive. As $s(|A|) = (-1)^n$ under DS, A is Q-invertible only if the signs of all cofactors are known. Now the cofactor A_{ij} includes the terms

$$(-1)a_{ji}\,a_{11}\ldots a_{i-1\,i-1}\,a_{i+1\,i+1}\ldots a_{j-1\,j-1}\,a_{j+1\,j+1}\ldots a_{nn}$$

and

$$(-1)^2 a_{jk}\,a_{ki}\,a_{11}\ldots a_{i-1\,i-1}\,a_{i+1\,i+1}\ldots a_{j-1\,j-1}\,a_{j+1\,j+1}\ldots$$
$$\ldots a_{k-1\,k-1}\,a_{k+1\,k+1}\ldots a_{nn};$$

the sign of the first is $(-1)^{n-2+1}s(a_{ji})$, and of the second $(-1)^{n-3+2}s(a_{jk}\,a_{ki})$. As the diagonal elements may be made arbitrarily large in absolute value, we may choose without violating the stability assumption numerical values so that other terms are arbitrarily small in absolute value relative to the above two terms. Then the sign of A_{ij}, and thus of A^{-1}, is indeterminate unless $s(a_{ji}) = s(a_{jk}\,a_{ki})$. Now this condition is merely the M-condition (5′) in section 1, from which it follows that a necessary condition for Q-invertibility in this case is that A should be a reduced M-matrix. Sufficiency of this condition follows from the Morishima theorem.

This identifies the sole class of matrices which are Q-invertible under DS in the interior case, though Bassett, Maybee, and Quirk [**1**] have extended this class in the boundary case, where if A is indecomposable with negative diagonal and some proper cycle positive (and $n > 2$), then it is Q-invertible under DS only if it is a reduced M-matrix; sufficiency of this again follows from the Morishima theorem. This then is the corollary of the result in the interior case; combining the two we have[13]

THEOREM 3.1. Q-invertibility under DS. *If A has negative diagonal and is* (a) *interior or* (b) *indecomposable with some proper*

(13) Bassett, Habibagahi, and Quirk [**1**] and Bassett, Maybee, and Quirk [**1**].

cycle positive, then it is Q-invertible under DS iff it is 2×2 *or a reduced M-matrix.*

This theorem concerns only matrices with no negative cycles; this, however, is no real restriction, for Bassett, Maybee, and Quirk [**1**] have shown that the negative cycle class is irrelevant here in that such matrices are Q-invertible under DS only if they are Q-invertible in the purely qualitative case. The similarities between this theorem and the theorem for Q-invertibility in the purely qualitative case (Theorem 2.1) are apparent, the requirements here being weaker (for the interior case). Also instructive is a comparison between these conditions and the conditions for Q-invertibility where Q-stability obtains (section 2.6), these conditions being stronger (again for the interior case).

For example, the Q-matrix

$$s(A) = \begin{bmatrix} - & + & + \\ - & - & 0 \\ 0 & + & - \end{bmatrix}$$

investigated above is neither interior nor indecomposable with some proper cycle positive, so it does not fit the requirements of the theorem. As, however, it has negative cycles and we know it to be Q-invertible in the purely qualitative case, it clearly is Q-invertible under DS.

However, the Q-matrix

$$s(B) = \begin{bmatrix} - & 0 & - \\ - & - & + \\ - & + & - \end{bmatrix}$$

does fit the requirements of the theorem because it is indecomposable with a positive proper cycle, $b_{13}b_{32}b_{21} > 0$; clearly it is also a reduced M-matrix (partitioned at the index 1), so satisfies the conditions of the theorem and is Q-invertible under DS. But this Q-matrix does not satisfy the conditions of Theorem 2.3 (since it has a non-zero proper cycle and is not boundary symmetric), so is not Q-stable in the purely qualitative case.

The above theorem gives conditions for the existence of a signed inverse, but, as Maybee and Quirk [**1**] have noted, in the indecomposable negative diagonal case all elements in an inverse signed under DS are non-zero. Further, it follows from the Morishima theorem that the inverse of a reduced indecomposable M-matrix under DS has all diagonal elements negative and all off-diagonal elements of opposite sign to the corresponding elements in the original matrix. This is a generalization of the established results that in the gross substitutes case, due to Mosak [**1**], and indecomposable weak gross substitutes case, due to Arrow [**2**] and Morishima [**3**], all elements of the inverse under DS are negative.

3.3. *Q-solvability under stability*

In the investigation of Q-solvability we again consider only matrices with negative diagonal, and commence with the restricted conjugate pairs case. In this case with the kth element b_k of b being non-zero, we have complete Q-solvability if the sign pattern of the kth column of the inverse is known, that is if all cofactors A_{ki} in the kth row of the matrix A are signed, since the assumption of DS implies that $|A|$ is signed with

$$s(|A|) = (-1)^n.$$

As has been demonstrated, all off-diagonal cofactors A_{ki} are signed only if all non-zero chains $a(i \to k)$ in A_{ki} are of the same sign. Further, Bassett, Maybee, and Quirk [**1**] show that the diagonal cofactor A_{kk} is signed only if there are no negative proper cycles containing the index k which have an index in common with a positive cycle in A_{kk}. Thus if A_{kk} is to be signed there can be no index common to a positive cycle of A_{kk} and a negative proper cycle of A. This, together with the chain condition of Q-invertibility, gives the required conditions in the conjugate pairs case.

In the more general case where b may be full, we assume without loss of generality that elements $b_1,\ldots, b_r$ of b are non-negative, and elements $b_{r+1},\ldots, b_n$ are non-positive. Then the system (1) is Q-solvable if columns $1,\ldots, r$ of A^{-1} have the same sign pattern and columns $r+1,\ldots, n$ have the same sign pattern, opposite to that of columns $1,\ldots, r$. For matrices with non-negative cycles the conjugate pairs result may then be extended to the more general case. Bassett, Maybee, and Quirk [**1**] thus obtain:

THEOREM 3.2. Q-solvability under DS. *If A has negative diagonal, $Ax = b$ is Q-solvable under DS iff*

(i) *in the conjugate pairs case where b_k is non-zero and where A is indecomposable:*

(a) *A is a reduced M-matrix, or*

(b) *all cycles of A of length less than n are non-positive and all chains $a(i \to k)$ in any cofactor A_{ki} are weakly of the same sign;*

(ii) *in the general case: after some identical permutation to A and b giving $\tilde{A}$ and $\tilde{b}$, $\tilde{A}$ is a reduced M-matrix, partitioned at r, and $\tilde{b}_1, \ldots, \tilde{b}_r$ are non-negative with $\tilde{b}_{r+1}, \ldots, \tilde{b}_n$ non-positive, or vice versa.*

This is the DS counterpart of Theorem 2.2 and the conditions are clearly weaker. For example the system investigated in connection with Theorem 2.2, that is $Ax = b$, or

$$\begin{bmatrix} - & + & + \\ - & - & 0 \\ 0 & + & - \end{bmatrix} s(x) = \begin{bmatrix} 0 \\ 0 \\ - \end{bmatrix},$$

clearly satisfies the conditions of (i) (b) since $b_2 = b_3 = 0$ and we know that all cycles of A, and thus of A_{11}, are non-positive, and all chains $a(j \to 1)$ in A_{12} and in A_{13} are weakly of the same sign. This system is then Q-solvable under DS.

If, however, we replace the element $s(a_{21})$ by $+$, we obtain the system $Bx = b$, or

$$\begin{bmatrix} - & + & + \\ + & - & 0 \\ 0 & + & - \end{bmatrix} s(x) = \begin{bmatrix} 0 \\ 0 \\ - \end{bmatrix},$$

which clearly does not satisfy the conditions of Theorem 2.2, since B has a positive cycle $b_{12}b_{21}$ and is thus not Q-solvable in the purely qualitative case. This system does, however, satisfy the condition (i) (a) of Theorem 3.2, since B is a weak gross substitutes matrix, and thus a reduced M-matrix partitioned at 0; alternatively it satisfies conditions (i) (b) of the theorem, since $s(B_{11}) = s(A_{11})$ and the chains $b(j \to 1)$ in B_{12} and B_{13} which are of opposite sign to the chains $a(j \to 1)$ in A_{12} and A_{13}

are still weakly of the same sign. Thus although not Q-solvable in the purely qualitative case, this system is Q-solvable under DS. It then follows that the system $Bx = c$, or

$$\begin{bmatrix} - & + & + \\ + & - & 0 \\ 0 & + & - \end{bmatrix} s(x) = \begin{bmatrix} - \\ - \\ - \end{bmatrix},$$

satisfies conditions (ii) of the theorem since B is a reduced M-matrix partitioned at 0 and $b_1,..., b_3$ are non-positive. Therefore this non-conjugate pairs system is Q-solvable under DS, though not in the purely qualitative case.

We have not discussed partial Q-solvability, for which the conditions are clearly weaker; in this case the conditions derived in the theorem need only apply to some of the cofactors A_{ki}.

Again no mention has been made of matrices with negative cycles in the general case, for we cannot extend the conjugate pairs results in this case. We do, however, have the particular result obtained by Bassett, Maybee, and Quirk [**1**] that if A is Q-invertible under DS and is indecomposable with some proper cycle negative, then (1) is always Q-solvable in the conjugate pairs case; it is noted, however, that in this case, A is Q-invertible under DS iff it is so without DS.

3.4. *Static stability*

Theorems 3.1 and 3.2 summarize our results under the DS assumption. As a link between this and the maximization hypothesis we may note the effects of assuming static or Hicksian stability (SS),(14) or of assuming that all principal minors of order i of the matrix A have sign $(-1)^i$. In the conjugate pairs case Maybee and Quirk [**1**] have shown that if A has negative diagonal and is indecomposable, then (1) is Q-solvable under the assumption of static stability iff it is Q-solvable under DS, though results on complete Q-solvability are not available in the general case. Since DS does not imply SS, or vice versa, this implies that if A satisfies DS and not SS, or vice versa, then (1) is not Q-solvable, or alternatively DS

(14) Hicks [**1**].

and SS are equivalent in Q-solvable systems. Partial Q-solvability under SS is, however, always available in the conjugate pairs case, for the definition of a Hicksian matrix immediately implies that x_k is non-positive if the only non-zero (positive) element of b is b_k, where A is weakly Hicksian, and that x_k is negative where A is Hicksian.

Thus static stability is a potentially more useful assumption for Q-solvability than is DS, though as Samuelson [**1**] has shown in general, it is neither necessary nor sufficient for (true) dynamic stability and so is less valid if we require our system to approach a new equilibrium position following a parameter change. Finally, as Morishima [**1**] has shown, in an important class of systems, those based on M-matrices, of which the Hicksian gross substitutes system is a special case, static and dynamic are equivalent.

3.5. *The maximization hypothesis*

We now consider the hypothesis that the equilibrium positions in the underlying model correspond to the regular extrema (maxima or minima) of some function; without loss of generality we consider only the maximum, for if the solution corresponds to the minimum of some function u then this is equivalent to the maximum of the function $-u$.

We continue to use the model (1), but now consider this as being obtained from the equations giving the change in equilibrium values of $\tilde{y}_1,\ldots, \tilde{y}_n$ when some parameter α changes, where $\tilde{y}_1,\ldots, \tilde{y}_n$ are the values corresponding to the regular local maximum of the objective function

$$u(y_1,\ldots, y_n, \alpha).$$

The conditions that u attain a maximum at the point $(\tilde{y}_1,\ldots, \tilde{y}_n)$ are firstly that

$$\frac{\partial u}{\partial y_i} = 0 \quad (i = 1,\ldots, n),$$

and secondly that the Hessian

$$A \equiv \left[\frac{\partial^2 u}{\partial y_i\, \partial y_j}\right] \quad (i, j = 1,\ldots, n)$$

be negative definite. We assume as usual that this is symmetric. The change in equilibrium values is then given by

$$A\left[\frac{\mathrm{d}y_i}{\mathrm{d}\alpha}\right] = -\left[\frac{\partial^2 u}{\partial y_j\,\partial\alpha}\right], \quad \text{or } Ax = b. \tag{1'}$$

We then investigate the Q-solvability of (1′) under the assumption that equilibrium values correspond to the unconstrained maximum of the function (UM), or that A is negative definite.

A similar problem arises if we consider the equilibrium positions as corresponding to the maximum of this function subject to the constraint

$$G(y_1,\ldots, y_n, \alpha) = 0;$$

we assume all $\partial G/\partial y_j$ are non-zero. (The maximum subject to more than one constraint may be discussed in a similar way.)

Let L be the Lagrangian expression

$$L = u(y_1,\ldots, y_n, \alpha)+\lambda G(y_1,\ldots, y_n, \alpha)$$

with λ a Lagrangian multiplier. The maximum conditions are firstly that

$$\frac{\partial L}{\partial y_j} = 0, \quad \frac{\partial L}{\partial \lambda} = 0 \quad (j = 1,\ldots, n)$$

and secondly that the bordered Hessian,

$$A^* \equiv \begin{bmatrix} A & c \\ c' & 0 \end{bmatrix} \equiv \begin{bmatrix} \dfrac{\partial^2 L}{\partial y_i\,\partial y_j} & \dfrac{\partial G}{\partial y_j} \\ \dfrac{\partial G}{\partial y_i} & 0 \end{bmatrix} \quad (i, j = 1,\ldots, n),$$

be negative definite under constraint. The change in equilibrium values is then given by

$$A^*\begin{bmatrix} \dfrac{\mathrm{d}y_i}{\mathrm{d}\alpha} \\ \cdots \\ \dfrac{\mathrm{d}\lambda}{\mathrm{d}\alpha} \end{bmatrix} = -\begin{bmatrix} \dfrac{\partial^2 L}{\partial y_j\,\partial\alpha} \\ \cdots\cdots \\ \dfrac{\partial^2 L}{\partial\lambda\partial\alpha} \end{bmatrix}, \quad \text{or } A^*x^* = b^*. \tag{2}$$

We then investigate the Q-solvability of (2) under the assumption that equilibrium values correspond to the constrained maximum of the function (CM), or that A^* is negative definite under constraint. We interpret Q-solvability and Q-invertibility under UM or CM analogously to Q-solvability under DS.

We first recall the established mathematical propositions due to Hicks [**1**] that under these conditions A^{-1} and A^{*-1} exist with A^{-1} negative definite and $A^{*-1} \equiv \begin{bmatrix} \hat{A} & \hat{c} \\ \hat{c}' & \hat{\delta} \end{bmatrix}$ negative definite under constraint, with $\hat{A}$ being negative semi-definite of rank $n-1$. These imply that all principal minors of order i of A have sign $(-1)^i$, and the determinant of the submatrix consisting of the first r $(r > 1)$ rows and columns of A bordered as in A^*, that is

$$\begin{vmatrix} a_{11} & \cdot & \cdot & \cdot & a_{1r} & c_1 \\ \cdot & & & & \cdot & \cdot \\ \cdot & & & & \cdot & \cdot \\ \cdot & & & & \cdot & \cdot \\ a_{r1} & \cdot & \cdot & \cdot & a_{rr} & c_r \\ c_1 & \cdot & \cdot & \cdot & c_r & 0 \end{vmatrix},$$

is of sign $(-1)^r$. This indicates the strong similarity with the assumption of static stability, for A is Hicksian. These properties, however, include further information, which makes the maximization assumption potentially more useful than that of static stability, and thus potentially more useful than that of dynamic stability.

Before considering these two main problems of determining the conditions on $s(A)$ or $s(A^*)$ for Q-solvability under UM or CM, we note a related result, discussed by Archibald [**3**], which applies to the solvability of the system under the maximization assumption, without qualitative information. This is Samuelson's 'theorem of conjugate pairs' that, under these conditions, (1′) is partially Q-solvable iff only one element of b is non-zero, which follows from the above properties of the inverse. Our qualitative investigation should bear in mind this result, which is obtained without qualitative information.

3.6. *Q-invertibility and Q-solvability under maximization*

We now turn to the main problem, starting with Q-invertibility. As we may always convert the CM case to the UM by substituting the constraint into the objective function, we concentrate on UM.

At the maximum point A is symmetric and Hicksian, and therefore dynamically stable. It then follows directly from Theorem 3.1 that if A is indecomposable it is Q-invertible under UM iff it is 2×2 or a reduced M-matrix. This is extended to the decomposable case by Quirk and Ruppert [**3**] to give:

THEOREM 3.3. Q-invertibility under UM. *A is Q-invertible under UM iff it is block diagonal (that is completely decomposable) with each block a reduced M-matrix.*

For example, the sign symmetric Q-matrix

$$s(A) = \begin{bmatrix} - & + & - \\ + & - & + \\ - & + & - \end{bmatrix}$$

is block diagonal only in the trivial sense, and this block (the matrix) has negative proper cycles, $a_{12}a_{23}a_{31}, a_{21}a_{13}a_{32} < 0$. It is not a reduced M-matrix and is not Q-invertible under UM by Theorem 3.3. On the other hand, the Q-matrix

$$s(B) = \begin{bmatrix} - & - & - \\ - & - & + \\ - & + & - \end{bmatrix}$$

is a reduced M-matrix, having all proper cycles non-negative, and is Q-invertible under UM.

For Q-solvability we first consider the conditions under UM in the conjugate pairs case, that is the conditions for some column of the inverse to be signed. Again using a similar argument to that in the DS case, Quirk and Ruppert [**3**] have shown that if A is indecomposable, some column of A is signed under UM iff all proper cycles are non-negative, that is iff A is a reduced M-matrix.

As under DS we can extend this result to the general case if b can be suitably partitioned and obtain:(15)

THEOREM 3.4. Q-solvability under UM. *$Ax = b$ is Q-solvable under UM in the indecomposable case iff after some identical permutation to A and b giving $\tilde{A}$ and $\tilde{b}$, $\tilde{A}$ is a reduced M-matrix*

(15) Quirk and Ruppert [**3**].

partitioned at r, and $\tilde{b}_1,\ldots,\tilde{b}_r$ *are non-negative with* $\tilde{b}_{r+1},\ldots,\tilde{b}_n$ *non-positive, or vice versa.*

By this theorem, the system

$$\begin{bmatrix} - & + & - \\ + & - & + \\ - & + & - \end{bmatrix} s(x) = s(b)$$

is not Q-solvable under UM for any $s(b)$, since the matrix of the system is not a reduced M-matrix. However, the matrix of the system

$$\begin{bmatrix} - & - & - \\ - & - & + \\ - & + & - \end{bmatrix} s(x) = \begin{bmatrix} + \\ - \\ - \end{bmatrix} \equiv s(c)$$

is a reduced M-matrix partitioned at 1, and $c_1 > 0$, c_2, $c_3 < 0$, so the conditions of the theorem are satisfied and the system is Q-solvable under UM.

If A is decomposable, the conditions of Theorem 3.4 may be weakened to require only at least one indecomposable block of A and the associated part of b to satisfy the conditions of the theorem, with the remaining elements in b zero. This theorem is the counterpart of Theorem 3.2 under DS; clearly the conditions of this theorem are identical with those of part (ii) of Theorem 3.2, since M-matrices are dynamically stable iff they are Hicksian, which is implied by UM.

Under CM, Quirk and Ruppert [**3**] have obtained a very restrictive result on Q-solvability:

THEOREM 3.5. Q-solvability under CM. $A^*x^* = b^*$ is *Q-solvable under CM in the case where* $n > 2$ *iff A is diagonal and only one element of* b^* *is non-zero.*

Consider, however, the example of a linear constraint, where we maximize $u(y_1,\ldots,y_n,\alpha)$ subject to $\sum_{i=1}^{n} p_i y_i = m$. This CM problem produces the system

$$\begin{bmatrix} u_{ij} & p_j \\ p_i & 0 \end{bmatrix} \begin{bmatrix} \dfrac{dy_j}{d\alpha} \\ \cdots \\ \dfrac{d\lambda}{d\alpha} \end{bmatrix} = - \begin{bmatrix} \dfrac{\partial u_i}{\partial \alpha} \\ \cdots \\ 0 \end{bmatrix} \quad (i,j = 1,\ldots,n). \tag{3}$$

If, however, we substitute the constraint into the preference function (eliminating y_n) we have the equivalent UM system,

$$[v_{ij}]\left[\frac{dx_j}{d\alpha}\right] = -[v_{i\alpha}] \quad (i, j = 1,\ldots, n-1), \tag{4}$$

where
$$v_{ij} = u_{ij} - u_{in}\frac{p_j}{p_n} - u_{nj}\frac{p_i}{p_n} + u_{nn}\frac{p_i}{p_n}\frac{p_j}{p_n}, \tag{5}$$

$$v_{i\alpha} = \frac{\partial u_i}{\partial \alpha} - \frac{\partial u_n}{\partial \alpha}\frac{p_i}{p_n}. \tag{6}$$

Now for Q-solvability under the appropriate constraints the above result of Quirk and Ruppert [**3**] requires all off-diagonal u_{ij} in the CM system to be zero, while Theorem 3.4 requires $[v_{ij}]$ in the UM system to be a reduced M-matrix, which is consistent with non-zero off-diagonal u_{ij}.

This apparent inconsistency arises because the conditions of Quirk and Ruppert guarantee complete Q-solvability, that is solvability for the signs of all $dy_j/d\alpha$ and $d\lambda/d\alpha$, under CM, but only for the signs of all $dy_j/d\alpha$ under UM. In many cases, however, Q-solvability for $d\lambda/d\alpha$ is not required, and has no interpretation. We should note then that Quirk and Ruppert's conditions are unnecessarily strict as they require that we sign an irrelevant additional variable. In this context it is interesting to note that in the context of utility theory, Theorem 3.5 implies that an additive form of the utility function (such as Frisch's 'want-independence' or Houthakker's 'addilog' functions) is necessary for complete Q-solvability for $dy/d\alpha$ and $d\lambda/d\alpha$.

Finally, we note that it is meaningless to consider Q-invertibility and Q-solvability in the system (3) unless we accept cardinal utility, for u_{ij} and $\partial u_i/\partial\alpha$ are not invariant in sign with respect to a monotonic transformation $F(u)$ of u. In fact the partial derivatives,

$$\frac{\partial^2 F(u)}{\partial y_i\,\partial y_j} = F'\frac{\partial^2 u}{\partial y_i\,\partial y_j} + F''\frac{\partial u}{\partial y_i}\frac{\partial u}{\partial y_j},$$

$$\frac{\partial^2 F(u)}{\partial y_i\,\partial \alpha} = F'\frac{\partial^2 u}{\partial y_i\,\partial \alpha} + F''\frac{\partial u}{\partial y_i}\frac{\partial u}{\partial \alpha},$$

may take any sign, because F'' is arbitrary, even though $F' > 0$.

On the other hand, the signs of v_{ij} and $v_{i\alpha}$ in (4) are independent of monotonic transformations because of (5) and (6), so it is legitimate to consider Q-invertibility and Q-solvability in the system (4).

3.7. *Conclusions*

This concludes our survey of stable qualitative systems. We must note that since the question of potential stability remains partially open we cannot obtain a complete answer to the questions of Q-solvability under stability. Within this limitation, however, it is apparent that in the larger-dimension cases the stability hypothesis is very strong for systems based on M-matrices, where it provides all the information required, though fairly weak in other cases, where it adds little. There is then a close connection between M-matrices and the qualitative scope of the correspondence principle. See Morishima [**1**].

If we interpret the system as a general equilibrium model of exchange we have, in the general small-dimension case, the result that if a system with three commodities including numeraire is dynamically stable for all speeds of adjustment, then a shift in demand from the numeraire to some commodity does not decrease the equilibrium price of that commodity (and increases it for some particular commodity), the direction of the change in the equilibrium price of the other commodity being unambiguously determined. Little useful knowledge, however, is obtainable in the general larger-dimension case.

For systems of larger dimensions based on M-matrices we have the complete result that if the system is dynamically stable, then a shift in demand from the numeraire to some commodity will result in the equilibrium price of this commodity rising, and the equilibrium price of any other commodity rising if it is a gross substitute for this commodity and falling if it is a gross complement. In the special case of this system, the gross substitutes system, it follows that all prices rise.

We note that the assumption of static stability has little relevance except in systems based on M-matrices, where it is equivalent to the dynamic stability assumption discussed above.

The mathematically similar maximization hypothesis again only yields fruitful results when applied to M-systems. However, if the system is not of the M-type qualitative analysis under the maximization hypothesis gives little information.

On the whole we have increased the strength of our results by incorporating the general quasi-qualitative restriction of stability and maximization; to strengthen these further we must incorporate some more specific restrictions.

4. Qualitative Economic Systems

4.1. *Introduction*

The above two sections have examined mathematical systems whose applicability is general, though they are particularly relevant in economics, where most results have been obtained. We now consider the general equilibrium model of exchange, which is examined for Q-solvability and Q-stability on the assumption that the numerical values of the elements in its Jacobian satisfy some particular conditions prevailing in competitive economies.

We continue to use the same model, but consider this as arising as follows. We have $n+1$ commodities X_i $(i = 0,\ldots, n)$, each with price y_i and the differentiable excess demand function

$$F_i(y_0,\ldots, y_n, \alpha)$$

where α is a parameter representing a shift in these demand functions; the model, $F_i(\tilde{y}_0,\ldots, \tilde{y}_n, \alpha) = 0$, is then considered as giving the equilibrium prices $\tilde{y}_i$ for some given value of the parameter α. This gives the comparative statics system

$$\left[\frac{\partial F_i}{\partial y_j}\right]\left[\frac{\mathrm{d}\tilde{y}_j}{\mathrm{d}\alpha}\right] = -\left[\frac{\partial F_i}{\partial \alpha}\right] \quad (i, j = 0,\ldots, n),$$

where partial derivatives are evaluated at the equilibrium point. If we choose X_0 as numeraire with price $y_0 \equiv 1$, we may write this as

$$\begin{bmatrix} a_{00} & a_0 \\ a^0 & A \end{bmatrix}\begin{bmatrix} 0 \\ x \end{bmatrix} = \begin{bmatrix} \beta \\ b \end{bmatrix},$$

where A is an $n \times n$ matrix, a_0 is a $1 \times n$ vector, and a^0, x, b are

$n \times 1$ vectors all defined over indices 1,..., n only, and a_{00}, β are scalars; we may equivalently write this as

$$A^*x^* = b^*, \tag{1}$$

where A^* is an $(n+1)\times(n+1)$ matrix and x^*, b^* are $(n+1)\times 1$ vectors, defined over indices 0,..., n.

We now introduce two dual restrictions on the model: firstly that Walras's law (WL) applies, that is,

$$\sum_{i=0}^{n} y_i F_i(y_0,..., y_n, \alpha) = 0 \quad \text{for all } y,$$

and secondly that excess demand functions are homogeneous of degree zero in all prices (HZ), that is,

$$F_i(\lambda y_0,..., \lambda y_n, \alpha) = F_i(y_0,..., y_n, \alpha) \quad \text{for all } \lambda > 0 \;\; (i = 0,..., n).$$

Defining physical units so that all $\tilde{y}_i = 1$ and differentiating, the two conditions WL and HZ become, respectively,

$$e'A = -a_0 \quad (\text{and } e'b = -\beta),$$

and

$$Ae = -a^0,$$

where e is an $n \times 1$ vector of unities.

We then investigate the Q-solvability and Q-stability of this system, under WL, under HZ, and under Walras's law and homogeneity together (WH). The concepts of Q-solvability and Q-stability under these restrictions are interpreted analogously to that of Q-solvability under DS in section 3. For example, the system (1) is said to be Q-solvable under WL if its solutions x are of the same sign pattern for all possible A^* and b^* which are of some assumed sign patterns and satisfy WL.

The statement of the restrictions of WL and HZ in the form above makes their duality clear, for they imply respectively zero column sums and zero row sums in A^*. We need not then consider both restrictions independently, for a condition applying to A under WL clearly applies to A' under HZ and vice versa; we thus only examine WL. Also it is clear that WH requires both WL and HZ, so necessary conditions under WH are necessary under WL and under HZ, and sufficient conditions under WL or under HZ are sufficient under WH.

4.2. *Summary of Quirk's results*

The problems of Q-invertibility, Q-solvability, and Q-stability under WL, under HZ, and under WH have been discussed by Quirk [**1**, **3**]. His results are well summarized by himself, so we merely review the main conclusions. Throughout this section we assume strong interdependence everywhere (or the interior case only), that is $a_{ij} \neq 0$ and $a_{0j} \neq 0$ (in the case of WL) or $a_{i0} \neq 0$ (in the case of HZ) for all i and j. Then under WL Quirk [**1**] obtains:

THEOREM 4.1. Q-invertibility and Q-solvability under WL. *With $n > 3$, A is Q-invertible under WL iff by the independent reindexing of its rows and multiplying by -1 of its columns A may be brought to the form $\tilde{A}$ such that $\tilde{A}$ is a gross substitutes matrix and $\tilde{a}_0 = -e'\tilde{A}$ is positive; the system $Ax = b$ is Q-solvable under WL iff by the above reindexing and multiplying procedure it is transformed into $\tilde{A}\tilde{x} = \tilde{b}$ such that all diagonal elements of $\tilde{A}$ are negative, $\tilde{a}_0$ is positive, all non-zero elements of $\tilde{b}$ have the same sign, and*

(i) *in the conjugate pairs case with the unique non-zero element b_k, all off-diagonal elements of the k-th column of $\tilde{A}$ have the same sign, all other off-diagonal elements being positive;*(16)

(ii) *in the general case, all off-diagonal elements of $\tilde{A}$ are positive.*

THEOREM 4.2. Q-stability under WL. *With $n > 2$, A is Q-stable under WL if A is a gross substitutes matrix and a_0 is positive.*

Theorems 4.1 and 4.2 exclude small-dimension cases for $n \leqq 3$ and $n \leqq 2$, respectively, which have also been examined by Quirk. Since the Q-invertibility part of Theorem 4.1 requires $\tilde{A}$ to have positive cycles whereas Theorem 2.1 on pure Q-invertibility precludes this, no matrix which is Q-invertible under WL is Q-invertible in the purely qualitative case. Further, any matrix satisfying the requirements of the Q-invertibility of Theorem 4.1 without any reindexing of rows and multiplying by -1 of columns is a dynamically stable matrix by Theorem 4.2,

(16) $\tilde{A}$ of such a sign pattern is referred to by Quirk as the generalized gross substitutes matrix.

so it follows from Theorem 3.1 that any interior matrix with $n > 3$ satisfying the requirements of the Q-invertibility under WL is Q-invertible under DS. The converse is not true, however, because dynamically stable M-matrices with negative off-diagonal elements cannot be transformed into the form required for Theorem 4.1 so that they are not Q-invertible under WL. This means that dynamic stability is more informative than WL.

Next under WH, Quirk [**3**] assumes $a_{ii} < 0$, $a_{ij} \neq 0$, $a_{0i} > 0$, and $a_{j0} > 0$ for all i and j, and obtains:(17)

THEOREM 4.3. Q-invertibility and Q-stability under WH. *A is Q-invertible (for $n > 3$) and Q-stable (for $n > 2$) under WH iff A is a gross substitutes matrix.*

Finally, Quirk considers the possibility of having negative elements in the numeraire row and column. Assuming gross substitutability between each pair of non-numeraire commodities he obtains:

THEOREM 4.4. Q-stability under WH (gross substitutes case). *Assume $a_{ii} < 0$, $a_{ij} > 0$ for all i and j $(i \neq j)$, and $a_{00} < 0$, $a_{i0} \neq 0$, $a_{0j} \neq 0$ for all i and j; then A is Q-stable under WH (for $n > 3$), iff* (i) $a_0 > 0$ *or* $a^0 > 0$, *or* (ii) *one element of a^0 is negative with the others positive and the corresponding element of a_0 is positive with the others negative, or vice versa.*

4.3. *Conclusions*

This ends our survey of qualitative economic systems. We may conclude that the particular quasi-qualitative economic restrictions we have incorporated significantly increase the scope of the qualitative model of section 2, but increase this less than the incorporation of the general quasi-qualitative restriction of stability in section 3.

We have then the result that if all commodities including the numeraire are substitutes and Walras's law or homogeneity applies, then a shift in demand from the numeraire to some commodity will raise the equilibrium price of all commodities,

(17) The small-dimension cases excluded by the theorem can be discussed directly.

the system being stable for all speeds of adjustment. Further, if all commodities including the numeraire except one, k, are substitutes and demand for commodity k obeys the rule

$$\frac{\partial F_k}{\partial y_j} > 0, \qquad \frac{\partial F_j}{\partial y_k} < 0, \qquad \frac{\partial F_k}{\partial y_k} < 0 \quad \text{for all } j,$$

then a shift in demand from the numeraire to commodity k raises the price of commodity k and diminishes the price of all other commodities if Walras's law applies. We may note that this requires strongly asymmetric income effects for commodity k, which precludes qualitative stability under Walras's law.

This concludes our examination of the results available in the explicitly qualitative literature. To obtain more concrete comparative statical laws we must move to related areas, using our qualitative results as a basis to work from. We do this in the final section.

5. Comparative Statics

5.1. *Introduction*

The preceding three sections have been concerned with specifying conditions, or the type of system, under which qualitative results are obtainable. In this final section we reverse the process, and take a number of given systems, which are economically interesting, then examine what qualitative information, in the form of comparative statical laws, we may derive from them.

We first consider three typical existing systems: the gross substitutes exchange system, the Leontief production system (these two being essentially equivalent mathematically), and the M-exchange system. We then present some new comparative statical results for these systems, which may be considered as the 'fourth and fifth Hicksian laws'. Finally, we reconsider the definitions of substitutability and complementarity.

5.2. *Existing systems*

We now summarize the main results available for existing systems, starting with the gross substitutes system. This concerns the model specified in section 4 where WL and HZ hold and all commodities, including the numeraire, are gross substitutes for one another, or equivalently the system $A^*x^* = b^*$ where

$$s(A^*) = s\left(\left[\begin{array}{c|c} a_{00} & a_0 \\ \hline a^0 & A \end{array}\right]\right) = \left[\begin{array}{c|ccc} - & & + & \\ \hline & - & & + \\ + & & \ddots & \\ & + & & - \end{array}\right]$$

(the negative diagonal being implied by WH). For clarity we refer to this as the extended gross substitutes system, distinguishing this from the system where only non-numeraire commodities are gross substitutes. It is immediate from Theorem 4.3 that A is Q-stable under WH; thus we may legitimately consider (in this extended gross substitutes system) comparative statical implications without specifying any further restrictions to ensure stability.

The comparative statics we are concerned with arise from a simple shift in demand from the numeraire to some non-numeraire commodity j, that is some shift in α such that $\partial F_j/\partial\alpha = -b_j > 0$ for some particular j, $\partial F_0/\partial\alpha = b_0 = -b_j$, all other $\partial F_i/\partial\alpha$ being zero, F_i denoting the excess demand for commodity i. This then is the conjugate pairs case, so it is immediate from Theorem **3.2** (part (i) (b)) that the (non-extended) system $Ax = b$ is Q-solvable. We have the result mentioned in section 4, or Hicks's first and second laws, that the prices of all commodities rise.(18) This is the only information which follows directly from the results of the preceding sections. Also well known, however, is Hicks's third law, that the price of commodity j increases proportionately more than the price of any other commodity. A separate well-known result in this case is Samuelson's LeChatelier principle; that the increases in all prices are less if the supply of some other good is adjusted so as to keep its price constant, than if no supply is adjusted and all prices are allowed to vary.(19)

(18) See Hicks [**1**] and Morishima [**3**]. That the directions of all price changes are unambiguously determined also follows from Theorem 3.2 (part (i) (a)), as we have stability, or from the result in section 3 connecting Q-solvability with Q-stability.

(19) Samuelson [**1**] and Morishima [**3**].

These results apply to the interior, or strong gross substitutes, case, and also to the boundary, or weak gross substitutes, case, if the main submatrix A is indecomposable. In the weak gross substitutes case where only the extended matrix A^* is indecomposable and at least one element of a_0 or a^0 is positive, the system is still stable, though the above comparative statics results, apart from Hicks's first law that the own-price increases, are weakened into the corresponding weak form: 'rises' must be replaced by 'does not fall'.

We now turn to a Leontief production system, retaining the same mathematical model $Ax = b$. Here, however, we interpret $x \geq 0$ as a vector of gross outputs from n industries, $-b \geq 0$ as a vector of the corresponding net outputs, or final demands, and $A = C - I$ where $C \geq 0$ is a matrix of input coefficients (c_{ij} being the amount of commodity i used in producing a unit amount of commodity j). Since $c_{ii} < 1$ for all i, A is a (weak) gross substitutes matrix; the assumption of productivity of C assures the stability of A.[20] In this system we have results equivalent to the three Hicksian laws and the LeChatelier principle: when A is indecomposable an increase in the final demand for commodity j gives rise to an increase in the outputs of all commodities with that of commodity j increasing by the largest proportional amount, and the increases in all outputs are less if other outputs are kept constant than if they may vary. When A is decomposable these results apply in their corresponding weak forms.[21]

The system $Ax = b$ discussed above is the output side of the Leontief system. We also have the dual price side, $pA = -v$ where p is a vector of prices and $v > 0$ the vector of value-added coefficients. We may transpose this system to obtain a system qualitatively equivalent to the output system, and thus immediately obtain the price versions of the three Hicksian laws and the LeChatelier principle.

(20) C is said to be productive if there is a positive x such that $x > Cx$. This assumption is equivalent to the Hawkins–Simon conditions, for which a sufficient condition is that column sums of A are non-positive, with some negative if A is indecomposable.

(21) See, for example, Morishima [**3**].

We finally turn to the M-system. This again concerns the model specified in section 4 where WH and the Hicks–Morishima chain rule

$$s(a_{ik}) = s(a_{ij}\,a_{jk}) \quad \text{for all distinct } i, j, k$$

apply. It is apparent from Theorem 4.3 that this system is not Q-stable, i.e. not necessarily stable on the basis of its sign pattern alone, except in the degenerate case of the extended gross substitutes system. Therefore, before we consider its comparative statical properties we first apply sufficient restrictions to ensure stability. As Morishima [4] has shown, appropriate restrictions are either

$$a_{i0}+2\sum_{j=k+1}^{n} a_{ij}\,p_j > 0 \quad (i = 1,\ldots, k),$$

$$a_{i0}+2\sum_{j=1}^{k} a_{ij}\,p_j > 0 \quad (i = k+1,\ldots, n), \tag{1}$$

or

$$a_{0j}+2\sum_{i=k+1}^{n} a_{ij}\,p_i > 0 \quad (j = 1,\ldots, k),$$

$$a_{0j}+2\sum_{i=1}^{k} a_{ij}\,p_i > 0 \quad (j = k+1,\ldots, n), \tag{2}$$

where p_i is the price of commodity i, p_0 being normalized at unity; these are referred to as the row and column stability conditions respectively.

Under HZ (1) is equivalent to the dominant diagonality conditions

$$\sum_{j=1}^{k} a_{ij}\,p_j - \sum_{j=k+1}^{n} a_{ij}\,p_j < 0 \quad (i = 1,\ldots, k),$$

$$-\sum_{j=1}^{k} a_{ij}\,p_j + \sum_{j=k+1}^{n} a_{ij}\,p_j < 0 \quad (i = k+1,\ldots, n), \tag{1$'$}$$

whilst under WL (2) is equivalent to

$$\sum_{i=1}^{k} a_{ij}\,p_i - \sum_{i=k+1}^{n} a_{ij}\,p_i < 0 \quad (j = 1,\ldots, k),$$

$$-\sum_{i=1}^{k} a_{ij}\,p_i + \sum_{i=k+1}^{n} a_{ij}\,p_i < 0 \quad (j = k+1,\ldots, n). \tag{2$'$}$$

Quirk [4] shows that an M-matrix is locally stable iff it has quasi-dominant diagonal, while Morishima [3] shows global stability of the M-system from modified versions of the restrictions (1) and (2).

Conditions (1) and (2) are restrictions on the numeraire similar to $a_0, a^0 > 0$ in the gross substitutes system; unlike these, however, they do not follow from the immediate extension of the system to cover the numeraire. The fact that these additional constraints are quantitative explains why the M-system could not be validly considered in the earlier qualitative discussion. It is, however, to some extent arbitrary how much 'more quantitative' these restrictions are than those for the gross substitutes system; in fact when $k = n$, they reduce to $a^0 > 0$ and $a_0 > 0$ respectively.

We may note here a controversy over the stability of the M-system. It has been suggested by Arrow and Hurwicz [**1**], Bassett, Habibagahi, and Quirk [**1**], and others that not only is the system not Q-stable, but also it is not P-stable. For example, summarized by Quirk [**3**, Theorem 10] this becomes:

> 'Let $A^* = \begin{bmatrix} A & a^0 \\ a_0 & a_{00} \end{bmatrix}$ satisfy the Morishima sign pattern conditions, [then] A is not a stable matrix for any choice of values satisfying these sign pattern conditions.'

This result is not, however, an important criticism of the system, for it applies only to the extended M-system—when the M-conditions apply to all commodities *including* the numeraire. Morishima [**4**] has shown that this is an unrealistic extension of the system, for it implies a contradiction between dynamic stability and more basic properties of the system, particularly WH, and he has shown that the proper M-system (which assumes the Hicks–Morishima chain rule only for the main submatrix A) does not suffer from these difficulties. This provides an illustration of the importance of specifying the system such that the basic stability requirements are fulfilled first.

The comparative statics we are concerned with arise from a simple shift in demand from the numeraire to some non-numeraire commodity, j. As we have ensured stability, it follows from Theorem 3.2 (part (i) (a)), that the prices of commodity j

and of its substitutes increase while the prices of its complements decrease.

5.3. *Global extensions*

So far in this and all preceding sections we have been exclusively concerned with local problems: stability and comparative statics in the small. In this subsection we now consider a few aspects of the global problem, or stability and comparative statics in the large. We first summarize the relevant existing results in the systems discussed earlier in this section, and then present some extensions.

Global stability has been established by Arrow and Hurwicz [**1**] in the gross substitutes system and by Morishima [4] in the M-system, under similar assumptions to those required for local stability. Morishima [**2**] has also shown that the comparative statical laws discussed above, i.e. the three Hicksian laws and Samuelson's LeChatelier principle, continue to hold in the large in the gross substitutes system, without assuming differentiability of the excess demand functions. In the M-system, equivalent global comparative statical results easily follow, if we assume differentiability, from repeated use of the corresponding local results.

The extensions concern the flexibility of the prices and confirm the local results due to Hicks [**1**] globally. We show that a change in equilibrium prices caused by a shift in demand for a good depends on the degree of substitutability–complementarity between the commodities as well as the slope of the demand curve of the good for which there is an autonomous increase in demand.

We consider the $n+1$ commodities X_i $(i = 0,..., n)$ with X_0 treated as numeraire, each with price p_i, with $p_0 \equiv 1$, and single-valued continuous excess demand function bounded from below:

$$F_i(1, p_1,..., p_n) \equiv F_i(1, p).$$

We assume that Walras's law and homogeneity apply, and that all commodities are gross substitutes; in the large we write these assumptions as, respectively,

$$F_0(1,p)+\sum_{i=1}^{n} p_i F_i(1,p) \equiv 0,$$

$$F_i(\lambda, \lambda p) = F_i(1,p) \quad \text{for all } \lambda > 0 \quad (i = 0,..., n),$$

$$F_i(1,p) < F_i(1,p') \quad \text{if } p_i = p_i' \text{ and } p \leq p' \; (p \neq p') \quad (i = 0,..., n).$$

It is well known that under these conditions there is a unique normalized equilibrium price vector $p^0 > 0$, such that

$$F_i(1,p^0) = 0 \quad (i = 0,..., n). \tag{3}$$

Now we consider a shift in the excess demand function of good s from F_s to F'_s such that

$$F'_s(1,p_1,..., p'_s,..., p_n) < (\text{or} >)\; F_s(1,p_1,..., p'_s,..., p_n) \tag{4}$$

for all prices $p_1,..., p'_s,..., p_n$, when $p'_s > (\text{or} <)\; p^0_s$. From this and the assumed continuity of F_s and F'_s we have

$$F'_s(1,p_1,..., p^0_s,..., p_n) = F_s(1,p_1,..., p^0_s,..., p_n)$$

at the equilibrium price p^0_s. This shift implies that the excess demand function of good s is rotated around the equilibrium point p^0 in such a way that the excess demand curve for s becomes steeper, or more downward sloping in terms of its own-price.

We thus have two systems, the second replacing the excess demand function F_s in the first system by F'_s, all other excess demand functions remaining unchanged. Suppose now there is an identical increase in the autonomous demand for good j in both systems, which results in the new equilibrium prices p^1 and p^2 respectively. We show that the price of every commodity is more flexible in the first system than in the second, that is that

$$|p^1_i - p^0_i| > |p^2_i - p^0_i| \quad (i = 1,..., n). \tag{5}$$

The two equilibrium price sets determined by

$$\left.\begin{aligned} F_j(1,p^1)+\beta_j &= 0 \\ F_i(1,p^1) &= 0 \quad (i \neq 0, j, s) \\ F_s(1,p^1) &= 0 \end{aligned}\right\}, \tag{6.1}$$

$$\left.\begin{aligned} F_j(1,p^2)+\beta_j &= 0 \\ F_i(1,p^2) &= 0 \quad (i \neq 0, j, s) \\ F'_s(1,p^2) &= 0 \end{aligned}\right\}, \tag{6.2}$$

are now compared with the original equilibrium price set p^0 fulfilling (3). As $\beta_j > 0$ and goods are assumed to be gross substitutes for each other, we have $p^1 > p^0$ and $p^2 > p^0$ from the first and second Hicksian laws. In particular we have $p_s^1 > p_s^0$ so from (4)

$$F'_s(1, p^1) < F_s(1, p^1).$$

Combining this with the equations for the other goods of (6.1) we have in the second system

$$\left.\begin{aligned} F_j(1,p^1)+\beta_j &= 0 \\ F_i(1,p^1) &= 0 \quad (i \neq 0,\, j,\, s) \\ F'_s(1,p^1) &< 0 \end{aligned}\right\}. \tag{7}$$

The last inequality may be replaced by the equation

$$F'_s(1,p^1)+\beta_s = 0 \tag{8}$$

for some appropriate positive β_s. Now the second system may move from the equilibrium (6.2) to another equilibrium described by the first $n-1$ equations of (7) and equation (8) simply by an autonomous increase in the demand for good s. It again follows from the first and second Hicksian laws that $p^1 > p^2$, so we have (5), or

THEOREM 5.1. *In the gross substitutes system all prices are less flexible the steeper is the excess demand curve of any commodity.*

We next consider a shift in the excess demand function of good r from F_r to F'_r such that

$$F'_r(1, p_1,..., p'_s,..., p_n) > (\text{or} <)\ F_r(1, p_1,..., p'_s,..., p_n) \tag{9}$$

for all $p_1,..., p'_s,..., p_n$, when $p'_s > (\text{or} <)\ p_s^0$, so that

$$F'_r(1, p_1,..., p_s^0,..., p_n) = F_r(1, p_1,..., p_s^0,..., p_n).$$

(The local equivalent of (9) is merely $\partial F'_r/\partial p_s > \partial F_r/\partial p_s > 0$.) We again compare the effects on equilibrium prices of an increase in the excess demand for good j in the two systems, one with F_i $(i = 1,..., n)$ and the other with F_i $(i = 1,..., r-1, r+1,..., n)$

and F'_r. The equilibrium prices p^1 and p^2 are determined by

$$\left.\begin{aligned} F_j(1,p^1)+\beta_j &= 0 \\ F_i(1,p^1) &= 0 \quad (i \neq 0, j, r) \\ F_r(1,p^1) &= 0 \end{aligned}\right\}, \tag{10.1}$$

$$\left.\begin{aligned} F_j(1,p^2)+\beta_j &= 0 \\ F_i(1,p^2) &= 0 \quad (i \neq 0, j, r) \\ F'_r(1,p^2) &= 0 \end{aligned}\right\}, \tag{10.2}$$

respectively. We have $p^1 > p^0, p^2 > p^0$ as before. Since $p^1_s > p^0_s$, it follows from (9) that

$$F'_r(1,p^1) > F_r(1,p^1) = 0, \tag{11}$$

so we obtain from (10.1) and (11) a set of equations

$$\left.\begin{aligned} F_j(1,p^1)+\beta_j &= 0 \\ F_i(1,p^1) &= 0 \quad (i \neq 0, j, r) \\ F'_r(1,p^1)+\beta_r &= 0 \end{aligned}\right\}, \tag{12}$$

with an appropriate negative β_r. Combining (12) with (10.2) we obtain $p^1 < p^2$, and thus $|p^2_i - p^0_i| > |p^1_i - p^0_i|$ for all i. We have then

THEOREM 5.2. *In the gross substitutes system all prices are more flexible the more substitutability there is between any pair of commodities.*

This theorem appears to contradict Hicks's result[22] that 'a given rise in demand will affect the price of [the commodity whose demand is increased] less the more substitutability or less complementarity there is between any pair of commodities in the system', for Theorem 5.2 shows that the effect is less the *less* substitutability (in the gross sense) there is. This, however, arises from the difference in definition of 'isolated' changes in substitutability. Walras's law and homogeneity both imply that a change in some off-diagonal element in the matrix of price substitution terms, F_{ij} say, be compensated somewhere else: in the jth column under Walras's law and in the ith row under homogeneity. It also gives rise to a change in F_{ji} with similar compensations under symmetry.

(22) Hicks [**1**, page 76].

We do not require symmetry in Theorem 5.2, and specify that all compensation is taken up by the numeraire, that is by F_{i0} and F_{0j}. Hicks, however, requires symmetry, and specifies that all compensation is taken up by the appropriate diagonal elements, the numeraire remaining unchanged; thus a change in F_{ij} is associated with a similar change in F_{ji} and an equal but opposite change in F_{ii} and F_{jj}, with F_{i0}, F_{j0}, F_{0i}, F_{0j} unchanged. Hicks's result then involves a combination of Theorems 5.1 and 5.2 and shows that, for the commodity whose demand is changed, the effect of a change in a diagonal element of the matrix is stronger than that of one in an off-diagonal element.

Theorems 5.1 and 5.2 are our two results in the gross substitutes system. By an argument analogous to that of Morishima [**3**] which derives results equivalent to the three Hicksian laws and the LeChatelier principle in the Leontief system, we may see that these results carry over to the Leontief system, *mutatis mutandis*. In this system, then, we observe that all outputs are more flexible (that is more responsive to a change in final demands) the greater the value of any input coefficient.

We next turn to the M-system and show that, with an allowance for complementarity, Theorems 5.1 and 5.2 continue to hold, provided that we now assume differentiability, so results equivalent to the first and second Hicksian laws hold in the large.

Theorem 5.1 carries over *mutatis mutandis*. Commodities are now grouped into two groups H and K, within each of which we have gross substitutability, while between each we have complementarity. We then have four cases to consider:

$$\text{(i) } j, s \in H; \quad \text{(ii) } j \in H, s \in K; \quad \text{(iii) } j \in K, s \in H;$$
$$\text{(iv) } j, s \in K.$$

Consider the second of these; the argument is essentially that of the gross substitutes case, and is only outlined here. The increase in the excess demand function for j now results in prices p^1 if there are no shifts in other excess demand functions and p^2 if the excess demand function of good s is shifted from F_s to F'_s. From the global version of the Morishima theorem we obtain the inequalities

$$p_i^1 > p_i^0, \quad i \in H; \qquad p_i^1 < p_i^0, \quad i \in K,$$

and
$$p_i^2 > p_i^0, \quad i \in H; \qquad p_i^2 < p_i^0, \quad i \in K.$$

As we assume that

$$F'_s(1, p_1,..., p'_s,..., p_n) > F_s(1, p_1,..., p'_s,..., p_n)$$

for any $(p_1,..., p'_s,..., p_n)$ such that $p'_s < p_s^0$, we have

$$F'_s(1, p^1) > F_s(1, p^1).$$

Note that $F_s(1, p)$ vanishes at $p = p^1$. Then we have

$$F_j(1, p^1) + \beta_j = 0,$$
$$F_i(1, p^1) = 0 \quad (i \neq 0, j, s),$$
$$F'_s(1, p^1) + \beta_s = 0,$$

for some appropriate negative β_s. Applying the Morishima theorem again in the comparison of the above hypothetical equilibrium system with the second equilibrium system,

$$F_j(1, p^2) + \beta_j = 0,$$
$$F_i(1, p^2) = 0 \quad (i \neq 0, j, s),$$
$$F'_s(1, p^2) = 0,$$

we obtain

$$p_i^1 > p_i^2, \quad i \in H; \qquad p_i^1 < p_i^2, \quad i \in K.$$

Hence,
$$|p_i^1 - p_i^0| > |p_i^2 - p_i^0| \quad (i = 1,..., n).$$

A similar argument may be employed in the other three cases.

On the other hand, Theorem 5.2 must be modified to allow for complementarity, so we may replace 'more substitutability' by 'more substitutability or more complementarity'. If r and s are substitutes they become more substitutable if (9) applies; if r and s are complements they become more complementary if the converse applies, that is if, under the same shift,

$$F'_r(1, p_1,..., p'_s,..., p_n) < (\text{or} >)\ F_r(1, p_1,..., p'_s,..., p_n) \qquad (13)$$

for all $p_1,..., p'_s,..., p_n$ when $p'_s >$ (or $<$) p_s^0 where r and s are complements. In the former case, r and s become more substitutive after the shift, while in the latter they become more complementary.

We now have four basic cases to consider (the other four being symmetric):

$$\text{(i) } j, r, s \in H; \quad \text{(ii) } j, r \in H,\ s \in K;$$
$$\text{(iii) } j, s \in H,\ r \in K; \quad \text{(iv) } j \in H,\ r, s \in K.$$

Again we sketch the argument for the second. The increase in the excess demand function for j now results in prices p^1 such that

$$p_i^1 > p_i^0, \quad i \in H; \qquad p_i^1 < p_i^0, \quad i \in K,$$

and a shift in the excess demand function of good $s \in K$ of the type (13) (so r and s become more complementary) causes a further change in p such that

$$p_i^2 > p_i^1, \quad i \in H; \qquad p_i^2 < p_i^1, \quad i \in K.$$

Hence,
$$|p_i^2 - p_i^0| > |p_i^1 - p_i^0| \quad (i = 1,\dots, n).$$

A similar argument may be employed in the other cases.

5.4. *Q-consistency between p- and q-definitions of substitutability and complementarity*

We now reconsider the definitions of the basic concepts of substitutability and complementarity in the exchange system. We assume that the consumer maximizes the value of a utility function,

$$u(y_0,\dots, y_n),$$

defined on the $n+1$ commodities $Y_0,\dots, Y_n$, subject to a budget constraint,

$$\sum_{i=0}^{n} p_i y_i = M, \tag{14}$$

where p_i is the price of commodity i, and $p_0 \equiv 1$. The equilibrium conditions in this problem are

$$r_i \equiv \frac{u_i}{u_0} = \frac{p_i}{p_0} = p_i \quad (i = 1,\dots, n). \tag{15}$$

Assuming a simple change in the price of commodity k and differentiating (14) and (15) with respect to p_k, we have

$$\sum_{i=0}^{n} r_i \frac{\partial y_i}{\partial p_k} = -y_k, \tag{16}$$

$$\sum_{j=0}^{n} r_{ij} \frac{\partial y_j}{\partial p_k} = \delta_{ik} \quad (i = 1,\dots, n), \tag{17}$$

where $r_{ij} = \partial r_i/\partial y_j$, δ_{ik} is the Kronecker delta (and $r_0 \equiv 1$). Then subtracting (16) multiplied by r_{i0} from each of (17) we have

$$\sum_{j=1}^{n} (r_{ij}-r_j r_{i0}) \frac{\partial y_j}{\partial p_k} = y_k r_{i0}+\delta_{ik} \quad (i = 1,..., n),$$

which we may write as

$$Cx = -y_k g+d^k,$$

where

$$C \equiv [r_{ij}-r_j r_{i0}], \quad x = [\partial y_j/\partial p_k], \quad g = [-r_{i0}], \quad d^k = [\delta_{ik}]$$
$$(i, j = 1,..., n).$$

This gives the Slutsky equation,

$$x = -y_k C^{-1}g+C^{-1}d^k, \tag{18}$$

whose first term, as usual, gives the income effects, and the second the substitution effects. Goods i and j are substitutes or complements in Hicks's *price* definition of substitutability–complementarity[23] according as the substitution term between i and j is positive or negative. The $n \times n$ matrix of price substitution terms (excluding numeraire 0) is

$$C^{-1}[d^1,..., d^n] = C^{-1}I = C^{-1},$$

so we have i and j as p-substitutes if $c^{ij} > 0$ and p-complements if $c^{ij} < 0$ (c^{ij} being the (i,j) element of C^{-1}).

Hicks's original definition of substitutability–complementarity was the quantity definition.[24] This gives i and j as substitutes if $r_i = u_i/u_0$ decreases when y_j is increased in substitution for y_0 in such a way as to leave u unchanged, with the quantities of all other commodities constant, that is, if

$$\frac{\mathrm{d}r_i}{\mathrm{d}y_j} = \frac{\partial r_i}{\partial y_j}+\frac{\partial r_i}{\partial y_0}\frac{\mathrm{d}y_0}{\mathrm{d}y_j} = r_{ij}-r_{i0}r_j < 0,$$

and i and j as complements if

$$\frac{\mathrm{d}r_i}{\mathrm{d}y_j} = r_{ij}-r_{i0}r_j > 0.$$

We thus have i and j as q-substitutes if $c_{ij} < 0$, and q-complements if $c_{ij} > 0$.

To examine the relationship between these two definitions we

(23) Defined in the appendix of Hicks [**1**] and named in Hicks [**2**].
(24) Given in the text of Hicks [**1**] and named in Hicks [**2**].

may first note that C and C^{-1} are negative definite from the stability conditions, and so we may apply Theorem 3.3 which concerns signed inverses under negative definiteness. In the indecomposable case this theorem immediately informs us that C is Q-invertible if and only if C is a reduced M-matrix, and also that C^{-1} is Q-invertible if and only if C^{-1} is a reduced M-matrix. Using these results and the Morishima theorem, we have in the first case

$$s(C) = \left[\begin{array}{ccc|ccc} - & & + & & & \\ & \ddots & & & - & \\ + & & - & & & \\ \hline & & & - & & + \\ & - & & & \ddots & \\ & & & + & & - \end{array}\right], \quad s(C^{-1}) = \left[\begin{array}{c|c} - & + \\ \hline + & - \end{array}\right],$$

and in the second

$$s(C^{-1}) = \left[\begin{array}{ccc|ccc} - & & + & & & \\ & \ddots & & & - & \\ + & & - & & & \\ \hline & & & - & & + \\ & - & & & \ddots & \\ & & & + & & - \end{array}\right], \quad s(C) = \left[\begin{array}{c|c} - & + \\ \hline + & - \end{array}\right].$$

The p- and q-definitions are Q-consistent (i.e. consistent for all values of c^{ij} or c_{ij} satisfying given sign pattern of C^{-1} or C) only in these two cases. In the first case commodities in the same group (that is partition of the matrix) are both q- and p-complements, whereas those in different groups are both q- and p-substitutes. In the second case, however, commodities in the same group are both p- and q-substitutes, whereas those in different groups are both p- and q-complements.

Clearly the second case is the M-system, for it satisfies the M-conditions on the matrix of price-substitution terms (where the conditions are defined), that is

$$s(c^{ij}) = s(c^{ik}c^{kj}) \quad \text{for distinct } i, j, k.$$

The first case, however, contradicts these conditions, and indeed satisfies the reverse, or 'anti-M' conditions

$$s(c^{ij}) = -s(c^{ik}c^{kj}) \quad \text{for distinct } i, j, k;$$

we thus call this the 'anti-M' system.(25) The above is, of course, all in the p-sense; clearly the reverse applies in the q-sense.(26)

Hicks appreciated that unless some stringent conditions are satisfied, his original q-definition may not be consistent with the p-definition, and proposed a revised form of the q-definition, based on the sign of $\mathrm{d}r_i/\mathrm{d}y_j$ where the quantities of all other commodities change so as to keep their marginal rates of substitution for the numeraire fixed at equilibrium prices. It was proposed that this new q-definition would always be consistent with the p-definition.(27)

Under this new definition we consider, say,

$$\frac{\mathrm{d}r_1}{\mathrm{d}y_2} = c_{12}+c_{13}\frac{\mathrm{d}y_3}{\mathrm{d}y_2}+\ldots+c_{1n}\frac{\mathrm{d}y_n}{\mathrm{d}y_2} \tag{19}$$

under the restrictions that

$$\frac{\mathrm{d}r_i}{\mathrm{d}y_2} = c_{i2}+c_{i3}\frac{\mathrm{d}y_3}{\mathrm{d}y_2}+\ldots+c_{in}\frac{\mathrm{d}y_n}{\mathrm{d}y_2} = 0 \quad (i = 3,\ldots, n). \tag{20}$$

This gives a system of $n-1$ equations in the $n-1$ variables $\frac{\mathrm{d}r_1}{\mathrm{d}y_2}, \frac{\mathrm{d}y_3}{\mathrm{d}y_2}, \ldots, \frac{\mathrm{d}y_n}{\mathrm{d}y_2}$, which we may solve to obtain

$$\frac{\mathrm{d}r_1}{\mathrm{d}y_2} = \frac{\begin{vmatrix} c_{12} & \cdots & c_{1n} \\ c_{32} & \cdots & c_{3n} \\ \vdots & & \vdots \\ c_{n2} & \cdots & c_{nn} \end{vmatrix}}{\begin{vmatrix} c_{33} & \cdots & c_{3n} \\ \vdots & & \vdots \\ c_{n3} & \cdots & c_{nn} \end{vmatrix}} = -\frac{C_{21}}{C_{1122}},$$

(25) In the anti-M system there prevail negatives of the Hicks–Morishima chain rules. For example, substitutes of substitutes are complements.

(26) There is no *a priori* reason why either the M- or the anti-M system should be the more realistic. In terms of the q-definitions, a plausible example of the M-system might be an economy consisting of tennis rackets, squash rackets, tennis balls, and squash balls, and of the anti-M system one of tennis rackets, tennis balls, golf clubs, and golf balls. It should be appreciated that both are special cases of a more general economy, which might consist of all these commodities. Such a system would not satisfy the conditions of Theorem 3.3, and thus, by the reasoning given above, not preserve Q-consistency between p- and q-definitions of substitutability–complementarity.

(27) This was originally proposed for factors in the theory of the firm in Hicks [**1**], and then extended to commodities in demand theory in Hicks [**2**].

where C_{ij} is the cofactor of c_{ij} in

$$|C| = \begin{vmatrix} c_{11} & \cdots & c_{1n} \\ \vdots & & \vdots \\ c_{n1} & \cdots & c_{nn} \end{vmatrix},$$

and C_{iijj} is the cofactor of c_{jj} in C_{ii}. From the stability conditions, C_{1122} has the same sign as $|C|$, and therefore

$$s\left(\frac{\mathrm{d}r_1}{\mathrm{d}y_2}\right) = -s\left(\frac{C_{21}}{|C|}\right).$$

$C_{21}/|C|$ is, however, merely the substitution term of the Slutsky equation of y_1 with respect to p_2.

This revised q-definition, although consistent with the p-definition, changes the fundamental nature of the definition, and makes it of less interest. Suppose the 'other commodities' 2,..., n form a composite commodity Y_c, such that any changes in y_i from some given y_i^* ($i = 2,..., n$) are in fixed proportions:

$$Y_c = [y_2^*+y_2', y_3^*+t_3 y_2',..., y_n^*+t_n y_2'].$$

Then the marginal rate of substitution of Y_c for y_0 is

$$\begin{aligned} r_c = -\mathrm{d}y_0/\mathrm{d}y_2 &= (u_2+t_3 u_3+...+t_n u_n)/u_0 \\ &= r_2+t_3 r_3+...+t_n r_n. \end{aligned}$$

Now applying the original q-definition between y_1 and Y_c, we have

$$\begin{aligned} \frac{\mathrm{d}r_1}{\mathrm{d}Y_c} &= \frac{\partial r_1}{\partial y_2}+\frac{\partial r_1}{\partial y_0}\frac{\mathrm{d}y_0}{\mathrm{d}y_2} \\ &= r_{12}+t_3 r_{13}+...+t_n r_{1n}-r_{10}(r_2+t_3 r_3+...+t_n r_n) \\ &= c_{12}+t_3 c_{13}+...+t_n c_{1n}. \end{aligned}$$

It is clear that this holds for any t_i, so we may take $t_i = \mathrm{d}y_i/\mathrm{d}y_2$ ($i = 3,..., n$), where these $\mathrm{d}y_i/\mathrm{d}y_2$ are determined by (20). Then $\mathrm{d}r_1/\mathrm{d}Y_c$ equals $\mathrm{d}r_1/\mathrm{d}y_2$ determined by (19), and the q-relationship between 1 and 2 according to the revised version of the q-definition gives the substitutability or complementarity not between commodities 1 and 2 but between 1 and the composite commodity Y_c, in the original sense. It is not surprising to find that there may be an inconsistency between the original q-definition concerning commodities 1 and 2 and the revised q-definition concerning 1 and 2 (that is the original q-definition concerning 1 and Y_c), and thus the p-definition concerning 1 and 2.

5.5. *Conclusions*

This section provides some new results by the authors, in addition to an over-all synthesis of existing comparative statical laws. We first note the established comparative statical results in a number of systems, and note that in spite of apparent differences, their qualitative structures are remarkably similar. The establishing of these comparative statical results, essentially versions of the three Hicksian laws and the LeChatelier principle, may be viewed as various applications of the more fundamental qualitative theory discussed in this chapter. We have also derived some new global results which we may term the fourth and fifth Hicksian laws.

Finally, on the definition of related goods we have identified the cases in which p- and q-definitions are qualitatively consistent, and shown why they may be inconsistent in the general case. This questions the suitability of the usual price definition of substitutability and complementarity.

II. The Qualitative Content of Maximizing Models

G. C. ARCHIBALD (1965)

1. Introduction

IT seems unfortunately to be the case that the general qualitative content of maximizing models is small, if not trivial. By 'general' here is meant explicitly 'knowing or assuming no more than that sufficient conditions for an extreme solution are satisfied'.(1) This is enough, as Samuelson [**1**] showed, to prove the basic theorem of conjugate pairs; but the case of conjugate pairs appears to be the only case in which an unambiguous qualitative prediction can be obtained, yet it is empirically not a very important case. A good deal of attention has been given in recent years to cases that are not conjugate pairs; and surprise and disappointment are often expressed at the discovery that the conventional—or 'general'—allowance of qualitative information is not sufficient for an unambiguously signed prediction to be obtained. Thus one object of this chapter is to gather together some of these cases, and to show that the reason for the lack of qualitative content is the same, that the theorem of conjugate pairs cannot be used, while another object is to set out systematically what can be got from the theorem, and to offer some assessment.

It is clear that the basic work is Samuelson's; but he himself was apparently uncertain of the scope of the theorem (as will be seen below), and could not, in any case, have anticipated its application to postwar theoretical developments, such as 'second best' and certain cases in imperfect competition.

A variable and a parameter in a given system are said to be a conjugate pair if the parameter appears only in the equation which determines the equilibrium value of that variable and in

(1) For discussion of the conditions for qualitative content in models whose equilibrium conditions are not obtained from a maximization assumption see Lancaster [**1, 2**], and Gorman [**1**].

no other equation. When that parameter is shifted, we may say that one 'curve' is shifted, while adjustment is completed by shifting *along* the other 'curves' of the system. Of the assumption that conjugate pairs exist, Samuelson wrote:

> Let us examine more closely the nature of our hypothesis . . . that each parameter shifts but one condition of equilibrium, leaving all others unchanged. In the first place this does not mean that a change in the i-th parameter results in a change in the i-th variable alone. On the contrary, a change in any parameter will typically result in a change in all variables. Our hypothesis merely says that this must come about through a shift in but one schedule with movements along the remaining schedules.
>
> *As I shall later argue, the assumption of this hypothesis does not involve any serious loss of generality and still includes the vast majority* (*in fact, it is hard to find exceptions*) *of relationships contained in current economic theory.*(2) [My italics.]

Samuelson was, however, clear that this was not the end of the matter. A few pages later he wrote: 'It must not be thought, however, that the assumption of our equilibrium as the solution of a maximum problem is the "open sesame" to the successful unambiguous determination of all possible questions which we may ask. For it is extremely easy to specify simple and important problems which cannot be answered even qualitatively without further knowledge.'(3) This seems to leave the scope and importance of conjugate pairs rather undecided. In this chapter we collect some of the unanswerable problems in a systematic way, and show that the necessary assumption for conjugate pairs leads only to the relatively trivial result that all derived demand curves slope down, and supply curves in perfect competition slope up, while in a substantial number of cases of interest, which have much occupied economists, the assumption cannot be made, with disastrous results for general qualitative theory.

2. The Theorem of Conjugate Pairs

Samuelson proved the familiar theorem of conjugate pairs,(4) and applied it to several cases. He did not, however, say very much about its limitations. The first step is, therefore, to restate

(2) Samuelson [1], p. 33. (3) Ibid., p. 41. (4) Ibid., pp. 30–9.

the theorem in order to obtain a clear statement of the necessary assumptions. We shall find that, in the general case, the direction of changes in the variables in response to a parameter change can *only* be determined for conjugate pairs, which turn out to be, practically speaking, rather uninteresting.

The assumed behaviour is that the economic unit maximizes some objective function U (with continuous first and second derivatives) subject to some constraint F, where the arguments of the functions are the variables $x_1,\ldots, x_n$ and some parameter a, selected as a shift parameter (there is in general some set of parameters, but we may suppress all but one without loss of generality).

For the Lagrangian function

$$V = U+\lambda F \tag{1}$$

to be at a maximum, it is necessary that

$$V_{x_i} = U_{x_i}+\lambda F_{x_i} = 0 \quad \text{and} \quad V_\lambda = F = 0 \quad (i = 1,\ldots, n). \tag{2}$$

Sufficient conditions for equations (2) to be a true maximum are that the bordered Hessian

$$H = \left|\begin{array}{c|c} V_{ij} & F_i \\ \hline F_i & 0 \end{array}\right|$$

evaluated at this point be negative definite under constraint, which implies that

$$(-1)^n H > 0$$

and that for each r $(1 \leqq r \leqq n)$,

$$(-1)^r \begin{vmatrix} V_{11} & \cdots & V_{1r} & F_1 \\ \vdots & & \vdots & \vdots \\ V_{r1} & \cdots & V_{rr} & F_r \\ F_1 & \cdots & F_r & 0 \end{vmatrix} > 0.$$

(Where there is no room for ambiguity, partial derivatives V_{x_i} will be written V_i.) The system is 'solved' if the variables can be expressed as functions of the parameters in the neighbourhood of equilibrium, that is, by forming the n equations

$$x_i = f^i(a) \quad (i = 1,\ldots, n). \tag{3}$$

The task of qualitative comparative statics (the qualitative calculus) is to find, where possible, the signs of the partial derivatives f_a^i, in order that directions of change in the variables in response to a parameter change may be predicted ($dx_i = f_a^i \, da$; the n expressions dx_i/da will be referred to as the solution vector).

The assumption that extremum conditions are satisfied is *alone* sufficient to obtain an unambiguous sign for one (and only one) element dx_i/da of the solution vector iff the following conditions are satisfied: (i) (obviously) the sign of V_{ia} is known;[5] (ii) (the conjugate-pair assumption) $V_{ja} = 0$ for all $j \neq i$, and $F_a = 0$.

That these conditions are sufficient means that the derivative of a variable with respect to its conjugate parameter is signed in the general case in which we do not have information about the signs or relative magnitudes of the off-diagonal elements (V_{ij}, $i \neq j$) of the Hessian other than that they are consistent with second-order conditions. What is particularly important, however, is that they are necessary as well as sufficient. Note particularly the following:

(i) the two conditions given above are not sufficient to sign any other element dx_j/da of the solution vector without further information, usually of a quantitative or semi-quantitative nature;

(ii) if the conditions that $V_{ja} = 0$ for all $j \neq i$ and/or $F_a = 0$ are violated, not even dx_i/da is qualitatively signed.

This may be interpreted. So long as we adhere to the 'general' assumption that the second-order cross-partial derivatives of V are non-zero (which is the case if we assume U_{ij} and/or F_{ij} to be non-zero), and we have no further information about these cross-partials, then we can never sign more than one element of the solution vector when a parameter is shifted, and that only if we can find a parameter that appears in only one of equations (2). If it appears in the ith equation and nowhere else, we may describe x_i and the parameter a as a conjugate pair. Thus it turns out

(5) If this condition is violated (because V_{ia} is unsigned, that is, either U_{ia} and/or F_{ia} are unsigned, or have opposite signs), obviously not even the conjugate pair can be signed. This is what may happen when a shift parameter is introduced into a monopolist's demand function or the supply function of a monopsonist (see H. W. Folk and J. N. Wolfe [**1**]).

that even conjugate pairs depend on a particular restriction on the functional forms of U and F: that there exists a parameter that appears in only one of the equilibrium equations (2). This restriction requires as much empirical justification as the restriction that some V_{ij}s are zero (or stand in some known relationship to each other). Just how these restrictions have been used in existing theory will emerge as we proceed.

For proof, we differentiate equations (2) totally with respect to all variables and the parameter in question. This gives $n+1$ simultaneous linear equations, which may be solved by Cramer's method. The equations may be written

$$\left[\begin{array}{c|c} V_{ij} & F_i \\ \hline F_i & 0 \end{array}\right] \cdot \begin{bmatrix} dx_1 \\ \cdot \\ \cdot \\ \cdot \\ dx_n \\ d\lambda \end{bmatrix} = -\begin{bmatrix} a_1 \\ \cdot \\ \cdot \\ \cdot \\ a_n \\ a_{n+1} \end{bmatrix} da, \qquad (4)$$

where the column vector

$$\alpha = \begin{bmatrix} a_1 \\ \cdot \\ \cdot \\ \cdot \\ a_n \\ a_{n+1} \end{bmatrix}$$

is composed of the elements of V_{ia}, the partial derivatives of V_i, V_λ with respect to a. Write H_{ij} for the cofactor of the ijth element in H. Then if $a_i < 0$ and all $a_{j\neq i} = 0$ $(j = 1,..., n+1)$,

$$\frac{dx_i}{da} = -a_i \frac{H_{ii}}{H} < 0,$$

because H_{ii} is a principal minor of H and therefore of opposite sign.

We see that the conditions are necessary as follows:

(1) $dx_j/da = -a_i(H_{ij}/H)$ is unsigned since H_{ij} is unsigned.

(2) Let any element of α, say a_k, be non-zero as well as a_i. Then (without consideration of the sign of a_k)

$$\frac{dx_i}{da} = -a_i \frac{H_{ii}}{H} - a_k \frac{H_{ki}}{H},$$

and
$$\frac{\mathrm{d}x_k}{\mathrm{d}a} = -a_k \frac{H_{kk}}{H} - a_i \frac{H_{ik}}{H}.$$

H_{ik} ($= H_{ki}$) is unsigned, so both $\mathrm{d}x_i/\mathrm{d}a$ and $\mathrm{d}x_k/\mathrm{d}a$ are unsigned. Further
$$\frac{\mathrm{d}x_j}{\mathrm{d}a} = -a_i \frac{H_{ij}}{H} - a_k \frac{H_{kj}}{H} \quad \text{(for all } j \neq i \text{ or } k\text{)},$$

which is unsigned. Hence no element of the solution vector is signed. If this is true when two elements of α are non-zero, it is true, *a fortiori*, when more than two are non-zero.

Some applications (to welfare economics and the theory of the firm) will be discussed below. The immediately obvious and best-known application is to the theory of consumer demand: the slope of the demand curve cannot be obtained 'in general' because the condition that all $a_{j \neq i} = 0$ is violated. Each price is an argument of the constraint as well as the relevant partial derivative of V, so that there are two non-zero elements in α, yielding the familiar substitution and income terms.

At this point it is convenient to ask what further qualitative information of a fairly general nature we might reasonably assume in order to give our theory a little more empirical content. One obvious candidate is to assume that cross-partial derivatives are zero, so that the off-diagonal elements of H are zero (except, of course, the border). This certainly increases the number of signed elements in the solution vector, but in rather embarrassing ways. In consumer theory, with a linear constraint, the off-diagonal elements are zero if the utility function is of the strongly independent or additive variety, so that it may be written

$$U(x_1, \ldots, x_n) = \sum_{i=1}^{n} u^i(x_i).$$

The embarrassing result is that, in this case, there can be no inferior goods and no complements, except in one (apparently very peculiar) case.(6) In monopolistic competition it is particularly

(6) H. A. J. Green [1] and references cited therein. The peculiar case is explored by Green. Stability conditions do not require that all u_{ii} are negative, but only that $(n-1)$ of them are. If the marginal utility of exactly one good is constant or increasing, which is permissible, then that good is normal, and the remainder are inferior! Furthermore, all other goods are either complements or unrelated to each other.

tempting to try to add to the meagre qualitative content of the maximizing model by assuming cross-partial derivatives to be zero. In one case, at least, putting an intrusive cross-partial equal to zero leads to the result that the equilibrium output of a firm is not altered by a change in an excise tax on that output.(7) Giving it the sign that appears 'reasonable', we avoid this embarrassment, but at the price of having no qualitative prediction about the direction of change in advertising.

This naturally raises the possibility of adding to the empirical content of our models by assuming cross-partial derivatives, and so on, to have the signs that appear 'reasonable' when we can obtain signs in the solution vector by this means. The difficulty is that empirical content gained in this way is largely illusory. Suppose a theory yields a prediction of the sort 'if a and b, then c', where a is some observable event (say, a change in a parameter), c is the observable result (change in a variable), and b is not independently observed (b is, for example, the condition that a cross-partial has a given sign). If we observe not-c, we can rescue the theory merely by saying, 'Ah, well, we made the wrong guess about b.' In this sort of situation, indeed, we can always 'rig up' the unobserved bits to make the theory predict as we wish, but, by so doing, we render the theory unfalsifiable.(8)

Before going on, one further introductory point should be clarified: there may be some information about maximands or constraints, beyond what is necessary for extremum conditions to be satisfied, that the reader would consider 'qualitative' (for example, that a production function is homogeneous). Where such additional information is available, more 'qualitative' predictions may well be obtained than follow from conjugate pairs alone. Nothing that is said here should be read as denying the

(7) See Archibald [**2**]. Write the demand function facing the firm as $v = f(p, x)$, where v is the quantity of advertising, p is product price, and x the amount taken. The cross-partial in question is f_{xp}.

(8) Except perhaps in one case. Suppose that we have 'rigged' b to be consistent with c (or not-c, as the case may be). If the theory yields some other prediction (d) in which b plays a similar role, then we may obtain some potential falsifiability by requiring consistency. On the general question of untested subsidiary assumptions see A. G. Papandreou [**1**].

proposition that, if more is known, more is known: on the contrary, the burden of the argument is that more must be known if worthwhile predictions are to be obtained.

3. Examples: Second Best

Lipsey and Lancaster [**1**] remarked, in 'The General Theory of the Second Best', that many writers had discovered particular examples of the problem, but had not realized that it was general. We may go a step further: The impossibility of piecemeal welfare economics is only a particular case of failing to satisfy the second necessary condition of the theorem of conjugate pairs.

That this has apparently not been noticed already is perhaps due to the fact that 'second best' is not generally thought of as a problem in comparative statics. It may, however, be easily put into this familiar form. Assume that there are at least two constraints preventing the fulfilment of the Paretian optimum conditions in two or more markets, that at least one constraint is immovable, while the other may be varied by policy, and that the constrained maximum (second-best optimum) has been found. Let the parameter of the policy constraint be k_g—a tax rate, tariff, or whatever. Then piecemeal welfare economics becomes the usual qualitative calculus operation: trying to predict the sign of $\mathrm{d}U/\mathrm{d}k_g$ in order to discover in which direction k_g should be varied. At the general qualitative level of analysis this is impossible.

This may be seen more clearly if we consider the way in which the parameters appear in the constraints. We maximize U subject to several constraints: the production frontier, and two or more non-Paretian conditions. The question is: how should these be written? If the only immovable constraint is one constant inequality k_i between price and marginal cost in the ith industry, then, as McManus [**1**] pointed out, a Paretian optimum may be achieved, given the full-employment assumption, by adopting the same k in all other industries. Lancaster and Lipsey [**1**] replied that, if the ith industry were in the hands of a monopolist, he would not 'hold still'; his profit-maximizing k_i would be a function of all other ks. They alternatively wrote the constraint as[9]

$$\frac{U_i}{U_n} = k_i \frac{F_i^{\mathrm{p}}}{F_n^{\mathrm{p}}}, \tag{5}$$

where U is the maximand, F^{p} the production constraint, and the nth industry is chosen as numeraire. McManus [**1**] also pointed out that the choice of n was not arbitrary: the nth industry must be perfectly competitive. For present purposes, we may bypass these problems. If the Paretian optimum is achieved by maximizing

$$V = U + \lambda F^{\mathrm{p}}, \tag{6}$$

the additional constraints may be written in the form

$$F^i(V_i, k_i) = 0, \tag{7}$$

or even more generally

$$F^i(V_i, V_j, k_i, k_j) = 0 \quad (j = 1,..., i-1, i+1,..., n). \tag{8}$$

Now a second-best optimum is achieved when U is maximized subject to F^{p}, one or more constraints F_i^i (in the form of (7) or (8)), and one particular constraint F^g of the same form, and containing the policy parameter k_g. The problem is to predict the sign of $\mathrm{d}U/\mathrm{d}k_g$ (it is immaterial whether k_g is originally unity or not. If it is, the sign of $\mathrm{d}U/\mathrm{d}k_g$ tells us whether utility is increased by a subsidy or a tax in the gth industry. If it is not, the sign of $\mathrm{d}U/\mathrm{d}k_g$ tells us whether k_g should be nearer to or further from unity). The difficulty is simply that

$$\frac{\mathrm{d}U}{\mathrm{d}k_g} = \sum_{i=1}^{n} U_i \frac{\mathrm{d}x_i}{\mathrm{d}k_g}. \tag{9}$$

To sign equation (9) without further information, the necessary and sufficient conditions are that all $U_i(\mathrm{d}x_i/\mathrm{d}k_g)$s have the same sign. The fact is that not a single one of them can be signed if we maintain the general assumption that all $V_{ij} \neq 0$ but are of unknown magnitude. As can be seen from the conditions for conjugate pairs, not even $\mathrm{d}x_g/\mathrm{d}k_g$ can be signed because the parameter k_g must appear in *at least* two equations of the equilibrium set, namely,

$$V_g = 0 \quad \text{and} \quad F^g = 0 \tag{10}$$

[9] Lipsey and Lancaster [**1**].

(if the constraints have the form of (8) or if some ks are functions of other ks, k_g will appear in more than two equations). Thus there are at least two non-zero elements in the α vector, and not a single element of the right-hand side of equation (9) can be signed without further information.[10]

A general comment on welfare economics may be added here. What Arrow did was to prove that successful anarchy is impossible, that is, that the 'irreducible element of coercion' in government *is* inescapable. (Arrow's volume[11] might well be published as the Technical Appendix to Mill's *Essay on Liberty*!) Thus society has to have a government (to prevent some undesired individual or combination from imposing his/their welfare function on the community). But government cannot be costless. Hence a government has to raise taxes. Hence, except perhaps in the uninteresting case of a poll tax, there must exist at least one unavoidable departure from the Paretian optimum conditions. Hence all welfare economics of any possible real-world relevance inescapably deals in second-best problems. But there is a more important conclusion still: so far as the case for *laissez-faire* and perfect competition rests on the argument that this ensures fulfilment of the Paretian optimum conditions, it is, even in the absence of external effects, an invalid application of piecemeal welfare economics. The existence of a government (necessary to police perfect competition) ensures that there will be at least one market in which the optimum conditions are not satisfied, since policing involves taxing; *ergo* there is no presumption in favour of satisfying the Paretian conditions in the remaining markets; *ergo* there is no welfare presumption in favour of *laissez-faire* plus perfect competition.[12]

(10) I am indebted to Professor Peter Pashigian for showing me an unpublished paper in which he imposes sufficient restrictions on F^{p} to sign not only $\mathrm{d}U/\mathrm{d}k_g$, but all the other derivatives $\mathrm{d}U/\mathrm{d}k_j$ ($j = 1,\ldots, n-2$; one k must be immovable). This he does by assuming that there are intermediate products such that the output of each final good is a function of the input of capital, labour, and one intermediate product only, a 'vertical-chain' assumption which provides a convenient batch of zeros. Consideration of this result materially advanced my own understanding of the problem.

(11) K. J. Arrow [**1**].

(12) We may also consider the currently fashionable studies of optimal growth paths. In these studies an objective function (for example, utility as

4. Examples: The Theory of the Firm

We may first consider the general case of a multiproduct, multiplant, multimarket firm that may vary quantities, qualities, prices, selling outlays, etc. The essential assumption is that there exists a well-defined demand surface (or, in the discriminating case, surfaces). The problem is, as usual, to maximize U subject to one or more market constraints F. U is commonly taken to be identical with $R-C$, but it may be remarked that there is no particular reason why the utility function should be cardinal; any monotonic increasing function of $R-C$ would serve perfectly well as the maximand.

Assuming that there are m independent markets ($m \geq 1$), we may write

$$V = \sum_{i=1}^{m} R^i - \sum_{i=1}^{k} C^i + \lambda_1 F^1 + \ldots + \lambda_m F^m, \tag{11}$$

where there are k (≥ 1) additive elements of the cost function. This means that there may be more than one plant with costs of production independent of each other, or that there may be selling outlays which are independent of the quantity or quality of some or all outputs. Let the arguments of the functions of equation (11) be elements of the vector $x = (x_1, x_2, \ldots, x_n)$, and some parameters which will not be specified yet, where $n \geq 2m$ (there is at least a price and output for each market; if quality and advertising variables are admitted, $n > 2m$). We have some restrictions on the way in which the elements of x may appear in the arguments of the functions:

(i) if any x_i is an argument of any C^i, it is an argument of at least one R^i (no input is used, or output made, which does not contribute to revenue);

a function of the present value of the future income stream) is maximized subject to some constraint or constraints determined by technology, factor endowments, savings ratios, etc. It is fashionable to solve the problem by finding the conditions for $U_{\max}$, or by proving that a solution exists, and to let it go at that. But the discovery of equilibrium conditions is not the end of analysis: we want to know something about the 'comparative static' solution vector as well. It is clear that the conditions for these models to have comparative content are those stated in section 2 above, and that, in general, these conditions will not be satisfied by qualitative considerations. (It is clear that the comparative technique is not confined to static models, nor are its limitations.)

(ii) the set of arguments of any R^i is identical with that of the ith market constraint F^i;

(iii) there exists one argument of every R^i that is not an argument of any C^i (production costs are independent of market prices);

(iv) a special restriction: the same argument of R^i is not an argument of any R^j (the markets are independent).

We have the usual first- and second-order conditions, so we may proceed immediately to comparative statics. If we shift some parameter a, we obtain

$$\begin{bmatrix} V_{ij} & [F_i^1][F_i^2]...[F_i^m] \\ \hline \{F_i^1\} & \\ \{F_i^2\} & \\ . & \\ . & 0 \\ . & \\ \{F_i^m\} & \end{bmatrix} \cdot \begin{bmatrix} dx_1 \\ dx_2 \\ . \\ . \\ . \\ dx_n \\ d\lambda_1 \\ d\lambda_2 \\ . \\ . \\ . \\ d\lambda_m \end{bmatrix} = - \begin{bmatrix} a_1 \\ . \\ . \\ . \\ . \\ . \\ . \\ a_{n+m} \end{bmatrix} da, \qquad (12)$$

where brackets denote a column vector and braces a row vector. We may at once apply conjugate pairs: iff a is an argument of one and only one element of V_i, say the ith, so that all $a_{j \neq i} = 0$, then if $a_i < 0$

$$\frac{dx_i}{da} = -a_i \frac{H_{ii}}{H} < 0. \qquad (13)$$

How can this condition be satisfied, and what does it mean? First, a must not be an argument of any R^i, since, by restriction (ii) above, it will then be an argument of F^i, and there will be at least two non-zero elements of α (*a fortiori*, a must not be an argument of two or more revenue functions). Second, then, a must be an argument of a cost function, and in such a fashion that it is an argument of only one partial derivative of C. This limits a to being a factor price or a specific tax on one output.

Thus the theorem of conjugate pairs tells us that all derived demand curves slope down, including the 'demand' for any particular output whose 'price' has risen (a 'demand' derived from maximization of U). This, I submit, is a pretty trivial result; but unless we can impose some more restrictions it is the only one we are going to get.

Before considering possible restrictions, however, we may clear up some other points. What happens if a is an argument of more than one C^i? The answer is that the condition that only one element of V_{ia} be non-zero still stands. This means that if a wage rate affects more than one element of the x-vector (more than one output; or the cost of quality as well as quantity), the conditions for conjugate pairs are not satisfied. As a particular case, we have no signs by conjugate pairs if a specific tax is imposed on all outputs and/or in all markets. What, then, happens if a is an *ad valorem* tax in one market, say the ith? The answer is, of course, that a appears in all the derivatives R^i_i, so that there are as many non-zero elements in α as there are arguments in R^i, and no element of the solution vector is signed.

One further consequence of this analysis may be pointed out. In general, the effects on price or prices of parameter changes are unpredicted. Even in the conjugate pairs case, where $\mathrm{d}x_i/\mathrm{d}a$ is signed, $\mathrm{d}p_i/\mathrm{d}a$ is an off-diagonal, and so unsigned; in no other case is any element of the solution vector signed at all. Our sole result, that derived demands slope down, is meagre indeed!

We must now ask if any of the restrictions on the functional forms discussed above lead to any elements of V_{ij} being zero, and, if so, if there can be enough zeros to sign any H_{ij}. The first two restrictions are plainly no help at all. Consider the third. This excludes prices from the cost functions. But, by restriction (ii), any price is an argument of an R^i and an F^i, so this is no help. Now consider restriction (iv), which looks more helpful. In the simplest case of price discrimination (two markets, one product, no quality variable, no advertising) we have, as is well known, qualitative content (the reader may verify for himself that the Hessian is a 6×6 containing 18 zeros). The introduction of quality or advertising variables robs the single-market case of qualitative content, and the addition of extra markets will not restore qualitative content to a model that lacks it.[13]

It may now be a relief to turn to perfect competition, where we expect rather more qualitative content. The object of this section is to clarify very briefly the relationship between qualitative content and the particular restrictions imposed on the functions in this case. First, consider the restrictions in the general case discussed in equation (11) above. The first and third obviously apply to perfect competition, *mutatis mutandis*. The fourth is irrelevant. The second, however, is altered. Let $R = px$. Now if we take the fixed price for our constraint $(F = p - p_0 = 0)$, x is an argument of R but not of F. If, on the other hand, we take the production function as the constraint $F = x - f(x_1, x_2) = 0$ (where x_1, x_2 are inputs) then p is an argument of R but not of F. The result, of course, is to enlarge the set of parameters with respect to which only one of the equilibrium equations yields a non-zero partial derivative, and to increase the number of zeros in the Hessian.

Let us first take the production function as the constraint, forming the equation

$$V = px - p_1 x_1 - p_2 x_2 - \lambda[x - f(x_1, x_2)] \tag{14}$$

(where p_1 and p_2 are the factor prices). The relevant bordered Hessian is (after interchange of the last two columns and the last two rows)

$$H = \left|\begin{array}{ccc|c} \lambda f_{11} & \lambda f_{12} & f_1 & 0 \\ \lambda f_{21} & \lambda f_{22} & f_2 & 0 \\ f_1 & f_2 & 0 & 1 \\ \hline 0 & 0 & 1 & 0 \end{array}\right| > 0. \tag{15}$$

This contains $(n \times n) = 16$ elements and 6 zeros, or $(n-1)!$ This is sufficient to sign every cofactor provided that the signs of the non-zero elements are known. The only one in doubt is f_{12}, which is not signed by the convexity condition (necessary

(13) It is clear that the examples of qualitative emptiness in maximizing models of the firm in non-perfect competition that I have discussed elsewhere (see Archibald [1], [2]) were merely examples of the limitations of conjugate pairs, although I did not recognize this at the time. There is no need to rehearse them all here.

in this case for cost minimization because the factor-price constraint is linear) which only requires that the indicated principal minor be negative. Thus if f_{12} is signed, all the elements of every solution vector are signed so long as there is only one non-zero element in the α vector. This condition is, however, the rather special one that changes in p_1 or p_2 induce no changes in p, and vice versa, which cannot be maintained for industry-wide changes.

We may alternatively use the market constraint

$$F = p - p_0 = 0,$$

where p_0 is the market price, and form the equation

$$v = pf(x_1, x_2) - p_1 x_1 - p_2 x_2 + \lambda(p - p_0). \tag{16}$$

The bordered Hessian is

$$H = \begin{vmatrix} 0 & f_1 & f_2 & 1 \\ f_1 & pf_{11} & pf_{12} & 0 \\ f_2 & pf_{21} & pf_{22} & 0 \\ 1 & 0 & 0 & 0 \end{vmatrix}, \tag{17}$$

which again contains $6 = (n-1)!$ zeros.

As a last illustration of the consequences of not requiring identical sets of arguments in F and R, consider

$$V = px - C(x) + \lambda(p - p_0), \tag{18}$$

where

$$H = \begin{vmatrix} 0 & 1 & 1 \\ 1 & -C'' & 0 \\ 1 & 0 & 0 \end{vmatrix} = \begin{vmatrix} 1 & 1 & 0 \\ 0 & C'' & 1 \\ 0 & 0 & 1 \end{vmatrix}, \tag{19}$$

which is triangular.

The situation may be summed up as follows. The assumption that maximum conditions are satisfied is sufficient to tell us that derived demand curves slope down, that other demand curves do unless income effects offset substitution effects, and apparently not much else (except in the special case of perfect competition where we obviously obtain upward-sloping short-run supply curves).

Part II · Separability

III. Demand and Supply under Separability

P. T. GEARY *and* M. MORISHIMA

1. Introduction

THE concept of separability has played an important role in several areas of economic theory from their earliest development. In the pioneering contributions to the theory of consumer behaviour of Gossen [**1**], Jevons [**1**], Marshall [**1**], and Walras [**1**], the utility function of the consumer was assumed to be additive (and, hence, cardinal). While some of the implications of the assumption led to its rejection and replacement by a completely general formulation as, for example, in the work of Hicks [**1**], this in turn generated dissatisfaction because of the relative paucity of its meaningful empirical implications. As a result, considerably increased attention has been paid in demand analysis both to additivity and particularly to less extreme forms of separability. These concepts have enriched the theory of consumer behaviour in a number of directions, perhaps the most celebrated of which has been the utility tree. In certain circumstances the utility tree can be interpreted in terms of Hicks's view [**2**] of the consumer as choosing first between objectives and then between the means of achieving them. When the relationship between means and objectives is seen as a technical one, as it is by Hicks, we have an integration of the theories of consumer behaviour and production. In empirical studies of consumer demand functions, of course, separability concepts inevitably play an important role due to the stronger restrictions they impose, and most studies in recent years have used separability assumptions (see below).

Two other areas in which separability plays an important role are the dynamic theory of consumer behaviour, particularly with reference to dynamic utility functions, and the theory of aggregation. Dynamic utility has involved separability concepts to a very large degree since the seminal work of Ramsay [**1**].

Most work in the theory of optimal economic growth uses Ramsay-type assumptions and separability concepts are also important in the work of Koopmans [**1**] and Koopmans, Diamond, and Williamson [**1**] on the concepts of impatience and time perspective. Separability is also central to the theory of aggregation. The existence of aggregate stocks of capital and labour and the aggregate production function depends critically on the separability assumptions. Separability concepts can be applied to the theory of the firm in the same way as they are applied in the theory of consumer behaviour and, except in empirical studies, there are no new problems specific to it.

The plan of the survey is as follows. Section 2 is entitled 'the mathematics of separability' and is concerned with an exposition and extension of the fundamental theorems of separability. In section 3 the comparative static implications of the various kinds of separability are presented and the problem of simultaneously additive direct and indirect utility functions is discussed. Finally section 4 deals with the applications of separability to the static and dynamic theories of consumer behaviour, to the theories of the firm and aggregation, and to the empirical estimation of demand functions.(1)

2. The Mathematics of Separability

2.1. *Introduction*

As we have observed, early contributions to the theory of consumer behaviour by such authors as Gossen [**1**], Jevons [**1**], and Walras [**1**] were characterized by the assumption that the utility function of the consumer was cardinal and additive, i.e. it could be written

$$U = \sum_{i=1}^{n} U_i(x_i), \tag{1}$$

where U is the utility of all goods consumed and U_i is the utility of the quantity of good i consumed. This was a very restrictive

(1) When our work was in final draft for publication, we were provided with the two important unpublished studies by Goldberger [**2**] and by Theil [**3**]. These three are obviously concerned with reviewing works in closely related areas. However, ours are complementary, rather than substitutive, with theirs.

assumption and its strong implications, both theoretical and empirical, which were spelled out by Samuelson [**1**], led to its replacement by the much more general formulation,

$$U = U(x_1, \ldots, x_n); \tag{2}$$

it was from this formulation that the work of Slutsky, Hicks, and Allen proceeded. A consequence of the great increase in generality, however, was a reduction in empirical content of sufficient magnitude to lead to a consideration of utility functions less restrictive than (1) while less general than (2). Further impetus in this direction came from work in the dynamic theory of consumer behaviour and on the aggregation problem (see below). In all of the new formulations the concept of *separability*, variously defined, was employed.

2.2 *The fundamental theorems of separability*

In spite of recent work on the subject, the basic contributions on separability remain those of Sono [**1**] and Leontief [**1**, **2**]. Sono's paper was published in Japanese in 1943, in *Kokumin Keizai Zasshi*, but it remained little known outside Japan until an English translation appeared in 1961. He presented his results in the context of utility theory. Leontief's work was undertaken completely independently and appeared in 1946–7; its context was primarily the theory of production. Since these papers were published the separability concepts have been widely employed in both of these areas.

The concept of separability which was studied by both Sono and Leontief, and since named *weak separability*, is defined as follows. Let $y = f(x)$ be a utility function (or a production function), where x is an n-dimensional vector with elements labelled by indices, 1,..., n. Denote the set of indices (or goods) by $N = \{1, \ldots, n\}$. Then a subset $N^* = \{1, \ldots, m\}$, $m < n$, is weakly separable from N (or from $\bar{N}^*$, the complement of N^* in N) in $f(x)$, iff the following conditions are fulfilled:

$$\frac{\partial}{\partial x_k}\left(\frac{f_i}{f_j}\right) = 0 \quad (i, j \in N^*,\ k \in \bar{N}^*), \tag{3}$$

where f_i and f_j indicate partial derivatives of f with respect to x_i and x_j.

These conditions imply that the marginal rate of substitution between goods i and j is independent of the goods in $\bar{N}^*$. They are equivalent to

$$\frac{f_{1k}}{f_1} = \frac{f_{2k}}{f_2} = \dots = \frac{f_{mk}}{f_m} \quad (k \in \bar{N}^*) \tag{4}$$

(where $f_{ik} = \partial^2 f/\partial x_i \, \partial x_k$), which follows from the evaluation of (3). Denoting the ratios in (4) by ν_k, we obtain

$$f_{ik} = \nu_k f_i \quad (i = 1,..., m;\ k = m+1,..., n), \tag{5}$$

where ν_k is, in general, a function of x. From these conditions, it can be shown that there follows *the First Fundamental Theorem of Separability.*

THEOREM 1. *A subset $N^* = \{1,..., m\}$ is weakly separable from the set N in $f(x)$ if and only if $f(x)$ is of the form*

$$f(x) = F(f^1(x^*), \bar{x}^*), \tag{6}$$

where $x^* = (x_1,..., x_m)$ and $\bar{x}^* = (x_{m+1},..., x_n)$.

Sono referred to $f^1(x^*)$ as the 'proper' utility function of x^*.(2) $\bar{N}^*$ is called a *free set* if no subsets of it, including itself, are separable from N (in the sense of Theorem 1).(3)

(2) The objection is sometimes raised that weak separability is an excessively unrealistic concept. A weaker form of separability has been proposed by Franklin Fisher [4] which he calls 'approximate separability'. Suppose a twice continuously differentiable function $F(x_1, x_2, x_3)$ is to be approximated by another such function, $G\{\phi(x_1, x_2), x_3\}$ drawn from a set of functions satisfying certain regularity conditions. A similar analysis would apply if we were to ask what functions, F, satisfying certain regularity conditions could be approximated by a given function G. Defining $H(x_1, x_2, x_3) \equiv F - G$, the standard of approximation is

$$|H(x_1, x_2, x_3)| < \epsilon$$

for some $\epsilon < 0$ and all points in a closed, bounded rectangular region. Fisher then proves a theorem, the essence of which is that, if a twice differentiable weakly separable function approximates a given reasonable-looking twice differentiable function, then either the given function approximately satisfies the First Fundamental Theorem of Separability or else the approximating function exhibits peculiar behaviour (see Fisher [4]).

(3) Gorman [6] defines N^* as separable from N if the conditional ordering N^* is the same for all $\bar{x}^*$. This is slightly weaker than the Sono definition; while the latter assumes $m \geqq 2$, all single-element sets are separable in ordinary cases according to the former.

Leontief also considered the concept of *additive* or *strong separability* and proved the following theorem that is valid locally:[(4)]

THEOREM 2. *If two weakly separable subsets N^* and N^{**} of N in $f(x)$, of which neither is a subset of the other, intersect, then the three non-overlapping subsets $N^* \cap N^{**}$, N^*-N^{**}, and $N^{**}-N^*$ are additively separable subsets of N in $f(x)$; denoting them, respectively, by N_1, N_2, and N_3, and the rest by N_c, there exist functions f^1, f^2, f^3, and F such that*[(5)]

$$f(x) = F(f^1(x^1)+f^2(x^2)+f^3(x^3), x^c), \tag{7}$$

where x^1, x^2, x^3, x^c are subvectors of x generated by the partition of N into N_1, N_2, N_3, and N_c.

This is *the Second Fundamental Theorem of Separability.* Leontief did not define additive separability in terms of the conditions which it imposes on the partial derivatives of f although he did so in the case of weak separability.[(6)] These conditions are presented in the following definition.

DEFINITION. Let $y = f(x)$ be a utility function (or a production function), where x is an n-element vector. Then the non-overlapping subsets N_1, N_2, N_3, defined as above, are additively or strongly separable subsets of N in $f(x)$ if the conditions

$$\text{(i)} \quad \frac{\partial}{\partial x_k}\left(\frac{f_i}{f_j}\right) = 0 \quad \text{for } i, j \in N_h,\ k \notin N_h \quad (h = 1, 2, 3),$$

$$\text{(ii)} \quad \frac{\partial}{\partial x_k}\left(\frac{f_i}{f_j}\right) = 0 \quad \text{for } i \in N_g,\ j \in N_h,\ k \notin N_g \cup N_h$$

$$(g \neq h \text{ and } g, h = 1, 2, 3) \tag{8}$$

are fulfilled.

This definition has a number of implications. First, (i) is no more than the conditions for weak separability. Second, (ii) is the strengthening condition which distinguishes strong from

(4) The global result was established by Gorman [**6**].

(5) Let S and T be two sets. $S-T$ means the complement of T in S, i.e. all elements of S not in T.

(6) But he proved the theorem by showing that the assumed weak separability into overlapping subsets implies (i) and (ii) below.

weak separability. Third, it is important that each of the subsets N_1, N_2, and N_3 is not empty. Fourth, the free set N_c may be empty. The latter two implications we examine in more detail. Assume that N_c is empty and consider the case in which one of the subsets N_1, N_2, and N_3 is also empty, say N_3. Then, instead of (7) we have

$$f(x) = F[f^1(x^1)+f^2(x^2)]. \tag{9}$$

This case, in which the set N is partitioned into *two* additively separable subsets, is by no means an implausible one, but it falls outside the scope of Leontief's theorem concerning additive separability as well as the Strotz–Gorman definition of strong separability (8) and so it was not investigated by them (see Strotz [**3**] and Gorman [**2**]). However, it was treated in detail by Sono under the title of 'independent goods'; the special case in which x^1 and x^2 each consist of a single variable and $F(t) = t$ was treated by Samuelson [**1**] and Allen [**1**] under the title of 'independent utilities'.

Sono was concerned with a special case of N_1 consisting of a single element and defined independent goods as follows.

DEFINITION. Let the utility function be denoted by $y = f(x)$, where x is an n-element vector, and let N be partitioned into two weakly separable subsets $N_1 = \{1\}$ and $N_2 = \{2,..., n\}$. Then good 1 is independent of the goods in N_2 if the following conditions are fulfilled:

$$\frac{\frac{\partial}{\partial x_1}\left(\frac{f_2}{f_1}\right)}{\frac{f_2}{f_1}} = \frac{\frac{\partial}{\partial x_1}\left(\frac{f_3}{f_1}\right)}{\frac{f_3}{f_1}} = \dots = \frac{\frac{\partial}{\partial x_1}\left(\frac{f_n}{f_1}\right)}{\frac{f_n}{f_1}} = \theta(x_1), \tag{10}$$

where θ is a function of x_1 alone or is constant.

These conditions state that the percentage rates of change of the marginal rate of substitution of an independent good x_1 for all goods from N^2, with respect to a change in the quantity of the independent good x_1, are equal; furthermore, their value θ is independent of N^2, i.e. it depends only on the independent good. In general, of course, θ would be a function of x. It can also be shown that independence is a symmetric relationship; x_1 independent of x^2 implies x^2 independent of x_1.[(7)]

Sono showed that from these conditions there follows *the Third Fundamental Theorem of Separability*:

THEOREM 3. *If conditions* (10) *hold, there exist functions* f^1, f^2, *and* F *such that*

$$f(x) = F(f^1(x_1)+f^2(x^2)). \tag{11}$$

The converse of this theorem is also true.

Samuelson proved the following theorem for the two-good case.

THEOREM. *The necessary and sufficient condition that there exist a utility index which can be written in the form*

$$f(x) = f^1(x_1)+f^2(x_2) \tag{9'}$$

is as follows:

$$\frac{\dfrac{\partial}{\partial x_1}\left(\dfrac{f_1^1}{f_2^2}\right)}{\dfrac{f_1^1}{f_2^2}} = \frac{\dfrac{\partial^2}{\partial x_1\,\partial x_2}\left(\dfrac{f_1^1}{f_2^2}\right)}{\dfrac{\partial}{\partial x_2}\left(\dfrac{f_1^1}{f_2^2}\right)} = \theta^*(x_1). \tag{10*}$$

Allen also derived this result. Its similarity to the Sono conditions (10) is evident.

Although Sono dealt only with the case of one independent

(7) Employing the extended Theorem 3 we shall demonstrate that

$$\frac{\dfrac{\partial}{\partial x_k}\left(\dfrac{f_1}{f_h}\right)}{\dfrac{f_1}{f_h}} = \frac{\dfrac{\partial}{\partial x_k}\left(\dfrac{f_2}{f_h}\right)}{\dfrac{f_2}{f_h}} = \dots = \frac{\dfrac{\partial}{\partial x_k}\left(\dfrac{f_m}{f_h}\right)}{\dfrac{f_m}{f_h}} = n(x^2) \quad (h, k = m+1,\dots, n).$$

Evaluate
$$\frac{\dfrac{\partial}{\partial x_k}\left(\dfrac{f_j}{f_h}\right)}{\dfrac{f_j}{f_h}} \quad (j = 1,\dots, m).$$

By Theorem 3,

$$\frac{\dfrac{\partial}{\partial x_k}\left(\dfrac{f_j}{f_h}\right)}{\dfrac{f_j}{f_h}} = \frac{\dfrac{\partial}{\partial x_k}\left(\dfrac{F'f_j^1}{F'f_h^2}\right)}{\dfrac{F'f_j^1}{F'f_h^2}} = \frac{f_h^2 f_{jk}^1 - f_j^1 f_{hk}^2}{(f_h^2)^2}\,\frac{f_h^2}{f_j^1} = -\frac{f_{hk}^2}{f_h^2}$$

since $f_{jk}^1 = 0$; this is independent of x_1, and clearly holds for all $j = 1,\dots, m$.

good, the concept of independence can be generalized to two or more goods. Here we deal with the two-good case; the many-good case follows, *mutatis mutandis*. In the two-good case we have, where x_1 and x_2 are independent of $(x_3,..., x_n)$:

$$\frac{\frac{\partial}{\partial x_1}\left(\frac{f_3}{f_1}\right)}{\frac{f_3}{f_1}} = ... = \frac{\frac{\partial}{\partial x_1}\left(\frac{f_n}{f_1}\right)}{\frac{f_n}{f_1}} = \theta_1(x_1, x_2), \tag{10'}$$

$$\frac{\frac{\partial}{\partial x_2}\left(\frac{f_3}{f_1}\right)}{\frac{f_3}{f_1}} = ... = \frac{\frac{\partial}{\partial x_2}\left(\frac{f_n}{f_1}\right)}{\frac{f_n}{f_1}} = \theta_2(x_1, x_2). \tag{10''}$$

Similarly

$$\frac{\frac{\partial}{\partial x_1}\left(\frac{f_3}{f_2}\right)}{\frac{f_3}{f_2}} = ... = \frac{\frac{\partial}{\partial x_1}\left(\frac{f_n}{f_2}\right)}{\frac{f_n}{f_2}} = \pi_1(x_1, x_2), \tag{10'''}$$

$$\frac{\frac{\partial}{\partial x_2}\left(\frac{f_3}{f_2}\right)}{\frac{f_3}{f_2}} = ... = \frac{\frac{\partial}{\partial x_2}\left(\frac{f_n}{f_2}\right)}{\frac{f_n}{f_2}} = \pi_2(x_1, x_2). \tag{10''''}$$

Goods $N_1 = \{1, 2\}$ are of course weakly separable from

$$N_2 = \{3,..., n\},$$

and vice versa.

First, it is easily seen that an additively separable function

$$u = f(\xi(x_1, x_2) + \eta(x_3,..., x_n))$$

satisfies conditions (10′)–(10′′′′). Secondly, the converse is proved as follows: If (10′) and (10″) hold,

$$\log \frac{f_k}{f_1} = -\log \theta(x_1, x_2) + \log \sigma_k(x_3,..., x_n) \quad (k = 3,..., n). \tag{12}$$

Similarly, (10‴) and (10′′′′) imply

$$\log \frac{f_k}{f_2} = -\log \pi(x_1, x_2) + \log \omega_k(x_3,..., x_n) \quad (k = 3,..., n). \tag{13}$$

Therefore, from (12) and (13),

$$\frac{f_2}{f_1} = \frac{\pi(x_1, x_2)}{\theta(x_1, x_2)} \frac{\sigma_k(x_3,..., x_n)}{\omega_k(x_3,..., x_n)}, \tag{14}$$

$$\frac{f_k}{f_h} = \frac{\sigma_k(x_3,..., x_n)}{\sigma_h(x_3,..., x_n)} = \frac{\omega_k(x_3,..., x_n)}{\omega_h(x_3,..., x_n)}. \tag{15}$$

f_2/f_1 is independent of $(x_3,..., x_n)$ since $N_1 = \{1, 2\}$ is a weakly separable subset. Therefore σ_k/ω_k is constant. Let $\phi(x_1, x_2)$ be π multiplied by σ_k/ω_k. (13) and (14) are then written as

$$\frac{f_k}{f_2} = \frac{\sigma_k(x_3,..., x_k)}{\phi(x_1, x_2)} \quad \text{and} \quad \frac{f_2}{f_1} = \frac{\phi(x_1, x_2)}{\theta(x_1, x_2)}, \tag{16}$$

respectively.

Now, the integrability of $\sum \sigma_k \, dx_k$ follows directly from the separability of $N_2 = \{3,..., n\}$ from N, so that

$$\frac{\partial \sigma_k}{\partial x_j} = \frac{\partial \sigma_j}{\partial x_k} \quad (j, k \in N_2).$$

On the other hand, the integrability of $\theta \, dx_1 + \phi \, dx_2$ can be shown by means of the condition

$$\frac{\theta_2}{f_2} = \frac{\pi_1}{f_1}, \tag{17}$$

which follows from (10″), (10‴), and the separability of N_1. Bearing (12), (13), and (16) in mind, we evaluate θ_2 and π_1. We then find that (17) implies

$$\frac{\partial \theta}{\partial x_2} = \frac{\partial \phi}{\partial x_1}. \tag{18}$$

Thus, both $\theta \, dx_1 + \phi \, dx_2$ and $\sigma_3 \, dx_3 + ... + \sigma_n \, dx_n$ are total differentials. Integrating, we obtain

$$\int [\theta \, dx_1 + \phi \, dx_2 + \sigma_3 \, dx_3 + ... + \sigma_n \, dx_n] = \xi(x_1, x_2) + \eta(x_3,..., x_n). \tag{19}$$

On the other hand,

$$df = f_1 \, dx_1 + ... + f_n \, dx_n = \frac{f_1}{\theta}(\theta \, dx_1 + \phi \, dx_2 + \sigma_3 \, dx_3 + ... + \sigma_n \, dx_n)$$

$$= \frac{f_1}{\theta}(d\xi + d\eta). \tag{20}$$

Therefore,

$$f(x) = F[\xi(x_1, x_2) + \eta(x_3,..., x_n)]. \tag{21}$$

Thus we obtain the additive separability into two groups.

2.3. *Extensions*

Goldman and Uzawa [**1**] re-examined the work of Sono and Leontief. All of Leontief's proofs were local and he assumed functions in C^3, i.e. with continuous first, second, and third derivatives. Goldman–Uzawa, like Sono, assumed functions in C^2 and obtained theorems which are proved globally. In their definitions of weak and strong separability they introduced 'separability with respect to a partition', which involved extending the Sono–Leontief results to the many-subset case. Their definitions and theorems of weak and strong separability are presented in the context of demand theory and are as follows.

DEFINITION. Let $\{N_1,\ldots, N_s\}$ be a partition of the set of n commodities $N = \{1,\ldots, n\}$ and $u(x)$ be a utility function for a preference relation, each indifference surface of $u(x)$ being connected in any subspace and $x = (x_1,\ldots, x_n)$ being a commodity bundle. The utility function $u(x)$ is weakly separable with respect to the partition $\{N_1,\ldots, N_s\}$ (or, alternatively, each of $N_1,\ldots, N_s$ is weakly separable from N in $u(x)$) if the conditions

$$\frac{\partial}{\partial x_k}\left(\frac{u_i(x)}{u_j(x)}\right) = 0 \quad \text{for all } i, j \in N_h,\ k \notin N_h \tag{22}$$

are fulfilled, where u_i and u_j indicate partial derivatives of u with respect to x_i and x_j.

THEOREM 1*. *A utility function $u(x)$ is weakly separable with respect to a partition, $\{N_1,\ldots, N_s\}$, if and only if $u(x)$ is of the form*

$$u(x) = \Phi(u^1(x^1),\ldots, u^s(x^s)), \tag{23}$$

where $(x^1,\ldots, x^s)$ is a corresponding partition of the commodity bundle x, $\Phi(u^1,\ldots, u^s)$ is a function of s variables, and, for each $h = 1,\ldots, s$, $u^h(x^h)$ is a function of subvector x^h alone.

DEFINITION. Let $s > 2$. The utility function $u(x)$ is strongly separable with respect to a partition $\{N_1,\ldots, N_s\}$ (or $N_1,\ldots, N_s$ are strongly separable from N in $u(x)$) if the conditions

$$\frac{\partial}{\partial x_k}\left(\frac{u_i(x)}{u_j(x)}\right) = 0 \quad \text{for all } i \in N_h,\ j \in N_t, \text{ and } k \notin N_h \cup N_t \tag{24}$$

are fulfilled.[8] If $s = 2$, $i \in N_1$, say, implies $k \in N_2$ and hence $j \in N_1$; then (24) reduces to the conditions for weak separability.

THEOREM 2*. *A utility function is strongly separable with respect to a partition* $\{N_1,..., N_s\}$ $(s > 2)$ *iff* $u(x)$ *is of the form*

$$u(x) = F[u^1(x^1)+...+u^s(x^s)] \tag{25}$$

where $F(t)$ *is a monotonically increasing function of one variable and for each* h, $u^h(x^h)$ *is a function of subvector* x^h *alone.*

Theorem 1* is easily derived from Sono's Theorem 1 by applying it repeatedly. As x^1 is separable, we can first write $u(x)$ in the form

$$u(x) = F\big(u^1(x^1), x^2,..., x^s\big).$$

Then, by virtue of the separability of x^2, this is further rewritten as

$$u(x) = G\big(u^1(x^1), u^2(x^2), x^3,..., x^s\big)$$

and so on, until we finally have (23).

Similarly, Theorem 2* is no more than a corollary of Sono's Theorem 3. Let $i \in N_h$ and j, $r \in N_t$. The weak separability of x^h implies that f_{ir}/f_i is independent of $i \in N_h$, so that

$$\frac{\partial}{\partial x_r}\left(\log\frac{f_i}{f_j}\right) = \frac{f_{ir}}{f_i} - \frac{f_{jr}}{f_j} = \theta_{jr} \quad \text{for all } i \in N_h \tag{26}$$

$$(h = 1,..., t-1, t+1,..., s).$$

On the other hand, the strong separability (24) implies that f_i/f_j is independent of all x^k other than x^h and x^t. Therefore,

$$\theta_{jr} = \theta_{jr}^{(h)}(x^h, x^t)$$

from (26). As this must hold for all h except t, we have

$$\theta_{jr} = \theta_{jr}^{(h)}(x^h, x^t) = \theta_{jr}^{(h')}(x^{h'}, x^t). \tag{27}$$

The first equation of (27) shows that θ_{jr} is independent of $x^{h'}$ so that $x^{h'}$ cannot appear as an argument of $\theta_{jr}^{(h')}(x^{h'}, x^t)$, as it is an

[8] Seemingly weaker conditions on the independence of the marginal rates of substitution are necessary and sufficient for additive separability. Gorman [5] proved the following results.

Let $a_{ht} = 1$ if u_i/u_j depends only on i, j, x^h, x^t (each $i \in h$, $j \in t$), otherwise $a_{ht} = 0$. Then, if $u(.)$ is well-behaved it is additively separable if and only if $A = \|a_{st}\|$ is indecomposable.

However, conditions (24) have also been proved to be necessary and sufficient, so that they and the indecomposability of A are equivalent.

alternative expression of the function θ_{jr}; hence

$$\theta_{jr} = \theta_{jr}(x^t). \tag{28}$$

(26) and (28) are no more than the condition that x^t be independent, in Sono's sense, of all other goods.

Thus the strong separability implies that each x^t is independent, $t = 1,\ldots, s$. (Conversely, we can show that the independence of each x^t from the others implies the strong separability of x with respect to the partition $\{N_1,\ldots, N_s\}$.) By Sono's Theorem 3, we have

$$\begin{aligned} u(x) &= F[u^1(x^1)+\eta^1(\bar{x}^1)] \\ &= G_i[u^i(x^i)+\eta^i(\bar{x}^i)] \quad (i = 2,\ldots, s), \end{aligned}$$

where $\bar{x}^i$ is the complement of x^i in x. Hence

$$u^1(x^1)+\eta^1(\bar{x}^1) = H_i[u^i(x^i)+\eta^i(\bar{x}^i)],$$

where $H_i = F^{-1}G_i$. Differentiating this equation with respect to an element of x^1, say x_1, we have

$$\frac{\partial u^1}{\partial x_1} = H_i' \frac{\partial \eta^i}{\partial x_1}.$$

Because both $\partial u^1/\partial x_1$ and $\partial \eta^i/\partial x_1$ are independent of x^i, H_i' must not be affected by x^i and this is possible only if $H_i(t)$ is a linear function. Therefore,

$$u^1(x^1)+\eta^1(\bar{x}^1) = a_i[u^i(x^i)+\eta^i(\bar{x}^i)]+b_i,$$

where a_i and b_i are constant. By differentiating both sides of this equation twice with respect to x_h and x_k ($h \in N_i$, $k \in N_j$; $i, j = 2,\ldots, s$) we obtain

$$\frac{\partial^2 \eta^1}{\partial x_h \, \partial x_k} = 0$$

for $h \in N_i$, $k \in N_j$ and for all $i, j = 2,\ldots, s$; $i \neq j$. Hence η^1 can be written in an additive form. That is to say, we have the Goldman–Uzawa form (25).

It is obvious that a function of the form (25) satisfies the conditions of independence (26) and (28) as well as strong separability (24). This proves the 'only if' part of Theorem 2*.

In this proof of Theorem 2* we have seen that when the whole set of commodities is partitioned into more than two subgroups, strong separability of the subgroups is equivalent to the Sono independence of each subgroup.

As was mentioned previously, however, the definition of strong separability is not applicable if there are only two subgroups, whilst Sono independence, which was originally defined for the two-subgroup case, can be extended so that it covers the case of the set of commodities being partitioned into many (more than two) subgroups. We must therefore conclude that Sono independence is more fundamental than Strotz–Gorman–Goldman–Uzawa strong separability.

By taking $F(t) \equiv t$, (25) can be written as

$$u(x) = \sum_i u^i(x^i).$$

$\sum_i u^i(x^i)$ is thus a 'normalized utility index'. The crude concept of cardinal utility can be justified if it is interpreted as the normalized utility index, which is obtained only if the conditions of strong separability hold. In fact, the utility functions of Gossen, Jevons, and Walras are the special case of $\sum_i u^i(x^i)$ in which each x^i contains only one element. Thus the addition of utilities of goods is permissible only if they are the normalized additive utilities which are obtained under strong separability. It is worth noting, however, that the concept of strong separability itself does not presume any cardinality; the separability with respect to a partition $\{N_1,\ldots, N_s\}$ is invariant under a general monotonic transformation of $u(x)$.

The concepts of weak and strong separability were combined by Pearce [**1**] to form what is now known as 'Pearce separability'. It is defined as follows.

Definition. The utility function $u(x)$ is Pearce-separable with respect to a partition $\{N_1,\ldots, N_s\}$ if the conditions

$$\frac{\partial}{\partial x_k}\left(\frac{u_i(x)}{u_j(x)}\right) = 0 \quad \text{for all } i, j \in N_h \text{ and } k \neq i, j \tag{29}$$

are fulfilled.

What these conditions state is that the marginal rate of substitution between any two goods in one subgroup of the partition is independent of all other goods, including other goods in the same subgroup. It is the latter property which distinguishes Pearce separability from weak separability.(9) With this definition Pearce [**3**] and Goldman–Uzawa [**1**] proved the following theorem.

THEOREM 4. *A utility function is Pearce separable with respect to a partition* $\{N_1, \ldots, N_s\}$ *iff it is of the form*

$$u(x) = \Phi[u^1(x^1), \ldots, u^s(x^s)], \tag{30}$$

where $\Phi[u^1, \ldots, u^s]$ *is a function of s variables and* $u^h(x^h)$ *is an additive function of* x^h *whenever the number of elements of* x^h *exceeds two*. Clearly, if the number of elements of x^h, for all h, is equal to two, Pearce separability reduces to weak separability.

The concepts of homothetic and homogeneous separability, which were introduced by Gorman [**2**] and Morishima [**3**] under closely related stimuli, are defined as follows.(10)

DEFINITION. A utility function is said to be homothetically separable if it is weakly separable and the proper utility functions are homothetic; it is said to be homogeneously separable if it is weakly separable and the proper utility functions are homogeneous of degree one. Thus homogeneous separability can be viewed as normalized homothetic separability.

The stimulus to Gorman came from Strotz [**2**], who wrongly attributed to weak separability of the utility function the implication that the consumer's budgetary process was such that he first allocated his income between the different *separable subsets* of commodities and then spent the allotted income optimally on the commodities in each particular subset, without further reference to the other subsets. Gorman investigated the conditions under which there exists a set of price indices for the different groups of commodities, which depend only on commodity prices *within* the group, such that expenditure on each

(9) A more detailed consideration of Pearce separability or, as he termed it, 'neutral want association' will be given in section 4. Although it amounts only to a combination of weak and strong separability, its implications for consumer behaviour are of some interest.

(10) Before Gorman and Morishima, the homogeneous separability was discussed by Shephard [**1**] in the context of the theory of production. See section 4 below.

group depends only on the price indices and total expenditure; i.e. the consumer does not have to know the actual prices of individual commodities in order to carry out his preliminary allocation. His results are contained in the following propositions, the first of which states *local* and the second *global* conditions.

PROPOSITION 1. *Local price aggregates exist if and only if the utility function can be written in one or other of the following forms:*

$$\left.\begin{array}{ll}\text{(i)} & u = F(v_1, v_2) \\ \text{(ii)} & u = F[v_1, f(v_2,\ldots, v_s)] \\ \text{(iii)} & u = v_1+\ldots+v_m+f(v_{m+1},\ldots, v_s) \quad (0 \leqslant m \leqslant s)\end{array}\right\}, \tag{31}$$

where $v_i = v_i(x^i)$, $i = 1,\ldots, s$ *is the proper utility function of group* i, F *and* f *are general functions but the arguments of* f *are homogeneous of degree one.*

PROPOSITION 2. *If there are more than two groups, and if not precisely* $(s-1)$ *of the proper utility functions are homogeneous, global price aggregates exist iff the utility function can be written in the form*

$$u = v_1+\ldots+v_m+f(v_{m+1},\ldots, v_s) \quad (0 \leqslant m \leqslant s), \tag{32}$$

where

$$\text{(i)} \qquad v_k = v_k(x^k) \quad (k = m+1,\ldots, s) \tag{33}$$

is homogeneous of degree one, and

$$\text{(ii)} \quad v_i = G_i(y_i/P_i)+Q_i(p_i) \text{ is in polar form} \quad (i = 1,\ldots, s), \tag{34}$$

where p_i *is the price vector for the i-th group of commodities,* P_i *the price index for group* i, y_i *the consumer's expenditure on commodities in group* i, *and*

$$P_i = P_i(p_i) \quad \text{is homogeneous of degree one,} \tag{35}$$

$$Q_i = Q_i(p_i) \quad \text{is homogeneous of degree zero.} \tag{36}$$

The polar form of v_i, $G_i(y_i/P_i)+Q_i(p_i) = g_i(y_i, p_i)$, is found by maximizing v_i subject to $p_i x^i = y_i$, when y_i is determined as $P_i v_i$ by maximizing u subject to $\sum P_i v_i = Y =$ consumer's total income. (34) then says that $g_i(y_i, p_i)$ must be additive and satisfy (35) and (36).

It should be noted that these propositions state conditions

on the form of the utility function which hold *after* normalization; it is required only that u can be put in the particular forms specified. Gorman uses the term 'homogeneous' in an extended sense; 'homogeneous' proper utility functions means that the proper utility functions are 'functions of a function which is homogeneous of degree one', i.e. homothetic. (See Gorman [**2**], footnote 1.)

If $m = 0$ in (32), i.e.

$$u = f(v_1, ..., v_s), \tag{32'}$$

conditions (34)–(36) are automatically satisfied; but these conditions are not automatically satisfied by the strongly separable part of (32). Thus strong separability is not sufficient for the existence of global price aggregates; it is, however, sufficient for the existence of local aggregates, as Gorman's Proposition 1 (iii) makes clear, and it was the local problem with which Strotz [**3**] was concerned. On the other hand, homothetic separability alone, as normalized in (32′), is sufficient for the existence of global price aggregates, provided there are more than two homothetically separable subsets. Gorman notes that if u can be written in the form (32′), the allocation problem reduces to the maximization of $f(v_1, ..., v_s)$ subject to $\sum P_i v_i = Y$; this holds iff each of the proper utility functions is homothetic. In a recent paper, Blackorby, Lady, Nissen, and Russell [**1**] present a technique for constructing global price aggregates P_i for a homothetically separable utility function and derive a two-stage budgeting strategy for the consumer which is consistent iff the utility function is homothetically separable. The price indices are defined as follows:

$$P_i = \frac{1}{g_i[\Phi_i(1, p_i)]}$$

where $x^i = \Phi_i(y_i, p_i)$ represent the partial demand functions for goods in group i, derived by maximizing $g_i(x^i)$ subject to $p_i x^i = y^i$. The g_i, which are homogeneous of degree one, are the normalized proper utility functions of groups i $(i = 1, ..., s)$; they clearly correspond to Gorman's v_i while $g_i[\Phi_i]$ corresponds to Gorman's g_i. The P_i so defined allow the consumer to solve the allocation problem $\max u = u[g_1(x^1),..., g_s(x^s)]$ subject to $\sum P_i g_i(x^i) = Y$. The solution yields optimal $g_i = g_i^*$; this gives the optimal $y_i = y_i^*$ from which the optimal $x^i = x^{*i}$ can be calculated. However, these Blackorby–Lady–Nissen–Russell results have already been obtained by Morishima [**3**].

Morishima's discussion of homogeneous separability was stimulated by Hicks's *Revision of Demand Theory* [**2**]. In Chapter 17 Hicks viewed the consumer as choosing between certain objectives and then choosing between alternative means of achieving those objectives. The relationship between the means and the objectives is a technical one, rather like a production function. Morishima [**3**] developed this idea. He assumed that the consumer pursues m objectives; the means to the attainment of the jth objective are the goods $i_j,..., i'_j$. These goods are assumed to be weakly separable from all other goods, i.e. from the means to the other objectives. Further, the *technical* nature of the relationship of means to objectives prompts the assumption that the proper preference functions are homogeneous of degree one, i.e. constant returns to scale. The utility function is thus

$$u(x) = u[f^1(x_{i_1},..., x_{i'_1}),..., f^m(x_{i_m},..., x_{i'_m})], \tag{37}$$

where the f^j $(j = 1,..., m)$ are homogeneous of degree one; $u(x)$ is then homogeneously separable. Obviously (37) is a special case of (31), (iii), or (32) which is obtained by neglecting the additive part $\sum v_i(x_i)$. Thus Gorman's global proposition applies to the Hicks–Morishima model and we may regard the consumer as Hicks and Morishima did, as first deciding between objectives and then choosing between alternative means of achieving those objectives.

In a well-known paper, Frisch [**1**] introduced into the demand analysis the idea of *want independence*, which he defined as follows.

Definition. Good i is *want-independent* of all other goods if the marginal utility of good i depends only on good i.

Letting $i = 1$, the utility function must be of the form

$$u(x) = \phi_1(x_1)+\phi_2(x_2,..., x_n), \tag{38}$$

which is a normalized version of (9), the case of independence discussed by Sono. An extension of Frisch's want independence was made by Barten [**1**] which gave rise to a utility function of the form

$$u(x) = \phi^1(x^1)+\phi^2(x^2)+...+\phi^s(x^s), \tag{39}$$

where $\partial^2\phi^h/\partial x_i\,\partial x_j$ are negligible for all $i, j \in N_h$, $i \neq j$, and some h. This is the case of the proper utility function $\phi^h(x^h)$ being 'almost additive preferences', and the utility function (39) is the normalized utility index associated with strong separability into subsets $N_1, N_2,..., N_s$.

However, Frisch and Barten employ concepts which are not invariant under a general monotonic transformation. Frisch defines the concepts of 'utility accelerations' and 'want elasticities' as follows.

DEFINITION. The utility acceleration of good i with respect to good k is given by

$$\tilde{u}_{ik} = \frac{\partial u_i(x_1,..., x_n)}{\partial x_k}\,\frac{x_k}{u_i(x_1,..., x_n)} \quad (i, k = 1,..., n), \tag{40}$$

where $u_i(x_1,..., x_n) = \partial u(x_1,..., x_n)/\partial x_i$, the marginal utility of good i.

DEFINITION. The want elasticity of good i with respect to good $k$is given by

$$\tilde{x}_{ik} = \frac{\partial x_i(u_1,..., u_n)}{\partial u_k}\,\frac{u_k}{x_i(u_1,..., u_n)} \quad (i, k = 1,..., n), \tag{41}$$

where the $x_i(u_1,..., u_n)$ are the inverses of the marginal utility functions, i.e.

$$u_i = u_i(x_1,..., x_n) \quad (i = 1,..., n) \tag{42}$$

has an inverse

$$x_i = x_i(u_1,..., u_n) \quad (i = 1,..., n). \tag{43}$$

Neither of these concepts, as Frisch remarked, is invariant under a monotonic transformation of the utility function; nor is want independence, as we now show.

Want independence of good i requires

$$u_{ik} = 0 \quad (i \neq k); \quad \text{i.e. } \frac{\partial u_i(x_1,..., x_n)}{\partial x_k} = 0.$$

Introduce the monotonic transformation $F = [u(x_1,\ldots,x_n)]^2$. Then

$$\frac{\partial^2 F}{\partial x_i\,\partial x_k} = \frac{\partial}{\partial x_k} 2u(x_1,\ldots,x_n)u_i$$
$$= 2u_k u_i + 2u(x_1,\ldots,x_n)u_{ik} = 2u_k u_i \neq 0.$$

Therefore want independence is not invariant under a monotonic transformation.

The related concepts of independence (Sono) and strong separability (Leontief) are, however, invariant under a monotonic transformation; they are thus properties of the indifference curve. Want independence, on the other hand, is the property of a *particular* utility function from the family of functions defined on the individual indifference map; the existence of such a utility function was the problem of Sono and Leontief. Thus the concept is unnecessarily cumbersome; this is underlined by the fact that all of Frisch's results can be obtained from Sono's independence which is free of cardinal concepts.

Debreu [**1**] and Gorman [**6**] proved the Fundamental Theorem of Weak and Strong Separability under much weaker assumptions than those encountered above. They assumed only a continuous complete preference ordering on a product space, each element of which was topologically separable and connected. (However, see Vind [**1**].) Their results are global. Apart from these points, Gorman's Lemma 1 is identical with our Theorem 1 by Sono, and his Theorem 1 with our Theorem 2 by Leontief. Pokropp [**1**] has now removed even the continuity and has replaced it by strict monotonicity in each variable.

2.4. *The utility tree*

In his 1947 paper Leontief [**2**] presented a detailed discussion of the structure of functions containing separable subsets of independent variables and described the structure by means of a *tree*. He presents the following example.

Let $f(x_1,\ldots,x_n)$ have the internal structure

$$f(x_1,\ldots,x_n)$$
$$= F\{f_1(x_1,x_2,x_3), f_2[f_{21}(x_4,x_5)+f_{22}(x_6)+f_{23}(x_7)], x_8\}. \quad (44)$$

In $N = \{1, 2, \ldots, 8\}$ there are three weakly separable subsets $N_1 = \{1, 2, 3\}$, $N_2 = \{4, 5, 6, 7\}$, $N_3 = \{8\}$. The free set containing only one element, $N_3 = \{8\}$, can be considered as a weakly separable subset, due to a proposition of Leontief [**2**] that 'each individual independent variable constitutes a subset weakly separable from X in $f(X)$'. The subset N_1 is then seen to contain three weakly separable subsets, $N_{11} = \{1\}$, $N_{12} = \{2\}$, $N_{13} = \{3\}$. Subset N_2 has a more complicated structure. It contains three strongly separable subsets: $N_{21} = \{4, 5\}$, $N_{22} = \{6\}$, and $N_{23} = \{7\}$. Leontief defines the subsets N_{21}, N_{22}, N_{23} as additively primitive subsets of N in $F(x)$ *because they cannot be partitioned into smaller additively separable subsets of N in $F(x)$*. The subset N_{21} itself contains weakly separable subsets $N_{211} = \{4\}$, $N_{212} = \{5\}$. Thus subsets N_{211} and N_{212} are separable from N_{21} in $f_{21}(x^{21})$, N_{21} is separable from N_2 in $f_2(x^2)$, and N_2 is separable from N in $f(x)$, where $x^{21} = (x_4, x_5)$, $x^2 = (x_4, \ldots, x_7)$, and $x = (x_1, \ldots, x_8)$. Subsets N_{211} and N_{212} are then said to be *separable subsets of the third order*, subsets N_{ij} ($i = 1, 2$; $j = 1, 2, 3$) are separable subsets of the *second order*, and N_1, N_2, N_3 are separable subsets of the *first order*. The order of a separable subset can then be defined.

Definition. The order of a separable subset within the set Z of all non-intersecting separable subsets of N in $f(x)$ is defined as being equal to the number of elements of Z from which it can be separated. The order of a separable function is the same as the order of the subset which it separates.

The structure of (44) can be illustrated by means of a tree diagram. The weakly separable subsets are indicated by , the strongly separable subsets by 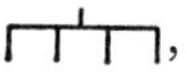, and the homogeneously separable subsets, if any, by . Then (44) will appear as Fig. 1. If $f_1(x^1)$ were homogeneous of degree one, the structure of N_1 would appear as Fig. 2. Any of the utility functions encountered above can be illustrated in this manner, for example, the three trees (31) discussed by Gorman are presented as in Fig. 3.

Strotz [**2**] referred to separable utility functions as utility trees, each proper function being a branch, but he made no

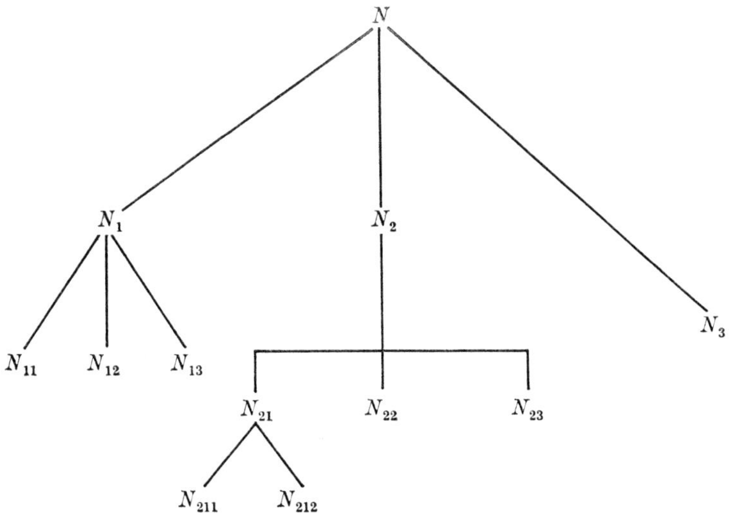

FIG. 1

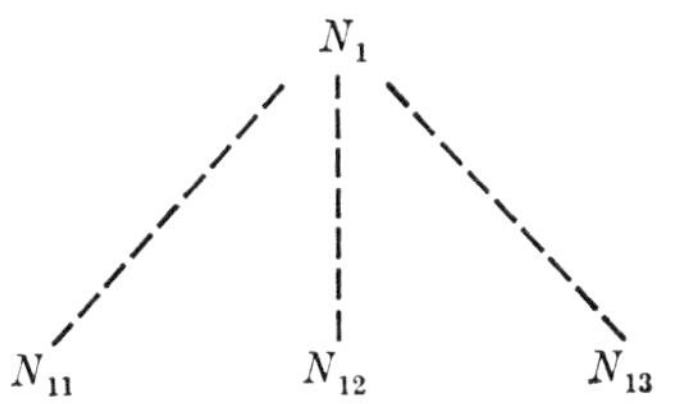

FIG. 2

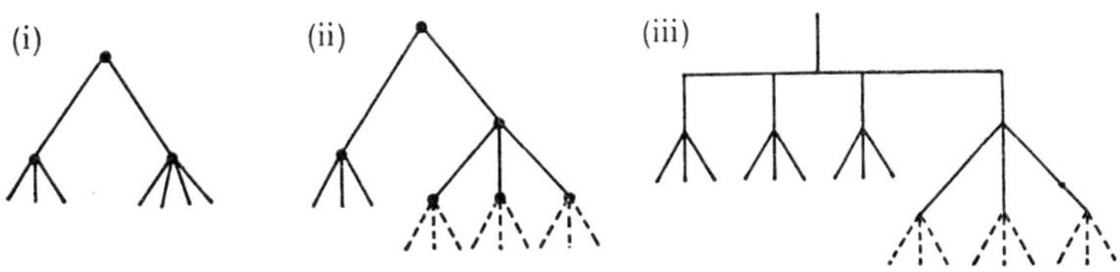

FIG. 3

reference to the concept of order of separability. Gorman [7] contains a rigorous analysis of the utility tree. He also presents an example similar to Leontief's and illustrates it as in Fig. 1; again, order of separability is not referred to.

3. The Comparative Statics of Separability

3.1. *The comparative statics of weak separability*

Much of the discussion of separability has taken place in the context of demand theory. The assumption of separability, of whatever type, involves restrictions on the partial derivatives of the utility function and must therefore have relevant implications for the comparative static aspects of the theory of demand. The implications of assuming weak separability were examined in detail by Sono [**1**].

In his analysis Sono employs a concept which he calls the 'point of common equilibrium'. Assume that there exists a weakly separable subset N^* of N in $f(x)$ such that

$$f(x) = F(f^1(x^*), \bar{x}^*)$$

(see (6) above). If some or all of the commodities in the subset $\bar{N}^*$ (the complement of N^* in N) are excluded from the preference field, the equilibrium quantities of commodities in N^* will change. However, Sono proves that, if I is the income of the consumer and I^* is the expenditure on those goods in N^*, the consumer would buy the same quantities of goods in N^* when his income was I^* and goods in $\bar{N}^*$ were excluded, as he would buy when goods in $\bar{N}^*$ were included and his income was I. This is the 'point of common equilibrium'; its existence is an implication of weak separability. He proceeds from this point to derive a number of comparative static properties which he calls 'laws of proportionality'; in what follows, 'general' denotes the case in which commodities in $\bar{N}^*$ are included; 'proper' denotes the case in which they are excluded.

Sono's laws of proportionality

(i) The general propensities to consume separable goods are proportional to the proper propensities to consume them, at the point of common equilibrium.

The propensity to consume any good j is $\partial x_j/\partial I$ where I is money income. We may also refer to it as the general income effect. Formally (i) is written:

$$\frac{\partial x_j}{\partial I} = \frac{\partial x_j}{\partial I^*}\frac{\partial I^*}{\partial I} \quad (j \in N^*). \tag{1}$$

(1) states that the general propensity to consume good j is equal to the product of the proper propensity to consume it, $\partial x_j/\partial I^*$, and of the aggregate propensity to consume the goods in N^*, $\partial I^*/\partial I$. Sono notes that whether or not the general and proper propensities to consume x_j have the same sign depends on $\partial I^*/\partial I$. If it is positive these signs are the same.

(ii) The rate of change of the equilibrium quantity of a good in the weakly separable subset N^* with respect to a change in the price of a good in $\bar{N}^*$ is, like the substitution term in the Slutsky equation, proportional to the proper propensity to consume the separable good at the point of common equilibrium.

This can be written as follows. For all $j \in N^*$, $k \in \bar{N}^*$,

$$\frac{\partial x_j}{\partial p_k} = \frac{\partial x_j}{\partial I^*}\frac{\partial I^*}{\partial p_k}, \tag{2}$$

$$K_{jk} = \frac{\partial x_j}{\partial I^*} w_k^*, \tag{3}$$

where

$$K_{jk} = \frac{\partial x_j}{\partial p_k} + x_k \frac{\partial x_j}{\partial I} \tag{4}$$

is the Slutsky term and

$$w_k^* = \frac{\partial I^*}{\partial p_k} + x_k \frac{\partial I^*}{\partial I} \tag{5}$$

is the equivalent term in the expression for the rate of change of expenditure on goods in N^* with respect to a change in the price of a good in $\bar{N}^*$.

Combining (1) and (3) we at once obtain the following result, which was also derived by Rajaoja [**1**].

$$\frac{K_{jk}}{K_{ik}} = \frac{\partial x_j/\partial I}{\partial x_i/\partial I} \quad \text{for } i, j \in N^*,\ k \in \bar{N}^*. \tag{6}$$

Combining (1) and (2) we obtain, except where $\partial I^*/\partial p_k = 0$, Houthakker's [**1**] result:

$$\frac{\partial x_j/\partial p_k}{\partial x_i/\partial p_k} = \frac{\partial x_j/\partial I}{\partial x_i/\partial I} \quad \text{for } i, j \in N^*,\ k \in \bar{N}^*. \tag{7}$$

To get this result Houthakker assumed additivity of the utility function, but clearly it is not necessary to do so, weak separability being sufficient.

(iii) The differences between the general and proper rates of change in the equilibrium quantities of goods in N^* with respect to a change in the price of a good in N^* are proportional to the respective proper propensities to consume them, at the point of common equilibrium. The same statement holds for the differences between the general and proper substitution terms.

Denoting the proper rates of change and substitution terms by $\partial x_j^*/\partial p_k$ and K_{jk}^* respectively, this can be written

$$\frac{\partial x_j}{\partial p_k}-\frac{\partial x_j^*}{\partial p_k} = \frac{\partial x_j}{\partial I^*}\frac{\partial I^*}{\partial p_k}, \qquad j,\, k \in N^* \tag{8}$$

$$K_{jk}-K_{jk}^* = -\frac{\partial x_j}{\partial I^*}w_k^{**}, \qquad j,\, k \in N^* \tag{9}$$

where
$$w_k^{**} = \frac{\partial(I-I^*)}{\partial p_k}+x_k\frac{\partial(I-I^*)}{\partial I} \tag{10}$$

is the 'substitution' term in the expression for the rate of change of expenditure on goods in $\bar{N}^*$ with respect to a change in the price of a good in N^*. Using the proper Slutsky equation

$$\left(\frac{\partial x_j}{\partial p_k}\right)^* = -x_k\frac{\partial x_j}{\partial I^*}+K_{jk}^*, \tag{11}$$

equation (8) can be written

$$\frac{\partial x_j}{\partial p_k} = -\left(x_k-\frac{\partial I^*}{\partial p_k}\right)\frac{\partial x_j}{\partial I^*}+K_{jk}^* \quad \text{for all } j,\, k \in N^*, \tag{12}$$

which is a result obtained by Pearce [**1**] for the more stringent case of Pearce separability (see his Theorem 4). In view of (9) it can be shown that the proper income effect, i.e. the first term of the right-hand side of (12), is the sum of the general income effect and the difference between the general and proper substitution effects, i.e. substituting from (4) for $\partial x_j/\partial p_k$ in (12) we find

$$-\left(x_k-\frac{\partial I^*}{\partial p_k}\right)\frac{\partial x_j}{\partial I^*} = -x_k\frac{\partial x_j}{\partial I}+K_{jk}-K_{jk}^*. \tag{13}$$

The difference between the general and proper substitution terms is of interest. The Hicksian substitution term K_{jk} is concerned with substitution which leaves the value of the *general* preference function unchanged. Sono considers substitution which leaves the value of the *proper* preference function unchanged and shows that substitution in terms of the proper preference function is equivalent to the proper substitution term, K^*_{jk}. Thus inspection of (4), (12), and (13) shows that if the Slutsky equation is written in Hicksian terms, (4), the difference between K_{jk} and K^*_{jk} is included in the *substitution* term, while if it is written in Sono terms, (12), $K_{jk}-K^*_{jk}$ is included in the *income* term. Sono shows in an example that it is possible for K_{jk} and K^*_{jk} to differ in sign; so cardigan and pullover, which are substitutive in terms of the proper utility function of clothing, may become complementary when food and other things are taken into account. From this viewpoint, Sono queried the suitability of Hicks defining substitutability and complementarity according to the sign of the general substitution term. Substitutability and complementarity may be defined in terms of the non-trivial proper utility functions of the highest order and the discrepancies of the proper substitution effects from the general ones may be included in the income effects.

One further theorem on weak separability was proved by Pearce [**1**] and Goldman and Uzawa [**1**]. They assumed that the utility function is strictly quasi-concave.(11)

THEOREM 1. *A strictly quasi-concave utility function is weakly separable with respect to a partition* $\{N_1,\ldots,N_s\}$ *iff the substitution terms* $K_{jk}(x)$ *are of the form*

$$K_{jk}(x) = a^{ht}(x)\frac{\partial x_j}{\partial I}\frac{\partial x_k}{\partial I}, \quad \textit{for all}\ j \in N_h,\ k \in N_t\ (h \neq t), \tag{14}$$

for all x, *with some functions* $a^{ht}(x)$ *defined for* $h \neq t$.

The necessity part of Theorem 1 is a corollary of Sono's Laws of Proportionality, although Sono did not derive it. From (3)

$$K_{jk} = w^*_k \frac{\partial x_j}{\partial I^*}.$$

(11) The necessity part of Theorem 1 and that of Theorem 3 below were first proposed and proved by Pearce, while the sufficiency parts were due to Goldman and Uzawa.

From (5)

$$w_k^* = \frac{\partial I^*}{\partial p_k} + x_k \frac{\partial I^*}{\partial I} = \sum_{t \in N^*} p_t \frac{\partial x_t}{\partial p_k} + x_k \frac{\partial I^*}{\partial I}$$

$$= \sum_{t \in N^*} p_t\left(-x_k \frac{\partial x_t}{\partial I} + K_{tk}\right) + x_k \frac{\partial I^*}{\partial I}$$

$$= \sum_{t \in N^*} p_t K_{tk}. \tag{15}$$

If $k \in N'$ is also separable, we have

$$K_{tk} = K_{kt} = w_t' \frac{\partial x_k}{\partial I'}$$

for $t \in N^*$; this, together with (15), yields

$$w_k^* = \left(\sum_t p_t w_t'\right) \frac{\partial x_k}{\partial I'}.$$

The expression $\sum_t p_t w_t'$ can be written $b^{*\prime}(x)$, which depends only on the groups N^* and N' and is common to all pairs of goods, $j \in N^*$ and $k \in N'$. Therefore, substituting into (3),

$$K_{jk} = b^{*\prime}(x) \frac{\partial x_j}{\partial I^*} \frac{\partial x_k}{\partial I'}. \tag{16}$$

Substituting from (1), we have the Pearce–Goldman–Uzawa result

$$K_{jk} = a^{*\prime}(x) \frac{\partial x_j}{\partial I} \frac{\partial x_k}{\partial I},$$

where $b^{*\prime}(x) = a^{*\prime}(x) \dfrac{\partial I^*}{\partial I} \dfrac{\partial I'}{\partial I}$.

3.2. *The comparative statics of independence*

In his investigation of the comparative statics of the one independent good case, Sono proves the following proposition.

PROPOSITION 1. *The rate of change of the equilibrium quantity of a good with respect to a change in the price of the independent good has the same or opposite sign as the substitution term, according as the elasticity of the marginal rate of substitution of the independent good for any other good, with respect to a change in the quantity of the independent good, is less or greater than one.*

Where good 1 is the independent good, we have

$$\frac{\partial x_j}{\partial p_1} = -(\epsilon_1 - 1)K_{j1} \tag{17}$$

where $$\epsilon_1 = -x_1 \frac{f_j}{f_1} \frac{\partial}{\partial x_1}\left(\frac{f_1}{f_j}\right), \quad j \in N_2 = \{2,\dots,x_n\}$$

is invariant under a monotonic transformation of the utility function. From (17) and the Slutsky equation we find that

$$K_{j1} = \frac{x_1}{\epsilon_1}\frac{\partial x_j}{\partial I}, \quad j \in N_2. \tag{18}$$

As $\dfrac{\partial x_j}{\partial I} = \dfrac{\partial x_j}{\partial I^2}\dfrac{\partial I^2}{\partial I}$ where I^2 is expenditure on goods in N_2, we have from (18)

$$K_{j1} = \frac{x_1}{\epsilon_1}\frac{\partial I^2}{\partial I}\frac{\partial x_j}{\partial I^2}, \tag{19}$$

which is Sono's Proposition 2 below. $\left(\text{Note that we can show } \dfrac{1}{\epsilon_1}\dfrac{\partial I^2}{\partial I} > 0.\right)$

PROPOSITION 2. *When the price of an independent good changes, the general substitution term K_{j1} has the same sign as the proper propensity to consume each good (except the independent good x_1) at the point of common equilibrium.*

Combining (17) and (18) we obtain, *except where* $\epsilon_1 = 1$,

$$\frac{\partial x_i/\partial p_1}{\partial x_j/\partial p_1} = \frac{\partial x_i/\partial I}{\partial x_j/\partial I} \quad \text{for } i, j \in N_2. \tag{20}$$

Where $\epsilon_1 = 1$, $\partial x_j/\partial p_1 = 0$ for all $j \in N_2$. This result is the same as Houthakker's [1] equation (10), with the important exception that he missed the proviso $\epsilon_1 \neq 1$. The case $\epsilon_1 = 1$ gave rise to the Hicksian exception to the Houthakker–Samuelson theorem on simultaneously additive direct and indirect utilities, which we discuss in section 3.4 below.

From Sono's Proposition 1 we can derive his third proposition, which can be stated:

PROPOSITION 3. *The rate of change of the expenditure on an independent good with respect to a change in its own price is positive, zero, or negative according as the elasticity of its marginal rate of substitution, ϵ_1, is greater than, equal to, or less than one.*

Let I^1 be expenditure on good 1 and I^2 expenditure on goods in N_2. Then we have

$$I^1 = p_1 x_1, \qquad I^2 = \sum_{i \neq 1} p_i x_i, \qquad I^1 + I^2 = I.$$

Therefore,
$$\frac{\partial I^1}{\partial p_1} = -\frac{\partial I^2}{\partial p_1}.$$

By the second Law of Proportionality (2)

$$\frac{\partial x_j}{\partial p_1} = \frac{\partial x_j}{\partial I^2}\frac{\partial I^2}{\partial p_1} = -\frac{\partial x_j}{\partial I^2}\frac{\partial I^1}{\partial p_1} \qquad (j \neq 1).$$

Therefore,
$$\frac{\partial I^1}{\partial p_1} = -\frac{\partial x_j}{\partial p_1}\Big/\frac{\partial x_j}{\partial I^2} = (\epsilon_1 - 1)\frac{x_1}{\epsilon_1}\frac{\partial I^2}{\partial I} \tag{21}$$

by equations (17) and (19). This is Sono's Proposition 3.

Sono's results for the one independent good case can be generalized to the case of strong separability. Suppose we have

$$f(x) = F[f^1(x^1) + f^2(x^2)], \qquad \begin{array}{l} x^1 = (x_1,..., x_m), \\ x^2 = (x_{m+1},..., x_n), \end{array} \tag{22}$$

where $f^2(x^2)$ itself may be separated into a set of additively separable proper utility functions. The definition of Sono's ϵ_1 can be extended in the following way, the property of invariance under a monotonic transformation of the utility function being preserved:

$$\epsilon_k = -x_k \frac{f_j}{f_h}\frac{\mathrm{d}}{\mathrm{d}x_k}\left(\frac{f_h}{f_j}\right), \qquad \text{for } h, k = 1,..., m, \; j = m+1,..., n \tag{23}$$

where $\frac{\mathrm{d}}{\mathrm{d}x_k}\left(\frac{f_h}{f_j}\right)$ is the solution to the set of equations generated by evaluating the derivatives $\frac{\mathrm{d}}{\mathrm{d}x_k}\left(\frac{f_h}{f_j}\right)$ $(h = 1,..., m)$ subject to the additional assumption that

$$\frac{\mathrm{d}}{\mathrm{d}x_k}\left(\frac{f_h}{f_j}\right) = \frac{f_h}{f_k}\frac{\mathrm{d}}{\mathrm{d}x_k}\left(\frac{f_k}{f_j}\right),$$

i.e. when x_k changes, the quantities of the goods in $N_1 = \{1,..., m\}$ are changed so that the marginal rates of substitution between them and j change in proportion to their marginal rates of substitution for j. The set of equations is written as follows, where, because of (22), $\dfrac{f_h}{f_j} = \dfrac{f_h^1}{f_j^2}$:

$$\begin{aligned}
\frac{\mathrm{d}}{\mathrm{d}x_k}\left(\frac{f_1^1}{f_j^2}\right) = \frac{f_1^1}{f_k^1}\frac{\mathrm{d}}{\mathrm{d}x_k}\left(\frac{f_k^1}{f_j^2}\right) &= \frac{\partial}{\partial x_1}\left(\frac{f_1^1}{f_j^2}\right)\frac{\mathrm{d}x_1}{\mathrm{d}x_k} + \frac{\partial}{\partial x_2}\left(\frac{f_1^1}{f_j^2}\right)\frac{\mathrm{d}x_2}{\mathrm{d}x_k} + \dots + \\
&\quad + \frac{\partial}{\partial x_k}\left(\frac{f_1^1}{f_j^2}\right) + \dots + \frac{\partial}{\partial x_m}\left(\frac{f_1^1}{f_j^2}\right)\frac{\mathrm{d}x_m}{\mathrm{d}x_k}, \\
\frac{\mathrm{d}}{\mathrm{d}x_k}\left(\frac{f_2^1}{f_j^2}\right) = \frac{f_2^1}{f_k^1}\frac{\mathrm{d}}{\mathrm{d}x_k}\left(\frac{f_k^1}{f_j^2}\right) &= \frac{\partial}{\partial x_1}\left(\frac{f_2^1}{f_j^2}\right)\frac{\mathrm{d}x_1}{\mathrm{d}x_k} + \frac{\partial}{\partial x_2}\left(\frac{f_2^1}{f_j^2}\right)\frac{\mathrm{d}x_2}{\mathrm{d}x_k} + \dots + \\
&\quad + \frac{\partial}{\partial x_k}\left(\frac{f_2^1}{f_j^2}\right) + \dots + \frac{\partial}{\partial x_m}\left(\frac{f_2^1}{f_j^2}\right)\frac{\mathrm{d}x_m}{\mathrm{d}x_k}, \qquad (24) \\
&\cdots\cdots\cdots\cdots \\
\frac{\mathrm{d}}{\mathrm{d}x_k}\left(\frac{f_m^1}{f_j^2}\right) = \frac{f_m^1}{f_k^1}\frac{\mathrm{d}}{\mathrm{d}x_k}\left(\frac{f_k^1}{f_j^2}\right) &= \frac{\partial}{\partial x_1}\left(\frac{f_m^1}{f_j^2}\right)\frac{\mathrm{d}x_1}{\mathrm{d}x_k} + \frac{\partial}{\partial x_2}\left(\frac{f_m^1}{f_j^2}\right)\frac{\mathrm{d}x_2}{\mathrm{d}x_k} + \dots + \\
&\quad + \frac{\partial}{\partial x_k}\left(\frac{f_m^1}{f_j^2}\right) + \dots + \frac{\partial}{\partial x_m}\left(\frac{f_m^1}{f_j^2}\right)\frac{\mathrm{d}x_m}{\mathrm{d}x_k}.
\end{aligned}$$

Solving (24) for $\dfrac{\mathrm{d}}{\mathrm{d}x_k}\left(\dfrac{f_k^1}{f_j^2}\right)$ by Cramer's rule, we get

$$\frac{\mathrm{d}}{\mathrm{d}x_k}\left(\frac{f_k^1}{f_j^2}\right) = -\frac{f_k^1}{f_j^2}\frac{D_0^{(1)}}{\lambda D_k^{(1)}}, \qquad (25)$$

where $D_0^{(1)}$ is the cofactor of 0 in

$$D^{(1)} = \begin{vmatrix} 0 & p_1 & \cdot & \cdot & \cdot & p_m \\ p_1 & f_{11}^1 & \cdot & \cdot & \cdot & f_{1m}^1 \\ \cdot & \cdot & & & & \cdot \\ \cdot & \cdot & & & & \cdot \\ \cdot & \cdot & & & & \cdot \\ \cdot & \cdot & & & & \cdot \\ p_m & f_{m1}^1 & \cdot & \cdot & \cdot & f_{mm}^1 \end{vmatrix},$$

$D_k^{(1)}$ is the cofactor of p_k in $D^{(1)}$, and λ is the Lagrange multiplier. From (23) and (25) we can express ϵ_k in terms of the normalized utility index as follows:

$$\epsilon_k = x_k \frac{D_0^{(1)}}{\lambda D_k^{(1)}}, \qquad (26)$$

where (26) and (23) are equivalent due to the invariance property. In the special case where $m = 1$ (Sono's case) (26) reduces to

$$\epsilon_k = -x_k \frac{f_{kk}}{f_k},$$

which is Sono's formula.

Sono's Propositions can be generalized as follows. The substitution term K_{jk} is given in terms of the normalized utility function as

$$K_{jk} = \frac{\lambda D_{jk}}{D}, \tag{27}$$

where

$$D_{jk} = (-1)^{j+k} \times$$

$$\times \left| \begin{array}{cccc|cccccc} 0 & p_1 & \cdots & p_m & p_{m+1} & \cdots & p_{j-1} & p_{j+1} & \cdots & p_n \\ p_1 & f^1_{11} & \cdots & f^1_{1m} & & & & & & \\ \vdots & \vdots & & \vdots & & & & & & \\ p_{k-1} & f^1_{k-1\,1} & \cdots & f^1_{k-1\,m} & & & 0 & & & \\ p_{k+1} & f^1_{k+1\,1} & \cdots & f^1_{k+1\,m} & & & & & & \\ \vdots & \vdots & & \vdots & & & & & & \\ p_m & f^1_{m1} & \cdots & f^1_{mm} & & & & & & \\ \hline p_{m+1} & & & & f^2_{m+1\,m+1} & \cdots & f^2_{m+1\,j-1} & f^2_{m+1\,j+1} & \cdots & f^2_{m+1\,n} \\ \vdots & & 0 & & \vdots & & \vdots & \vdots & & \vdots \\ p_n & & & & f^2_{n\,m+1} & \cdots & f^2_{n\,j-1} & f^2_{n\,j+1} & \cdots & f^2_{nn} \end{array} \right|.$$

Therefore,

$$K_{jk} = \frac{\lambda D^{(1)}_k}{D^{(1)}_0} \frac{D_j}{D} = \frac{\lambda D^{(1)}_k}{D^{(1)}_0} \frac{\partial x_j}{\partial I}, \quad \text{for } k \in N_1,\ j \in N_2. \tag{28}$$

Therefore,

$$\frac{\partial x_j}{\partial p_k} = -x_k \frac{\partial x_j}{\partial I} + K_{jk}$$

$$= -\left[x_k \frac{D^{(1)}_0}{\lambda D^{(1)}_k} - 1\right] K_{jk} = -[\epsilon_k - 1] K_{jk}, \tag{17$'$}$$

which generalizes (17). From (17′) and the Slutsky equation it follows at once that

$$K_{jk} = \frac{x_k}{\epsilon_k} \frac{\partial x_j}{\partial I} \quad \text{for } k \in N_1,\ j \in N_2, \tag{18$'$}$$

which generalizes (18) and therefore Sono's Proposition 2. Similarly, Proposition 3 can be generalized to

$$\frac{\partial I^1}{\partial p_k} = (\epsilon_k - 1)\frac{x_k}{\epsilon_k}\frac{\partial I^2}{\partial I}, \quad k \in N_1, \tag{21'}$$

where $$I^1 = \sum_{i=1}^{m} p_i x_i.$$

From (17′) and (18′) we have the extended Houthakker result:

$$\frac{\partial x_i/\partial p_k}{\partial x_j/\partial p_k} = \frac{\partial x_i/\partial I}{\partial x_j/\partial I} \quad \text{for } k \in N_1;\ i, j \in N_2, \tag{20'}$$

provided that $\epsilon_k \neq 1$.

The Engel elasticity $E_k = \dfrac{I}{x_k}\dfrac{\partial x_k}{\partial I}$ and (18′) give

$$K_{jk} = \frac{I}{\epsilon_k E_k}\frac{\partial x_k}{\partial I}\frac{\partial x_j}{\partial I}, \quad \text{for } k \in N_1,\ j \in N_2, \text{ or } j \notin N_1. \tag{29}$$

The term $\dfrac{I}{\epsilon_k E_k}$ is independent of good k; using the normalized form of the utility function $\dfrac{I}{\epsilon_k E_k}$ can be shown to be equal to $\dfrac{\lambda D}{D_0}$, which is independent of k. Therefore we can write (29) as

$$K_{jk} = a(x)\frac{\partial x_k}{\partial I}\frac{\partial x_j}{\partial I}, \quad k \in N_1,\ j \in N_2, \text{ or } j \notin N_1. \tag{29'}$$

(29′) is the necessity part of a theorem proved by Goldman and Uzawa for the case of strong separability.

THEOREM 2. *A strictly quasi-concave utility function* $u(x)$ *is strongly separable with respect to a partition* $\{N_1, \ldots, N_s\}$, $s > 2$, *iff the substitution terms* K_{jk} *are of the form*

$$K_{jk}(x) = a(x)\frac{\partial x_k}{\partial I}\frac{\partial x_j}{\partial I}$$

for $k \in N_t$, $j \in N_h$ $(h \neq t)$ *and for all* x.[12]

[12] Pearce [**1**] and Goldman and Uzawa [**1**] also proved for the case of Pearce separability the following:

THEOREM 3. *A strictly quasi-concave utility function* $u(x)$ *is Pearce separable with respect to a partition* $\{N_1, \ldots, N_s\}$ *iff the substitution terms* $K_{jk}(x)$ *are of the form*

$$K_{jk} = a^{ht}(x)\frac{\partial x_j}{\partial I}\frac{\partial x_k}{\partial I}, \quad \text{for } j \in N_h,\ k \in N_t \text{ and for all } x$$

with some functions a^{ht} *defined for all* h *and* t, *including* $h = t$.

Since $\frac{\partial\lambda}{\partial I} = -\frac{D_0}{D}$, the term $a(x) = \frac{\lambda D}{D_0}$ can be rewritten as $-\frac{\lambda}{\partial\lambda/\partial I}$ so that (29′) becomes

$$K_{jk} = -\frac{\lambda}{\partial\lambda/\partial I}\frac{\partial x_k}{\partial I}\frac{\partial x_j}{\partial I} \quad \text{for } k \in N_1,\ j \in N_2, \text{ or } j \notin N_1. \qquad (29'')$$

This is Houthakker's [1] Theorem 1 which he obtained under the assumption of additivity of the utility function but this can be weakened to strong separability. Multiplying (29″) by $\frac{I}{\lambda}\Big/\frac{I}{\lambda}$ we obtain

$$K_{jk} = -\left(I\Big/\frac{\partial\lambda}{\partial I}\frac{I}{\lambda}\right)\frac{\partial x_k}{\partial I}\frac{\partial x_j}{\partial I} \quad \text{for } k \in N_1,\ j \in N_2, \text{ or } j \notin N_1$$

$$= -\frac{I}{\hat{\omega}}\frac{\partial x_k}{\partial I}\frac{\partial x_j}{\partial I}, \qquad (29''')$$

where $\hat{\omega}$ is Frisch's 'money flexibility'. From (29‴) and (17′) we obtain

$$\frac{\partial x_j}{\partial p_k} = (\epsilon_k - 1)\frac{I}{\hat{\omega}}\frac{\partial x_k}{\partial I}\frac{\partial x_j}{\partial I}.$$

Therefore, $$\frac{p_k}{x_j}\frac{\partial x_j}{\partial p_k} = e_{jk} = \frac{\epsilon_k}{\hat{\omega}}\alpha_k E_j E_k - \frac{1}{\hat{\omega}}\alpha_k E_j E_k, \qquad (30)$$

where E_j and E_k are Engel elasticities and $\alpha_k = \frac{p_k x_k}{I}$. From (29) and (29‴) it follows that $\epsilon_k E_k = -\hat{\omega}$; it therefore follows that

$$e_{jk} = -E_j\alpha_k\left(1 + \frac{E_k}{\hat{\omega}}\right), \qquad (31)$$

which is a result obtained by Frisch. By the homogeneity condition,

$$p_j\frac{\partial x_j}{\partial p_j} = -\sum_{k\neq j} p_k\frac{\partial x_j}{\partial p_k} - I\frac{\partial x_j}{\partial I}, \qquad (32)$$

or, in elasticity terms,

$$e_{jj} = -\sum_{k\neq j} e_{jk} - E_j. \qquad (32')$$

If good j is independent of all other goods, (32′) becomes

$$e_{jj} = -E_j\left(\alpha_j - \frac{1-\alpha_j E_j}{\hat{\omega}}\right), \tag{33}$$

because of (31), of $\sum_{k=1}^{n} \alpha_k = 1$, and of $\sum_{k=1}^{n} \alpha_k E_k = 1$ which is the Engel aggregation condition. (33) was also obtained by Frisch.

Equations (29″), (29‴), (31), and (33) hold only for the normalized utility index and so are not invariant with respect to a monotonic transformation of the utility function. However, equation (29), which follows from Sono's extended propositions, is invariant with respect to a monotonic transformation, so that the Frisch–Houthakker results, which are only variations on (29), employ cardinality unnecessarily; cardinal concepts are not required to obtain the additional restrictions on demand functions.

A final point concerns the conclusion of Samuelson [**2**] where he presents some comparative static results which are obtained on the assumption of additivity. They are, however, incorrect and should be amended as follows:

$$h_{ij} = \frac{1}{p_i}\left(1-p_i\frac{\partial x_i}{\partial I}\right)\left(\frac{\partial x_i}{\partial p_j}+x_j\frac{\partial x_i}{\partial I}\right)+\frac{\partial x_j}{\partial I}\left(\frac{\partial x_i}{\partial p_i}+x_i\frac{\partial x_i}{\partial I}\right) \equiv 0 \quad (i \neq j),$$

$h_{11} \equiv h_{22} \equiv \ldots \equiv h_{nn}$, where

$$h_{ii} = \frac{\dfrac{\partial x_i}{\partial I}\left(1-p_i\dfrac{\partial x_i}{\partial I}\right)}{p_i\left(\dfrac{\partial x_i}{\partial p_i}+x_i\dfrac{\partial x_i}{\partial I}\right)} = \frac{\hat{\omega}}{I}.$$

Samuelson's original formula contradicts the results of Frisch as well as those of Sono.

3.3. *The comparative statics of homogeneous separability*

A detailed discussion of the comparative statics of homogeneous separability appears in Morishima [3]. He proved the following propositions.(13)

(13) In a much later paper Muth [**1**], apparently unaware of Morishima's article, rederived some of the comparative static properties of homogeneous separability.

PROPOSITION 1. *If the utility function $u(x)$ is homogeneously separable with respect to a partition $N = \{N_1,\ldots,N_s\}$, i.e. if in $u(x) = u[f^1(x^1),\ldots,f^s(x^s)]$, each $y_k = f^k(x^k)$ is homogeneous of degree one, then the conditions*

$$\frac{I}{x_j}\frac{\partial x_j}{\partial I} = \frac{I}{y_k}\frac{\partial y_k}{\partial I} \quad \textit{for all } j \in N_k \tag{34}$$

are fulfilled.

In other words, all goods in the subgroup N_k have the same income elasticity which is equal to the income elasticity of the group as a whole. This implication of homogeneous separability was noted by Gorman [**2**]. Taking the example of clothes, he is unhappy with the conclusion that if the proper utility function of clothes is homogeneous of degree one, then an income rise which leads to a doubling of expenditure on clothes will lead the consumer to buy twice as many blue jeans as before, and twice as many evening suits. He states that homogeneity of the proper utility functions precludes the grouping together of luxuries and necessities, if the concept is to be meaningful. Muth [**1**] argues, however, that while much evidence suggests that within the commodity grouping usually encountered there are commodities of different income elasticities, the demand for some commodities purchased by the household is, in fact, a composite demand. He quotes the example of the household's demand for fuel which is a composite of the derived demand for fuel for cooking and for heating, or for fuel used to produce food and fuel used to produce housing. In these cases the income elasticity of the household's *total* demand for fuel is not the relevant elasticity when homogeneous separability is being considered. It is very doubtful, though, whether all differences in income elasticities could be accounted for in this way. Thus, in the analysis of those subgroups which are amenable to the Hicks–Morishima view of objectives and means, homogeneous separability plays an important role, while to those subgroups which include necessities and luxuries to which the composite demand idea does not apply, homogeneous separability is of questionable relevance.

PROPOSITION 2. *If a utility function $u(x)$ is homogeneously separable with respect to a partition $\{N_1,\ldots, N_s\}$ of N, the conditions*

$$K_{rv} = \frac{x_r x_v}{y_j y_k} K'_{jk} \quad \text{for } r \in N_j,\ v \in N_k,\ j \neq k, \tag{35}$$

where K'_{jk} is the objectives-substitution term, are fulfilled.

This means that the substitution effect of the change in the price of good r on the demand for good v *which serves a different objective to* r does not include a means-substitution effect. Using (34), (35) can be rewritten:

$$K'_{jk}\Big/\left(\frac{\partial y_j}{\partial I}\frac{\partial y_k}{\partial I}\right) = K_{rv}\Big/\left(\frac{\partial x_r}{\partial I}\frac{\partial x_v}{\partial I}\right) = a^{jk}, \quad r \in N_j,\ v \in N_k,\ j \neq k \tag{36}$$

by Theorem 1, as y_j and y_k are weakly separable in $u(x)$. This means that the result $a^{jk} = K_{rv}\Big/\left(\frac{\partial x_r}{\partial I}\frac{\partial x_v}{\partial I}\right)$ in the case of weak separability is strengthened in the case of homogeneous separability to $a^{jk} = K'_{jk}\Big/\left(\frac{\partial y_j}{\partial I}\frac{\partial y_k}{\partial I}\right)$.

PROPOSITION 3. *If a utility function $u(x)$ is homogeneously separable with respect to a partition, the conditions*

$$K_{rs} = \frac{x_r x_s}{y_j y_j} K'_{jj} + y_j K''_{rs} \quad \textit{for } r, s \in N_j \tag{37}$$

are fulfilled.

This states that where two goods from the same subgroup or two means towards the same objective are considered, the substitution effect of a change in the price of one on the quantity of the other is a combination of *objectives substitution*—a change in p_r affects the cost of objective j—and *means substitution* within j. The former is given by the first term, the latter by the second; K''_{rs} is the means-substitution effect. Muth expressed (37) in elasticity terms, but his expression (equation (2) of his paper) is incomplete; it should read, in his notation:

$$H_{ij} = s_{g,j}(p_g x_g S_{g,ij} + H_{gg}), \tag{37'}$$

where

$$s_{g,j} = p_j y_j \Big/ \sum_{k \in g} p_k y_k = s_j / s_g$$

is the share of commodity (means) j in producing good (objective) g; $S_{g,ij}$ is the partial elasticity of substitution of commodity (means) i for commodity (means) j in the production of good (objective) g, and thus corresponds to K''_{rs} in (37); H_{gg} is the own price elasticity of demand for good j and thus corresponds to K'_{jj} in (37); and H_{ij} is the elasticity of demand for commodity i with respect to the price of commodity j, and corresponds to K_{rs} in (37). Note that Muth's x is our y, his y our x, and his p_g corresponds to our q_j.

Multiplying (37) by p_s and p_r and summing over s and r respectively, we obtain

$$\sum_r \sum_s p_r p_s K_{rs} = \left(\sum_r p_r \frac{x_r}{y_j}\right)\left(\sum_s p_s \frac{x_s}{y_j}\right) K'_{jj} = q_j q_j K'_{jj}, \quad (38)$$

where $\sum_r p_r \dfrac{x_r}{y_j} = \sum_s p_s \dfrac{x_s}{y_j} = q_j$, and the second term vanishes because $\sum_r p_r K''_{rs} = 0$, by the homogeneity condition. Therefore,

$$\sum_r \sum_s \frac{p_r}{q_j} \frac{p_s}{q_j} K_{rs} = K'_{jj}, \quad r, s \in N_j, \quad (39)$$

so that the objectives-substitution term is a weighted sum of the general substitution terms of the pairs of goods r, $s \in N_j$.[14]

The sufficiency of conditions (34) and (37) for homogeneous separability can be demonstrated as follows.

Let $$q_j = \frac{\sum_r p_r x_r}{y_j} \neq 0, \quad r \in N_j.$$

Therefore, $$\frac{x_r}{y_j} \neq 0 \quad \text{for some } r.$$

[14] It is interesting to compare the results for homogeneous separability, particularly (39), with the result obtained by Hicks [**1**] for the case of composite goods. Hicks derived a similar formula for the substitution term of a group of commodities. In his derivation, he assumed that the prices of all goods belonging to a group changed in the same proportion but he did not impose any restriction on the form of the utility function. Here, however, we impose homogeneous separability on the utility function but make no assumption about prices.

Consider, first, $\dfrac{\partial y_j}{\partial I} = 0$. We have

$$\frac{\partial y_j}{\partial p_r} = \frac{\partial y_j}{\partial q_j}\frac{\partial q_j}{\partial p_r} = \frac{\partial y_j}{\partial q_j}\frac{x_r}{y_j} = K'_{jj}\frac{x_r}{y_j}. \tag{40}$$

Also

$$\frac{\partial y_j}{\partial p_r} = \sum_t y_{jt}\frac{\partial x_t}{\partial p_r} = \sum_t y_{jt}K_{rt} = \sum_t y_{jt}\frac{x_r}{y_j}\frac{x_t}{y_j}K'_{jj} + \sum_t y_{jt}K''_{rt}y_j \tag{41}$$

by (37), for $t \in N_j$, where $y_{jt} = \dfrac{\partial y_j}{\partial x_t}$. As y_{jt}s are proportional to p_ts in equilibrium, we find that $\sum y_{jt}K''_{rt}$ vanishes; therefore,

$$\frac{\partial y_j}{\partial p_r} = \left(\sum_t y_{jt}\frac{x_t}{y_j}\right)K'_{jj}\frac{x_r}{y_j}. \tag{42}$$

Therefore, since $K'_{jj} < 0$, $\dfrac{x_r}{y_j} \neq 0$, we have from (40) and (42)

$$\sum_t y_{jt}\frac{x_t}{y_j} = 1.$$

Therefore y_j is homogeneous in x_t, by Euler's theorem.

Now consider $\dfrac{\partial y_j}{\partial I} \neq 0.$

$$\frac{\partial y_j}{\partial I} = \sum_t y_{jt}\frac{\partial x_t}{\partial I} = \sum_t y_{jt}\frac{x_t}{y_j}\frac{\partial y_j}{\partial I}, \quad \text{by (34);}$$

therefore,
$$\frac{\sum y_{jt}x_t}{y_j} = 1,$$

so that y_j is homogeneous of degree one.

Finally, consider the case of $x_r = 0$ for all $r \in N_j$. Since $y_j = f^j(x^j)$ is homogeneous of degree one if some $x_r \neq 0$, we have $0 = f^j(0)$ in the limit when $x^j \to 0$.

3.4. *Additivity and separability of direct and indirect utility functions*

In his paper, 'Additive Preferences', Houthakker [**1**] discusses additivity of both the direct and the indirect utility function. The indirect utility function is an alternative way of describing a preference ordering to the usual or direct utility function, $u(x)$. It is based on the fact that, assuming quasi-concavity of $u(x)$, the elements of x are completely determined by income and prices, i.e. demand functions, $x_i = x_i(p_1,..., p_n, I)$, are derived. The value of u is therefore indirectly a function of the p_i and I, so that we can write the indirect utility function

$$\psi(p_1,..., p_n, I) = u[x_1(p_1,..., p_n, I),..., x_n(p_1,..., p_n, I)], \quad (43)$$

where the $x_i(p_1,..., p_n, I)$ are homogeneous of degree zero; we can then rewrite (43):

$$\psi(p_1,..., p_n, I) = \psi(z_1,..., z_n), \quad (43')$$

where $z_i = I/p_i$. Minimization of the indirect utility function with respect to normalized prices with given quantities is the dual of the more usual maximization of the direct utility function with respect to quantities with given prices and income.

Additivity of the direct utility function means that we can write

$$u(x) = u_1(x_1)+...+u_n(x_n), \quad (44)$$

while additivity of the indirect utility function means that we can write

$$\psi(z) = \psi_1(z_1)+...+\psi_n(z_n). \quad (45)$$

The question of the compatibility of direct and indirect additivity was considered by Houthakker and, in greater detail, by Samuelson [**2**]. Samuelson discussed the conditions for simultaneously additive direct and indirect utilities and also for 'quasi-simultaneously' additive direct and indirect utilities. The latter refers to the case in which one of the utility functions is additive and the other could be put in that form by an admissible monotonic transformation. Quasi-simultaneity clearly includes simultaneity but not vice versa.

The conditions under which the indirect utility function is additive were derived by Houthakker. He proved the following theorem.

THEOREM 4. *The indirect utility function can be written in the additive form iff the cross elasticities with respect to any price are the same for all commodities.*

This can be written

$$\frac{\partial x_i/\partial p_k}{\partial x_j/\partial p_k} = \frac{x_i}{x_j}. \tag{46}$$

Combining (46) and (20′) we obtain

$$\frac{I}{x_i}\frac{\partial x_i}{\partial I} = \frac{I}{x_j}\frac{\partial x_j}{\partial I} = 1, \quad \text{if } \epsilon_k \neq 1 \text{ for at least two goods.} \tag{47}$$

This leads to

THEOREM 5. *If a preference ordering is quasi-simultaneously additive, the Engel curves derived from it are straight lines through the origin, if* $\epsilon_k \neq 1$ *for at least two goods.*

To obtain utility functions which satisfy the conditions of direct and indirect additivity quasi-simultaneously and simultaneously, Samuelson used (47), Houthakker's Theorem 5, but without the revision we have incorporated; that is, he did not take account of the restriction on ϵ_k. An exception to his result was found by Hicks [**5**]; Samuelson [**3**] corrected his argument to cover the Hicks exception. Ideally, however, the argument should proceed in full recognition of the restrictions on ϵ_k.

Suppose $\epsilon_k \neq 1$ for at least two goods. Then by Houthakker's theorem quasi-simultaneous direct and indirect additivity imply that the utility function is homothetic so that it can be transformed into a homogeneous function by means of an appropriate monotonic transformation. Bergson [**1**] has shown that homogeneity plus additivity means that the direct (or indirect) utility function can be written as a sum of powers of the variables:

$$f(u(x)) = b + \sum_{i=1}^{n} a_i x_i^m \quad (m < 1). \tag{48}$$

This is a CES function and includes the Cobb–Douglas utility function as the limiting case as $m \to 0$; i.e.

$$f(u(x)) = b + \sum_{i=1}^{n} a_i \log_e x_i. \tag{48′}$$

Next suppose that $\epsilon_k = 1$ for all k. By definition,

$$\epsilon_k = \frac{-x_k u_k''}{u_k'} = 1 \quad (k = 1,\ldots, n),$$

for the normalized utility function. This implies that

$$u_k(x_k) = b_k + a_k \log_e x_k. \tag{49}$$

Hence the normalized utility function must be of the Cobb–Douglas form.

Finally, consider $\epsilon_1 \neq 1$, and $\epsilon_k = 1$, $k = 2,..., n$. In this case we have

$$u(x) = u_1(x_1) + \sum_{i=2}^{n} a_i \log_e x_i, \tag{50}$$

where $u_1(x_1)$ is an arbitrary monotonically increasing concave function. This is the case which was pointed out by Hicks as an exception to the original Samuelson case. Thus we have the quasi-simultaneously direct and indirect additivity property iff the normalized utility function is either a member of the Bergson family (48) or (48′) or is of the Hicksian type (50).

In the more stringent case of simultaneity, all members of the Bergson family other than the Cobb–Douglas are ineligible, but the Hicks case (50) remains eligible.

So far, we have implicitly assumed that $n \geq 3$. If $n = 2$, the Houthakker theorem is not applicable because it assumes two different goods i and j, as well as good k. But Samuelson has observed that if the direct utility function is of one of the forms:

$$\left.\begin{array}{ll} \text{(i)} & u(x) = b + a_1 \log x_1 + a_2 \log x_2 \\ \text{(ii)} & u(x) = b + a_1 x_1^m + a_2 x_2^m \\ \text{(iii)} & u(x) = u_1(x_1) + \alpha_2 \log x_2 \end{array}\right\}, \tag{51}$$

then the indirect utility function is also quasi-simultaneously additive. More specifically, when the utility function is of the form (51 i) or (51 iii) we have simultaneous direct and indirect additivity. However, whether there is any other form of the direct utility function under which we have either simultaneous or quasi-simultaneous direct and indirect additivity is an open question which was left by Samuelson [**3**] for further research.

Lau [**1**] proved the following theorems about simultaneous strong and weak separability of the direct and indirect utility functions.

THEOREM 6. *A strictly quasi-concave utility function is strongly separable with respect to a commodity partition and the corre-*

sponding price partition in the direct and indirect forms, respectively, only if

(i a) *it is homothetic, with respect to proper utilities and each proper utility function is homogeneous of the same degree, or*

(i b)
$$u(x) = \sum_{i=1}^{s} \log u^i(x^i), \tag{52}$$

where each u^i is homogeneous; or

(ii)
$$u(x) = u^1(x^1) + \sum_{i=2}^{s} \log u^i(x^i), \tag{53}$$

where each u^i $(i = 2,\ldots, s)$ is homogeneous.

Lau shows that (i) implies that $u(x)$ is homothetic; (ii) corresponds to the Hicksian special case for strong separability.

THEOREM 7. *A strictly quasi-concave utility function is weakly separable with respect to a commodity partition and the corresponding price partition in the direct and indirect forms, respectively, only if each proper utility function is homothetic, i.e. the utility function is homothetically separable.*(15)

In these important extensions of the Houthakker–Samuelson results it is seen that homotheticity plays a significant role.

Arrow [**1**] examined the weakest conditions under which the additive logarithmic demand functions proposed by Houthakker are derivable from a utility function. Later the general solution of Arrow's problem was more carefully discussed by Gorman [**4**] who showed that we obtain the additive logarithmic demand function of the Houthakker–Arrow type if goods can be classified into several groups, the expenditure on each good within a group being a constant proportion of group expenditure, and if the aggregate demand function for each group of goods is additive logarithmic. It is interesting to note that where

(15) Lau also proves the following theorems concerning homogeneous and homothetic direct utility functions.

THEOREM 8. *A strictly quasi-concave homogeneous direct utility function is weakly separable with respect to a commodity partition iff the indirect utility function is weakly separable with respect to the corresponding price partition.*

THEOREM 9. *A strictly quasi-concave homogeneous direct utility function is strongly separable with respect to a commodity partition iff the indirect utility function is strongly separable with respect to the corresponding price partition.*

Gorman's conditions are satisfied, the utility function must be homogeneously separable.

Goldberger [**1**] showed that if the utility function is directly additive and expenditure functions display constant marginal budget shares, the utility function must be of the Stone–Geary form:

$$u = \sum_i u^i(x_i) = \sum_i \beta_i \log(x_i - \gamma_i) + \alpha_i \quad (i = 1,..., n), \qquad (54)$$

the β_i, γ_i, and α_i being parameters, while Pollak [**2**] was concerned with a more general case where marginal budget shares were independent of income but not necessarily of prices. Theil [**2**] added the assumption of constant income flexibility to those of additive direct utility and constant marginal budget shares. Interestingly, this leads (54) to be specialized to the Cobb–Douglas utility function,

$$u = \sum_i \alpha_i + \sum_i \beta_i \log x_i, \qquad (54')$$

which was shown by Samuelson to imply simultaneous direct and indirect additivity.

Unlike most of the other authors, but like von Neumann–Morgenstern [**1**], Debreu [**1**], and others, Fishburn [**2**, **3**] discussed additivity of utility where choice takes place under uncertainty. He examines the notion of independence among the coordinates of $X = \prod_{i=1}^{n} X_i$, in a formulation where basic preferences are between simple probability distributions in the space $\mathscr{P}$ of all such distributions defined on the subsets of X. The X_is can be interpreted as commodity sets (Sono, Strotz, Pearce, and others), sets of attributes (Lancaster [**1**]), sets of performance characteristics (Hicks, Morishima), sets of consumption programmes in different time periods (Koopmans and others), and so on. Fishburn [**3**] also contains a detailed treatment of additivity of utility under conditions of certainty, based on the axiomatic approach of Debreu and other authors.

Finally, we may add that Goldberger [**2**] and Theil [**3**] review recent studies by the so-called Rotterdam School as well as now classical contributions by Geary and Stone.

4. Applications of Separability

4.1. *The static theory of consumer behaviour*

The classification of commodities into weakly separable subsets is a natural specialization of the general Hicksian theory of consumer demand. The interpretation of weak separability —that the marginal rate of substitution between two goods in a weakly separable subset is independent of the quantity of all goods not in that subset—suggests many examples in which the concept is entirely plausible or, at worst, a working approximation. To cite an example, food, clothing, and housing might be considered to be weakly separable subgroups, in which case the marginal rate of substitution between stout and lager would be independent of the quantity of shoes, but not independent of the quantity of pork pies, which are in the food subgroup. A less convincing example, on the other hand, can be found by considering the marginal rate of substitution between woollen sweaters and cotton shirts; it is unlikely to be completely independent of the quantity of house heaters. That such examples will occur is one inevitable consequence of any specialization of the completely general case.

A pioneering application of weak separability was made by Yasui [**1**] and Morishima [**1**]. They assumed that 'monetary goods' (money and bonds) and consumption goods are weakly separable from one another. On the basis of this assumption, and others about the role of money and bonds, the following results are obtained by Morishima: (1) If a consumer's initial assets are positive and the marginal propensity to hold cash and bonds (with respect to an increase in the initial assets) is less than one, the demand for proper superior consumption goods decreases and the demand for proper inferior goods increases when all prices rise proportionally. (2) If an increase in the rate of interest leads to an increase in a consumer's savings, it will decrease his demand for proper superior consumption goods and increase his demand for proper inferior consumption goods; if savings are unaffected, the demand for all consumption goods is unchanged; if savings fall, demand for proper superior consumption goods rises and demand for proper inferior consumption goods falls. These results are based on Sono's 'laws of proportionality'.

Negishi [**1**] showed that the assumption that money is weakly separable from goods in the utility function, together with the assumptions of identical and homogeneous utility functions, implies the neutrality of money. If money is neutral, we can first obtain the equilibrium relative prices in the barter economy and then substitute into the excess demand equation for money in the monetary economy to solve for the absolute price level. Patinkin's [**1**] criticism of the classical dichotomy, i.e. the inconsistency between the homogeneity postulate and the real balance effect, does not apply in this case.

When the assumption of weak separability is strengthened to strong or homogeneous separability, the two-stage budgetary process becomes optimal. This means that consumers may first allocate expenditure among the several budget categories and then decide how best to spend each budget allotment on the commodities within the category, with no further reference to purchases in other categories. When strong separability is assumed, this property only holds locally; Gorman [**2**], Strotz [**3**], and Rajaoja [**1**] considered this implication of strong separability. Gorman showed, however, that if there is homogeneous separability, the two-stage budgetary process is globally optimal. The additional implication of homogeneous separability, that all goods in each category have the same income elasticity, led Gorman to express doubts about its usefulness because, in his view, most budgetary categories contained necessities and luxuries whose income elasticities had been observed to be different. However, as we noted above, Muth argued in favour of homogeneous separability on the grounds of the existence of composite demands for certain goods.

The view that the consumer chooses between certain objectives and then decides between alternative means of achieving those objectives was introduced by Hicks [**2**]. The relative valuations of those goods which are means of reaching the same objective are determined by their relative contributions to that objective, and are independent of the remaining goods which are devoted to other objectives. The relation between the means and the objective is of a technical character, rather like a production function. Morishima [**3**] assumed that the functions which give the relations between means and objectives are homogeneous of degree one, i.e. the utility function of the consumer is homogeneously separable. This application of homogeneous separability can be seen as providing a synthesis of the theories of demand and the firm.

4.2. *Empirical estimation of demand function*

Strotz [**2**] was concerned with the implications of separability for the estimation of demand functions. He showed that weak separability of the utility function implies the following restrictions on the price coefficients of the demand functions: for any two commodities in a particular branch of the utility tree, the coefficients of the prices of commodities not in that branch will be proportional to the income coefficients (Sono's law of proportionality). However, these restrictions are not subjected to empirical test. Frisch [**1**] explored in detail the implications of the much stronger assumption of want independence. He showed that when good i is want-independent of all other goods, it follows that

$$e_{ii} = -E_i\left(\alpha_i - \frac{1-\alpha_i E_i}{\hat{\omega}}\right), \tag{1}$$

$$e_{ik} = -E_i \alpha_k\left(1+\frac{E_k}{\hat{\omega}}\right), \tag{2}$$

where e_{ii} and e_{ik} are price elasticities, E_i is an Engel elasticity, α_i is a budget share, and $\hat{\omega}$ is the money flexibility in terms of the normalized utility function (see equations (33) and (31) in section 3). From these expressions it follows that if a satisfactory estimate of $\hat{\omega}$ exists, the own and cross price elasticities of demand for all want-independent goods can be computed from the knowledge of the Engel elasticities and budget shares, which usually can be obtained more easily than price elasticities. This procedure clearly involves a substantial reduction of costs in empirical estimation. If $\hat{\omega}$ is not known, Frisch suggests that the own price elasticity be estimated for a 'representative' group of want-independent goods. These elasticities, together with the Engel elasticities and budget proportions, allow $\hat{\omega}$ to be computed; if the independence assumption is realistic, the values of $\hat{\omega}$ should be approximately equal. If they are, an approximate $\hat{\omega}$ can be used to compute the remaining elasticities. Frisch quotes as an example a study by Johansen [**1**] in which commodities of widely differing Engel elasticities and budget proportions gave rise to very consistent values of $\hat{\omega}$.

Houthakker's discussion of additive preferences [**1**], conducted for the most part in terms of slopes rather than elasticities, is very similar to Frisch's in many respects. He finds that all the Slutsky terms can be computed from the income slopes and the money flexibility. Indirect additivity, on the other hand, is shown to imply that the cross elasticities of demand, with respect to any price, are the same for all affected commodities. Using direct and indirect utility functions of the 'addilog' form and cross-section data, Houthakker estimates demand equations for four sets of commodities. He finds that the error sum of squares turns out to be generally lower for the direct addilog case.

Pearce's analysis of neutral want association [**1**, **3**] has many points of contact with Frisch [**1**] and Houthakker [**1**]. He shows that the number of parameters of the complete set of demand functions which must be estimated is reduced from $\frac{1}{2}(n^2+3n)$ to $\frac{1}{2}g(g+1)+n$ when the utility function is Pearce-separable, where n is the number of commodities and g the number of groups. The reduction is due to the fact that the demand functions can be written in terms of the income slopes and a set of parameters related to Frisch's money flexibility. Pearce carries the analysis further. He proves that for any pair of goods i, j within a group, we have

$$\frac{\mathrm{d}x_i}{\left(\sum_s C_s \lambda^{rs}\right)\frac{\partial x_i}{\partial I}} - \frac{\mathrm{d}x_j}{\left(\sum_s C_s \lambda^{rs}\right)\frac{\partial x_j}{\partial I}} = \frac{\mathrm{d}p_j}{p_j} - \frac{\mathrm{d}p_i}{p_i} \tag{3}$$

for $i, j \in N_r$, $k \in N_s$,

where $C_s = \sum p_k\, (\partial x_k/\partial I)$ for all k in group N_s, λ^{rs} is a parameter related to Frisch's money flexibility, and dp and dx are observed price and quantity changes. He suggests that (3) may be used to determine whether any two commodities are in neutral want association with all others. The approach is as follows: (3) is an equation in two variables,

$$k_i = 1\Big/\left[\left(\sum_s C_s\lambda^{rs}\right)\frac{\partial x_i}{\partial I}\right] \quad \text{and} \quad k_j = 1\Big/\left[\left(\sum_s C_s\lambda^{rs}\right)\frac{\partial x_j}{\partial I}\right].$$

Four successive observations of price quantity data yield three equations which must be consistent with some unique value of the variables. If they are consistent, the hypothesis of neutral want independence is not contradicted. A group may be formed by testing any pair for neutrality; once a pair is found any other good neutral with both can be added to the group, and so on. In his empirical work Pearce [**2**] chooses fifteen commodities which he assumes to form a group so that there is only one λ. He estimates the k_i from British expenditure data, and uses the estimates to compute λ^{rs} and the price and income elasticities. These are then used to predict the consumption of commodities within the period.

Barten [**1**] considers the case in which preferences are 'almost additive'. He expresses this by postulating that the matrix of second-order partial derivatives of the utility function takes the form

$$u^* = -\bar{u}(I+\theta)\bar{u}, \tag{4}$$

where $\bar{u}$ is a diagonal matrix and θ is an $n\times n$ matrix with zeros on the diagonal. The elements of θ are postulated to be sufficiently small so that

$$u^{*-1} \cong -\bar{u}^{-1}(I-\theta)\bar{u}^{-1}. \tag{5}$$

Barten analyses the implications of 'almost additivity' in terms of elasticities and reduces the number of unconstrained elasticities to be estimated to $n+\frac{1}{2}\sum m_i$ where n is the number of commodities and m_i is the number of commodities in the ith group. Using Dutch data he arrives at the tentative conclusion that there is somewhat more evidence against complete additivity than was previously supposed. In his later and comprehensive treatment of the estimation of complete sets of demand functions Barten [**2**] finds that he is unable to reject the hypothesis of 'groupwise independence' (strong separability) although the homogeneity and symmetry restrictions are not supported by the evidence.

Ayanian [**1**] used Barten's data to compute own and cross price elasticities using the method of Frisch [**1**]. He found that the results, in particular the own price elasticities, are sensitive to the choice of value of the money flexibility. K. Sato [**1**] considered a class of additive utility functions which yield logarithmic demand functions and estimated their parameters using Japanese data; Powell [**1**] estimated demand functions for Australia derived from an additive utility function. Parks [**1**] and Yoshihara [**1**] used the indirect addilog model and compared the results to those obtained by using the Linear Expenditure System (L.E.S.) of Stone [**1**]. Using Swedish data, Parks found that a third alternative, not involving an additivity assumption, fared better than either, although in some cases the L.E.S. was superior; Yoshihara found that the L.E.S. was superior to the indirect addilog system, using Japanese data.

An interesting paper by Byron [**1**] states the restrictions placed on the elasticities when demand functions are derived under the assumptions of additivity, groupwise additivity (strong separability), weak separability, and Pearce separability of the utility functions. He applies these restrictions to log linear demand functions, where the (non-linear) restrictions are evaluated at the mean budget shares for the sample. Byron's data are the Dutch expenditure data used by Barten. His results lead to a rejection of all the separability hypotheses, additivity faring worst, followed by Pearce separability, strong separability, and weak separability. He suggests that the negative conclusions may be due to inappropriate grouping, shifting of the utility function, or the undue severity of the method of testing the hypotheses—the mean budget share evaluations do not hold at every moment of time.

4.3. *Dynamic utility*

Koopmans [1] discussed the problem of defining preference for advanced timing—Fisher's 'impatience'—in terms of an ordinal utility function. He formulated postulates about the utility function of a consumption programme for an *infinite* future which logically imply impatience at least for certain broad classes of programmes. The postulates are as follows. (i) The existence of a continuous utility function $U({}_1x)$ defined for all infinite programmes ${}_1x = (x_1, x_2, \ldots)$, where $x_t = (x_{t1}, \ldots, x_{tn})$ represents a vector of commodities to be consumed in period t. (ii) Sensitivity of the utility function to changes in the consumption vector of some designated period, i.e. there must exist first-period consumption vectors x_1, x_1' and a programme ${}_2x$ from the second period on, such that $U(x_1, {}_2x) > U(x_1', {}_2x)$. (iii) Stationarity of the utility function, i.e. the passage of time does not affect preferences. This can be expressed formally: for some x_1 and all ${}_2x$, ${}_2x'$, $U(x_1, {}_2x) \geqq U(x_1, {}_2x')$ iff $U({}_2x) \geqq U({}_2x')$. (iv) The existence of a best programme ${}_1\bar{x}$ and a worst programme ${}_1\underline{x}$, i.e. there must exist ${}_1\underline{x}$ and ${}_1\bar{x}$ such that $U({}_1\underline{x}) \leqq U({}_1x) \leqq U({}_1\bar{x})$ for all ${}_1x$. (v) Weak separability (Koopmans's 'limited non-complementarity'), i.e. the particular sequence of bundles of commodities to be consumed from the second period on has no effect on the preference between alternative bundles in the first period, and conversely. Formally, for all x_1, x_1', ${}_2x$, ${}_2x'$,

$$\left.\begin{aligned} &\text{(a)}\ \ U(x_1, {}_2x) \geqq U(x_1', {}_2x) \Rightarrow U(x_1, {}_2x') \geqq U(x_1', {}_2x') \\ &\text{(b)}\ \ U(x_1, {}_2x) \geqq U(x_1, {}_2x') \Rightarrow U(x_1', {}_2x) \geqq U(x_1', {}_2x') \end{aligned}\right\}. \tag{6}$$

The final postulate is of some interest. It follows from (6), (a) and (b), that the utility function can be written in the form

$$U({}_1x) = V[u_1(x_1), U_2({}_2x)], \tag{7}$$

where $V[u_1, U_2]$ is a continuous and increasing function of u_1 and U_2, i.e. period 1 consumption is weakly separable from all future consumption and vice versa. This result was proved by Koopmans. However, (6) is very similar to Sono's Propositions 1 and 3 except in that U is a function of an infinite number of variables, so that (7) amounts to a generalization of the First

Fundamental Theorem of Separability to the infinite number of variables case. Evidently

$$V[u_1(x_1), U_2({}_2x)] > V[u_1(x_1), U_2({}_2x')] \quad \text{iff } U_2({}_2x) > U_2({}_2x').$$

On the other hand, the stationarity postulate (iii) implies that

$$V[u_1(x_1), U_2({}_2x)] > V[u_1(x_1), U_2({}_2x')] \quad \text{iff } U({}_2x) > U({}_2x').$$

Therefore, we may replace U_2 by U:

$$U({}_1x) = V[u_1(x_1), U({}_2x)].$$

As

$$U({}_2x) = V[u_1(x_2), U({}_3x)],$$

we obtain

$$U({}_1x) = V[u_1(x_1), V\{u_1(x_2), U({}_3x)\}]$$
$$= \ldots\ldots\ldots, \tag{8}$$

so that goods to be consumed in period t are weakly separable from all future consumption and from all past consumption. We write (8)

$$U({}_1x) = F(u_1(x_1), u_2(x_2),\ldots). \tag{9}$$

Koopmans strengthened postulate (v) so that, in addition to (6), we have

$$\left.\begin{aligned} &\text{(a)}\ U(x_1, x_2, {}_3x) \geqq U(x_1', x_2', {}_3x) \\ &\qquad\qquad \Rightarrow U(x_1, x_2, {}_3x') \geqq U(x_1', x_2', {}_3x') \\ &\text{(b)}\ U(x_1, x_2, {}_3x) \geqq U(x_1', x_2, {}_3x') \\ &\qquad\qquad \Rightarrow U(x_1, x_2', {}_3x) \geqq U(x_1', x_2', {}_3x') \end{aligned}\right\}. \tag{6$'$}$$

Now from (a) it can be seen that (x_1, x_2) is weakly separable from ${}_3x$, so that the marginal rate of substitution between a good in x_1 and a good in x_2 is independent of goods in ${}_3x$. From (b) we have $(x_1, {}_3x)$ weakly separable from (x_2) so that the marginal rate of substitution between a good in x_1 and a good in ${}_3x$ is independent of goods in x_2. Therefore $U({}_1x)$ is strongly separable, so that we can write

$$U({}_1x) = u_1(x_1)+u_2(x_2)+U_3({}_3x), \tag{10}$$

by the Debreu–Gorman generalization of Leontief's Theorem 2, or by Sono's extended theory of independence if U is twice differentiable. Combining (10) with the stationarity postulate (iii) we obtain

$$U({}_1x) = \sum_{t=1}^{\infty} \alpha^{t-1}u(x_t) \quad (0 < \alpha < 1). \tag{11}$$

This result can be obtained as follows. By the stationarity of preferences,

$$u_1(x_1)+u_2(x_2)+U_3({}_3x) > u_1(x_1)+u_2(x_2')+U_3({}_3x')$$

iff $U({}_2x) > U({}_2x')$. Therefore,

$$\begin{aligned} u_2(x_2)+U_3({}_3x) &= F[U({}_2x)] \\ &= F[u_1(x_2)+u_2(x_3)+U_3({}_4x)]. \end{aligned} \tag{12}$$

Hence,
$$\frac{\partial u_2}{\partial x_{2i}} = F' \frac{\partial u_1}{\partial x_{2i}}, \tag{13}$$

$$\frac{\partial U_3}{\partial x_{3i}} = F' \frac{\partial u_2}{\partial x_{3i}}. \tag{14}$$

From (13), F' can depend only on x_2; from (14), F' cannot depend on x_2. Therefore F' must be constant, so that F is linear. Therefore

$$u_2(x_2)+U_3({}_3x) = \alpha[u_1(x_2)+u_2(x_3)+U_3({}_4x)]+\beta. \tag{15}$$

Therefore $u_2(x_2)$ is a linear function of $u_1(x_2)$: $u_2 = \alpha u_1+\gamma_1$. Also, $U_3({}_3x)$ is a linear function of $u_2(x_3)+U_3({}_4x)$. Therefore

$$\begin{aligned} U_3({}_3x) &= \alpha[u_2(x_3)+U_3({}_4x)]+\gamma_2 \\ &= \alpha u_2(x_3)+\alpha[\alpha\{u_2(x_4)+U_3({}_5x)\}+\gamma_2]+\gamma_2 \\ &= \cdots \\ &= \alpha u_2(x_3)+\alpha^2u_2(x_4)+\alpha^3u_2(x_5)+\ldots. \end{aligned} \tag{16}$$

Since $u_2 = \alpha u_1+\gamma_1$,

$$\begin{aligned} U({}_1x) &= u_1(x_1)+u_2(x_2)+U_3({}_3x) \\ &= u_1(x_1)+\alpha u_1(x_2)+\alpha^2u_1(x_3)+\alpha^3u_1(x_4)+\ldots \\ &= \sum_{t=1}^{\infty} \alpha^{t-1}u_1(x_t). \end{aligned} \tag{17}$$

This form of the utility function, involving a constant discount factor, is widely used in the literature. For example Ramsay [**1**] employed it with the restriction that $\alpha \equiv 1$ and most of the subsequent optimal savings literature employs it with $0 < \alpha < 1$. Strotz [**1**] and Frisch [**2**] used it and both noted that (17) is not invariant under a general monotonic transformation; it is, in fact, the normalized utility index. Frisch, in particular, strongly emphasized its cardinality, and claimed that cardinality was necessary for developing a sensible sort of dynamic analysis. However, it is obvious that their results could have been derived from any non-normalized strongly separable utility function

$$U({}_1x) = F^*\Big[\sum_{t=1}^{\infty} \alpha^{t-1} u(x_t)\Big]. \tag{18}$$

Furthermore, Morishima [**4**] and Pollak [**1**] have shown that even strong separability is not necessary for the particular results obtained by Frisch.

Hakansson [**1**] employed a utility function of the form (17), $0 < \alpha < 1$, in his study of the individual's economic decision problem under risk, with the additional restriction that either the relative risk aversion index $-xu''(x)/u'(x)$ or the absolute risk aversion index $-u''(x)/u'(x)$ is a positive constant for all $x \geq 0$, i.e. $u(x) = x^{\gamma}$, $0 < \gamma < 1$, $u(x) = -x^{-\gamma}$, $\gamma > 0$, $u(x) = \log x$, or $u(x) = -e^{-\gamma x}$. In the first three cases, optimal consumption behaviour satisfies the permanent income hypothesis precisely. This result is consistent with the results of Yaari [**1**] and Thompson [**1**]. Thompson showed that a proportional relationship between consumption C_t, C_{t+1},... and wealth W_t, W_{t+1},... implied a utility function of the form

$$U_t(C_t, C_{t+1}, \ldots) = V_t\Big[\sum_{i=0}^{\infty} (1-r)^i u(C_{t+i})\Big] \tag{18'}$$

with $u(C_{t+i}) = \log C_{t+i}$, while Yaari showed that unitary elasticities of all consumptions with respect to initial wealth implied either $u(C_{t+i}) = \log C_{t+i}$ or C^{β}_{t+i}, $0 < \beta < 1$—a result similar to Houthakker's and Samuelson's in section 3.4.

4.4. *The theory of the firm and the aggregation problem*[16]

Leontief applied the concept of weak separability to the firm's production function. He considers the example of the

[16] A survey of the aggregation literature up to 1962 is to be found in H. A. J. Green [**1**]. He provides a survey of separability concepts too. Attention should also be paid to Fisher [**5**].

production function of steel. The set of inputs can be divided into those used in the production of coal, those used in the production of iron ore, and those used in the steel plant itself. The over-all production function of steel can then be viewed as a function of intermediate products which are functions of inputs. Thus the internal structure of a production function can effectively be analysed by separating the over-all production function into a number of intermediate production functions.

The theory of separability plays an important role in the theory of aggregation, too. In his now classic article, Klein [**1**] inquired into the conditions under which there exists an aggregate production function $\phi(X, N, Z) = 0$ such that

$$X = G(x_{11},..., x_{m1},..., x_{1A},..., x_{mA}),$$
$$N = H(n_{11},..., n_{r1},..., n_{1A},..., n_{rA}),$$
$$Z = I(z_{11},..., z_{s1},..., z_{1A},..., z_{sA}),$$

where $x_{i\alpha}$ is the ith output of the firm α, $n_{i\alpha}$ the ith labour employed by α, and $z_{i\alpha}$ the ith capital services utilized by α. There are A firms, each of which has a microeconomic production function:

$$F_\alpha(x_{1\alpha},..., x_{m\alpha}, n_{1\alpha},..., n_{r\alpha}, z_{1\alpha},..., z_{s\alpha}) = 0 \quad (\alpha = 1,..., A).$$

Klein found that the aggregative functions G, H, and I must be chosen so as to satisfy the following conditions:

$$\text{(i)} \quad \frac{\partial x_{1\alpha}}{\partial x_{i\alpha}} = -\frac{\partial G/\partial x_{i\alpha}}{\partial G/\partial x_{1\alpha}} \quad (i = 2,..., m;\ \alpha = 1,..., A).$$

$$\text{(ii)} \quad \frac{\partial x_{1\alpha}/\partial n_{i\alpha}}{\partial x_{1\beta}/\partial n_{j\beta}} = \frac{\partial H/\partial n_{i\alpha}}{\partial H/\partial n_{j\beta}} \frac{\partial G/\partial x_{1\beta}}{\partial G/\partial x_{1\alpha}}$$
$$(i,j = 1,..., r;\ \alpha, \beta = 1,..., A).$$

$$\text{(iii)} \quad \frac{\partial x_{1\alpha}/\partial z_{i\alpha}}{\partial x_{1\beta}/\partial z_{j\beta}} = \frac{\partial I/\partial z_{i\alpha}}{\partial I/\partial z_{j\beta}} \frac{\partial G/\partial x_{1\beta}}{\partial G/\partial x_{1\alpha}}$$
$$(i,j = 1,..., s;\ \alpha, \beta = 1,..., A).$$

But as Nataf [**1**] and Okamoto and Morishima [**1**] have pointed out, these conditions imply that it is impossible to obtain such functions G, H, I unless the microeconomic production functions are weakly separable. In fact, the right-hand side of (i) is independent of $n_{1\alpha},..., n_{r\alpha}, z_{1\alpha},..., z_{s\alpha}$; therefore, (i) implies that the marginal rate of substitution between any two outputs is independent of inputs. Similarly, by putting $\alpha = \beta$ in (ii) and (iii), we find that $n_{1\alpha},..., n_{r\alpha}$ are separable from outputs and the other inputs and that $z_{1\alpha},..., z_{s\alpha}$ are similarly separable. Pokropp [**1**] has recently established necessary and sufficient conditions for the Klein–Nataf aggregation to be possible without any assumption of differentiability or continuity of the individual production functions.

The aggregation problem consists of two parts:[17] aggregation with respect to goods and aggregation with respect to agents. The former deals with reducing a large set of variables in a single function (say a utility or a production function) to a small, manageable number of variables, while the latter deals with consolidation of a set of functions into a single function (say, the welfare function or an aggregate production function). The theory of separability deals mainly with the former, that is the theory of groups of commodities.

By confining his interest to the case of prices of a number of commodities changing proportionately, Hicks [**1**] formulated an important theorem: Any group of commodities whose relative prices do not change can be lumped together into one commodity. This theorem does not require any specification of the utility or production function but does not hold if prices change in an arbitrary way.

In a 1950 article in Japanese, Okamoto and Morishima [**1**] developed a theory of groups of commodities which is not

[17] In a comment on Gorman [**1**], Wold [**1**] suggests that it is not always fruitful to consider aggregation in exact terms. In economics, micro-relationships are not exact, i.e. they can be written

$$\text{(a)} \quad u = u(x, y, z) + \epsilon,$$

where ϵ is a disturbance term. Denoting by capitals the aggregate of the u functions, we write

$$\text{(b)} \quad U = U(X, Y, Z) + E,$$

where E can now be considered as including both the aggregated ϵ terms and the aggregation error itself. As long as the approximation involved in (b) is sufficient for the purpose in hand, exact aggregation from (a) without ϵ to (b) without E seems, in Wold's view, rather academic. It is interesting to compare this with Fisher's approximate separability; see p. 90, n. 2 above.

affected by a disproportional change in prices. They were interested in a case where a set of commodities is grouped into several groups, each of which satisfies the following conditions: (i) the marginal rate of substitution between any two commodities in a group is independent of commodities belonging to any other group; (ii) each group has a standard commodity, for which the marginal rate of substitution of a commodity in the same group is independent of the quantity of the standard commodity. Then the production function can be written as

$$f(\xi_1, \xi_2, \dots, \xi_s) = 0, \tag{19}$$

where $\xi_i = x_{1i} + \theta_i(x_{2i}, \dots, x_{mi})$, ξ_i is the quantity of the ith composite commodity, x_{1i} the quantity of the standard commodity, and $x_{2i}, \dots, x_{mi}$ quantities of other component commodities of the same composite commodity. The marginal conditions are

$$\frac{\partial f}{\partial \xi_i} \Big/ \frac{\partial f}{\partial \xi_1} = p_i/p_1 \quad (i = 2, \dots, s), \tag{20}$$

where p_i is the price of the ith standard commodity. Thus the aggregate quantities $\xi_1, \dots, \xi_s$ which maximize profits can be determined by (19) and (20) without information on prices, p_{ji}, of non-standard commodities. When these prices are known, x_{ij}s are determined by the marginal conditions

$$\frac{\partial \theta_i}{\partial x_{ji}} = p_{ji}/p_i \quad (j = 2, \dots, m). \tag{20$'$}$$

It is important to note that θ_i may or may not be homogeneous of degree one in the variables $x_{2i}, \dots, x_{mi}$. If θ_i is homogeneous of degree one, the theoretical quantity index ξ_i determined by (20) equals the conventional one $X_i = x_{1i} + \sum_{j=2}^{m} \frac{p_{ji}}{p_i} x_{ji}$ determined by (20) and (20′). However, if θ_i is not homogeneous of degree one and increases more (or less) than proportionately when $x_{2i}, \dots, x_{mi}$ increase in the same proportion, then

$$\theta_i < (\text{or} >) \sum_{j=2}^{m} \frac{\partial \theta_i}{\partial x_{ji}} x_{ji}$$

respectively, so that the conventional index X_i exceeds (or falls short of) the theoretical aggregate ξ_i.

Later, Shephard [**1**] was rightly concerned with the case of $\Gamma_i \xi_i = \sum_{j=1}^{m} p_{ji} x_{ji}$, where Γ_i is the price index of ξ_i which depends on $p_{1i},..., p_{mi}$ only, by assuming that each

$$\xi_i = \theta_i(x_{1i}, x_{2i},..., x_{mi}) \quad (i = 1, 2,..., s),$$

is homogeneous of degree one. This is perhaps the first explicit discussion of homogeneous separability to appear in the economic literature.

In relation to the controversy with Joan Robinson, Solow [**1**] was concerned with the following problem. Let the output of firm i be denoted by Y_i and be given by the production function

$$Y_i = f_i(K_{1i},..., K_{ni}, L_i),$$

where K_{ji} is the amount of the jth capital good utilized by firm i and L_i the amount of labour employed by i. Total output Y is defined as

$$Y \equiv \sum Y_i = \sum_{i=1}^{m} f_i(K_{1i},..., K_{ni}, L_i),$$

which is maximized subject to

$$\sum_{i=1}^{m} K_{ji} \leqq K_j^* \quad (j = 1,..., n),$$

$$\sum_{i=1}^{m} L_i \leqq L^*,$$

where K_j^* and L^* are given positive numbers. Varying the total inputs $K_1^*,..., K_n^*, L^*$ and calculating the maximal output Y^* corresponding to them, we can trace out an aggregate production function, $Y^* = F(K_1^*,..., K_n^*, L^*)$. Then Solow's problem was to determine the conditions under which there exists an index of the quantity of capital $K^* = J(K_1^*,..., K_n^*)$ such that

$$Y^* = F(K_1^*,..., K_n^*, L^*) = G(K^*, L^*)$$

for all possible $K_1^*,..., K_n^*, L^*$.

Clearly, the problem is closely related to Sono's and Leontief's separability: the necessary and sufficient condition for the existence of the function J is that the marginal rate of substitution between any two capital goods in the production of Y^* be independent of L^*. Solow's novelty, however, lies in the fact that he carried out the discussion in terms of discrete 'activities'. Let there be m activities, each of which, say activity i, produces a unit of output with inputs c_{1i} of K_1, c_{2i} of $K_2,\ldots, c_{ni}$ of K_n, and l_i of L. Consider a linear programming problem to maximize

$$Y = \sum_{i=1}^{m} y_i$$

subject to

$$\begin{pmatrix} \Gamma \\ \\ \\ \\ \Lambda \end{pmatrix} \begin{pmatrix} y_1 \\ \cdot \\ \cdot \\ \cdot \\ \cdot \\ y_m \end{pmatrix} \leqq \begin{pmatrix} K_1^* \\ \cdot \\ \cdot \\ K_n^* \\ \\ L^* \end{pmatrix}, \qquad y_i \geqq 0, \tag{21}$$

where Γ is the $n \times m$ matrix (c_{ij}) and Λ the m-dimensional row vector (l_i). The maximum output Y^* can obviously be written as $Y^* = F(K_1^*,\ldots, K_n^*, L^*)$.

Then Solow asks whether the above linear programming problem with $n+1$ constraints can be collapsed into one with two constraints. He presents a sufficient condition: the problem is collapsible if, after transformation of variables, the matrix $(\Gamma', \Lambda')'$ can be transformed into the form

$$\begin{pmatrix} C & 0 \\ -D & B \\ 0 & A \end{pmatrix}, \tag{22}$$

where B and D have only a single row. But he has not shown the conditions under which the original matrix can be transformed into the above form.

This open question can be settled in the following way. Let us classify m activities into s groups, each of which consists of the same number of activities, say r. Suppose now $(\Gamma', \Lambda')'$ can be partitioned into

$$\begin{pmatrix} \Gamma \\ \Lambda \end{pmatrix} = \begin{pmatrix} b_1 C & b_2 C & . & . & . & b_s C \\ a_1 D & a_2 D & . & . & . & a_s D \end{pmatrix} \tag{23}$$

where C is an $n \times r$ matrix, D a $1 \times r$ vector, and the a_is and b_is are scalars. Correspondingly, write $(y_1,\ldots,y_m)$ in a partitioned vector form as

$$(y_1,\ldots,y_m) = (y^{(1)\prime},\ldots,y^{(s)\prime})$$

where each $y^{(i)}$ is an r-dimensional column vector.

We then consider the following two linear programming problems.

(i) Maximize $K = Dx$ subject to

$$Cx \leqq \begin{pmatrix} K_1^* \\ \cdot \\ \cdot \\ \cdot \\ K_n^* \end{pmatrix}, \qquad x \geqq 0, \tag{24}$$

where x is an r-dimensional column vector.

(ii) Maximize $Z = \sum_{i=1}^{s} z_i$ subject to

$$\begin{pmatrix} B \\ \\ \\ \\ A \end{pmatrix} \begin{pmatrix} z_1 \\ \cdot \\ \cdot \\ \cdot \\ z_s \end{pmatrix} \leqq \begin{pmatrix} K^* \\ \\ \\ \\ L^* \end{pmatrix}, \qquad z_i \geqq 0, \tag{25}$$

where $A = (a_1,\ldots,a_s)$, $B = (b_1,\ldots,b_s)$, and K^* is a maximal value of the K of problem (i). It is obvious that the solution Z^* of the second-stage maximization problem (ii) after (i) is equal to the maximum value of Z of the Solow problem, i.e.

maximize $Z = \sum_{i=1}^{s} z_i$ subject to

$$\begin{pmatrix} C & 0 \\ & \\ & \\ & \\ -D & B \\ 0 & A \end{pmatrix} \begin{pmatrix} x \\ \\ \\ \\ \\ z \end{pmatrix} \leqq \begin{pmatrix} K_1^* \\ \cdot \\ \cdot \\ \cdot \\ K_n^* \\ 0 \\ L^* \end{pmatrix}. \tag{26}$$

We can also prove that Z^* is exactly the same as the solution of the following problem:

(iii) Maximize $Y = \sum_{i=1}^{m} y_i$ subject to

$$\begin{pmatrix} b_1 C & b_2 C & . & . & . & b_s C \\ a_1 D & a_2 D & . & . & . & a_s D \end{pmatrix} \begin{pmatrix} y_1 \\ . \\ . \\ . \\ . \\ y_m \end{pmatrix} \leqq \begin{pmatrix} K_1^* \\ . \\ . \\ K_n^* \\ L^* \end{pmatrix}, \qquad y_i \geqq 0. \quad (27)$$

(Put $x = \sum_{i=1}^{s} b_i y^{(i)}$ and $z_i = Dy^{(i)}$, $i = 1,..., s$ in (26); then it is reduced to (27).) It is thus seen that iff $(\Gamma', \Lambda')'$ can be partitioned into the form (23), it is transformable into the form (22), the original problem being equivalent to the Solow problem.

After Solow, the same idea was pursued by Fisher [**1**], [**2**], Diamond [**1**], Hall [**1**], and Stigum [**1**]. They explicitly took the immobility of capital goods into account and considered the following problem. Let $Y(v)$ be the amount of output Y obtained from capital of vintage v, $K(v)$, and labour $L(v)$ allocated to that capital. All $Y(v)$ are of the same kind of output, all $K(v)$ are fixed, and $L(v)$, $v = 1,..., n$, are adjusted so as to maximize $Y = \sum_{v=1}^{n} Y(v) = \sum_{v=1}^{n} f^{(v)}[K(v), L(v)]$ subject to $\sum_{v=1}^{n} L(v) = L$.

The value of Y obtained in this way is denoted by Y^*. Then, under what conditions does there exist an aggregate production function $G(K, L)$ and a capital aggregate $K = J[K(1),..., K(n)]$ such that $G = Y^*$? Fisher [**1**] showed that on the assumption of constant returns to scale, the heterogeneous capital may be aggregated under the following conditions: (i) if there are two factors, a necessary and sufficient condition for aggregation is that when labour is allocated to maximize output, i.e. its marginal product in all uses is the same, the average product of labour in all uses is the same; (ii) more generally, capital-augmenting technical change is necessary and sufficient to permit aggregation of the heterogeneous capital stock.[18] Later Fisher considered the aggregation of labour and of output for the same model (see Fisher [**3**] and Stigum [**2**]). Gorman also investigated the conditions under which the short-run production possibility set for the economy as a whole, $S(y)$, where y represents immovable inputs distributed among firms, can be written in the form $\tilde{S}(Y(y))$ with aggregates Y of y. Then Fisher extended the model so as to admit both immovable and movable capital goods. Unfortunately, the conditions for aggregation obtained were more or less as restrictive as (23) in the discrete case.

Whitaker [**1**] was concerned with a case where optimality conditions need not hold. They are replaced by some allocation rules concerning labour, which include, as a special case, the optimality allocation rule. One of Whitaker's results is that, when constant returns to scale prevail, aggregation in terms of the orthodox fixed weights, $\sum w_v K(v)$, is possible only if labour is always allocated optimally. However, he found his own aggregation condition quite restrictive.

Finally, a short note on the aggregation of demand functions may be added. Using demand equations of the type suggested by Theil [**1**], i.e.[19]

$$\bar{\omega}_{it}\Delta\log x_{it} = A_i + B_i\Big(\Delta\log Y_t - \sum_k \bar{\omega}_{kt}\Delta\log p_{kt}\Big) + \\ + \sum_j C_{ij}\Big(\Delta\log p_{jt} - \sum_k B_k\Delta\log p_{kt}\Big) + u_{it}, \quad (28)$$

Barten and Turnovsky [**1**] show that under the assumption of almost additive preferences it is possible to construct group demand functions such that the aggregate possesses the same properties as demand equations for single commodities. A

(18) This result is also cited in Ferguson [**1**], as is the Robinson–Solow controversy.

(19) Where $\omega_{it} = \dfrac{p_{it}\,x_{it}}{Y_t}$, $\bar{\omega}_{it} = \frac{1}{2}(\omega_{it}+\omega_{i,t-1})$, B_i is the marginal propensity to spend on good i out of income Y_t, C_{ij} is the 'specific' substitution effect in elasticity terms, weighted by ω_i, the term 'specific' being used in the sense of Houthakker [**1**] and Theil [**1**] to refer to that part of the substitution effect which depends on the combination (i, j) and not on quantities specific for i and j separately, and u_{it} is an error term.

condition is that a certain type of price index be used whose weights are marginal allocation coefficients of a partial kind:

$$\Delta \log \bar{p}_{ht} = \sum_{r \in h} \beta_r \Delta \log p_{rt}, \tag{29}$$

where β_r = marginal propensity to spend on good r out of expenditure on group h.

IV. Separability and Intrinsic Complementarity

M. MORISHIMA (1959)

1. Introduction

THE traditional theory of the consumer's behaviour says that two goods r and s are substitutes or complements to one another depending on whether the demand for r is increased or decreased by an income-compensated rise in the price of s.(1) The demand for two complements (x_r and x_s) may, however, change in opposite directions from causes other than income-compensated price variations. For instance, if r is a normal good and s inferior, a rise in income will increase x_r and decrease x_s. Therefore, in order to analyse 'intrinsic' complements which are such that an increase in demand for r, *from whatever cause*, is linked with an increase in demand for s, we must abandon the traditional definition and use a new method of approach.(2)

A chapter in J. R. Hicks's book, *A Revision of Demand Theory* suggests such a new approach.(3) The present chapter deals with a translation of his verbal theory into the mathematical language of Slutsky. The traditional theory does not specify the particular shape of the utility function (except for those features which derive diminishing marginal rates of substitution), but the development of consumer theory by Hicks makes such a specification necessary. In this chapter it is assumed that the utility function satisfies the condition for the 'separability' of goods, due to Sono and Leontief;(4) it is

(1) For complementarity and substitution, Hicks gave two definitions, the p- and q-definitions. See Hicks [**2**], p. 156. The definition in the text corresponds to his p-definition. As to the usefulness of the q-definition, see Morishima [**2**].

(2) Hicks [**2**], p. 16. After the publication of the original version of this chapter, K. Lancaster proposed a 'new' approach, but it is essentially no more than a revival of Hicks. See Lancaster [**1**].

(3) Hicks [**2**], pp. 16–18.

(4) See Sono [**1**], Leontief [**2**], and Morishima [**1**]. Leontief dealt with the problem of separability of goods quite independently of Sono. I was not

shown that the amalgamated theory of Hicks and Sono–Leontief, besides throwing some light on the nature of intrinsic complementarity, may be considered a synthesis of traditional demand theory and theory of the firm, which have in most cases been sharply separated up to now.(5) It is also shown that if we apply the theory of 'linear programming' instead of the traditional, marginal theory of the firm to analysis of the technical part of consumer demand, we can make much deeper researches in the nature of intrinsic complementarity between goods.

2. The Objective–Means Analysis of Consumer's Behaviour

We consider an individual with a given money income M, who is offered consumption goods at fixed prices $p_1, p_2, \ldots, p_n$. Let $x_1, x_2, \ldots, x_n$ be the amounts he consumes. Then, as is well known, these amounts will be determined by the maximization of his utility function

$$u = u(x_1, x_2, \ldots, x_n) \tag{1}$$

subject to the budget constraint

$$M = p_1 x_1 + p_2 x_2 + \ldots + p_n x_n. \tag{2}$$

This is, of course, no more than the traditional theory of consumer behaviour. But Hicks has recently suggested the new idea 'that we ought to think of the consumer as choosing, according to his preferences, between certain *objectives*; and then deciding, more or less as the entrepreneur decides, between alternative *means* of reaching those objectives'.(6) We begin by introducing this idea into traditional consumer theory.

Let there be m objectives which the consumer pursues; and let the goods $i_j, \ldots, i'_j$, be means to the attainment of the jth objective. Goods which are consumed for different objectives

aware of Leontief's article until several months after the publication of mine. This is the reason why it was not cited in my paper.

(5) From a different point of view, Makower and Baumol [1], Graaff [1], and Tanaka [1] synthesized the theory of consumer's behaviour and the theory of the firm.

(6) Hicks [2], p. 166.

are treated as different goods, even though they are of the same kind, so that each good contributes to only one objective. Then we shall have the following arrangement of goods $(1, 2, \ldots, i, \ldots n)$ and objectives $(1, 2, \ldots, j, \ldots, m)$:

$$\begin{array}{ll} \text{goods:} & 1 = \underbrace{i_1, \ldots, i'_1}_{1}, \ldots, \underbrace{i_j, \ldots, i'_j}_{j}, \ldots, \underbrace{i_m, \ldots, i'_m}_{m.} = n, \\ \text{objectives:} & \end{array}$$

Since the goods $i_j, \ldots, i'_j$ are means of reaching the same objective j, the valuation of those goods relative to one another is determined by their relative contributions to the objective j, and independently of the remaining goods which are devoted to other objectives. Consequently, we may assume that the marginal rates of substitution between goods $i_j, \ldots, i'_j$ are independent of all the other goods, i.e. that goods $i_j, \ldots, i'_j$ are 'separable' from each of goods $i_k, \ldots, i'_k$ $(k \neq j)$, using the terms in the sense of Sono and Leontief. Thus all the sets of goods $(i_1, \ldots, i'_1), \ldots, (i_j, \ldots, i'_j), \ldots, (i_m, \ldots, i'_m)$ are mutually separable, and according to the Sono–Leontief theorem, we can write the utility function (1) in the form(7)

$$u = u[f^1(x_{i_1}, \ldots, x_{i'_1}), \ldots, f^j(x_{i_j}, \ldots, x_{i'_j}), \ldots, f^m(x_{i_m}, \ldots, x_{i'_m})]. \quad (3)$$

Next, let us take into account the fact that the relation between the means and the objective is of a technical character, being very similar to the relation between factor inputs and commodity outputs. Then we may assume that the functions

$$y_j = f^j(x_{i_j}, \ldots, x_{i'_j}) \quad (j = 1, \ldots, m), \quad (4)$$

which give us m relations between means and objectives, are homogeneous of the first degree in the variables $x_{i_j}, \ldots, x_{i'_j}$. We obtain, therefore, the relations

$$1 = f^j(z_{i_j}, \ldots, z_{i'_j}) \quad (5.j)$$

$(j = 1, \ldots, m)$, where z_r $(r = i_j, \ldots, i'_j)$ stands for the amount of x_r required per unit of y_j, i.e. x_r/y_j. $(5.j)$ implies, of course, that the means have constant returns to scale. It is a restrictive assumption, but may be accepted as the first approximation.

(7) See Morishima [**1**].

3. A Digression

In Morishima [**1**] (reprinted below, Chapter VIII), I developed a theory of consumer demand for money based on the assumption that all the monetary goods (cash and bonds) and all the consumption goods are separable from one another; that is to say, I assumed a utility function of the form

$$u = U[\phi(x_1,\ldots,x_n),\ \psi\{q(H, B, p_1,\ldots, p_n, p_b;\ \xi)\}],$$

where x_i represents the demand for the ith consumption good, H and B the quantities of cash and bonds held by the consumer at the end of the period, ξ is an index of the future living standard desired by the consumer, $p_1, p_2,\ldots, p_n$ are the prices of the goods, and p_b is the price of bonds. Here ϕ is called the proper utility function of consumption goods. q is the probability of the future living standard ξ, depending on the consumer's present resources (H and B) and on present prices. ψ, which is a functional of the distribution $q(\xi)$, is called the choice function of the future life. In Hicks's language our theory can be restated as follows: the consumer has two objectives, enjoyment in the current period and security for the future. All the consumption goods are means of pursuing utility and all the monetary goods means of making the future life preferable. This illustrates the closeness of my old theory to Hicks's new idea.

4. Equilibrium and Stability Conditions

Now the consumer is supposed to maximize his utility (3), subject to the condition (2). The conditions for consumer equilibrium are therefore

$$u_j f_r^j = \lambda p_r \quad (r = i_j,\ldots, i_j';\ j = 1,\ldots, m), \tag{6}$$

where $u_j = \dfrac{\partial u}{\partial y_j}$, $f_r^j = \dfrac{\partial f^j}{\partial x_r}$, and λ is a Lagrange multiplier. The stability condition is that the quadratic form

$$\sum_{j=1}^{m} \sum_{r=i_j}^{i_j'} \sum_{s=i_j}^{i_j'} u_j f_{rs}^j \, \mathrm{d}x_r \, \mathrm{d}x_s +$$

$$+ \sum_{j=1}^{m} \sum_{k=1}^{m} \sum_{r=i}^{i_j'} \sum_{s=i_k}^{i_k'} u_{jk} f_r^j f_s^k \, \mathrm{d}x_r \, \mathrm{d}x_s \tag{7}$$

is negative for all values of $\mathrm{d}x_1,\ldots, \mathrm{d}x_n$ such that

$$\sum_{j=1}^{m} \sum_{r=i_j}^{i'_j} u_j f_r^j \,\mathrm{d}x_r = 0.$$

In the expression (7) we write

$$f_{rs}^j \text{ for } \frac{\partial^2 f^j}{\partial x_r \partial x_s} \quad \text{and} \quad u_{jk} \text{ for } \frac{\partial^2 u}{\partial y_j \partial y_k}.$$

When λ is eliminated from equations (6) we have $n-1$ equations, which together with equation (2) determine the n quantities $x_1, x_2,\ldots, x_n$.

The above equilibrium and stability conditions are at first sight very peculiar and complicated; but, as will be shown below, they can be expressed in more familiar forms. First, denoting u_j/λ by μ_j, we shall have from (6) the following m sets of simultaneous equations:

$$\mu_j f_r^j = p_r \quad (r = i_j,\ldots, i'_j), \tag{8.j}$$

where $j = 1,\ldots, m$, and we call these equations the f^j-equilibrium conditions. Next, multiplying both sides of equations (6) by x_r and summing over all rs of the commodity-group in question, we obtain m equations:

$$u_j\Big[\sum_{r=i_j}^{i'_j} f_r^j x_r\Big] = \lambda \Big[\sum_{r=i_j}^{i'_j} p_r x_r\Big] \quad (j = 1, 2,\ldots, m). \tag{9}$$

But since the functions (4) are homogeneous of degree one, we have by Euler's theorem,

$$y^j = \sum_{r=i_j}^{i'_j} f_r^j x_r \quad (j = 1, 2,\ldots, m). \tag{10}$$

Together with (10), equations (9) lead to the following u-equilibrium conditions:

$$u_j = \lambda q_j \quad (j = 1, 2,\ldots, m), \tag{11}$$

where

$$q_j = \sum_{r=i_j}^{i'_j} p_r z_r. \tag{12.j}$$

Using (12.j) we can easily rewrite the budget equation (2) in the form

$$\sum_{j=1}^{m} q_j y_j = M. \tag{13}$$

Now equations (11) and (8.j) ($j = 1, 2,..., m$) give us $m+n$ equations. Eliminating $\mu_1, \mu_2,..., \mu_m$ and λ, we obtain $n-1$ equations, which, together with the $1+m$ equations (13) and (5.j) ($j = 1, 2,..., m$), determine the $m+n$ quantities $z_1, z_2,..., z_n$, $y_1,..., y_m$, and hence the n quantities $x_1, x_2,..., x_n$.

Let us now consider the stability condition. Since it implies that (7) must be negative for all values of $dx_1,..., dx_n$ such that

$$\sum_{j=1}^{m} \sum_{r=i_j}^{i'_j} u_j f_r^j \, dx_r = 0,$$

it follows that (7) is negative also for all values of $dx_1, dx_2,..., dx_n$ such that

$$\sum_{r=i_j}^{i'_j} f_r^j \, dx_r = 0 \quad (j = 1, 2,..., m). \tag{14}$$

Further, by virtue of (14) the terms in the second line of the expression (7) must vanish. It follows that each of the m expressions

$$\sum_{r=i_j}^{i'_j} \sum_{s=i_j}^{i'_j} f_{rs}^j \, dx_r \, dx_s \quad (j = 1, 2,..., m)$$

must be negative under the constraints (14). Therefore,

$$(-1)^{k-1} \begin{vmatrix} 0 & f_{i_j}^j & \cdot & \cdot & \cdot & f_{i_j+k}^j \\ f_{i_j}^j & f_{i_j i_j}^j & \cdot & \cdot & \cdot & f_{i_j, i_j+k}^j \\ \cdot & \cdot & & & & \cdot \\ \cdot & \cdot & & & & \cdot \\ \cdot & \cdot & & & & \cdot \\ f_{i_j+k}^j & f_{i_j+k, i_j}^j & \cdot & \cdot & \cdot & f_{i_j+k, i_j+k}^j \end{vmatrix} > 0$$

$$(k = 1, 2,..., i'_j - i_j;\ j = 1, 2,..., m).$$

We shall refer to these conditions as the f^j-stability conditions.

Next it follows from the homogeneity of the functions (4) that each f_r^j is homogeneous of degree zero in variables $x_{i_j},..., x_{i'_j}$. We can therefore infer from Euler's theorem that, if variables $x_{i_j},..., x_{i'_j}$ change proportionately, the terms in the first line of (7) vanish necessarily. Thus, as long as $x_{i_j},..., x_{i'_j}$ move *pari passu*, our stability condition merely requires that the quadratic form

$$\sum_{j=1}^{m} \sum_{k=1}^{m} u_{jk} \, dy_j \, dy_k$$

be negative for all values of $\mathrm{d}y_1,\ldots, \mathrm{d}y_m$ such that

$$\sum_{j=1}^{m} u_j \,\mathrm{d}y_j = 0.$$

This implies that the following inequalities are fulfilled:

$$(-1)^k \begin{vmatrix} 0 & u_1 & \cdot & \cdot & \cdot & u_k \\ u_1 & u_{11} & \cdot & \cdot & \cdot & u_{1k} \\ \cdot & \cdot & & & & \cdot \\ \cdot & \cdot & & & & \cdot \\ \cdot & \cdot & & & & \cdot \\ u_k & u_{k1} & \cdot & \cdot & \cdot & u_{kk} \end{vmatrix} > 0 \quad (k = 2, 3,\ldots, m).$$

We shall call the condition in this form the u-stability condition.

So far we have shown that the equilibrium conditions are split into the f^j- and the u-equilibrium conditions, and similarly the stability conditions into the f^j- and the u-stability conditions. Using these f^j- and u-conditions, we can restate the above theory of consumer behaviour as follows. First, since the f^j-stability conditions hold, each of the f^j-equilibrium points $(j = 1, 2,\ldots, m)$ represents a minimum of (12.j) subject to (5.j). We can, of course, interpret (12.j) as the average cost of objective y_j, when (5.j) gives us the technical relation between means $i_j,\ldots, i'_j$ and objective j. Thus, as was asserted by Hicks, the consumer decides between alternative means for the attainment of objectives just as the entrepreneur decides between the inputs of production;[8] the f^j-equilibrium conditions (8.j) $(j = 1, 2,\ldots, m)$ determine the means-input coefficients (i.e. the amounts of means per unit of the objective y_j), $z_1, z_2,\ldots, z_n$, which correspond to the production coefficients of the Walrasian theory of general equilibrium.

Secondly, since all the zs are already determined, the consumer is faced with a set of determined qs. Now, together with the u-stability conditions, the u-equilibrium conditions (11) give us the point at which u is a maximum subject to (13). Thus, the consumer selects the most preferred set of objectives $y_1, y_2,\ldots, y_m$ according to his scale of preference. Needless to say, this part of the theory has a perfect counterpart in the

(8) Hicks [2], p. 166.

traditional theory of consumer behaviour. The twin assumptions, basic to general equilibrium theory, that consumers maximize utility and entrepreneurs minimize average costs of production are both related to the present theory. In fact, a consumer acts as an entrepreneur in selecting the most efficient means of reaching objectives. As will be explained in the next section, the distinction between consumption analysis and production analysis disappears, and the two are merged into the study of a composite entity, the 'consumer–producer'.

5. Another Digression

The new approach to consumer behaviour is not so much a departure from traditional theory as a generalization of it. This may be seen as follows. If the functions (4) are of the special form

$$y_j = x_j \quad (j = 1, 2, \ldots, m),$$

our problem of maximizing $u = u(y_1, \ldots, y_m)$ subject to $\sum q_j y_j = M$ is equivalent to the traditional problem of maximizing $u = u(x_1, \ldots, x_m)$ subject to $\sum p_j x_j = M$. Thus the traditional consumer theory tacitly assumes that each objective itself is a means of reaching it.

The new approach may be considered also as a generalization of the traditional theory of the firm. Suppose that the utility function (3) takes the form

$$u = (P_1 - q_1)y_1 + (P_2 - q_2)y_2 + \ldots + (P_m - q_m)y_m,$$

where P_j represents the price of the jth objective or the jth output. An entrepreneur who has a given capital M available for expenditure and has opportunities for producing m outputs, $y_1, y_2, \ldots, y_m$, minimizes the cost q_j of each output under the technical constraints (5.j), and maximizes the total profit u subject to the capital limitation (13). If the jth output is most profitable among m outputs, i.e. if P_j/q_j is the maximum of $P_1/q_1, \ldots, P_m/q_m$, the total profit u is a maximum subject to $\sum q_j y_j = M$, at the point $(0, \ldots, 0, y_j^*, 0, \ldots, 0)$ where $y_j^* = M/q_j$. Therefore, the theory reduces to

$$\min = p_{i_j} x_{i_j} + \ldots + p_{i'_j} x_{i'_j},$$

subject to $$y_j^* = f^j(x_{i_j},\ldots,x_{i'_j}).$$

It goes without saying that this is the traditional theory itself.

6. The Effect of a Change in Price

Let us now consider the effect of a change in a price on the amounts consumed. First, it follows immediately from (11) and (13) that y_k reacts to changes in q_j according to the familiar Slutsky equation

$$\frac{\partial y_k}{\partial q_j} = -y_j \frac{\partial y_k}{\partial M} + X'_{jk} \quad (j,k = 1,2,\ldots,m), \tag{15}$$

where $X'_{jk} = \lambda U_{jk}/U$, U denotes the last of the determinants appearing in the u-stability condition, and U_{jk} is the cofactor of u_{jk} in U. Secondly, from (5.j) and (8.j) we have

$$\frac{\partial z_s}{\partial p_r} = X''_{rs} \quad (r,s = i_j,\ldots,i'_j) \tag{16}$$

and $$\sum_{s=i_j}^{i'_j} p_s X''_{rs} = 0 \quad (r = i_j,\ldots,i'_j), \tag{17}$$

where $X''_{rs} = \mu_j F^j_{rs}/F^j$, F^j denotes the last of the determinants appearing in the f^j-stability condition, and F^j_{rs} is the cofactor of the f^j_{rs} in F^j.

Taking into account (16) and (17), we easily obtain the relations

$$\frac{\partial q_j}{\partial p_r} = z_r \quad (r = i_j,\ldots,i'_j). \tag{18}$$

Combining (15) and (18), we find by virtue of $z_r\, y_j = x_r$ that

$$\frac{\partial y_k}{\partial p_r} = -x_r \frac{\partial y_k}{\partial M} + z_r X'_{jk}. \tag{19}$$

Next, since z_s stands for x_s/y_k $(s = i_k,\ldots,i'_k)$, we have

$$\frac{\partial z_s}{\partial p_r} = \frac{y_k(\partial x_s/\partial p_r) - x_s(\partial y_k/\partial p_r)}{y_k^2} \quad (r = i_j,\ldots,i'_j;\ s = i_k,\ldots,i'_k)$$

and therefore

$$\frac{\partial x_s}{\partial p_r} = z_s \frac{\partial y_k}{\partial p_r} + y_k \frac{\partial z_s}{\partial p_r}, \tag{20}$$

where it has to be remembered that $\partial z_s/\partial p_r = 0$ if goods r and s belong to distinct groups, j and k, respectively. On account of (16) and (19), equation (20) leads to

$$\frac{\partial x_s}{\partial p_r} = -x_r z_s \frac{\partial y_j}{\partial M} + z_r z_s X'_{jj} + y_j X''_{rs} \quad (r, s = i_j, \ldots, i'_j) \tag{21}$$

and

$$\frac{\partial x_s}{\partial p_r} = -x_r z_s \frac{\partial y_k}{\partial M} + z_r z_s X'_{jk} \quad (r = i_j, \ldots, i'_j;\ s = i_k, \ldots, i'_k;\ j \neq k). \tag{22}$$

Equations (21) and (22) give us the effects of a change in price p_r on the amounts consumed, x_s $(s = 1, 2, \ldots, n)$.

So far we have deduced the Slutsky equations (21) and (22) from the f^j- and the u-equilibrium conditions; normally, of course, they are deduced immediately from (2) and (6). The familiar procedure of Slutsky and Hicks gives the equations in the form

$$\frac{\partial x_s}{\partial p_r} = -x_r \frac{\partial x_s}{\partial M} + X_{rs}.$$

But, since we can easily prove that

$$\frac{\partial x_s}{\partial M} = z_s \frac{\partial y_k}{\partial M} \quad (s = i_k, \ldots, i'_k;\ k = 1, 2, \ldots, m), \tag{23}$$

we know that the first terms on the right-hand sides of (21) and (22) represent the income effects and the other terms the substitution effects. Therefore, concerning the substitution effects, we have the following relations:

$$X_{rs} = z_r z_s X'_{jj} + y_j X''_{rs} \quad (r, s = i_j, \ldots, i'_j), \tag{24}$$

$$X_{rs} = z_r z_s X'_{jk} \quad (r = i_j, \ldots, i'_j;\ s = i_k, \ldots, i'_k;\ j \neq k). \tag{25}$$

The economic meaning of the first term of (24) is completely elucidated in Hicks's verbal explanation that a reduction in the price p_r reduces the cost of the objective j for which good r is a means, and accordingly sets up a tendency for the objective j to be substituted for others. The meaning of the second term, according to his explanation, is that a reduction in p_r reduces the cost of r-intensive methods of attaining y_j relative to other methods, and accordingly sets up a tendency for good r to be substituted for others.[(9)] The first term may be called the objectives-substitution term, and the second term the means-substitution term. As will be seen from equation (25), the substitution effect of a change in the price of r on the demand for a good s which serves an objective k *other* than that attained by r, does not include the *means*-substitution effect. This is not surprising, since the change in the price of r leaves all the cost of all the methods of attaining k unaltered.

We can deduce some economic laws from equations (23), (24), and (25). First, since $z_s = x_s/y_k$, it follows from (23) that

$$\frac{M}{x_{i_k}}\frac{\partial x_{i_k}}{\partial M} = \dots = \frac{M}{x_{i'_k}}\frac{\partial x_{i'_k}}{\partial M} = \frac{M}{y_k}\frac{\partial y_k}{\partial M}. \qquad (26)$$

In other words, goods which serve the same objectives have equal income elasticities. It is noted that even if the utility function is separable, this equality of the income elasticities does not follow unless the production function f^k is homogeneous of degree one.

Secondly, it follows from the u- and f^j-stability conditions that both X'_{jj} and X''_{rr} must be negative. Therefore (24) gives us $X_{rr} < 0$.

Thirdly, let us make the following distinctions. Two goods r and s are 'revealed substitutes' (or 'revealed complements') if $X_{rs} > 0$ (or < 0). Two goods r and s serving the same objective j are 'means-substitutes' (or 'means-complements') if $X''_{rs} > 0$ (or < 0). Two goods r and s serving different objectives j and k are 'objectives-substitutes' (or 'objectives-complements') if $X'_{jk} > 0$ (or < 0). Given a positive y_j, it follows from (24) that, in the trivial case of coefficients z_r and z_s being zero, the fact that r and s are means-complements implies that they are revealed complements, and conversely, but if *both* coefficients are positive, revealed complementarity no longer implies means-complementarity, though the opposite is still true. Moreover, it follows from (25) that if z_r and z_s are both positive, objectives-complementarity implies revealed complementarity and conversely; but if either of them vanishes, the two goods are necessarily independent of each other, i.e. $X_{rs} = 0$.

(9) Hicks [**2**], pp. 166–7.

7. Quasi-Intrinsic Complementarity

In this section we shall deal with the problem of intrinsic (or complete) complementarity which was discussed by Lange and Hicks.(10) If two goods r and s are *complete* complements, the consumption of s increases in the same proportion as the consumption of r. But this is not so in any of the definitions suggested above. Consequently, the need for another definition is keenly felt.

As may be seen from such examples as pen and ink and petrol and lubricating oil, almost all intrinsic complements are complementary means of reaching the same objective; and if the prices of commodities remain constant and there is an increase in the demand for a means r of attaining a particular objective j, there will be a proportionate increase in the demand for all those commodities s which are required as intrinsically complementary means to that objective. Accordingly, we shall define s as a *quasi-intrinsic* complement of r if X''_{rs} is not only negative but also satisfies the following condition:

$$\frac{X''_{rr}}{x_r} = \frac{X''_{rs}}{x_s}, \quad \text{or} \quad \frac{X''_{rr}}{z_r} = \frac{X''_{rs}}{z_s} \quad (r, s = i_j, \ldots, i'_j). \tag{27}$$

Since, as is easily shown, X''_{rr} (or X''_{rs}) represents an increase in the demand for r (or s) due to a 'solitary' increase in the marginal rate of substitution,(11) f^j_r/f^j_w $(w = i_j, \ldots, i'_j;\ w \neq r)$, of means r for other means, the relation (27) implies that a solitary increase in the demand for r increases the demand for s proportionally. If two goods are such quasi-intrinsic complements, it follows from (24) that

$$X_{rs} = z_r z_s X'_{jj} + y_j X''_{rr} = \frac{z_s}{z_r}(z_r^2 X'_{jj} + y_j X''_{rr})\frac{z_s}{z_r}.$$

As the part in parenthesis equals X_{rr}, the above equation immediately gives us the relation

$$\frac{X_{rr}}{z_r} = \frac{X_{rs}}{z_s}.$$

(10) Lange [**1**, **2**]; Hicks [**3**, **4**].

(11) Ichimura [**1**].

Therefore we obtain at once[12]

$$\frac{p_r}{x_r}\left(\frac{\partial x_r}{\partial p_r}+x_r\frac{\partial x_r}{\partial M}\right)=\frac{p_r}{x_s}\left(\frac{\partial x_s}{\partial p_r}+x_r\frac{\partial x_s}{\partial M}\right). \tag{28}$$

Thus if s is a quasi-intrinsic means-complement of r, they are so in the revealed sense; an income-compensated change in the price p_r gives rise to a proportionate change in x_r and x_s.

Now let us take into consideration the equation (26). Then it follows at once from (28) that

$$\frac{p_r}{x_r}\frac{\partial x_r}{\partial p_r}=\frac{p_r}{x_s}\frac{\partial x_s}{\partial p_r},$$

that is to say, the p_r-elasticities of quasi-intrinsic complements are equal to each other.

These are all the results to which the argument of quasi-intrinsic complementarity can lead us. It is true that they are quite satisfactory at first sight; but we must point out that there are some difficulties.

First, as mentioned above, and stated by Hicks, *true-intrinsic* complements are goods which are such that an increase in the consumption of s goes with an increase in the consumption of r, whatever has been the cause of the first increase. Hence, true-intrinsic complements have not only the same income and p_r-elasticities, but also the same p_t-elasticities ($t \neq r$). It is true that if t is a good other than $i_j,\ldots, i'_j$, it follows immediately from

$$\left.\begin{aligned} X_{tr} &= z_t z_r X'_{kj} \\ X_{ts} &= z_t z_s X'_{kj} \end{aligned}\right\} \quad (r,s=i_j,\ldots,i'_j;\ t=i_k,\ldots,i'_k;\ k\neq j) \tag{25'}$$

that $X_{tr}/z_r = X_{ts}/z_s$; therefore, considering

$$\frac{M}{x_r}\frac{\partial x_r}{\partial M}=\frac{M}{x_s}\frac{\partial x_s}{\partial M} \quad (r,s=i_j,\ldots,i'_j), \tag{26'}$$

we find

$$\frac{p_t}{x_r}\frac{\partial x_r}{\partial p_t}=\frac{p_t}{x_s}\frac{\partial x_s}{\partial p_t} \quad (t\neq i_j,\ldots,i'_j), \tag{29}$$

[12] Since the elasticity of substitution is defined as

$$\sigma_{rs}=\frac{M}{x_r x_s}\left(\frac{\partial x_s}{\partial p_r}+x_r\frac{\partial x_s}{\partial M}\right),$$

equation (28) means that the elasticity of substitution between x_s and x_r is equal to the elasticity of substitution of x_r for itself.

that is to say, r and s have the same elasticities with respect to the price of any good t which is not an element of the group $(i_j,..., i'_j)$. But, as can easily be proved, equation (29) does not apply if t $(t \neq r)$ is an element of the group $(i_j,..., i'_j)$. Furthermore, we obtain

$$\frac{p_s}{x_r}\frac{\partial x_r}{\partial p_s} \neq \frac{p_s}{x_s}\frac{\partial x_s}{\partial p_s},$$

which implies that even if s is a quasi-intrinsic complement of r, r is not necessarily a quasi-intrinsic complement of s.[13]

Secondly, all of X''_{rr}, X''_{rs}, x_r, and x_s are dependent on income and prices; consequently, even if the relation (27) is satisfied in one income–price situation, it does not necessarily hold in another income–price situation. Thus a pair of goods, r and s, which are quasi-intrinsic complements in one income–price situation may not be quasi-intrinsic complements in another. We must say therefore that our definition of quasi-intrinsic complementarity is not truly intrinsic.

These are defects of our definition and the reasons for a further search for a more adequate treatment.

8. True-intrinsic Complementarity

In order to analyse true-intrinsic complementarity, we introduce into our system a device of the theory of 'linear programming'. Let us assume that there are k methods of reaching the objective j; and let y_{jh} units of the objective j be realized by the hth method. Then we have

$$y_{j1}+y_{j2}+...+y_{jk} = y_j. \tag{30}$$

If we assume that, in order for one unit of the objective j to be realized by the method h, the goods $i_j,..., i'_j$ are consumed in the amounts $a_{i_jh},..., a_{i'_jh}$ respectively, we have

$$\left.\begin{array}{l} x_{i_j} = a_{i_j1}y_{j1}+a_{i_j2}y_{j2}+...+a_{i_jk}y_{jk} \\ \cdot \quad \cdot \quad \cdot \quad \cdot \quad \cdot \quad \cdot \quad \cdot \quad \cdot \quad \cdot \quad \cdot \quad \cdot \\ x_{i'_j} = a_{i'_j1}y_{j1}+a_{i'_j2}y_{j2}+...+a_{i'_jk}y_{jk} \end{array}\right\}, \tag{31}$$

where the as are assumed to be constant. From (31) we obtain

$$p_{i_j}x_{i_j}+...+p_{i'_j}x_{i'_j} = c_{j1}y_{j1}+...+c_{jk}y_{jk} \tag{32}$$

[13] Note that (27) does not imply $X''_{ss}/x_s = X''_{sr}/x_r$.

where

$$c_{jh} = p_{i_j} a_{i_j h} + \ldots + p_{i'_j} a_{i'_j h} \quad (h = 1, 2, \ldots, k).$$

Let v_{jh} represent y_{jh}/y_j. Then we have from (30) and (32)

$$\left.\begin{aligned} v_{j1} + v_{j2} + \ldots + v_{jk} &= 1 \\ q_j \equiv p_{i_j} z_{i_j} + \ldots + p_{i'_j} z_{i'_j} &= c_{j1} v_{j1} + \ldots + c_{jk} v_{jk} \end{aligned}\right\}. \tag{33}$$

Now we think of the consumer as selecting the method which makes q_j a minimum; then the problem of finding the most profitable method reduces to a problem of linear programming in the simplest form. In fact we easily find from (33) that the method whose c is minimum is selected as the most profitable method. Of course, two cases may arise; *either* one and only one c, say c_{jg}, is minimum among the cs *or* a number of cs are equal minima. In what follows we rule out the second case for the sake of simplicity.

If c_{jg} is minimum, $v_{jg} = 1$ and all the other vs vanish. Hence it follows from (31) that

$$z_{i_j} = a_{i_j g},$$

$$\cdot \quad \cdot \quad \cdot \quad \cdot$$

$$z_{i'_j} = a_{i'_j g}.$$

Since the second equation of (33) gives us the values q_j, the equations

$$q_1 y_1 + \ldots + q_m y_m = M,$$

$$u(y_1, \ldots, y_m) = \max,$$

determine the values y_j; and taking into account $y_{jg} = y_j$ and $y_{jh} = 0$ $(h \neq g)$, we get from equations (31) the values of our ultimate unknowns, xs.

The above argument provides us with a theory of intrinsic complements. Taking into account that each of $c_{j1}, c_{j2}, \ldots, c_{jk}$ is a linear and increasing function of p_r $(r = i_j, \ldots, i'_j)$, we get Fig. 4, where the segments $0d_h$ $(h = 1, 2, \ldots, k)$ stand for the values $c_{jh} - p_r a_{rh}$ $(h = 1, 2, \ldots, k)$, and the slopes of the lines $d_h c_{jh}$ $(h = 1, 2, \ldots, k)$ equal the values a_{rh} $(h = 1, 2, \ldots, k)$. As is easily found, if the price of good r is less than p'_r, the first method of reaching the objective j is cheapest; but if the price is greater than p'_r but less that p''_r, the second method is cheapest, whereas if the price is greater than p_r'', the third is cheapest. So long as the price of r changes within a range, say (p_r', p_r''), the same method (say the second method) will be selected as the efficient one. Although a change in q_j, due to the change in p_r, gives rise to substitutions among objectives $y_1, y_2, ..., y_m$, the demand for all the means of attaining the same objective will move

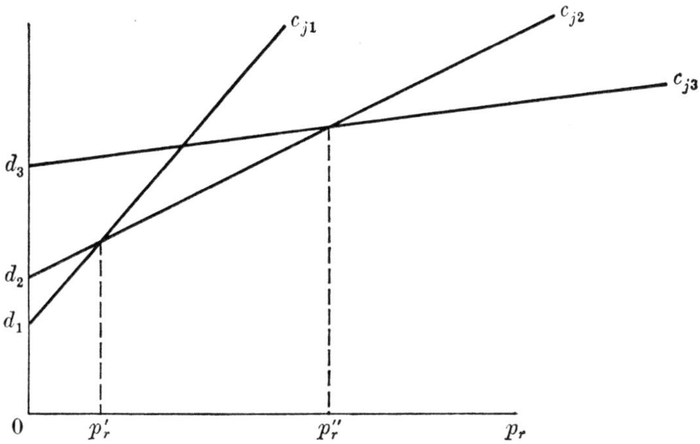

FIG. 4

proportionately. Thus we find that all the goods which are means of reaching the same objective constitute a group of intrinsic complements. But if the price of r rises from a point within a range (p_r', p_r'') to a point within another range, say (p_r'', ∞), there arises a substitution of the third method for the second method, which breaks the complementarities between goods.

The above argument holds for any of the prices p_r $(r = i_j, ..., i_j')$. We can say, therefore, that if a change in any of the prices is restricted within a certain (possibly narrow) range, it necessarily gives rise to a proportionate change in all the means of reaching the same objective. We may call such a complementarity *an intrinsic complementarity in the small.*

Next, let us assume that there exists one method, say the gth method, which satisfies conditions

$$a_{rg} \leq a_{rh} \quad (r = i_j, ..., i_j';\ h = 1, ..., g-1, g+1, ..., k). \quad (34)$$

In this case we can rule out substitution between methods. Hence, however much any of the prices may be increased or decreased, the consumer adopts the same method g in order to attain the single objective; the demand for the goods used by the method changes proportionately in any circumstances;

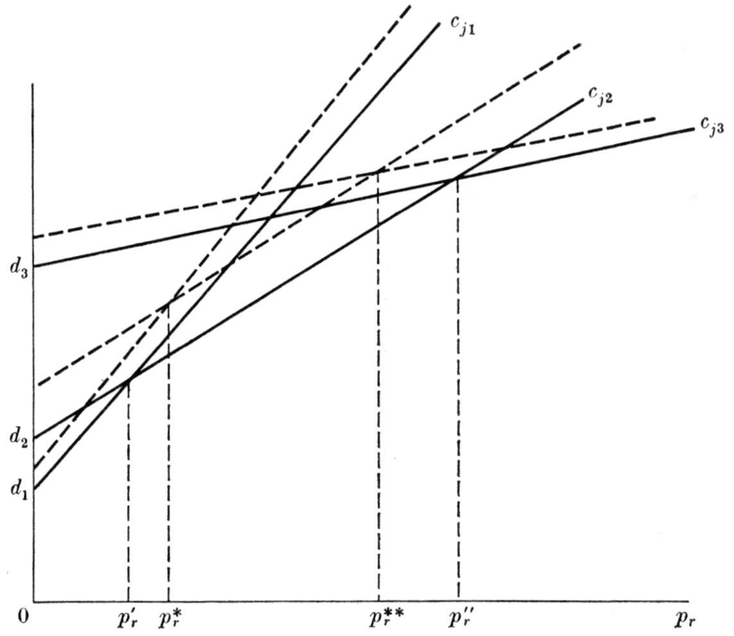

FIG. 5

that is to say, they are *intrinsic complements in the large.* In this case f^j is a CES function with the elasticity of substitution 0.

Thus, unless special, stringent conditions (34) are satisfied, goods which serve the same objective do not constitute a group of intrinsic complements in the large. They can, at best, be intrinsic complements within a certain range depending on prices, as is shown in the following. Since the segments $0d_h$ $(h = 1, 2,..., k)$ in Fig. 4 are elastic with respect to changes in prices other than p_r, a rise in p_t $(t = i_j,..., r-1, r+1,..., i_j')$ will shift the lines $d_h\, c_{jh}$ $(h = 1, 2,..., k)$ upwards; and therefore, we get Fig. 5. In the new situation after the rise in p_t, the means of attaining the same objective are complementary with one another so long as p_r changes within each of the new ranges $(0, p_r^*)$, (p_r^*, p_r^{**}), and (p_r^{**}, ∞). Thus the ranges are not inelastic, but may be narrowed or widened by changes in prices other than p_r.

Part III · Consumption

V. Demand for Commodities under Uncertain Expectation

C. LLUCH *and* M. MORISHIMA

1. Introduction

A STANDARD and immediate extension of the static Slutsky theory of demand is the one made by Tintner [**1**] and Hicks [**1**] which enables us to investigate the individual's consumption plans over time. They are concerned with a consumer who plans for the points of time 0, 1,..., T, on the assumptions that the consumption goods are all perishable and that he has precise price-expectations.(1) In Chapter VI the first assumption is removed so as to derive the demand functions for consumer durables. In this chapter we deal with a weaker individual whose price-expectations are subject to uncertainty.

Section 2 is devoted to summarizing the Tintner–Hicks analysis in the case of continuous time; we shall derive all the properties Hicks obtains in the discontinuous case. Section 3 discusses, in the discontinuous case, the demand for commodities under the more realistic and general assumption that the individual's price-expectations may be uncertain.

2. The Tintner–Hicks Theory

Suppose that consumer preferences can be represented by

$$\int_0^T \alpha(t)u[q(t)]\,\mathrm{d}t \tag{1}$$

where $q(t)$ is an n-vector of consumption flows; $\alpha(t)$, a subjective discount function; $u(q(t))$, a time-invariant instantaneous utility function which is concave. Let us represent the budget constraint as

$$\dot{w}(t) = \rho w(t) + y(t) - p'q(t) \quad (0 \leq t \leq T), \tag{2}$$

where the dot indicates the differentiation with respect to time

(1) Their model may allow for uncertainty in a restrictive way. See Hicks [**1**], pp. 124–5.

and the prime the transposition of vector p. At $t = 0$, this is the actual budget constraint. For $0 < t \leq T$, viewed at the point of time 0, this is the anticipated budget constraint. In (2), $w(t)$ represents wealth (a scalar); ρ is the (constant) expected rate of interest (rate of reproduction of wealth); $y(t)$ is the expected flow of labour income; and p is an n-vector of (constant) expected prices of goods in terms of the numeraire (wealth). It is noted that expectations of prices and the rate of interest are assumed to be stationary.(2)

Now we find $q(t) \geqq 0$, $0 \leqq t \leqq T$, which maximizes the utility functional over time (1) subject to the budget constraint (2) with given(3)

$$w(0) = w(T) = 0.$$

We set up the Lagrangian expression

$$\int_0^T \phi[q(t), w(t), \dot{w}(t), \lambda(t); y(t)]\,\mathrm{d}t$$

where

$$\phi = \alpha(t)u[q(t)] + \lambda(t)[\rho w(t) + y(t) - p'q(t) - \dot{w}(t)]$$

and treat $q(t)$, $w(t)$, and $\lambda(t)$ as if they are independent variables; $y(t)$ is a prescribed function on $0 \leqq t \leqq T$. Then we obtain the Euler differential equations necessary for a maximum;(4)

$$\frac{\partial\phi}{\partial q_i} = 0 \quad (i = 1,\dots, n), \quad \frac{\mathrm{d}}{\mathrm{d}t}\left(\frac{\partial\phi}{\partial\dot{w}}\right) - \frac{\partial\phi}{\partial w} = 0, \quad \frac{\partial\phi}{\partial\lambda} = 0,$$

or

$$\left.\begin{aligned} &\text{(a)}\quad \alpha(t)u_i(q(t)) = \lambda(t)p_i \quad (i = 1,\dots, n) \\ &\text{(b)}\quad \dot{\lambda}(t) = -\rho\lambda(t) \\ &\text{(c)}\quad \dot{w} = \rho w(t) + y(t) - p'q(t) \end{aligned}\right\}, \qquad (3)$$

where $u_i = \partial u/\partial q_i$. Equations (3a) are the Tintner–Hicks

(2) Tintner and Hicks are concerned with a more general case of changing expectations; but it is easy to relax the assumption.

(3) This is the 'wealth-constraint' problem in Yaari [**1**], for $q(t)$ a scalar.

(4) The inequality constraint $q(t) \geqq 0$ is ignored by assuming that the utility function has the property

$$\frac{\partial u[q(t)]}{\partial q_i} = \infty \qquad \text{if } q_i(t) = 0.$$

marginal conditions for optimality stating that the marginal rate of substitution between two commodities planned to be bought at given future dates must equal the ratio of their discounted prices.

Let us now define the truncated Laplace transform of $x(t)$ as

$$L(x) = \int_0^T e^{-\rho t} x(t)\, dt.$$

Then the basic formula

$$[e^{-\rho t} x(t)]_0^T = -\rho L(x) + L(\dot{x}) \tag{4}$$

follows from

$$\frac{d[e^{-\rho t} x(t)]}{dt} = -\rho\, e^{-\rho t} x(t) + e^{-\rho t} \dot{x}(t).$$

Putting now $x(t) = w(t)$ and bearing $w(0) = w(T) = 0$ in mind, we have from (4)

$$L(\dot{w}) = \rho L(w).$$

On the other hand we have from (2)

$$L(\dot{w}) = \rho L(w) + L(y) - p' L(q).$$

Hence we obtain the budget equation over time:

$$p' L(q) = L(y). \tag{5}$$

We can now derive the dynamic Slutsky equation from (3a) and (5). Differentiating them with respect to p_j, we have

$$\left.\begin{aligned} &\text{(a)} \quad U(t)\frac{\partial q(t)}{\partial p_j} - p\frac{\partial \mu(t)}{\partial p_j} = \mu(t)\delta_j, \quad 0 \leqq t \leqq T \\ &\text{(b)} \quad p' L\left(\frac{\partial q}{\partial p_j}\right) = -L(q_j) \end{aligned}\right\}, \tag{6}$$

where $U(t) = n \times n$ matrix $[u_{ij}(q(t))]$; $\mu(t) = \lambda(t)/\alpha(t)$; and

$$\delta_j = \begin{bmatrix} \delta_{1j} \\ \delta_{2j} \\ \cdot \\ \cdot \\ \cdot \\ \delta_{nj} \end{bmatrix},$$

where δ_{ij}s are Kronecker deltas. Defining

$$\begin{bmatrix} A(t) & B(t) \\ D(t) & C(t) \end{bmatrix} = [p'L(U^{-1})p]^{-1}\times$$

$$\times\left[\begin{array}{c:c} p'L(U^{-1})pU(t)^{-1} - U(t)^{-1}pp'L(U^{-1}) & U(t)^{-1}p \\ \hdashline p'L(U^{-1}) & -1 \end{array}\right]$$

we can show that

$$\left.\begin{array}{lll} \text{(a)} & \dfrac{\partial q(t)}{\partial p_j} = \mu(t)A(t)\delta_j - L(q_j)B(t), & 0 \leqq t \leqq T \\ \text{(b)} & \dfrac{\partial \mu(t)}{\partial p_j} = -\mu(t)D(t)\delta_j + L(q_j)C(t), & 0 \leqq t \leqq T \end{array}\right\} \tag{7}$$

are the solutions to (6). We can also show

$$\left.\begin{array}{ll} \text{(a)} & \dfrac{\partial q(t)}{\partial L(y)} = B(t) \\ \text{(b)} & \dfrac{\partial \mu(t)}{\partial L(y)} = -C(t) \end{array}\right\}, \tag{8}$$

so that the second terms of (7a) and (7b) may be interpreted as representing effects of the lifetime wealth $L(y)$. It can be seen that the 'residual' terms of the Slutsky equations of the form (7a), $A(t)$, satisfy the Cournot aggregation condition, $A(t)p = 0$, and the 'wealth' terms, $B(t)$, the Engel aggregation condition $p'L(B(t)) = 1$.[5] However, the 'residual' terms (unlike the substitution terms of the usual static Slutsky equations) are not symmetric[6] because the second term of the expression

$$A(t) = U(t)^{-1} - [p'L(U^{-1})p]^{-1}U(t)^{-1}pp'L(U^{-1})$$

is not symmetric. Moreover, the diagonal elements of the residual term matrix $A(t)$ are not necessarily negative.

Effects of a change in price p_j on demands $q(t)$ may be analysed in a different (and more convenient) way. At $t = 0$, the demands in the future, $q(t)$, $0 < t \leqq T$, are determined simultaneously with the current demands $q(0)$. But the whole plan is not implemented at once. The future part is a pure plan and is not carried out at $t = 0$ but may be revised before it is finally

(5) Note $L(U(t)^{-1}p) = L(U(t)^{-1})p$.

(6) This means that the 'residual' term contain some income effects.

implemented. In the following, therefore, we concentrate our attention upon that part of system (3) which is relevant to $q(0)$. Throughout the following we denote $y(0)$, $q(0)$, and $\lambda(0)$ by y, q, λ, respectively; we may then write the 'present' part of the subjective equilibrium conditions (3a) as[7]

$$U_q(q) = \lambda p. \tag{9}$$

In view of formula (4) the budget equation (5) can be written

$$p'q = Y \tag{10}$$

where $$Y = y+L(\dot{y})-p'L(\dot{q})-e^{-\rho T}[y(T)-p'q(T)].$$

The budget equation (10) implies that total consumption at the beginning of the plan equals 'quasi-income' Y which is defined as income at the beginning of the plan, *plus* the present value of expected income changes, *minus* the present value of changes in optimal consumption expenditures, *minus* the present value of the savings at time T. Thus, our problem to maximize the utility over time allows for income, y, to be distinguished from consumption expenditures—an impossible distinction in currently applied static demand theory—and allows for an explicit definition of savings, S, as an excess of y over Y,

$$S = y-Y = p'L(\dot{q})-L(\dot{y})+e^{-\rho T}[y(T)-p'q(T)].$$

Notice that (10) reduces to the usual budget constraint, $p'q = y$, if (i) the optimal consumption is stationary, i.e.

$$q(t) = q; \quad L(\dot{q}) = 0; \tag{11}$$

(ii) the present value of expected income change is zero, i.e.

$$L(\dot{y}) = 0; \tag{12}$$

and (iii) the time horizon of the individual is sufficiently far, so that

$$e^{-\rho T}[y(T)-p'q(T)] \text{ is negligible.} \tag{13}$$

The implication is that the general conditions (3) plus assumptions (11)–(13) are the basis of currently applied demand theory.

(7) Note $\alpha(0) = 1$.

Now consider the solution to (9) and (10):

$$\left.\begin{aligned} &\text{(a)} \quad q = q(p, Y(p, y, \rho;\, \dot{q}, \dot{y}, T)) \\ &\text{(b)} \quad \lambda = \lambda(p, Y(p, y, \rho;\, \dot{q}, \dot{y}, T)) \end{aligned}\right\}. \tag{14}$$

Equations (14a) constitute the complete system of demand functions at $t = 0$, under intertemporal utility maximization. In a manner completely parallel to the one first presented by Barten [**1**], we can derive the general laws of demand. First of all, the differential of (9) and (10) can be written in matrix form as

$$\begin{bmatrix} U & p \\ p' & 0 \end{bmatrix} \begin{bmatrix} Q_p & q_\rho & q_y \\ -\lambda_p & -\lambda_\rho & -\lambda_y \end{bmatrix} = \begin{bmatrix} \lambda I & 0 & 0 \\ Y_p - q' & Y_\rho & Y_y \end{bmatrix} \tag{15}$$

which is the 'fundamental equation of demand theory in matrix form', extended to allow for wealth accumulation. In (15), the following notation is used: U is the $n \times n$ matrix $[u_{ij}]$, the Hessian of the utility function; Q_p is the $n \times n$ matrix of (uncompensated) price slopes, $[\partial q_i/\partial p_j]$; q_y and q_ρ are $n \times 1$ vectors of income and interest-rate derivatives $\{\partial q_i/\partial y\}$, $\{\partial q_i/\partial \rho\}$; λ_p and Y_p are $1 \times n$ vectors of price derivatives, $\{\partial \lambda/\partial p_i\}$, $\{\partial Y/\partial p_i\}$; and λ_y, λ_ρ, Y_y, Y_ρ are derivatives with respect to y and ρ.

Solving (15), we obtain Q_p, q_p, q_y. As they satisfy the budget constraint (10), we have the following aggregation conditions:

$$\left.\begin{aligned} &\text{(a)} \quad p'q_y = Y_y \\ &\text{(b)} \quad p'q_\rho = Y_\rho \\ &\text{(c)} \quad p'Q_p = Y_p - q' \end{aligned}\right\}. \tag{16}$$

In particular, notice that if $L(\dot{y}) = L(\dot{q}) = 0$ independently of income and prices and T is sufficiently large, then (16b) disappears and (16a), (16c) reduce to

$$\left.\begin{aligned} &\text{(a)} \quad p'q_y = 1 \\ &\text{(b)} \quad p'Q_p = -q' \end{aligned}\right\}, \tag{17}$$

the familiar Engel and Cournot aggregation conditions of demand theory.

The symmetry restriction also applies. Let

$$M = \begin{bmatrix} U & p \\ p' & 0 \end{bmatrix}^{-1};$$

then we have from (15)

$$\begin{bmatrix} Q_p \\ -\lambda_p \end{bmatrix} = M \begin{bmatrix} \lambda I \\ Y_p - q' \end{bmatrix} \tag{18}$$

and

$$\begin{bmatrix} q_y \\ -\lambda_y \end{bmatrix} = M \begin{bmatrix} 0 \\ Y_y \end{bmatrix}. \tag{18'}$$

Dividing (18′) by Y_y and multiplying by $Y_p - q'$, we get

$$\begin{bmatrix} Y_y^{-1} q_y (Y_p - q') \\ -Y_y^{-1} \lambda_y (Y_p - q') \end{bmatrix} = M \begin{bmatrix} 0 \\ Y_p - q' \end{bmatrix}.$$

Subtracting this from (18), we obtain

$$\begin{bmatrix} Q_p^* \\ \lambda_p^* \end{bmatrix} = M \begin{bmatrix} \lambda I \\ 0 \end{bmatrix}, \tag{19}$$

where

$$Q_p^* = Q_p - Y_y^{-1} q_y (Y_p - q') \tag{20}$$

and

$$\lambda_p^* = \lambda_p - Y_p^{-1} \lambda_y (Y_p - p'). \tag{20'}$$

Since M is symmetric (because the matrix U is symmetric), it is at once seen from (19) that Q_p^* is symmetric, i.e.

$$Q_p^* = (Q_p^*)'. \tag{21}$$

Equation (20) is an extension of the Slutsky equation. If

$$Y \equiv y,$$

then $Y_y = 1$ and $Y_p = 0$; therefore, (20) reduces to

$$Q_p = -q_y q' + Q_p^*, \tag{22}$$

the usual Slutsky equation in matrix form. The first term gives the income effect and the second the substitution effect. Notice that as $u(q)$ is concave, the elements in the main diagonal of Q_p^* are negative.

A form of the homogeneous restriction can also be obtained. We have the identity

$$\begin{bmatrix} U & p \\ p' & 0 \end{bmatrix} \begin{bmatrix} 0 \\ 1 \end{bmatrix} = \begin{bmatrix} p \\ 0 \end{bmatrix}$$

or

$$\begin{bmatrix} 0 \\ 1 \end{bmatrix} = M \begin{bmatrix} p \\ 0 \end{bmatrix}. \tag{23}$$

On the other hand, the postmultiplication of (19) by p yields

$$\begin{bmatrix} Q_p^* p \\ \lambda_p^* p \end{bmatrix} = \lambda M \begin{bmatrix} p \\ 0 \end{bmatrix}.$$

Comparing this with (23), we have

$$Q_p^* p = 0 \qquad \text{and} \qquad \lambda_p^* p = \lambda.$$

Therefore, in view of (20), we finally obtain

$$Q_p p + q_Y(Y - Y_p p) = 0 \tag{24}$$

because $q_Y = Y_y^{-1} q_y$ by the differential identity and $Y = p'q$ by (10). (24) is a generalized form of the homogeneity constraint of demand theory:

$$Q_p p + q_y y = 0; \tag{25}$$

in fact, (24) reduces to (25) if $Y \equiv y$, or if

$$L(\dot{y}) = L(\dot{q}) = \mathrm{e}^{-\rho T} = 0,$$

so that $q_Y = q_y$ and $Y_p = 0$.

Let us next inquire what happens when the rate of interest increases. A relationship immediately derived from (15) is

$$q_\rho = Y_\rho Y_y^{-1} q_y \tag{26}$$

because (15) implies that q_ρ and Y_ρ are proportional to q_y and Y_y. However, (26) is not very useful because we do not know about the sign of Y_ρ at all, although it is plausible that $Y_y > 0$. Therefore, we return to the original system (3a) and (5), differentiation of which with respect to ρ yields

$$U(t)\frac{\partial q(t)}{\partial \rho} - p\frac{\partial \mu(t)}{\partial \rho} = 0, \qquad 0 \leqq t \leqq T,$$

$$p'L\left(\frac{\partial q}{\partial \rho}\right) = \int_0^T \tau\, \mathrm{e}^{-\rho\tau}\{p'q(\tau) - y(\tau)\}\, d\tau.$$

Solving, we obtain[8]

$$\frac{\partial q(t)}{\partial \rho} = B(t)\left[\int_0^T \tau\, \mathrm{e}^{-\rho\tau}\{p'q(\tau) - y(\tau)\}\, d\tau\right]$$

$$= \frac{\partial q(t)}{\partial L(y)}\left[\int_0^T \tau\, \mathrm{e}^{-\rho\tau}\{p'q(\tau) - y(\tau)\}\, d\tau\right]. \tag{27}$$

Now define the present value of savings at time t as

$$s(t) = \mathrm{e}^{-\rho t}[y(t) - p'q(t)].$$

(8) Because of the timewise additive separability of the utility over time, there is no (intertemporal) substitution term in (27). This is the only deviation of our result from Hicks's. Otherwise (27) is completely parallel to his equation.

Because of the budget equation over time (5), we have

$$\int_0^T s(\tau)\, d\tau = 0.$$

Therefore, if the stream $\{s(t)\}_0^T$ is monotonically decreasing, then the part in the square brackets of (27) is positive, while it is negative in the opposite case. Following Hicks, persons who have a monotonically decreasing savings stream $\{s(t)\}_0^T$ are said to be of the lender type and those having a monotonically increasing stream $\{s(t)\}_0^T$ are of the borrower type. Then we find from (27) that when the rate of interest is increased, a person of the lender type (or the borrower type) increases (or decreases) his demand for superior goods and decreases (or increases) his demand for inferior goods.[9]

3. Demand under Uncertainty

We have so far explained the Tintner–Hicks theory on the assumption that price and interest-rate expectations of the individual are stationary. It is not difficult to remove this assumption and replace it by a more general one that expected prices and interest rates are functions of the current prices and the current rate of interest. It seems, however, that their theory cannot get rid of the more basic assumption of precise expectations so long as the method of one-stage maximization of utility over time continues to be used.

In this section we reformulate the Tintner–Hicks theory so as to be able to allow for uncertainty. We propose a theory that views the individual's demands as being determined by a procedure of two-stage maximization of the utility function over time. For the sake of convenience we formulate it in the discrete time case; that is, it is assumed that the individual purchases commodities at points of time, $0, 1, ..., T$.

Let the individual's preferences be described by the utility function

$$u[q, q(1), ..., q(T)], \tag{28}$$

where q is the vector of current demands, $q(t)$ the vector of

[9] As usual, good i is called superior at t if $\partial q_i(t)/\partial L(y) > 0$ and inferior at t if $\partial q_i(t)/\partial L(y) < 0$.

expected demands in period t, and u is assumed to satisfy the von Neumann–Morgenstern axioms. Let p be the vector of current prices, and $p(1),..., p(T)$, T vectors of discounted future prices. The budget equation over time may then be written in the form

$$p'q+\sum_{1}^{T} p(t)'q(t) = Y, \tag{29}$$

where Y is the present value of the stream of current and expected incomes, y, $y(1),..., y(T)$, i.e. $Y = y+\sum_{1}^{T}\beta(t)y(t)$; the discount factors $\beta(1),..., \beta(T)$ are defined as

$$\beta(1) = \frac{1}{1+\rho_0}, \quad ..., \quad \beta(T) = \frac{1}{1+\rho_0}\frac{1}{1+\rho_1}\cdots\frac{1}{1+\rho_{T-1}},$$

where ρ_t is the rate of interest in period t.

With q being given arbitrarily, we first maximize (28), with respect to $q(1),..., q(T)$, subject to (29). The maximum point thus yielded is a function of $p(1),..., p(T)$, $Y-p'q$, and q prescribed, i.e.

$$Q = f(P, Y-p'q;\, q), \tag{30}$$

where

$$Q = [q(1),..., q(T)] \quad \text{and} \quad P = [p(1),..., p(T)].$$

Eliminating Q from (28) by the use of (30), we get the 'semi-indirect' utility function

$$u[q, f(P, Y-p'q;\, q)],$$

which is of the von Neumann–Morgenstern type.

We are now in a position to introduce uncertainty. It is assumed that the individual considers there to be a finite number, say m, of possible sets of expected prices and attaches a subjective probability $\pi(s)$ to the expected price set $P(s)$, $s = 1,..., m$. It is, however, assumed that he can expect his incomes and the interest rates in the future precisely. The individual may expect satisfaction at the level of

$$V = \sum_{s=1}^{m} \pi(s)u[q, f(P(s), Y-p'q;\, q)], \tag{31}$$

when he buys commodities in the quantities q at time 0. At the second stage of maximization, he will determine q such that the expected utility (31) is maximized. Evidently, the first- and second-order conditions for a maximum are given as

$$V_i = 0 \quad (i = 1,\ldots,n), \tag{32}$$

$$\sum_1^n \sum_1^n V_{ij}\, \mathrm{d}q_i\, \mathrm{d}q_j < 0 \tag{33}$$

where $V_i = \partial V/\partial q_i$ and $V_{ij} = \partial V_i/\partial q_j$.

The subjective equilibrium conditions (32) determine q as a function of current prices p, the present value of the individual's present and future incomes Y, and the probability distribution of expected prices $\pi(s)$, $s = 1,\ldots, m$. But, unlike the current demands q, the future demands Q are not determined exactly, because price expectations are not precise; Q will be

$$f(P(s), Y-p'q;\, q)$$

if expectations $P(s)$ happen to prevail. As the probability that $P = P(s)$ is $\pi(s)$, the means of the future demands Q are

$$\bar{Q} = \sum_{s=1}^{m} \pi(s) f(P(s), Y-p'q;\, q).$$

Thus the present part, q, of the entire plan $[q, q(1),\ldots, q(T)]$ is determined exactly (or deterministically), but the future part Q only probabilistically. Our present model is unusual among decision models, since most of them (including portfolio models as well as the Tintner–Hicks) are deterministic in spite of the fact that some of them claim to allow for uncertainty and risk.

Let us now note that (30) is a vector representation of Tn functional relationships; for a particular element $q_j(t)$, we may write

$$q_j(t) = f_{jt}(P, M, q) \quad (j = 1,\ldots, n;\ t = 1,\ldots, T),$$

where $M = Y-p'q$. We denote the partial derivative of $q_j(t)$ with respect to M by $f_{jt,M}$ and the one with respect to q_i of q, with M constant, by $f_{jt,i}$. These partial derivatives satisfy the following restrictions:

$$\left.\begin{aligned} &\text{(a)} \quad \sum_{t=1}^{T} \sum_{j=1}^{n} p_j(t) f_{jt,i} = 0 \\ &\text{(b)} \quad \sum_{t=1}^{T} \sum_{j=1}^{n} p_j(t) f_{jt,M} = 1 \end{aligned}\right\}, \tag{34}$$

which follow from the first-stage maximization. In view of the proportionality between $\partial u/\partial q_j(t)$ and $p(t), j = 1,\ldots, n;\ t = 1,\ldots, T$, that is necessary for the first-stage maximization, we have from (34)

$$\left.\begin{aligned} &\text{(a)} \quad \sum_1^T \sum_1^n u_{jt} f_{jt,i} = 0 \\ &\text{(b)} \quad \sum_1^T \sum_1^n u_{jt} f_{jt,M} = \lambda \end{aligned}\right\}, \tag{35}$$

where $u_{jt} = \partial u/\partial q_j(t)$ and λ represents the proportionality factor.

Differentiating V with respect to q_i, we may now evaluate V_i as

$$V_i = \sum_{s=1}^m \pi(s)\Big(u_i + \sum_1^T \sum_1^n u_{jt} f_{jt,i} - \sum_1^T \sum_1^n u_{jt} f_{jt,M}\, p_i\Big), \tag{36}$$

where u_i is the partial derivative of u of (28) with respect to the ith element of q. It is noted that in (36) all partial derivatives depend on $P(s)$. As the formulae (35) hold for each $P(s)$, with λ depending on $P(s)$ (so that λ is denoted as $\lambda(s)$ hereunder), we may now simply write

$$V_i = \sum_1^m \pi(s)[u_i(s) - \lambda(s) p_i]. \tag{37}$$

As intertemporal substitutability and complementarity are allowed for, the marginal utilities of current commodities depend on future events. The subjective equilibrium conditions (32) imply that their means $\sum_1^m \pi(s) u_i(s)$, $i = 1,\ldots, n$, are proportional to the current prices, $p_1,\ldots, p_n$, with the proportionality factor $\sum_1^m \pi(s)\lambda(s)$.

Now suppose p_k to vary, other prices, income, and the probability distribution remaining unchanged. Since u_{jt} and $f_{jt,M}$ are functions of P, $Y - p'q$, q, it follows from (35b) that λ too depends on them. Thus we have

$$\lambda(s) = \lambda(P(s), Y - p'q, q):$$

therefore,

$$V_i = \sum_1^m \pi(s)[u_i(P(s), Y - p'q, q) - \lambda(P(s), Y - p'q, q) p_i].$$

We now differentiate (37) with respect to p_k; then

$$\sum_1^n V_{ij}\frac{\partial q_i}{\partial p_k}+\sum_1^m \pi(s)[u_{iM}(s)-\lambda_M(s)p_i](-q_k)-\sum_1^m \pi(s)\lambda(s)\delta_{ik}=0 \qquad (i=1,\ldots,n), \qquad (38)$$

where u_{iM} and λ_M are partial derivatives of u_i and λ with respect to $M = Y-p'q$, and δ_{ik} is Kronecker's delta. It is noted that in evaluating the derivatives $V_{ij} = \partial V_i/\partial q_j$, not only the last argument q of u_i and λ but also the q in $Y-p'q$ are considered to change.

Equations (38) give us the Slutsky equation

$$\frac{\partial q}{\partial p_k}=-q_k H\begin{bmatrix}a_1\\ \cdot\\ \cdot\\ \cdot\\ a_n\end{bmatrix}+bH\begin{bmatrix}\delta_{1k}\\ \cdot\\ \cdot\\ \cdot\\ \delta_{nk}\end{bmatrix}, \qquad (39)$$

where $a_i = \sum_1^m \pi(s)(\lambda_M(s)p_i-u_{iM}(s))$, $b=\sum_1^m \pi(s)\lambda(s)$, and

$$H=\begin{bmatrix}V_{11} & \cdot & \cdot & \cdot & V_{1n}\\ \cdot & \cdot & \cdot & \cdot & \cdot\\ V_{n1} & \cdot & \cdot & \cdot & V_{nn}\end{bmatrix}^{-1}.$$

The first term of (39) gives the income effect and the second the substitution effect. As $V_{ij} = V_{ji}$, H is symmetric; and the negative definiteness of the quadratic form $\sum_1^n\sum_1^n V_{ij}\,z_i\,z_j$ as is implied by (33) yields the negative definiteness of H. Thus we have the familiar laws of the substitution terms

$$\text{(i) } H = H' \quad \text{and} \quad \text{(ii) } z'Hz < 0 \quad \text{for all} \quad z \neq 0.$$

That H_{kk} (the kth diagonal element of H) is negative is no more than a corollary of (ii).

Next we consider effects of a change in expectations on current demands in the case of current prices and income remaining unchanged. Suppose that the probability attached to the set of expected prices $P(r)$ is increased while the probabilities attached to all other sets are diminished proportionally. Then

$$\frac{\partial \pi(v)}{\partial \pi(r)}=-\frac{\pi(v)}{1-\pi(r)} \quad \text{for all} \quad v\neq r \qquad (40)$$

as $\sum_{s=1}^{m} \pi(s) = 1$. Differentiating (32) and considering (37), we get

$$\sum_{j=1}^{n} V_{ij} \frac{\partial q_j}{\partial \pi(r)} + \sum_{s=1}^{m} \frac{\partial \pi(s)}{\partial \pi(r)} [u_i(s) - \lambda(s)p_i] = 0 \quad (i = 1,..., n). \tag{41}$$

Taking (40) into account and considering $V_i = 0$, (41) can be put in the form

$$\sum_{j=1}^{n} V_{ij} \frac{\partial q_i}{\partial \pi(r)} + \frac{1}{1-\pi(r)} [u_i(r) - \lambda(r)p_i] = 0 \quad (i = 1,..., n). \tag{42}$$

Let q^0 be the subjective equilibrium point before the change. At q^0, $\sum_{s=1}^{m} \pi(s)u_i(s)$ equals $\sum_{s=1}^{m} \pi(s)\lambda(s)p_i$ for each i, but each $u_i(s)$ is not necessarily equated with $\lambda(s)p_i$. Our attention is concentrated on the following two particular (but basic) cases, combination of which may exhaust all possibilities. First, if

$$\begin{aligned} u_k(r) &= u_k[q^0, f(P(r), Y - p'q^0, q^0)] \\ &< \lambda[q^0, f(P(r), Y - p'q^0, q^0)]p_k = \lambda(r)p_k, \end{aligned} \tag{43}$$

while

$$\begin{aligned} u_i(r) &= u_i[q^0, f(P(r), Y - p'q^0, q^0)] \\ &= \lambda[q^0, f(P(r), Y - p'q^0, q^0)]p_i = \lambda(r)p_i \end{aligned} \tag{44}$$

for all $i \neq k$, then the demand for good k is said to tend to be over-satisfied at q^0, when $P(r)$ happens to prevail. The second case is the case which is obtained when the sense of the inequality of (43) is reversed and in which the demand for good k will be under-satisfied at q^0 when $P(r)$ happens to prevail.

We now solve (42) with respect to $\partial q_j / \partial \pi(r)$ $(j = 1,..., n)$:

$$\frac{\partial q}{\partial \pi(r)} = -\frac{1}{1-\pi(r)} H[u(r) - \lambda(r)p],$$

where $u(r)$ is the column vector of $u_1(r),..., u_n(r)$ and p the column vector of $p_1,..., p_n$. If (43) and (44) are additionally assumed, we get

$$\frac{\partial q_k}{\partial \pi(r)} < 0$$

as $H_{kk} < 0$. That is to say, as the probability that $P(r)$ happens becomes larger, so it becomes more probable that the demand for good k tends to be 'over-satisfied'; therefore, the demand for good k is decreased. Evidently, we have the opposite conclusion in the case of 'under-satisfaction'.

Finally we consider effects on the current demands, q, of a proportional change in the current prices, p, and the present value of the individual's income stream, Y. p and Y change to αp and αY, where α is greater (or less) than one when we have a proportional increase (or decrease). We suppose that such a change induces a change in the probability distribution such that to $\alpha P(s)$ will be associated the same $\pi(s)$ as that which is presently associated to $P(s)$.[10] As $f(P(s), Y-p'q; q)$ is homogeneous of degree zero in $P(s)$ and $Y-p'q$, we get

$$f(P(s), Y-p'q; q) = f(\alpha P(s), \alpha Y-\alpha p'q; q),$$

so that

$$u_i[q, f(P(s), Y-p'q; q)] = u_i[q, f(\alpha P(s), \alpha Y-\alpha p'q; q)];$$

that is to say, $u_i(s)$ is homogeneous of degree zero in $P(s)$, p, and Y. Similarly, we can show $\lambda(s)$ is homogeneous of degree -1 in $P(s)$, p, and Y, so that $\lambda(s)p_i$ is homogeneous of degree zero in the same variables. Moreover, by assumption, $\pi(s)$s remain unchanged when p and Y (and hence $P(s)$) change proportionally; therefore, we have no change in V_is of (37) and the V_is vanish at the same q. Thus a proportional change in Y and p gives rise to no influence on q, provided that it induces a horizontal shift of the probability distribution at the same rate. This conclusion corresponds to Hicks's for the case of the elasticities of expectations being all unity.

(10) This means that the probability distribution shifts horizontally at the rate α.

VI. Durable Goods as a Generalizer of Demand Theory

M. J. MARTIN

1. Introduction

EXISTING demand theory is, today, seen to be a particular interpretation of a general choice problem. The beginning of this interpretation is associated with perishable goods which were representative of the essential nature of the goods for which a demand theory was sought by the early theorists. Today durable goods play a far more important role in the typical consumer's budget. Many economists, since, have attempted to accommodate the newcomer.(1) We here attempt to provide a simple approach to durable goods which endeavours to remain faithful to the Hicksian tradition, from which we may develop a perspective of the problems when dealing with a 'durable' world.

What do we understand by the word 'durable' in the context of consumer theory? And what problems are associated with durables? We have the following conventional definition, that goods which are 'used up' in the act of consumption are perishables. And, therefore, goods which can be used to provide services required by the consumer, and still survive in such a way as still to be able to provide services at a later act of consumption, are durable. But, suppose that we assume that the planning period for an individual is broken up into suitable purchasing periods, then there is no point in distinguishing between perishables and those durables which do not survive the purchasing period if we are only interested in their intertemporal role.

In what follows we will explicitly consider goods which are durable, in the sense that in a depreciated form they may carry over into the next purchasing period. As a simplifying assump-

(1) See particularly: Chow [**1**], Cramer [**1**], Harberger (ed.) [**1**], Shibuya [**1**], and Stone and Rowe [**1**].

tion we take the depreciation rate to be fixed, although we recognize it to be part of the consumer's choice problem.[2] By making this assumption we are able to assume that the relevant entities over which the consumer defines his preferences are the quantities *available for use* within any purchasing period, these quantities being made up from the stocks received from the previous purchasing period and the *acquisitions* in the period. The depreciation rate is assumed to be such that the depreciated quantities from the previous period are equivalent, as the consumer sees it, to the new goods of the present period.[3]

As we have indicated, the proper context for a consideration of durable goods is a multi-period expenditure plan. The purchase of a good which survives the present purchasing period is evidently made with expectations about its role in future periods' consumption plans. That is, a utility function defined on the choice variables of the purchasing period, acquisitions, is not invariant with respect to changes in the initial stocks, which have survived from previous purchasing periods.

In our development of a simple model encompassing these points, we will be assuming that the utility function is differentiable and that durable goods are perfectly divisible. This last assumption may not reflect qualities associated with the real world, but may be approved of as a first approximation.

2. Basic Model

Let us now formulate this approach in a more explicit fashion. We begin by envisaging that the individual consumer maximizes a multi-period utility function of the form

$$v[s(0)+q^*(0), s(1)+q^*(1),\ldots, s(T)+q^*(T), s(T+1)]$$

where $s(t)$ is an n-vector of goods held at the beginning of the period (purchasing period) t and $q^*(t)$ is an n-vector of purchases (or sales for negative elements) for the period t. $s(T+1)$ is an n-vector of goods which are held over for the next planning period, the planning period being $T+1$ purchasing periods.

(2) Aspects of this problem are taken up in Chapter VII below.

(3) This assumption is in line with that made in neo-classical growth theory.

The vector of goods held at the beginning of the period t, $s(t)$, is given by[4]

$$s(0) = \bar{q}(0),$$
$$s(t) = \hat{c}[s(t-1)+q^*(t-1)]+\bar{q}(t) \quad (t = 1,..., T),$$
$$s(T+1) = \hat{c}[s(T)+q^*(T)]$$

where $\bar{q}(t)$ is an n-vector of endowments, as 'manna from heaven', and $\hat{c}$ is a diagonal matrix of 'carry-over' rates whose diagonal elements are c_i, that is $I-\hat{c} = \hat{d}$ is the diagonal matrix of depreciation rates. These rates are assumed to be fixed over the planning period.

In words, the consumer is assumed to possess a preference relation defined over the amounts of the n goods available for use in the periods over the planning period which may be represented by a utility function. For any particular period t, the quantities of the goods available for use is the sum of the initial stocks, $s(t)$, and the purchases or sales of the period, $q^*(t)$. At the end of the period a proportion, net of depreciation, will carry over into the next period to be a part of that period's initial stocks. The depreciation rate is taken to be the rate of decrease in the ability of a unit of a good to provide services of a particular quality after one period's use. As a consequence, goods are measured in terms of efficiency units relative to new goods. Evidently, the depreciation rate, as defined, is a subjective concept, but in what follows, it will be assumed that it coincides with the individual's expectation concerning the market's evaluation. The endowments, $\bar{q}(t)$ $(t = 1,..., T)$, are not essential for the model, but since it may happen that there is a carry-over from the previous planning period, $\bar{q}(0)$, we continue to include the endowment components of initial stocks, so providing a more general treatment.

By substituting for $s(T+1)$ into the utility function v and letting $x(t) = s(t)+q^*(t)$ $(t = 0,..., T)$, the availability of goods in period t for use (holdings), it is clear that maximizing $u[x(0),..., x(T)]$ is equivalent to maximizing v. Also, let

$$q(t) = q^*(t)+\bar{q}(t),$$

[4] These equations are a simplified form of those used by Stone and Rowe.

the acquisition of goods in period t, then from the equations for initial stocks we have the relationship between availability and acquisition:

$$x(0) = q(0),$$
$$x(t) = \hat{c}x(t-1)+q(t) \quad (t = 1,\ldots, T).$$

More conveniently, perhaps, we may rewrite the $T+1$ n-vector equations as $x = Cq$ where

$$x = \begin{bmatrix} x(0) \\ x(1) \\ \cdot \\ \cdot \\ \cdot \\ \cdot \\ x(T) \end{bmatrix}, \quad q = \begin{bmatrix} q(0) \\ q(1) \\ \cdot \\ \cdot \\ \cdot \\ \cdot \\ q(T) \end{bmatrix}, \quad C = \begin{bmatrix} I & 0 & \cdot & \cdot & 0 \\ \hat{c} & I & 0 & & 0 \\ \hat{c}^2 & \hat{c} & I & \cdot & \cdot \\ \cdot & & & & \\ \cdot & & & & \\ \cdot & & & & 0 \\ \hat{c}^T & \hat{c}^{T-1} & \cdot & \hat{c} & I \end{bmatrix}$$

and

$$C^{-1} = \begin{bmatrix} I & 0 & \cdot & \cdot & \cdot & 0 \\ -\hat{c} & I & 0 & \cdot & \cdot & 0 \\ 0 & -\hat{c} & I & \cdot & \cdot & \cdot \\ \cdot & & & & & \\ \cdot & & & & & \\ \cdot & & & & & 0 \\ 0 & \cdot & \cdot & 0 & -\hat{c} & I \end{bmatrix}.$$

As a consequence, we have two equivalent representations of the consumer's preferences, $u(x)$ defined over availability (holdings) and $f(q) = u[Cq]$ defined over acquisition.

In maximizing his utility function the individual is restricted by a set of $T+1$ budget restrictions

$$\alpha^{-1}W(t-1)+y(t) = \pi(t)'[q(t)-\bar{q}(t)]+W(t)$$

where $W(t)$ is the money balances of the period t which the individual is assumed to lend at the market rate of interest, i, and $y(t)$ is the exogenous labour income for the period. $\alpha = (1+i)^{-1}$ is the discount factor and $\pi(t)$ is the n-vector of goods' prices in period t. Expectations with respect to the income stream and the set of prices are assumed to be held with certainty. The interest rate on his money balances which the individual carries over from the previous planning period is already known to him. The consumer is assumed to expect that this interest rate will continue indefinitely.

If we assume that there exists a capital market such that the individual can borrow as well as lend at the market rate of interest, i, then we can collapse the $T+1$ budget restrictions into one wealth constraint for the planning period. Multiply through the budget constraint for period t by α^t and sum over all t and we have

$$\alpha^{-1}W(-1)+\sum_{t=0}^{T}\alpha^t y(t) = \sum_{t=0}^{T} p(t)'[q(t)-\bar{q}(t)]+\alpha^T W(T).$$

$W(-1)$ is the terminal money balances of the previous planning period, $W(T)$ the terminal balances of the present planning period, and $p(t) = \alpha^t\pi(t)$ is the vector of discounted purchase prices for period t. We, further, assume that the individual imposes upon himself the constraint that the discounted terminal money balances, $\alpha^T W(T)$, should equal his initial money balances, $\alpha^{-1}W(-1)$. As a consequence, the wealth constraint for the individual for the present planning period reduces to

$$W = \sum_{t=0}^{T}\alpha^t y(t) = \sum_{t=0}^{T} p(t)'[q(t)-\bar{q}(t)].$$

We may rewrite the wealth constraint as $W = p'(q-\bar{q})$, and since $x = Cq$, if we define $\bar{x} = C\bar{q}$, we may write the wealth constraint in terms of availability, $W = r'(x-\bar{x})$ where $r' = p'C^{-1}$.

We now see that we have two equivalent expressions of the consumer choice problem. We may conceive of the consumer as maximizing the utility index $f(q)$ subject to $W = p'(q-\bar{q})$, an approach which may be termed the 'acquisition–goods price' approach (q-mode). On the other hand, the consumer may be envisaged to maximize $u(x)$ subject to $W = r'(x-\bar{x})$, which may be characterized as the 'availability–rent' approach (x-mode). We are assured, as Samuelson has shown, that an extremum is invariant with respect to a non-singular transformation, C, of the independent variables, q.[(5)] Hence, the two modes are dual modes. While, if $\hat{c} = 0$, such that $C = I$, then

(5) Samuelson [**1**], pp. 125–41.

all goods are perishables, in the sense of not surviving the purchasing period, and then the two modes are identical to the conventional Hicksian multi-period problem. Therefore, our model is of greater generality than the conventional approach while still being able to encompass the essential problem.

As seen from the present, the consumer may be envisaged, in the x-mode, to purchase $x(t)$ at the beginning of the period t at prices $p(t)$ and to sell these amounts at the end of the period for $\hat{c}p(t+1)$; the difference, $r(t) = p(t) - \hat{c}p(t+1)$, being the discounted cost of one period's use. Alternatively, we may think of $x(t)$ as being rented for the period t, and $r(t)$ as being the rents. The undiscounted rental prices for period t will be denoted by $\rho(t)$, where $\alpha^{-t}r(t) = \rho(t)$. Now

$$\rho(t) = \alpha^{-t}[p(t) - \hat{c}p(t+1)] = \pi(t) - \alpha\hat{c}\pi(t+1),$$

that is, the difference between the purchase price and the discounted selling price. Further decomposition produces $\hat{d}\pi(t) + \hat{c}[\pi(t) - \alpha\pi(t+1)]$ so that the rental prices are the sum of the depreciation costs, $\hat{d}\pi(t)$, and the costs of holding the surviving goods. The last component, which may be rewritten as $i\alpha\hat{c}\pi(t) + \alpha\hat{c}[\pi(t) - \pi(t+1)]$, is the present value of the interest forgone and the present value of the capital loss on the wealth held in the form of goods. Now, if $\pi(t+1) = \pi(t)(1+i)$, the cost of holding wealth in the form of goods is zero, and, hence, the cost of availability for use is simply the depreciation cost. But, if expected price rises are greater than the interest rate, then conceivably the rental price may become negative. This constitutes a limitation on our model; that is $\pi(t) \geqq \alpha\pi(t+1)$. This restriction implies that rental prices are always non-negative even if the depreciation rate is zero. For if price rises are greater than the interest rate, it would seem probable that the consumer would add an extra dimension to the choice problem and hold goods as assets. But, in such a case, one would expect that there would be a different depreciation rate from that appropriate when the goods are kept for consumption or use. So, if the price rises are greater than the interest rate and the depreciation rate on holding goods in the form of assets, there will be a switching of income-bearing wealth from cash into goods. We should, however, recognize the limitations on such behaviour. If the consumer's expectations concerning the interest rate are reasonably accurate, then he should take into account the expected price increases. None the less, if we assume a constant rate for the planning period, then the above behaviour may emerge for some periods. Even if one were to consider a moving rate through the planning period, it would still not eliminate the possibility for a subset of goods in each period. If such possibilities occur, it is obvious that our model provides no bound to the consumption plan as an infinite amount may be borrowed at a lower rate of interest than the return from holding goods. That is, there is a negative real rate of interest. Needless to say, we assume that no such inconveniences arise.

As we are dealing with a multi-period expenditure plan, with an over-all wealth constraint for the planning period, income is not necessarily exhausted on consumption expenditure. On substituting $x(t)-\hat{c}x(t-1)$ for $q(t)$ in our budget equation for period t, we have, after rearrangement,

$$\{y(t)+iW(t-1)\}+\{\pi(t)'\hat{c}x(t-1)+\pi(t)'\bar{q}(t)+W(t-1)\}$$
$$= \{\pi(t)'x(t)+W(t)\}.$$

Here we will assume $\bar{q}(t) = 0$ for $t = 1,..., T$, and therefore we may rewrite the budget equation as

$$\{y(t)+iW(t-1)\}+\{\pi(t)'s(t)+W(t-1)\} = \pi(t)'x(t)+W(t).$$

That is, income, the first bracket, plus initial wealth equals the value of holdings, $\pi(t)'x(t)$, plus the amount on loan for the period. The value of holdings may be decomposed into $\pi(t)'\hat{d}x(t)$, the total depreciation cost, and $\pi(t)'\hat{c}x(t)$, the value of wealth held in the form of goods during period t. Hence it may seem natural to define consumption as $\pi(t)'\hat{d}x(t)$ and final wealth as $\pi(t)'\hat{c}x(t)+W(t)$. However, as we have observed previously, the consumption process involves the holding of goods and, hence, the opportunity cost of consumption is $\rho(t)'x(t)$, the cost of depreciation plus the cost of holding wealth in the form of goods. Consequently, the appropriate form of the budget equation is

$$\{y(t)+iW(t-1)\}+\{\pi(t)'s(t)+W(t-1)\}$$
$$=\rho(t)'x(t)+\{\alpha\pi(t+1)'s(t+1)+W(t)\}$$

(i.e. income+initial wealth = consumption+final wealth) where, because $\bar{q}(t) = 0$ $(t = 1,..., T)$, $s(t) = \hat{c}x(t-1)$. Therefore, saving for the period t, $\sigma(t)$, is given by

$$\sigma(t) = y(t)+iW(t-1)-\rho(t)'x(t),$$

or, alternatively, as the difference between final and initial wealth, i.e.

$$\sigma(t) = \{W(t)-W(t-1)\}+\{\alpha\pi(t+1)'s(t+1)-\pi(t)'s(t)\}.$$

Now, the saving in goods component may be written as

$$\pi(t)'[s(t+1)-s(t)]+[\alpha\pi(t+1)-\pi(t)]'\hat{c}x(t).$$

Therefore, if prices increase at a rate equal to the interest rate, then savings in the form of goods is simply the difference between final stocks and initial stocks. While, if price changes differ from the interest rate, then there is an additional component to savings, whose decomposition is

$$\alpha[\pi(t+1)-\pi(t)]'s(t+1)-i\alpha\pi(t)'s(t+1),$$

that is, the present value of capital gains minus the present value of the interest forgone on the wealth held in the form of goods.

3. Demand Functions

If the goods' price and income expectations are given for all periods, then the maximizing problem, in the x-mode, is formally identical to our traditional problem. Therefore, we may resort to these well-known results of traditional theory, albeit in a more general context. If we assume that $dx'U\,dx < 0$ subject to $(\partial u/\partial x)\,dx = 0$ where $U = \partial^2 u/\partial x\partial x'$, then we are assured that there exists a unique solution for $x = x(r, W+r'\bar{x})$, the availability–demand function, on solving the necessary conditions for a maximum. By the method of differentiating the first-order conditions with respect to the parameters we have the Hicks–Slutsky equation

$$\frac{\partial x}{\partial r} = K - \frac{\partial x}{\partial W}(x - \bar{x})'.$$

The above second-order or stability condition provides us with our restrictions on the demand functions, which can be summarized in the requirement that K, the substitution matrix for the x-mode, be negative definite subject to $r'K = 0$.(6)

As for the 'purchase–goods price' approach (q-mode) the problem is to maximize $f(q)$ subject to $W = p'(q - \bar{q})$. And since $f(q) = f[C^{-1}x] = u(x)$, then $(C')^{-1}FC^{-1} = U$ where

$$F = \frac{\partial^2 f}{\partial q \partial q'}.$$

Since a matrix's properties of negative definiteness and symmetry are invariant with respect to the congruent transformation C, F is negative definite subject to $\frac{\partial f}{\partial q} C^{-1}C\, \mathrm{d}q = \frac{\partial u}{\partial x}\, \mathrm{d}x = 0$. Hence we are assured of the existence of a unique acquisition–demand function, $q = q(p, W + p'\bar{q})$, which satisfies the condition that L, the substitution matrix for the q-mode, is negative definite subject to $p'L = 0$.

The relationship between the two, the acquisition–demand function and the availability–demand function, is seen from the following:

$$\frac{\partial x}{\partial r} = \frac{\partial x}{\partial q}\frac{\partial q}{\partial r} = C\frac{\partial q}{\partial r} = C\frac{\partial q}{\partial p}\frac{\partial p}{\partial r} = C\frac{\partial q}{\partial p}C',$$

$$\frac{\partial q}{\partial p} = C^{-1}\frac{\partial x}{\partial r}(C')^{-1},$$

$$\frac{\partial x}{\partial W} = \frac{\partial x}{\partial q}\frac{\partial q}{\partial W} = C\frac{\partial q}{\partial W} \quad \text{and} \quad \frac{\partial q}{\partial W} = C^{-1}\frac{\partial x}{\partial W},$$

and, therefore, as

$$\frac{\partial q}{\partial p} = C^{-1}\frac{\partial x}{\partial r}(C')^{-1} = C^{-1}\left[K - \frac{\partial x}{\partial W}(x - \bar{x})'\right](C')^{-1}$$

$$= C^{-1}K(C')^{-1} - \frac{\partial q}{\partial W}(q - \bar{q})',$$

(6) Samuelson [**1**], Chapter V.

we have also $L = C^{-1}K(C')^{-1}$. Hence, we can easily transform the results of one mode into those of the other.

It is common in currently applied demand theory that the restrictions on the demand functions are formulated as follows.(7)

Engel aggregation: $$r'\frac{\partial x}{\partial W} = 1.$$

Cournot aggregation: $$r'\frac{\partial x}{\partial r} = -(x-\bar{x}).$$

Symmetry: $$K = K'.$$

Homogeneity: $$\frac{\partial x}{\partial r}r = -\frac{\partial x}{\partial W}W.$$

Negative definiteness: $\xi' K\xi < 0$ subject to $\xi' K \neq 0$.

We have similar statements in the q-mode.

A useful, but not always a satisfactory, classification of goods is based on the income (wealth) derivatives and the substitution terms of the Hicks–Slutsky equation. In the present context, if $\partial x_i(t)/\partial W$ is positive (negative) then we may speak of good i in period t being x-superior (x-inferior) at the present level of W. And, if $K^{i(t)}_{j(s)}$, the substitution component of $\partial x_i(t)/\partial r_j(s)$, is positive (negative), then we may speak of good i in period t as being an x-substitute for (x-complement of) good j in period s for $j \neq i$ or $s \neq t$. In an analogous way we may define a q–p classification. Now, it is not the case, in general, that these classifications are invariant with respect to a transformation from one mode into the other, therefore giving rise to 'classification inversions'.

The problem of inversions of income classifications is seen if we recall
$$\frac{\partial q(t)}{\partial W} = \frac{\partial x(t)}{\partial W} - \hat{c}\,\frac{\partial x(t-1)}{\partial W}.$$

If, say, there is an increase in labour income such that the holdings for periods t and $t-1$ are x-superior, with the increase for period $t-1$ being greater than that for period t, then an inversion may occur depending on the magnitudes of the

(7) Barten [1].

depreciation rates. That is, in the event of an inversion in the income classification, the carry-over into the period t, net of depreciation, is greater than desired holdings for the period. Such a situation would give rise to classifying the goods of period t as q-inferior goods, as the consumer plans to sell in period t when income increases. Therefore, even if the system, all goods in all periods, is x-superior we are not assured the system is q-superior. The converse, though, is unambiguous. If the system is q-superior, then the system is also x-superior, as we can see from

$$\frac{\partial x(t)}{\partial W} = \frac{\partial q(t)}{\partial W} + \hat{c}\,\frac{\partial q(t-1)}{\partial W} + \ldots + \hat{c}^{t}\,\frac{\partial q(0)}{\partial W}.$$

For the case of perishable goods no such inversions arise, as is also the case when we are considering the current period, because holdings and acquisitions then coincide. The latter case is, obviously, of special importance as the current period is the main focus of our analysis.

When we turn to the relationship between the substitution terms of the two modes, the situation becomes a little more complex. We have as the substitution component of $\partial q(t)/\partial r(s)$ the expression $K_{t,s} - \hat{c}K_{t-1,s}$. So, even if good $j(s)$ is a substitute for goods $i(t)$ and $i(t-1)$, we are not assured that the substitution term of $\partial q_i(t)/\partial r_j(s)$ will be positive. It is not even possible to unambiguously sign the own-price substitution term of $q_i(t)$ for $r_i(t)$ because $K_{i(t)}^{i(t-1)}$ may be negative if good i in periods t and $t-1$ is complementary. In completing the transformation into the q-mode, we use

$$\frac{\partial q(t)}{\partial p(s)} = \frac{\partial q(t)}{\partial r(s)} - \frac{\partial q(t)}{\partial r(s-1)}\,\hat{c}$$

and, therefore, the substitution term, $L_{t,s}$, of $\partial q(t)/\partial p(s)$ may be written as

$$L_{t,s} = K_{t,s} - \hat{c}K_{t-1,s} - K_{t,s-1}\,\hat{c} + \hat{c}K_{t-1,s-1}\,\hat{c}.$$

Evidently, a restriction making the system x-substitutive does not impose any unambiguous signings on the elements of $L_{t,s}$. The only *a priori* restriction we may impose is that $L_{t,s}$

is negative definite, which does permit us to say something about

$$L_{i(t)}^{i(t)} = K_{i(t)}^{i(t)} - c_i K_{i(t)}^{i(t-1)} - c_i K_{i(t-1)}^{i(t)} + c_i^2 K_{i(t-1)}^{i(t-1)}.$$

From the symmetry property $K_{i(t)}^{i(t-1)} = K_{i(t-1)}^{i(t)}$, and since $K_{i(t)}^{i(t)}$ and $K_{i(t-1)}^{i(t-1)}$ are negative, there is a limit on the x-complementarity of a good in adjacent periods. The converse relationship permits of an easier characterization. The general nature of the transformation is seen from

$$\begin{bmatrix} K_{0,0} & K_{0,1} \\ K_{1,0} & K_{1,1} \end{bmatrix} = \begin{bmatrix} L_{0,0} & L_{0,1} + L_{0,0}\hat{c} \\ L_{1,0} + \hat{c}L_{0,0} & L_{1,1} + \hat{c}L_{0,1} + L_{1,0}\hat{c} + \hat{c}L_{0,0}\hat{c} \end{bmatrix}.$$

If we assume there is general q-substitutiveness, then we are assured that matrices $K_{s,t}$ will have non-negative off-diagonal elements. But, again, we have the possibility that a good in different periods is its own x-complement; that is, $K_{i(s)}^{i(t)} < 0$. In as much as our main attention is addressed to the current period, there is no possibility of substitution inversions, as $L_{0,0} = K_{0,0}$ irrespective of whether the goods are durables or perishables.

So far the relationship between the two modes has been discussed at a general level, especially using the assumption that all goods are durable. On the other hand, if all goods are perishable, then the traditional Hicks–Slutsky equation is relevant with the question of inversions not arising. It is of interest, though, to look at the intermediate cases of the consequence of the change in demand for a durable caused by a price change in a perishable and vice versa. Let good i be a durable and good j be a perishable, then

$$\frac{\partial q_i(t)}{\partial p_j(s)} = (K_{j(s)}^{i(t)} - c_i K_{j(s)}^{i(t-1)}) - \left(\frac{\partial x_i(t)}{\partial W} - c_i \frac{\partial x_i(t-1)}{\partial W}\right)\{x_j(s) - \bar{x}_j(s)\}.$$

For $s = t$, where we assume that goods i and j are substitutes, still leaves us with the usual possibilities of substitution and income inversions. However, it seems unreasonable to assume that if goods are within-period substitutes (car and bus-rides) they will be between-period complements. While, on the other hand, it seems reasonable to assume that within-period complements (car and petrol) are between-period substitutes in the x-sense. Suppose there is an increase in the price of petrol, then as cars and petrol are within-period x-complements, there will be a net decrease in holdings of cars for the period. But the car–petrol combination is now relatively cheaper in other periods; therefore, cars and petrol will be between-period x-substitutes. If we assume, for illustrative purposes, that the $K_{j(s)}^{i(t)}$ and $K_{j(s)}^{i(t-1)}$ are of similar absolute values, and the same for the income derivatives, then, on the assumption of a general between-period substitutiveness,

$$\frac{\partial q_i(t)}{\partial p_j(t)} \simeq (1-c_i)K_{j(t)}^{i(t)}-(1-c_i)\frac{\partial x_i(t)}{\partial W}\{x_j(t)-\bar{x}_j(t)\}$$

if goods i and j are within-period x-substitutes and

$$\frac{\partial q_i(t)}{\partial p_j(t)} \simeq (1+c_i)K_{j(t)}^{i(t)}-(1-c_i)\frac{\partial x_i(t)}{\partial W}\{x_j(t)-\bar{x}_j(t)\}$$

if goods i and j are within-period x-complements. Therefore, the substitution effect is relatively larger in absolute values when we are dealing with within-period x-complements as the increase in holdings of the previous period caused by the increase in price of good j (petrol) in period t accentuates the change in holdings of good i (cars) from period $t-1$ to period t.

The other special case which may be of interest is what happens to the purchase of a perishable when the price of a durable changes. The relevant Hicks–Slutsky equation is then

$$\frac{\partial q_i(t)}{\partial p_j(s)} = (K_{j(s)}^{i(t)}-c_j\,K_{j(s-1)}^{i(t)})-$$
$$-\frac{\partial x_i(t)}{\partial W}[\{x_j(s)-\bar{x}_j(s)\}-c_j\{x_j(s-1)-\bar{x}_j(s-1)\}],$$

which may be compared with the previous special case.

We have, so far, considered price changes in terms of discounted prices rather than in terms of undiscounted prices. Obviously, this is more convenient when one is not interested in changes in the interest rate. But if we are, further decomposition is required.

$$\text{Let}\qquad \hat{a} = \begin{bmatrix} I & 0 & \cdot & \cdot & \cdot & 0 \\ 0 & \alpha I & & & \cdot & \cdot \\ \cdot & & \cdot & & & \cdot \\ \cdot & & & \cdot & & \cdot \\ \cdot & & & & \cdot & 0 \\ 0 & \cdot & \cdot & \cdot & 0 & \alpha^T I \end{bmatrix},$$

where the Is are $n \times n$ identity matrices, then we may write r as $\hat{a}\rho$ and p as $\hat{a}\pi$. Therefore, the effect on availability of a change in the undiscounted prices is

$$\frac{\partial x}{\partial \rho} = \frac{\partial x}{\partial r}\hat{a} = K\hat{a} - \frac{\partial x}{\partial W}(x-\bar{x})'\hat{a}$$

for unchanging α. We will notice that we have now lost the symmetry of our substitution matrix; however, it is easily seen that homogeneity is retained.

The effect of a change in α, the discount factor, on holdings is given by

$$\frac{\partial x}{\partial \alpha} = K\frac{\partial r}{\partial \alpha} + \frac{\partial x}{\partial W}\left[\frac{\partial W}{\partial \alpha} - (x-\bar{x})'\frac{\partial r}{\partial \alpha}\right]$$

on substituting the Hicks–Slutsky equation. However, the effect of a change in α can be analysed more conveniently in the q-mode rather than in the x-mode. We have

$$\frac{\partial q}{\partial \alpha} = C^{-1}\frac{\partial x}{\partial r}(C')^{-1}\frac{\partial p}{\partial \alpha} = C^{-1}K(C')^{-1}\frac{\partial p}{\partial \alpha} + \frac{\partial q}{\partial W}\left[\frac{\partial W}{\partial \alpha} - (q-\bar{q})'\frac{\partial p}{\partial \alpha}\right]$$

because $q = C^{-1}x$, $\bar{q} = C^{-1}\bar{x}$, and $r = (C')^{-1}p$. We also have

$$\frac{\partial W}{\partial \alpha} - (q-\bar{q})'\frac{\partial p}{\partial \alpha} = \alpha^{-1}\sum_{t=0}^{T} tE(t) = e$$

where $$E(t) = \alpha^t y(t) - p(t)'[q(t)-\bar{q}(t)],$$

that is, the excess discounted labour income over the discounted expenditure for the period t. The budget equation for the planning period implies that $\sum_{t=0}^{T} E(t) = 0$. As an expository assumption let the series $\{E(0), E(1),..., E(T)\}$ be monotonic. If the series is increasing, then $e > 0$, while if it is decreasing then $e < 0$. We may characterize individuals as either 'planning to be lenders' if $e < 0$ or 'planning to be borrowers' if $e > 0$. These characterizations are those used by Hicks in his theory of tilting.[8] We have

$$\frac{\partial q}{\partial \alpha} = L\alpha^{-1}\tilde{p} + \frac{\partial q}{\partial W}e$$

(8) Hicks [1], pp. 213–17, 227–36.

where $$\tilde{p} = \begin{bmatrix} 0 \\ p(1) \\ 2p(2) \\ \cdot \\ \cdot \\ Tp(T) \end{bmatrix}.$$

Now, as $L\alpha^{-1}p = 0$ we may write

$$\frac{\partial q(s)}{\partial \alpha} = \alpha^{-1} \sum_{t=0}^{T} L_{s,t}[tp(t) - sp(t)] + \frac{\partial q(s)}{\partial W} e.$$

If we assume general q-substitutiveness, then the off-diagonal elements of L are all non-negative. Therefore, the substitution matrices for different periods can be simply related if we assume their monotonicity over the planning period. If $s = 0$, we observe that

$$\alpha^{-1} \sum_{t=0}^{T} L_{s,t}[tp(t) - sp(t)] > 0,$$

while the term is negative if $s = T$. Thus, we can describe the pattern of substitution effects as giving rise to a downward 'tilt' in the stream of purchases over the planning period.

The effect produced by the income term is a simple function of whether the goods are superior or inferior in the q-sense, and whether the individual is planning to be a lender or a borrower.

Even though we assume substitutiveness in the x-mode, we do not have the tilting theory applying to x if π is constant, because

$$\frac{\partial x}{\partial \alpha} = K\frac{\partial r}{\partial \alpha} + \frac{\partial x}{\partial W} e$$

where $$\frac{\partial r(t)}{\partial \alpha} = \alpha^{-1}[tr(t) - \hat{c}p(t+1)].$$

As the focus of our attention is for the main part the current period, we may consider

$$\frac{\partial x(0)}{\partial \alpha} = \alpha^{-1} \sum_{t=0}^{T} K_{0,t}[tr(t) - \hat{c}p(t+1)] + \frac{\partial x(0)}{\partial W} e.$$

The first part of the substitution effect, $\alpha^{-1} \sum_{t=0}^{T} K_{0,t}\, tr(t)$, is positive if we assume x-substitutiveness. The second part, though, is ambiguous in sign. The two components correspond to the double appearance of the discount factor in discounted rental prices. Again, of course, $\frac{\partial x(0)}{\partial \alpha}$ is identical to $\frac{\partial q(0)}{\partial \alpha}$ and, therefore, if we assume q-substitutiveness we may be assured that

$$\alpha^{-1} \sum_{t=0}^{T} K_{0,t}[tr(t) - \hat{c}p(t+1)] > 0.$$

The savings of any period t, $\sigma(t)$, have been defined as

$$\sigma(t) = y(t) + iW(t-1) - \rho(t)'x(t).$$

The influence of a change in an element of the income stream is as follows:

$$\frac{\partial \sigma(t)}{\partial y(s)} = \begin{cases} i\,\frac{\partial W(t-1)}{\partial y(s)} - \rho(t)'\,\frac{\partial x(t)}{\partial W}\,\alpha^s & \text{if } s \neq t, \\ 1 + i\,\frac{\partial W(t-1)}{\partial y(s)} - \rho(t)'\,\frac{\partial x(t)}{\partial W}\,\alpha^s & \text{if } s = t. \end{cases}$$

For $t = 0$, we have $\partial W(t-1)/\partial y(s) = 0$ as $W(-1)$ is a parameter of the planning period. If we assume that goods are x-superior in the current period, then we will expect a decrease in savings for an increase in $y(s)$, $s \neq 0$. But when $s = 0$ it is probable that there will be an increase in savings for the current period as the increase in the total cost of holding goods is probably less than the increase in $y(0)$.

The effect on savings due to a change in the discount factor is

$$\frac{\partial \sigma(t)}{\partial \alpha} = -\alpha^{-2}W(t-1) - \rho(t)'\,\frac{\partial x(t)}{\partial \alpha} - x(t)'[-\hat{c}\pi(t+1)],$$

that is, a reduction in the interest rate changes savings by changing the return on money balances and the cost of holding wealth in the form of goods, given unchanging levels of holdings, and by changing the cost of holding goods due to the change in holdings. When we consider the current period, the rate of interest paid on previous planning periods' money balances is taken as given; as $q(0) = x(0)$

$$\frac{\partial \sigma(0)}{\partial \alpha} = -\rho(0)'\,\frac{\partial x(0)}{\partial \alpha} + \pi(1)'\hat{c}x(0)$$

$$= -\rho(0)'\alpha^{-1}L\tilde{p} - \rho(0)'\,\frac{\partial x(0)}{\partial W}\,e + \pi(1)'\hat{c}x(0).$$

Therefore, if we assume q-substitutiveness a decrease in the interest rate gives rise to a decrease in savings through the substitution effects. The influence of the income effects, again, depends on whether the current period's goods are x-superior or not, and whether the individual plans to be a borrower or a lender. Finally, provided $x(0)$ is constant, savings increase because a rise in α reduces the cost of holding goods.

Is there any useful purpose served by our use of the two classifications? Given the depreciation rates and the initial stocks for the planning period, the classifications in the q-sense reflect the underlying choices of the consumer facing different price–wealth situations, just as much as they do in the x-sense which is the sense which most naturally reflects the traditional classification. Of course, if there are no inversions, then both classifications characterize the same aspects of the consumer's choices. In as much as the inter-period substitution terms are to an order less in absolute value than those for within periods, then the likelihood of inversions of the substitutes–complements is lessened. And, if the consumption pattern differs little from a stationary pattern, then the number of income classification inversions will be reduced. Of course, inversions decrease in likelihood with the increase in the depreciation rate and, hence, with an increase in the length of the purchasing period.

Finally, we may highlight the discussion above by emphasizing that the duality of the two modes is dependent on the assumption of perfect second-hand markets. The transformation of the wealth constraint $W = p'(q-\bar{q})$ into $W = r'(x-\bar{x})$ is the point where this assumption first intrudes. If we assume instead that there are no second-hand markets, we notice that the value of goods previously purchased is zero. Therefore we must dichotomize x into $s+q$, their associated prices being, respectively, 0 and p. The duality of the previous case is now destroyed. The latter case is characterized by only possessing a q-mode. Second-hand markets bound the problem to x being non-negative, while the lack of second-hand markets bounds the problem to q being non-negative. The basic structure of the q-demand functions is, however, unchanged, but q will no longer have any negative elements, exhibiting entry into the second-hand markets.

4. Stock Adjustment Equation

A common element in the work on consumer durables has been the use of a stock adjustment equation, its use being a response to the seemingly evident fact that the adaptive behaviour of the consumer, in the context of durables, takes time and encompasses more than one purchasing period. Stone and Rowe's contribution is probably the most well-known in this field.[9] As our basic assumptions concerning the nature of the consumer's decision problems relating to durable goods closely resemble theirs, we have no difficulty in placing this idea in our model.

We have so far defined the 'acquisition' demand for good i in period t as

$$q_i(t) = x_i(t) - c_i x_i(t-1)$$

which may be rewritten as

$$q_i(t) = d_i x_i(t) + c_i[x_i(t) - x_i(t-1)].$$

That is, if we assume that there are no endowments so that $\bar{q}_i(t) = 0$, $t = 1,\ldots, T$, then the amount purchased in any period is the sum of the replacement demand, equal to the depreciation of the period, and net investment, $c_i[x_i(t) - x_i(t-1)]$. As $x_i(t) = s_i(t) + q_i(t)$ and $s_i(t+1) = c_i x_i(t)$ we have that[10]

$$q_i(t) = d_i[s_i(t) + q_i(t)] + [s_i(t+1) - s_i(t)].$$

Stone and Rowe, at this point, assumed that the net investment component is given by

$$s_i(t+1) - s_i(t) = \beta_i[s_i^0 - s_i(t)],$$

where s_i^0 is the optimum stock level, given prices and the wealth position, and β_i is the speed of adjustment, $0 < \beta_i < 1$. An alternative stock adjustment equation is obtained by multiplying through by c_i^{-1}, so that

$$x_i(t) - x_i(t-1) = \beta_i[x_i^0 - x_i(t-1)],$$

[9] Stone and Rowe [**1**], and references therein.

[10] Stone and Rowe assume that the depreciation on purchases may be less than that on initial stocks, presumably due to lags in delivery.

a form which we will find more appropriate for our purposes. Obviously, a stationary consumption plan is envisaged for equilibrium, such that when the consumer has adjusted to the optimum stock level, the equilibrium purchase, q_i^0, will equal the depreciation of the period, $d_i[s_i^0+q_i^0]$.

Using this framework as a basis, Stone and Rowe proceeded to their empirical investigations in the market context. The stock adjustment is assumed to be characteristic of the market's behaviour. However, there is no micro-foundation for this characteristic given by Stone and Rowe. The question is, then, whether it is possible in the market to 'observe' such an adaptive behaviour from micro-theoretical considerations. As a partial answer to this question we assume that individual consumers adjust to the optimum stock levels by a process that is analogous to the quantity adjustment process of Morishima.[11] The focus of the following discussion then becomes the quest for reasonable assumptions which permit the 'observation' of the Stone and Rowe postulate at the market level.

Before proceeding, a rearrangement of our notation will be found to be useful. Define the following index sets as follows:

$$I = \{1(0),..., n(0), 1(1),..., n(T)\},$$
$$I_1 = I-\{1(0)\},$$
$$S = \{1(0),..., n(0)\},$$
$$S_1 = S-\{1(0)\},$$
$$F = I-S,$$

and let

$$x_1(0) = x_1, \qquad r_1(0) = 1,$$
$$(x_2(0),..., x_n(T))' = x, \qquad (r_2(0),..., r_n(T))' = r,$$
$$(x_2(0),..., x_n(0))' = x(0), \qquad (r_2(0),..., r_n(0))' = r(0),$$
$$(x_1(1),..., x_n(T))' = x(F), \qquad (r_1(1),..., r_n(T))' = r(F).$$

Let us assume that there are N individuals exchanging n durable goods, or rather, renting n durable goods under conditions of perfect competition over $T+1$ periods. That is, there is assumed to exist for each good a 'spot' market and T 'futures'

(11) Morishima [2].

markets such that an individual can simultaneously trade in the renting of all goods for all periods in his planning period. We assume that

$$\sum_{t=0}^{T} \alpha^t y(t) = 0$$

for all individuals, or that labour is a commodity to be included in the set I. Good 1 in period 0 is taken to be the numeraire. The demand functions for individual j, say, are

$$x_k = h_k(r, r'x^0 + x_1^0) \quad \text{for all } k \in I_1,$$

where (x^0, x_1^0) denotes the initial endowments of all goods in the set I. The wealth constraint for the jth consumer is

$$r'x + x_1 = r'x^0 + x_1^0.$$

All consumers are assumed to hold with certainty the expectation that discounted rental prices, which reflect the idea of trading in futures markets, are constant (fixed) at r^*.

The individual who is not holding the optimal stock levels, given the existing prices, cannot instantaneously adjust to the optimal levels. There will be some passage of time before the consumer will be in (subjective) equilibrium. We assume, specifically, that the consumer adjusts in the following manner:

$$\dot{x}_k = \phi[R_k(x, x_1) - r_k^*] \quad \text{for all } k \in I_1$$

with the numeraire adjusting to satisfy the wealth constraint. That is, the consumer increases (decreases) his demand for the kth good if his demand price for the good is above (below) the market price, where the demand prices are the prices at which his present holdings would be optimal. $R_k(x, x_1)$ is the marginal rate of substitution of good k for the numeraire, and ϕ, in the spirit of Lange,[12] is called the 'flexibility of demand' which is taken to be a scalar constant, for simplicity. Let us expand the right-hand side by Taylor's theorem around (x^*, x_1^*), the optimal holdings for r^*, retaining only the linear part. Eliminate $x_1 - x_1^*$ using $(x - x^*)'R^* + (x_1 - x_1^*) = 0$ where R^* is the vector of marginal rates of substitution evaluated at (x^*, x_1^*). Then

$$\dot{x} = \phi B(x - x^*)$$

(12) Lange [**1**], pp. 94–7.

where $$B = \frac{\partial R}{\partial x} - \frac{\partial R}{\partial x_1} R'$$
evaluated at (x^*, x_1^*).

We assume at this juncture that the futures demands are perfectly flexible in the sense that $x(F)$ at once takes on the values to satisfy

$$R_k(x(0), x(F), x_1) - r_k^* = 0 \quad \text{for all } k \in F.$$

Therefore

$$\dot{x}(0) = \phi B_{00}[x(0) - x^*(0)] + \phi B_{0F}[x(F) - x^*(F)],$$
$$0 = \phi B_{F0}[x(0) - x^*(0)] + \phi B_{FF}[x(F) - x^*(F)],$$

where B_{00}, B_{0F}, B_{F0}, and B_{FF} are appropriate submatrices of B. This assumption may be thought to be reasonable since it implies that the adjustments of the demands for the present goods $x(0)$ are imperfect, while there is no inertia working in deciding the futures demands $x(F)$. Apart from its reasonableness, the assumption suffices in 'isolating' a subjective adjustment process for the spot market; that is

$$\dot{x}(0) = \phi[B_{00} - B_{0F} B_{FF}^{-1} B_{F0}][x(0) - x^*(0)].$$

At this point, we recognize that B is the inverse of the matrix, K, of substitution terms for all goods in I_1. From this fact we can determine that $[B_{00} - B_{0F} B_{FF}^{-1} B_{F0}] = K_{00}^{-1}$ where K_{00} is the matrix of substitution terms of the goods in the index set S_1 for individual j. Since K_{00}^{-1} is negative definite we are assured that the adjustment process for the jth individual is dynamically stable, as the latent roots of the characteristic equation $|K_{00}^{-1} - \lambda I| = 0$ are negative.

If we were to assume that all individuals, $j = 1,..., N$, were homogeneous, in the sense that they have the same K_{00} and ϕ, then we may write

$$\dot{X}(0) = \phi K_{00}^{-1}[X(0) - X^*(0)],$$

where $X(0)$ represents the sum of $x(0)$ over individuals $j = 1,..., N$. This description of a market adjustment process is on the basis of fixed or inflexible prices. Of course, this is not always the case. The opposite situation would be that prices are flexible and that the individual's adjustment of x to x^* is perfectly flexible, such that $x = x^*$ instantaneously. Following

Lange and Samuelson,[13] we may assume that prices respond to disequilibrium situations in the following manner:

$$\dot{r} = \theta[X(r, r'X^0 + X_1^0) - X^0]$$

where θ is the price flexibility which, for simplicity, is taken to be a scalar constant. Such an adjustment process is dependent on the distribution of initial holdings among individuals. However, given a particular distribution, we may write

$$\dot{r} = \theta A[r - r^0]$$

when we linearize around r^0, the equilibrium set of prices, using Taylor's theorem, where $A = \partial X/\partial r$ is evaluated at equilibrium values. As we are assuming that the tatonnement process starts in the neighbourhood of X^0, we may be justified in neglecting the income effects so that $A = NK$, which is negative definite. Consequently, the market adjustment process is stable.

We have $$\dot{X} = A\dot{r} = \theta A[X - X^0],$$

a process which we know to be stable because of the demonstrated stability of $\dot{r}$. Now we modify the model by introducing a simplifying assumption that the prices $r(F)$ are rigid. That is, the θs corresponding to $X(F)$ are all zero. (We continue to assume that all $X(0)$s have the same non-zero θ.) There is no rationale for this assumption, other than the analytical one that it serves for isolating the spot markets from the futures. Then the above equation is reduced to

$$\dot{X}(0) = \theta A_{00}[X(0) - X^0(0)],$$

where A_{00} represents the appropriate submatrix of A. Since the income effects have been neglected ($A_{00} = NK_{00}$), we have that the 'isolated' adjustment process for the spot markets is

$$\dot{X}(0) = \theta NK_{00}[X(0) - X^0(0)].$$

This process differs from the one generated from the assumption of the individuals having a subjective adjustment process in that K_{00} enters in its inverse form. The diagonal elements of K_{00} have the same sign as the diagonal elements of K_{00}^{-1} because

(13) Lange [1], pp. 94–7 and Samuelson [1], pp. 269–76.

both are negative definite. As for the off-diagonal elements we can say nothing; therefore these adjustment processes have different paths. For example, in the case of all goods being substitutive for each other, the off-diagonal elements are positive in K_{00} and negative in K_{00}^{-1}.

The two adjustment processes are very different from each other. One assumes that prices are constant and quantities are flexible, while the other assumes that prices are flexible and quantities instantaneously adjust to these prices. We may, therefore, conceive of the following general case. That is, we envisage a situation where individuals adjust in accordance to their subjective adjustment process, but where the optimum quantities, x^*, will, themselves, be changing owing to the operation of the Walrasian adjustment process causing prices to change.

Again, we specifically consider the jth individual, whose subjective adjustment process is

$$\dot{x}_k = \phi[R_k(x, x_1) - r_k^*] \quad \text{for all } k \in I_1,$$

where r_k^* will be written as r_k from now on, for simplicity. Upon differentiating with respect to tatonnement time (τ) we obtain

$$\ddot{x} = \phi[B\dot{x} - \dot{r}].$$

The imposition of the assumption of perfect flexibility of the futures demands,

$$R_k - r_k = 0 \quad \text{for all } k \in F,$$

permits us to write

$$\ddot{x}(0) = \phi B_{00}\dot{x}(0) + \phi B_{0F}\dot{x}(F) - \phi\dot{r}(0),$$

$$0 = \phi B_{F0}\dot{x}(0) + \phi B_{FF}\dot{x}(F) - \phi\dot{r}(F).$$

We have

$$\dot{r} = \theta[X - X^0],$$

which upon the reintroduction of the assumption of rigidity with respect to futures prices gives $\dot{r}(F) = 0$. Therefore

$$\ddot{x}(0) = \phi\{[B_{00} - B_{0F}B_{FF}^{-1}B_{F0}]\dot{x}(0) - \dot{r}(0)\},$$

where $B_{00} - B_{0F}B_{FF}^{-1}B_{F0} = K_{00}^{-1}$. If individuals are homogeneous then

$$\ddot{X}(0) = \phi\{K_{00}^{-1}\dot{X}(0) - N\theta[X(0) - X^0(0)]\}$$

as

$$\dot{r}(0) = \theta[X(0) - X^0(0)].$$

In order to show the stability of this system, let us introduce the Liapunov function

$$V(0) = \dot{X}(0)'\dot{X}(0)+[X(0)-X^0(0)]'[X(0)-X^0(0)]N\theta\phi$$

which, upon differentiating with respect to time, gives

$$\dot{V}(0) = 2\dot{X}(0)'\ddot{X}(0)+2[X(0)-X^0(0)]'\dot{X}(0)N\theta\phi.$$

On substituting for $\ddot{X}(0)$ we have

$$\dot{V}(0) = 2\dot{X}(0)'K_{00}^{-1}X(0) < 0$$

as K_{00}^{-1} is negative definite, and, therefore, the process is stable.

When individuals possess a subjective adjustment process and accept prices as being fixed during the adjustment process, a simple stock adjustment process can be 'isolated' for the spot markets. This process is in the spirit of the Stone and Rowe model for durables. However, on accepting the conventional Walrasian market adjustment process a similar process is identified but which in general has a different sign pattern associated with the matrix of adjustment coefficients. Therefore, in principle, there is some difference between the two processes. We have seen in the general case, albeit under specializing assumptions, that the interaction of the two processes does not lead to any destabilizing forces in the neighbourhood of equilibrium. Given that our subjective process is in principle identifiable and stands up to the stability test, we may proceed to close the gap between its present formulation and that of Stone and Rowe.

Before we can state a particular hypothesis about the adjustment process in the market context we must relate adjustment time, τ, to period time. A polar assumption is to assume that there is only one adjustment round per period. We will be assuming that for each individual the optimum holdings plan is stationary, with prices and initial endowments expected to be stationary also. Stationarity of initial endowments for each period is achieved if we assume that the depreciation is compensated for by 'manner' income.

The adjustment process for the market can now be represented by the difference equation

$$X(\tau+1)-X(\tau) = \phi K_{00}^{-1}[X(\tau)-X^*(\tau)],$$

where $X^*(\tau)$ is regarded as a constant vector equal to $X^*(0)$. The characteristic equation of this difference equation is

$$|(\lambda-1)I-\phi K_{00}^{-1}| = 0.$$

As K_{00}^{-1} is symmetric and negative definite we are assured that all the latent roots are real and less than unity. Also, we may write

$$|(\lambda+1)I-(\phi K_{00}^{-1}+2I)| = 0$$

so that if $\phi K_{00}^{-1}+2I$ is positive definite, then there is no $\lambda+1 \leqq 0$. Hence $\lambda > -1$, and, therefore, $|\lambda| < 1$ which implies that the difference form of the stock adjustment equation is stable.

The Stone and Rowe postulate may be considered to be the special case of ϕK_{00}^{-1} being diagonal, where the diagonal elements are $-\beta_1, -\beta_2, \ldots$. Their assumption that $0 < \beta_j < 1$ is sufficient for stability but not necessary since in the diagonal case the latent roots are $\lambda_j = 1-\beta_j$. Therefore, even though $\beta_j > 1$, we have stability provided $\beta_j < 2$ because $|\lambda_j| < 1$.

In interpreting the adjustment equation one must exercise some care. The vector $X(\tau)$ is the vector of aggregate demands, which for any particular purchasing period during the adjustment process will not equate with stationary aggregate supply $X^0(\tau) = X^0(0)$. Consequently, at the market level the adjustment process will be frustrated to the extent that the stock of available goods must be held by the sum of individuals. The aggregate demand $X(\tau)$ may also deviate from stationary optimum holdings $X^*(0)$, although the former approaches the latter eventually. If $X^*(0) \neq X^0(0)$, then $X(\tau) \neq X^0(\tau)$ for all $\tau \geqq$ some τ^0, as $\lim_{\tau\to\infty} X(\tau) = X^*(0)$ and $X^0(\tau) = X^0(0)$; that is, the frustration is persistent, unless prices are adjusted.(14)

(14) In the case of the Walrasian adjustment process,

$$X(\tau+1)-X(\tau) = \theta A_{00}[X(\tau)-X^0(0)],$$

there will be no persistent frustration, because $X(\tau)$ will approach $X^0(0)$.

An alternative Walrasian process is obtained if we assume (i) that the spot prices change according to the Samuelson–Lange formula,

$$\dot{r}_k = \theta[X_k(r, r'X^0+X_1^0)-X_k^0] \quad \text{for all } k \in S_1,$$

(ii) that individuals have perfect foresight with respect to the futures prices in the sense that $r(F)$ are adjusted so that

$$X_k(r, r'X^0+X_1^0)-X_k^0 = 0 \quad \text{for all } k \in F,$$

The above pure exchange discussion really needs to be modified to take account of production possibilities. Then, the supply of goods must be related to the income received by individuals. If the supply is equal to the depreciation of the goods, then the above will still obtain. If, however, output levels differ from this, then initial endowments from one period to the next will be changing and, consequently, optimum holdings will be changing. During the adjustment process aggregate demand will still, typically, diverge from aggregate supply. If we were to assume that producers supply any amount at the going price, then if aggregate demand is less than aggregate supply the producers will only need to supply a part of the depreciated amounts. In the converse situation, the additional supply over depreciation will add to initial endowments for the next period, and so the optimal holdings will be changing. A detailed consideration of the effect of production is beyond the scope of this paper. None the less, we recognize that the adjustment process observed at the market level will be considerably influenced by the behaviour of the production sector.

and (iii) that income effects are negligible. In this case

$$\dot{X}(0) = \theta[A_{00} - A_{0F}\, A_{FF}^{-1}\, A_{F0}][X(0) - X^0(0)]$$
$$= \theta B_{00}[X(0) - X^0(0)]$$

or

$$X(\tau+1) - X(\tau) = \theta B_{00}[X(\tau) - X^0(0)]$$

and the stability implies $\lim_{\tau \to \infty} X(\tau) = X^0(0)$; no long-run frustration, again.

VII. Demand for Durable Goods: A Note

M. MORISHIMA

In the last chapter, old durable goods that have been damaged in various degrees from past use are considered to be equivalent to some smaller amounts of new durable goods of the same kind, and the rates of depreciation or the rates of conversion of old into new goods are constant, because they are assumed to be independent of the use of goods. However, in reality the speed of depreciation of a good depends on its utilization; its economic and physical life spans may differ from each other; and the theory of durable goods should be able to answer the problem of obsolescence. In this note we show that the problem can be nicely solved by applying the von Neumann device of treating new and old goods as qualitatively different;(1) the resulting model is very similar to the one which has been discussed at the end of Chapter IV above.

Following von Neumann, we treat used durable goods left over for the future as by-products of the consumption activity in the current period and regard them as being qualitatively different from the same sort of goods before use. Let there be m new and old durable goods. Each good may be used in several different ways; so that there are n ways of utilization or 'consumption activities', altogether.

Let x_t be the vector of intensities of utilization of durable goods in period t. Denote by S a $k \times n$ matrix whose elements in the jth column, s^j, represent the amounts of services obtained per unit of activity j. The consumer enjoys the amount of services $s_t = Sx_t$ in period t, the substitution of which into his utility function $u = v(s_0, s_1, \ldots, s_T)$ gives

$$u = v(Sx_0, Sx_1, \ldots, Sx_T). \tag{1}$$

(1) For the von Neumann treatment of durable goods, see M. Morishima [1], pp. 89–114.

Next let A be an $m \times n$ matrix whose elements in the jth column, a^j, represent the amounts of durable goods required per unit of activity j, and B an $m \times n$ matrix whose elements in the jth column, b^j, represent the amounts of durable goods left over to the next period, after the use of a^j in the current period. C denotes an $h \times n$ matrix whose elements in the jth column c^j represent the amounts of perishable goods (lubricating oil, fuel, etc.) required per unit of activity j for the utilization of durable goods. Finally, y_t (an m-dimensional vector) denotes the amounts of durable goods bought in period t; p_t (an m-dimensional vector) and q_t (an h-dimensional vector) are the discounted prices of durable and perishable goods in period t, respectively.

The consumer maximizes his utility (1), subject to the feasibility conditions

$$
\begin{aligned}
Bx_{-1}+y_0 &\geqq Ax_0, \\
Bx_0+y_1 &\geqq Ax_1, \\
\cdot \quad \cdot \quad \cdot & \quad \cdot \quad \cdot \quad \cdot \\
Bx_{T-1}+y_T &\geqq Ax_T,
\end{aligned}
$$

and the budget condition

$$M \geqq p_0' y_0 + p_1' y_1 + \ldots + p_T' y_T + q_0' Cx_0 + q_1' Cx_1 + \ldots + q_T' Cx_T,$$

where M is the total discounted amount of money available to the consumer in $T+1$ periods. Obviously this is an extension of the model for the analysis of true-intrinsic complementarity given in the last part of Chapter IV; in fact, the present model is reduced to it if $B = 0$, i.e. if all goods are perishable. By applying the Kuhn–Tucker theorem, we find, roughly speaking, that the consumer adopts the consumption activities of minimum cost and the marginal utilities from them are proportional to their costs.

Part IV · Money

VIII. Consumer Behaviour and Liquidity Preference

M. MORISHIMA (1952)

1. Fundamental Notions

THE orthodox theory of demand originating from Slutsky and completed by Allen and Hicks has thoroughly elucidated consumer behaviour in an abstract non-monetary economy. In an actual monetary economy, however, individuals can and do buy commodities for money, so that not only consumption of goods but also the demand for cash balances needs to be explained. Moreover, if there are bonds and securities in addition to cash, individuals can choose between these alternative means of saving. Many theorists such as Hicks, Samuelson, Leser, and Patinkin tried to expand the traditional theory so as to enable it to deal with the monetary aspect of consumer behaviour too. But, in spite of their efforts, there remains room for a new model placing major emphasis on the analysis of the substitution between cash and bonds and aiming at full explanation of consumer behaviour in a monetary economy.

1.1. *Budget equation*

We adopt the following notation: x_i represents the consumer's demand for good i in the current period ($i = 1, 2, ..., n-1$), and y represents his supply of labour in the same period, which is treated as negative demand, writing x_n for $-y$. Let M and H be the quantities of cash held by the consumer at the beginning and end of the period, respectively. For simplicity, let us assume that all bonds are perpetuities paying one dollar per period. $\bar{B}$ expresses the number of bonds held at the beginning of the period, while B represents those held at the end. $\bar{B}$ and B can take on negative values. That is, when $B > 0$ the consumer is a lender, and when $B < 0$ he is a borrower. Then the budget equation of the consumer takes the form

$$\sum_{i=1}^{n} p_i x_i + H + p_b B = M + (1+p_b)\bar{B} \equiv I, \tag{1}$$

where p_i is the current price of the ith good and p_b is the price of bonds, which is equal to the reciprocal of the rate of interest, r.

1.2. *Probability of the future living standard*

Let us next introduce the notion of the probability of the future standard of living. First we assume that the consumer is able to place any two future livings in one of the following mutually exclusive categories: (a) the living L^0 preferred to the living L^1, (b) L^1 preferred to L^0, (c) L^0 and L^1 equally preferred. We attach to each living a positive real number ξ, and the rule of numbering is as follows:

$$\begin{aligned} \xi(L^1) &< \xi(L^0) \quad \text{when (a) is the case,} \\ \xi(L^0) &< \xi(L^1) \quad \text{when (b) is the case,} \\ \xi(L^1) &= \xi(L^0) \quad \text{when (c) is the case,} \end{aligned}$$

and $\xi = 0$ for the lowest living standard. The numbers $\xi(L^0)$, $\xi(L^1)$,... are called indices of the future living standard or, briefly, living standard indices.

Next, we assume that the consumer knows the probability that, when he holds the amount H of cash and the amount B of bonds at the prices $p_1, p_2,..., p_n, p_b$, his future living standard will be *at least* as high as the given level ξ; denote it by

$$q(\xi) = q(H, B, p_1,..., p_n, p_b; \xi), \tag{2}$$

which is called the cumulative probability of the future living standard or, briefly, the living standard probability.(1) Of course, we have

$$q(\xi) \geqslant 0, \qquad q(0) = 1,$$

and $q(\xi)$ is a non-increasing function of ξ; i.e. when $\xi > \xi'$, $q(\xi) \leqslant q(\xi')$.

1.3. *Utility function*

Let X be a combination composed of a bundle of commodities, promised with certainty, and a probability distribution of the future living standard, i.e.

$$X = [x_1, x_2,..., x_n, q(\xi)].$$

(1) If some goods are durable, then $q(\xi)$ depends also on the current demand for durable consumption goods. But if all goods are non-durable, $q(\xi)$ is independent of them. We assume, for the sake of simplicity, that all goods are non-durable.

We postulate that the consumer is able to place any two combinations in one of the following mutually exclusive categories: (i) X^0 preferred to X^1, (ii) X^1 preferred to X^0, (iii) X^0 and X^1 equally preferred.(2) We attach to each X a positive real number u, and the rule of numbering is as follows:

$$u(X^1) < u(X^0) \quad \text{when (i) is the case,}$$
$$u(X^0) < u(X^1) \quad \text{when (ii) is the case,}$$
$$u(X^0) = u(X^1) \quad \text{when (iii) is the case.}$$

The numbers $u(X^0)$, $u(X^1)$,... are called utility indices, and $f(u)$ is also a utility index when and only when the function $f(u)$ is a monotonically increasing function of u.(3) Taking into account (2), we can put the consumer's utility function in the form

$$u = u[x_1,..., x_n, q(H, B, p_1,..., p_n, p_b;\ \xi)]. \tag{3}$$

Note that u is a function of all xs and a functional of $q(\xi)$.

1.4. *Separability postulate*

In his paper issued in 1943, Sono [**1**] for the first time defined 'separability of goods' as follows. Goods X_1, X_2..., X_l are said to be separable from each of goods X_{l+1}, X_{l+2}, .., X_m, when and only when the marginal rates of substitution between X_1, X_2,..., X_l are independent of quantities of X_{l+1}, X_{l+2},..., X_m, viz.

$$\frac{\partial}{\partial x_i}\left(\frac{g_j}{g_1}\right) = 0 \quad (j = 2,..., l;\ i = l+1,..., m), \tag{4}$$

where $g = g(x_1, x_2,..., x_m)$ is a utility function and subscripts denote partial differentiation, i.e. $g_j = \partial g/\partial x_j$. If X_1,..., X_l are separable from each of X_{l+1},..., X_m from the point of view of a particular consumer, then his utility function has the following properties.

PROPERTY I. The indifference relations between X_1,..., X_l are not disturbed by quantities of X_{l+1},..., X_m; that is to

(2) In his paper [**1**], J. Marschak postulated complete ordering of probability space. Our postulate is the one of complete ordering of commodity–probability space.

(3) The following discussions are unaltered by the substitution of $f(u)$ for u, so that they are independent of the cardinal character of u.

say, if two bundles of goods $(\bar{x}_1, \bar{x}_2,..., \bar{x}_l, x'_{l+1},..., x'_m)$ and $(\bar{\bar{x}}_1, \bar{\bar{x}}_2,..., \bar{\bar{x}}_l, x'_{l+1},..., x'_m)$ satisfy the condition

$$g(\bar{x}_1,..., \bar{x}_l, x'_{l+1},..., x'_m) = g(\bar{\bar{x}}_1,..., \bar{\bar{x}}_l, x'_{l+1},..., x'_m),$$

then the condition

$$g(\bar{x}_1,..., \bar{x}_l, x_{l+1},..., x_m) = g(\bar{\bar{x}}_1,..., \bar{\bar{x}}_l, x_{l+1},..., x_m)$$

holds for any values of $x_{l+1},..., x_m$.

Proof. From the separability conditions (4), we obtain

$$\frac{g_{1i}}{g_1} = \frac{g_{2i}}{g_2} = ... = \frac{g_{li}}{g_l} = v_i \quad (i = l+1,..., m),$$

where
$$g_{ji} = \frac{\partial^2 g}{\partial x_j \partial x_i}.$$

Therefore

$$\frac{\partial}{\partial x_i}\Big(\sum_{j=1}^{l} g_j \, dx_j\Big) = \sum_{j=1}^{l} g_{ji} \, dx_j = v_i\Big(\sum_{j=1}^{l} g_j \, dx_j\Big) \quad (i = l+1,..., m).$$

Consequently, if

$$\sum_{j=1}^{l} g_j \, dx_j = 0, \quad \text{then} \quad \frac{\partial}{\partial x_i}\Big\{\sum_{j=1}^{l} g_j \, dx_j\Big\} = 0 \quad (i = l+1,..., m),$$

that is to say, the indifference relations remain unchanged with respect to a change in x_i $(i = l+1,..., m)$. Q.E.D. (See Sono [**1**], pp. 243–4.)

Property II. The utility function g can be written in the form

$$g = G[h(x_1,..., x_l), x_{l+1},..., x_m], \tag{5}$$

where h is called by Sono the proper utility function of $X_1,..., X_l$.

Proof. Let a particular bundle of goods $X_{l+1},..., X_m$ be $(a_{l+1},..., a_m)$ and write

$$g(x_1,..., x_l, a_{l+1},..., a_m) = h(x_1,..., x_l).$$

If $h(\bar{x}_1,..., \bar{x}_l) = h(\bar{\bar{x}}_1,..., \bar{\bar{x}}_l)$, then it follows from Property I that

$$g(\bar{x}_1,..., \bar{x}_l, x_{l+1},..., x_m) = g(\bar{\bar{x}}_1,..., \bar{\bar{x}}_l, x_{l+1},..., x_m)$$

for any $x_{l+1},..., x_m$. Thus, only one value of g is determined corresponding to the arbitrary set of values, $h, x_{l+1},..., x_m$. Consequently, g is a function of $h, x_{l+1},..., x_m$. Q.E.D. (See Sono [**1**], p. 245.)

Conversely, we can easily prove that, if the consumer's utility function takes the form (5), then $X_1,\ldots, X_l$ are separable from $X_{l+1},\ldots, X_m$ from his viewpoint. Therefore, we may say that $X_1,\ldots, X_l$ are separable from $X_{l+1},\ldots, X_m$ when and only when the indifference relations between $X_1,\ldots, X_l$ are not disturbed by quantities of $X_{l+1},\ldots, X_m$.

Now, let us introduce the above notion of separability into our monetary system.(4) First, we may assume very reasonably that all of the real goods $x_1, x_2,\ldots, x_n$ are separable from $H, B, p_1,\ldots, p_n, p_b$, because the marginal rate of substitution between any two real goods (say, coffee and tea) is determined by the consumer's 'tastes' for them and may, therefore, be regarded as being independent of $H, B, p_1,\ldots, p_n, p_b$.(5) Hence, by Property II, our utility function (3) can be written as

$$u = U[\phi(x_1,\ldots,x_n), q(H, B, p_1,\ldots,p_n,p_b; \xi)], \tag{6}$$

where ϕ is called the proper utility function of real goods.

Next we make an assumption concerning the effect of a change in x_i $(i = 1,\ldots,n)$ on the marginal rate of substitution between cash and bonds. Since cash and bonds are desired by a consumer, not as consumption goods, but as means of securing his future subsistence, then the marginal rate of substitution between them is determined by (a) his expectation of the purchasing power of money in the future, (b) his expectation of the future price of bonds, and (c) his willingness to bear risks. On the assumption of perfect competition, (a) and (b) are independent of the individual demand for real goods; and on the assumption that all real goods are non-durable, (c) is independent of the xs. Thus we may assume

$$\frac{\partial}{\partial x_i}\left(\frac{U_B}{U_H}\right) = 0 \quad (i = 1, 2,\ldots, n),$$

i.e.

$$\frac{U_{Bi}}{U_B} = \frac{U_{Hi}}{U_H} \quad (i = 1, 2,\ldots, n),$$

(4) The separability postulate was introduced first into the field of the consumer's demand for cash by Yasui [**1**].

(5) Because of this assumption we must exclude goods demanded for their ostentatious value (diamonds, etc.) from our list of the real goods, because the desire for diamonds (the marginal rate of substitution for rice of a given quantity of diamonds) depends on the price of diamonds.

where $$U_H = \frac{\partial U}{\partial H} = \int_0^\infty U'[\phi, q(\xi); \mu] \frac{\partial q(\mu)}{\partial H} \, \mathrm{d}\mu,$$

$$U_B = \frac{\partial U}{\partial B} = \int_0^\infty U'[\phi, q(\xi); \mu] \frac{\partial q(\mu)}{\partial B} \, \mathrm{d}\mu,$$

$$U_{Hi} = \frac{\partial^2 U}{\partial H \partial x_i} = \frac{\partial \phi}{\partial x_i} \int_0^\infty U'_\phi[\phi, q(\xi); \mu] \frac{\partial q(\mu)}{\partial H} \, \mathrm{d}\mu = U_{iH}, \quad (7)$$

$$U_{Bi} = \frac{\partial^2 U}{\partial B \partial x_i} = \frac{\partial \phi}{\partial x_i} \int_0^\infty U'_\phi[\phi, q(\xi); \mu] \frac{\partial q(\mu)}{\partial B} \, \mathrm{d}\mu = U_{iB}, \quad (8)$$

and U' is the functional derivative of U with respect to q at the point μ and U'_ϕ is the functional derivative of $\partial U/\partial \phi$ with respect to q at μ.

2. Equilibrium and Stability Conditions

2.1. *Equilibrium conditions*

Since the consumer's behaviour is to select the most preferable plan under the condition of his budget constraint, our first problem is to maximize (6) subject to (1). If $p_1, p_2, \ldots, p_n, p_b$, and I are assumed to be constant, we derive the following equations as the necessary conditions for a maximum or the subjective equilibrium conditions:

$$\frac{U_1}{p_1} = \frac{U_2}{p_2} = \ldots = \frac{U_n}{p_n} = \frac{U_B}{p_b} = U_H = \lambda, \quad (9)$$

where $U_i = \partial U/\partial x_i = (\partial U/\partial \phi)(\partial \phi/\partial x_i)$ and λ is a Lagrange multiplier. In other words, our equilibrium conditions are as follows. (i) The marginal rate of substitution of any real commodity for cash is equal to the price of that commodity. (ii) The marginal rate of substitution of bonds for cash is equal to the price of bonds (or the reciprocal of the rate of interest).

2.2. *Stability conditions*

A point which satisfies (1) and (9) is called an equilibrium point. In order that u should be a true maximum at an equilibrium point, $\mathrm{d}^2 u$ must be negative definite under the constraint

$\sum_{i=1}^{n} p_i \, dx_i + dH + p_b \, dB = 0$. Now let us define

$$U_{ij} = \frac{\partial^2 U}{\partial x_j \partial x_i} = \frac{\partial U}{\partial \phi} \frac{\partial^2 \phi}{\partial x_j \partial x_i} + \frac{\partial^2 U}{\partial \phi^2} \frac{\partial \phi}{\partial x_i} \frac{\partial \phi}{\partial x_j} = U_{ji}, \qquad (10)$$

$$U_{HH} = \frac{\partial^2 U}{\partial H^2}, \quad U_{BB} = \frac{\partial^2 U}{\partial B^2}, \quad U_{BH} = \frac{\partial^2 U}{\partial H \partial B} = \frac{\partial^2 U}{\partial B \partial H} = U_{HB},$$

and let U^0_{ij}, U^0_{iH}, U^0_{iB}, U^0_{HH}, U^0_{BB}, U^0_{BH} denote, respectively, the values that U_{ij}, U_{iH}, U_{iB}, U_{HH}, U_{BB}, U_{BH} take on at the equilibrium point. Write

$$D = \begin{vmatrix} 0 & p_1 & . & . & . & p_n & 1 & p_b \\ p_1 & U^0_{11} & . & . & . & U^0_{1n} & U^0_{1H} & U^0_{1B} \\ . & . & . & . & . & . & . & . \\ p_n & U^0_{n1} & . & . & . & U^0_{nn} & U^0_{nH} & U^0_{nB} \\ 1 & U^0_{H1} & . & . & . & U^0_{Hn} & U^0_{HH} & U^0_{HB} \\ p_b & U^0_{B1} & . & . & . & U^0_{Bn} & U^0_{BH} & U^0_{BB} \end{vmatrix},$$

whose principal minor of order k is represented by D^k. Then the secondary conditions for a maximum are

$$(-1)^k D^k < 0 \quad (k = 3, 4, \ldots, n+3). \qquad (11)$$

Next let us postulate that $d^2u < 0$ for all values of $x_1, \ldots, x_n$, H, B, $p_1, \ldots, p_n$, p_b, $dx_1, \ldots, dx_n$, dH, and dB such that $du = 0$; i.e.

$$(-1)^k \Delta^k < 0 \quad (k = 3, 4, \ldots, n+3) \qquad (12)$$

identically in $x_1, \ldots, x_n$, H, B, $p_1, \ldots, p_n$, p_b, where Δ^k represents the principal minor of order k of the determinant

$$\begin{vmatrix} 0 & U_1 & . & . & . & U_n & U_H & U_B \\ U_1 & U_{11} & . & . & . & U_{1n} & U_{1H} & U_{1B} \\ . & . & . & . & . & . & . & . \\ U_n & U_{n1} & . & . & . & U_{nn} & U_{nH} & U_{nB} \\ U_H & U_{H1} & . & . & . & U_{Hn} & U_{HH} & U_{HB} \\ U_B & U_{B1} & . & . & . & U_{Bn} & U_{BH} & U_{BB} \end{vmatrix}.$$

We call (12) the subjective stability conditions, which imply that the marginal rate of substitution between goods (including cash and bonds) must diminish for substitutions in every direction.

Then, by the stability conditions, a point that satisfies the necessary conditions for a maximum (9) also satisfies the secondary conditions for a maximum (11). Therefore, the equilibrium point gives us a true maximum of the utility function, and the consumer chooses the plan that corresponds to the equilibrium point.

2.3. *A restatement of the traditional theory of consumer behaviour*

The traditional method of economic analysis has mainly been concerned with the 'real' economic phenomena by handing over the analysis of the monetary phenomena to the monetary specialists. Following this tradition, the orthodox consumer theory, developed by Slutsky, Allen, Hicks, and others, has also analysed only the 'real' plan of a consumer. Therefore it must be taken as only a part of the whole theory of consumer behaviour.

In the following we shall demonstrate that the traditional theory is identical with that part of our consumer theory which is concerned with the 'real' plan of a consumer.

First, putting $U_i = (\partial U/\partial\phi)(\partial\phi/\partial x_i)$ in equations (9) and eliminating $\partial U/\partial\phi$ between them, we obtain

$$\frac{\partial\phi/\partial x_1}{p_1} = \frac{\partial\phi/\partial x_2}{p_2} = \ldots = \frac{\partial\phi/\partial x_n}{p_n}, \tag{13}$$

where each $\partial\phi/\partial x_i$ depends only on $x_1, x_2,..., x_n$.

Secondly, considering (10) and assuming $\partial U/\partial\phi > 0$, we have from (12)

$$(-1)^k J^k < 0 \quad (k = 3, 4,..., n+1), \tag{14}$$

where J^k is the principal minor of order k of the determinant

$$J = \begin{vmatrix} 0 & \dfrac{\partial\phi}{\partial x_1} & \cdot & \cdot & \cdot & \dfrac{\partial\phi}{\partial x_n} \\ \dfrac{\partial\phi}{\partial x_1} & \dfrac{\partial^2\phi}{\partial x_1^2} & \cdot & \cdot & \cdot & \dfrac{\partial^2\phi}{\partial x_n\,\partial x_1} \\ \cdot & \cdot & \cdot & \cdot & \cdot & \cdot \\ \dfrac{\partial\phi}{\partial x_n} & \dfrac{\partial^2\phi}{\partial x_1\,\partial x_n} & \cdot & \cdot & \cdot & \dfrac{\partial^2\phi}{\partial x_n^2} \end{vmatrix}.$$

Thirdly, let us denote the solutions of (1) and (9) by x_1^0, $x_2^0,\ldots, x_n^0$, H^0, B^0 and rewrite our budget equation (1) as

$$\sum_{i=1}^{n} p_i x_i = E, \tag{15}$$

where $E \equiv I - H^0 - p_b B^0 =$ the consumer's net expenditure on real commodities.

We can then easily prove that the solutions of (13) and (15) are $x_1^0, x_2^0,\ldots, x_n^0$, and, because of (14), they give us a true maximum of ϕ under the constraint (15). That is, if $x_1,\ldots, x_n$ are separable from $q(\xi)$, the values of the xs for which ϕ is a maximum subject to (15) are identical with the values of the xs for which U is a maximum subject to (1).

Since (13) and (14) are regarded as the traditional equilibrium conditions and the traditional stability conditions respectively, we may say that $x_1^0, x_2^0,\ldots, x_n^0$ denote the traditional equilibrium point.

Consequently, we may interpret the traditional consumer theory as follows.

1. The traditional budget condition is not (1) but (15) where H^0 and B^0 are taken as determined by the monetary consumer theory.

2. The traditional theory presumes that $x_1, x_2,\ldots, x_n$ are separable from $q(\xi)$, that is, the preference relations between real commodities are not disturbed by any change in H, B, $p_1,\ldots, p_n, p_b$. Hence it follows that there exists the proper utility function ϕ of real commodities.

3. According to the theory, a consumer's behaviour is said to be rational when he maximizes his proper utility function of real commodities under his budget condition (15). Therefore, the amounts of real commodities bought by a rational consumer are determined by equations (13) and (15).

3. The Effect of a Change in Price

Now suppose p_k to vary, other prices, interest rate, and I remaining unchanged. Let the reciprocal determinant of D be

$$\begin{vmatrix} D_0 & D_i \\ D_j & D_{ij} \end{vmatrix} \quad (i,j = 1,\ldots,n, H, B),$$

and write

$$Z_i = D_i/D \quad (i = 0, 1, ..., n, H, B),$$

$$Z_{ij} = D_{ij}/D \quad (i, j = 1, ..., n, H, B).$$

Then, differentiating (1) and (9) with respect to p_k we get the solutions

$$\frac{\partial x_i}{\partial p_k} = -x_k Z_i + \lambda Z_{ki} - \sum_{j=1}^{B} U^0_{j[k]} Z_{ji}, \quad (16)$$

$$\frac{\partial H}{\partial p_k} = -x_k Z_H + \lambda Z_{kH} - \sum_{j=1}^{B} U^0_{j[k]} Z_{jH}, \quad (17)$$

$$\frac{\partial B}{\partial p_k} = -x_k Z_B + \lambda Z_{kB} - \sum_{j=1}^{B} U^0_{j[k]} Z_{jB}, \quad (18)$$

where $U^0_{j[k]}$ is the value which $\partial U_j/\partial p_k$ takes on at the equilibrium point ($j = 1, ..., n, H, B$), and the summation of each equation runs from 1 to B.

In each of (16), (17), and (18) the first term represents the effect of the deficiency (or excess) of I, which would arise if the consumer did not change his plan in spite of an increase (or a decrease) in p_k, and the other terms represent the effect due to the disturbances in the subjective equilibrium conditions caused by the change in p_k. Especially the last term expresses the effect that arises when the change in p_k shifts the marginal rates of substitution. Let us call these equations the generalized Slutsky equations.

In this subsection we examine the relationship between the generalized Slutsky equation (16) and the original Slutsky equation which Hicks called 'the fundamental equation of value theory'.(6)

By Laplace's theorem of the expansion of a determinant, we have, first of all,

$$\sum_1^n p_j Z_j + Z_H + p_b Z_B = 1, \quad (19)$$

$$p_i Z_0 + \sum_1^n U^0_{ij} Z_j + U^0_{iH} Z_H + U^0_{iB} Z_B = 0 \quad (i = 1, ..., n), \quad (20)$$

(6) The following analysis is substantially identical with the partition analysis by Lewis [**1**].

$$\sum_{j=1}^{n} p_j Z_{ij} + Z_{iH} + p_b Z_{iB} = 0 \quad (i = 1,\dots,n, H, B), \tag{21}$$

$$p_t Z_i + \sum_{j=1}^{n} U_{tj}^0 Z_{ij} + U_{tH}^0 Z_{iH} + U_{tB}^0 Z_{iB} = \begin{cases} 0 & (t \neq i) \\ 1 & (t = i) \end{cases} \tag{22}$$

$$(t,\, i = 1,\dots,n, H, B;\ p_H = 1).$$

Next define

$$V = \begin{vmatrix} 0 & p_1 & . & . & . & p_n \\ p_1 & \phi_{11}^0 & . & . & . & \phi_{1n}^0 \\ . & . & . & . & . & . \\ p_n & \phi_{n1}^0 & . & . & . & \phi_{nn}^0 \end{vmatrix},$$

$$X_0 = V_0/V, \qquad X_i = V_i/V, \qquad X_{ij} = V_{ij}/V,$$

where ϕ_{ij}^0 represents the value which $\partial^2\phi/\partial x_j\,\partial x_i$ takes on at the point $(x_1^0,\dots,x_n^0)$, and V_0, V_i, V_{ij} are, respectively, the cofactors of 0, p_i, ϕ_{ij}^0 in V. Since $U_{ij}^0 = (\partial U/\partial\phi)\phi_{ij}^0 + (\partial^2 U/\partial\phi^2)\phi_i^0\,\phi_j^0$, it follows (by Laplace's theorem) that

$$\sum_{j=1}^{n} p_j X_{ji} = 0, \tag{23}$$

$$p_t X_i + \left(\frac{\partial U}{\partial\phi}\right)^{-1} \sum_{j=1}^{n} U_{tj}^0 X_{ij} = \begin{cases} 0 & (t \neq i) \\ 1 & (t = i) \end{cases} \quad (t,\, i = 1,\dots,n). \tag{24}$$

In view of (7), (8), and $U_{j[k]} = (\partial\phi/\partial x_j)(\partial^2 U/\partial p_k\,\partial\phi)$, equation (23) yields

$$\left.\begin{aligned} \sum_{j=1}^{n} U_{jH}^0 X_{ji} &= 0 \quad (i = 1,\dots,n) \\ \sum_{j=1}^{n} U_{jB}^0 X_{ji} &= 0 \quad (i = 1,\dots,n) \end{aligned}\right\}, \tag{25}$$

$$\sum_{j=1}^{n} U_{j[k]}^0 X_{ji} = 0 \quad (i = 1,\dots,n). \tag{26}$$

Therefore, Z_i, Z_{ki}, Z_{Hi} $(i, k = 1,\dots,n)$ can be transformed as follows:

$$Z_i = X_i - \left(\sum_{1}^{n} p_t Z_t + Z_H + p_b Z_B\right) X_i + Z_i \qquad \text{(from (19))}$$

$$= X_i - (Z_H + p_b Z_B) X_i + \left(\frac{\partial U}{\partial\phi}\right)^{-1} \sum_{t=1}^{n} \left(\sum_{j=1}^{n} U_{jt}^0 X_{ji}\right) Z_t$$

(from (24))

$$= X_i - (Z_H + p_b Z_B)X_i + \left(\frac{\partial U}{\partial \phi}\right)^{-1} \sum_{j=1}^{n} \left(p_j Z_0 + \sum_{t=1}^{n} U^0_{jt} Z_t\right) X_{ji}$$

(from (23))

$$= X_i - (Z_H + p_b Z_B)X_i - \left(\frac{\partial U}{\partial \phi}\right)^{-1} \sum_{j=1}^{n} (U^0_{jH} Z_H + U^0_{jB} Z_B) X_{ji}$$

(from (20))

$$= X_i - (Z_H + p_b Z_B)X_i. \qquad \text{(from (25)),} \quad (27)$$

$$Z_{ki} = -(Z_{kH} + p_b Z_{kB})X_i - \left(\sum_{j=1}^{n} p_j Z_{kj}\right) X_i + Z_{ki} \qquad \text{(from (21))}$$

$$= -(Z_{kH} + p_b Z_{kB})X_i + \left(\frac{\partial U}{\partial \phi}\right)^{-1} \sum_{t=1}^{n} \left(\sum_{j=1}^{n} U^0_{jt} X_{ji}\right) Z_{kt}$$

(from (24))

$$= \left(\frac{\partial U}{\partial \phi}\right)^{-1} X_{ki} - (Z_{kH} + p_b Z_{kB})X_i +$$

$$+ \left(\frac{\partial U}{\partial \phi}\right)^{-1} \left[\sum_{j=1}^{n} \left(p_j Z_k + \sum_{t=1}^{n} U^0_{jt} Z_{kt}\right) X_{ji} - X_{ki}\right]$$

(from (23))

$$= \left(\frac{\partial U}{\partial \phi}\right)^{-1} X_{ki} - (Z_{kH} + p_b Z_{kB})X_i -$$

$$- \left(\frac{\partial U}{\partial \phi}\right)^{-1} \sum_{j=1}^{n} (U^0_{jH} Z_{kH} + U^0_{jB} Z_{kB}) X_{ji} \qquad \text{(from (22))}$$

$$= \left(\frac{\partial U}{\partial \phi}\right)^{-1} X_{ki} - (Z_{kH} + p_b Z_{kB})X_i. \qquad \text{(from (25)),} \quad (28)$$

$$Z_{Hi} = Z_{Hi} - \left(\sum_{j=1}^{n} p_j Z_{Hj} + Z_{HH} + p_b Z_{HB}\right) X_i \qquad \text{(from (21))}$$

$$= -(Z_{HH} + p_b Z_{HB})X_i + \left(\frac{\partial U}{\partial \phi}\right)^{-1} \sum_{j=1}^{n} \left(\sum_{t=1}^{n} U^0_{tj} X_{ti}\right) Z_{Hj}$$

(from (24))

$$= -(Z_{HH} + p_b Z_{HB})X_i +$$

$$+ \left(\frac{\partial U}{\partial \phi}\right)^{-1} \left[\sum_{t=1}^{n} p_t X_{ti} Z_H + \sum_{j=1}^{n} \left(\sum_{t=1}^{n} U^0_{tj} X_{ti}\right) Z_{Hj}\right]$$

(from (23))

$$= -(Z_{HH} + p_b Z_{HB})X_i -$$

$$- \left(\frac{\partial U}{\partial \phi}\right)^{-1} \sum_{t=1}^{n} (U^0_{tH} Z_{HH} + U^0_{tB} Z_{HB}) X_{ti} \qquad \text{(from (22))}$$

$$= -(Z_{HH} + p_b Z_{HB})X_i. \qquad \text{(from (25)),} \quad (29)$$

Similarly, we have

$$Z_{Bi} = -(Z_{BH}+p_b Z_{BB})X_i \quad (i = 1,..., n). \tag{30}$$

Now, substituting (27), (28), (29), and (30) into (16) and considering (26), we can write equation (16) in the form

$$\frac{\partial x_i}{\partial p_k} = -x_k X_i+\lambda' X_{ki}-\left(\frac{\partial H}{\partial p_k}+p_b \frac{\partial B}{\partial p_k}\right)X_i,$$

where $\lambda' = (\partial U/\partial \phi)^{-1}\lambda$.

In this expression the first and the second terms are, respectively, the traditional income effect and the traditional substitution effect (Hicks [**1**], p. 309), and the third term is the indirect income effect, which arises when H and B are affected by a change in p_k.

Since I is constant, we have $(\partial H/\partial p_k)+p_b(\partial B/\partial p_k) = -\partial E/\partial p_k$. In the traditional Slutsky equation, the third term is neglected by the assumption of constancy of E. As $H+p_b B-I$ ($\equiv -E$) is saving, the premise that E is constant is identical with the elasticity of saving with respect to the price p_k being zero.

By a similar procedure, we can transform (17) and (18) into

$$\frac{\partial H}{\partial p_k} = -\frac{\partial E}{\partial p_k}(p_b U^0_{HB}-U^0_{BB})/W+p_b(p_b U^0_{H[k]}-U^0_{B[k]})/W, \tag{31}$$

$$\frac{\partial B}{\partial p_k} = -\frac{\partial E}{\partial p_k}(U^0_{BH}-p_b U^0_{HH})/W-(p_b U^0_{H[k]}-U^0_{B[k]})/W, \tag{32}$$

where $$W = \begin{vmatrix} 0 & 1 & p_b \\ 1 & U^0_{HH} & U^0_{HB} \\ p_b & U^0_{BH} & U^0_{BB} \end{vmatrix}.$$

In each of (31) and (32), the first term represents the income effect that arises when a change in p_k gives rise to a change in the net expenditure E, while the second term represents the substitution effect that is obtained when the marginal rate of substitution between cash and bonds responds to a change in p_k. Since the second terms of (31) and (32) are opposite in sign, H and B must change in opposite directions so far as the substitution effect is concerned. We can thus say that cash and bonds are substitutive.

Let us now make a very realistic assumption that the marginal rate of substitution of bonds for cash decreases when B is increased and increases when H is increased, i.e.

$$\frac{\partial}{\partial B}\left(\frac{U_B}{U_H}\right) < 0, \qquad \frac{\partial}{\partial H}\left(\frac{U_B}{U_H}\right) > 0.$$

Then we have

$$U_{BB}\,U_H - U_{HB}\,U_B < 0, \qquad U_{HH}\,U_B - U_{BH}\,U_H < 0,$$

so that at the equilibrium point

$$U^0_{BB} - U^0_{HB}\,p_b < 0, \qquad U^0_{HH}\,p_b - U^0_{BH} < 0.$$

On the other hand, we have

$$\frac{\partial}{\partial p_k}\left(\frac{U^0_H}{U^0_B}\right) = (U^0_{H[k]}\,p_b - U^0_{B[k]})/\lambda p_b^2,$$

and $W > 0$ by the stability conditions. Consequently, we have the following comparative statical rules:

$\frac{\partial E}{\partial p_k}$	Income effect on: H	B	$\frac{\partial}{\partial p_k}\frac{U^0_H}{U^0_B}$	Substitution effect on: H	B
+	—	—	+	+	—
0	0	0	0	0	0
—	+	+	—	—	+

Following Sono, let us call the ith consumption good a 'proper' superior good (or a 'proper' inferior good) if X_i is positive (or negative) and a 'general' superior good (or a 'general' inferior good) if Z_i is positive (or negative). It is evident that if a good is superior (or inferior) in the Hicksian sense, then it is a proper superior good (or a proper inferior good) and vice versa. Then, what relation does there exist between the proper and the general superiority–inferiority of goods? Since

$$1 - Z_H - p_b\,Z_B = 1 - (\partial H/\partial I) - p_b(\partial B/\partial I),$$

it follows from (27) that

$$\frac{Z_1}{X_1} = \frac{Z_2}{X_2} = \dots = \frac{Z_n}{X_n} = 1 - \left(\frac{\partial H}{\partial I} + p_b\frac{\partial B}{\partial I}\right).$$

Hence if the extreme right-hand side of this expression is positive, that is, if it is the case that when the consumer's initial assets are increased by one unit of cash, less than the entire unit will be devoted to the acquisition of cash and bonds, then the above two definitions are consistent, i.e. a proper superior good is a general superior good and a proper inferior good is a general inferior good. Conversely, if the extreme right-hand side is negative, then the two definitions are inconsistent, i.e. a proper superior good is a general inferior good and a proper inferior good is a general superior good (Sono [**1**], p. 249).

Next we shall define substitute and complementary goods as follows: if $\lambda' X_{ki}$ is positive (or negative), k and i are called 'proper' substitutes (or 'proper' complements); and if Z_{ki} is positive (or negative), k and i are 'general' substitutes (or 'general' complements). Obviously, our proper substitutive–complementary relation is identical with the conventional one due to Hicks. In the following, we shall examine the 'proper' and the 'general' definitions of substitutiveness and complementarity for the relationship between them.

Since the determinant D is symmetrical, we have

$$Z_{Hk} = Z_{kH}, \qquad Z_{Bk} = Z_{kB}.$$

Therefore, it follows from (28), (29), and (30) that

$$\lambda Z_{ki} - \lambda' X_{ki} = \lambda (Z_{HH} + 2p_b Z_{HB} + p_b^2 Z_{BB}) X_i X_k,$$

where the part in the parentheses on the right-hand side is necessarily negative, because $\sum_{i=1}^{B} \sum_{j=1}^{B} h_i h_j Z_{ij}$ is a negative definite quadratic form by the familiar property of the substitution terms (Hicks [**1**], pp. 310–11). Consequently, we obtain the following rules (Sono [**1**], pp. 261–5).

1. The case in which both k and i are proper superior goods or proper inferior goods: If k and i are proper complementary goods, they are necessarily general complementary goods, but if they are proper substitutes they are not necessarily general substitutes. Similarly, if k and i are general substitutes, they are necessarily proper substitutes, but if they are general complementary goods they are not necessarily proper complementary goods.

2. The case in which one of k and i is a proper superior good and the other is a proper inferior good: If k and i are proper substitutes, they are necessarily general substitutes, but if they are proper complementary goods they are not necessarily general complementary goods. Likewise, if k and i are general complementary goods, they are necessarily proper complementary goods, but if they are general substitutes they are not necessarily proper substitutes.

3. For any good, $\lambda Z_{kk} < \lambda' X_{kk}$, that is, the general self-substitution effect is greater, in modulus, than the corresponding proper effect (the LeChatelier principle).

4. A Proportional Change in All Prices

In order to simplify the analysis of the effects of a proportional change of all current prices, we introduce the following assumption: the probability that a consumer who holds the amount H of cash and the amount B of bonds at the prices $p_1,..., p_n, p_b$ may expect a future living which will be at least as high as the given level ξ is equal to the probability that he may expect the same future living when he holds the amount ϵH of cash and the amount ϵB of bonds at the prices $\epsilon p_1,..., \epsilon p_n, p_b$. This case is not identical with the case of unit elasticity of price expectation discussed by Hicks, although they are closely related to each other.

If this assumption holds for any ξ the probability distribution of the future living standard remains unchanged when H, B, $p_1,..., p_n$ are changed proportionally. Therefore, U is homogeneous of order zero in H, B, $p_1,..., p_n$ or

$$\frac{\partial U}{\partial H}H+\frac{\partial U}{\partial B}B+\sum_{k=1}^{n}\frac{\partial U}{\partial p_k}p_k = 0 \tag{33}$$

identically in $x_1,..., x_n$, H, B, $p_1,..., p_n, p_b$.

Differentiating (33) partially with respect to x_j, we have

$$U_{jH}H+U_{jB}B+\sum_{k=1}^{n}U_{j[k]}p_k = 0, \tag{34}$$

that is to say, the marginal utility of the jth real commodity is homogeneous of order zero in H, B, $p_1,\ldots, p_n$ $(j = 1, 2,\ldots, n)$. Differentiating (33) partially with respect to H,

$$-U_H = U_{HH}\,H+U_{HB}\,B+\sum_{k=1}^{n} U_{H[k]}\,p_k. \tag{35}$$

Similarly,

$$-U_B = U_{BH}\,H+U_{BB}\,B+\sum_{k=1}^{n} U_{B[k]}\,p_k. \tag{36}$$

That is, the marginal utilities of cash and bonds are homogeneous of order -1 in H, B, $p_1,\ldots, p_n$.

Suppose now there is a proportional change in all prices, so that

$$\frac{\mathrm{d}p_1}{p_1} = \frac{\mathrm{d}p_2}{p_2} = \ldots = \frac{\mathrm{d}p_n}{p_n} = \mathrm{d}\theta.$$

Then we have

$$\begin{aligned}
\mathrm{d}x_i &= \sum_{k=1}^{n} \frac{\partial x_i}{\partial p_i}\,\mathrm{d}p_k = \left(\sum_{k=1}^{n} \frac{\partial x_i}{\partial p_k} p_k\right) \mathrm{d}\theta \\
&= \Big[-\Big(\sum_{k=1}^{n} p_k\,x_k\Big)Z_i+\lambda \sum_{k=1}^{n} p_k\,Z_{ki} - \\
&\qquad - \sum_{j=1}^{B}\Big(\sum_{k=1}^{n} U^0_{j[k]}\,p_k\Big)Z_{ji}\Big]\,\mathrm{d}\theta \qquad \text{(from (16))} \\
&= \Big[-(I-H-p_b\,B)Z_i+\lambda\Big(\sum_{k=1}^{n} p_k\,Z_{ki}+Z_{Hi}+p_b\,Z_{Bi}\Big)+ \\
&\qquad + \sum_{j=1}^{B} (U^0_{jH}\,H+U^0_{jB}\,B)Z_{ji}\Big]\,\mathrm{d}\theta \\
&\qquad\qquad \text{(from (34), (35), (36), and (9))} \\
&= \Big[-IZ_i+\Big(Z_i+\sum_{j=1}^{B} U^0_{jH}\,Z_{ji}\Big)H+ \\
&\qquad +\Big(p_b\,Z_i+\sum_{j=1}^{B} U^0_{jB}\,Z_{ji}\Big)B\Big]\,\mathrm{d}\theta. \qquad \text{(from (21))}, \quad (37)
\end{aligned}$$

But, since

$$Z_i+\sum_{j=1}^{B} U^0_{jH}\,Z_{ji} = p_b\,Z_i+\sum_{j=1}^{B} U^0_{jB}\,Z_{ji} = 0 \quad (i = 1,\ldots, n),$$

the last two terms of (37) vanish. Furthermore, considering (27) we finally obtain

$$\mathrm{d}x_i = -I(1-Z_H-p_b\,Z_B)X_i\,\mathrm{d}\theta = -I\left(1-\frac{\partial H}{\partial I}-p_b\frac{\partial B}{\partial I}\right)X_i\,\mathrm{d}\theta. \tag{38}$$

The demand for cash balances is influenced in the following way:

$$\mathrm{d}H = \left(\sum_{k=1}^{n} \frac{\partial H}{\partial p_k} p_k\right) \mathrm{d}\theta = \Big[-IZ_H + \Big(Z_H + \sum_{j=1}^{B} U_{jH}^0 Z_{jH}\Big) H + \\ + \Big(p_b Z_H + \sum_{j=1}^{B} U_{jB}^0 Z_{jH}\Big) B\Big] \,\mathrm{d}\theta.$$

But, since $Z_H + \sum_{j=1}^{B} U_{jH}^0 Z_{jH} = 1$ and $p_b Z_H + \sum_{j=1}^{B} U_{jB}^0 Z_{jH} = 0$, we have

$$\mathrm{d}H = (-IZ_H + H)\,\mathrm{d}\theta = H\left(1 - \frac{I}{H}\frac{\partial H}{\partial I}\right) \mathrm{d}\theta. \tag{39}$$

Similarly,

$$\mathrm{d}B = (-IZ_B + B)\,\mathrm{d}\theta = B\left(1 - \frac{I}{B}\frac{\partial B}{\partial I}\right) \mathrm{d}\theta. \tag{40}$$

Under the realistic assumption that all of H, $\partial H/\partial I$, $\partial B/\partial I$ are non-negative, we now derive from (38), (39), and (40) the following laws.

1. If I (the initial assets of the consumer) is 0, then $\mathrm{d}x_i = 0$ ($i = 1,..., n$) and $\mathrm{d}H = H\,\mathrm{d}\theta$, $\mathrm{d}B = B\,\mathrm{d}\theta$; that is to say, the demand for any consumption good and the supply of labour are unchanged in spite of the proportional change in all prices, while the demand for cash balances and the demand for bonds change in the same proportion as prices.

2. Suppose $I > 0$; then we have the following possibilities. If $(\partial H/\partial I) + p_b(\partial B/\partial I) < 1$, a proportional rise in all prices gives rise to a decrease or an increase in the demand for a 'real' commodity, according as it is superior or inferior in the 'proper' sense. If $(\partial H/\partial I) + p_b(\partial B/\partial I) > 1$, the reverse is the case, and if $(\partial H/\partial I) + p_b(\partial B/\partial I) = 1$, the demand for any 'real' commodity remains constant.

If the income elasticity of the demand for cash balances, $\epsilon_H = (I/H)\partial H/\partial I$, is zero, the demand for cash balances is increased in the same proportion as prices; if $0 < \epsilon_H < 1$, it increases less than proportionally when $\mathrm{d}\theta > 0$; and if $\epsilon_H > 1$, it decreases when $\mathrm{d}\theta > 0$. The demand for cash balances does not change in spite of the proportional change in prices when $\epsilon_H = 1$.

If $B > 0$ (i.e. if the consumer is a lender), the number of bonds held by him at the end of the period will change as follows. If the income elasticity of the demand for bonds, $\epsilon_B = (I/B)\partial B/\partial I$, is 0, B is increased in the same proportion as prices; but if $0 < \epsilon_B < 1$, it increases less than proportionally when $d\theta > 0$; and if $\epsilon_B > 1$, it decreases when $d\theta > 0$. The number of bonds B is unchanged in spite of the proportional change in prices when $\epsilon_B = 1$.

If $B < 0$ (i.e. if the consumer is a borrower), the number of bonds issued by him $(-B)$ increases proportionally or more than proportionally when $d\theta > 0$ because ϵ_B is non-positive in this case.

3. Lastly, let $I < 0$. What has been said in item 2 all holds *mutatis mutandis*. For example, if $(\partial H/\partial I)+p_b(\partial B/\partial I) < 1$, then the demand for a proper superior 'real' commodity is increased when there is a proportional rise in all prices. If $\partial H/\partial I > 0$, then $\epsilon_H < 0$ because $I < 0$; therefore, the demand for cash balances increases more than proportionally when $d\theta > 0$. If the consumer is a borrower with $\epsilon_B < 1$, the number of bonds issued by him $(-B)$ increases less than proportionally when $d\theta > 0$.

We may now consider an exchange economy in which there are v consumers (denoted by $1, 2,\ldots, v$) and no firms. Then, from the above laws it follows that if $I^j = 0$ $(j = 1,\ldots, v)$, or if $\partial H^j/\partial I^j = 0$ and $p_b\,\partial B^j/\partial I^j = 1$ $(j = 1,\ldots, v)$, then the market demand for each 'real' commodity is homogeneous of degree zero in $p_1,\ldots, p_n$ and the market demand for cash balances is homogeneous of degree one in the same variables. However, since the sum of $\bar{B}^j$ is zero for the entire community (credits and debts cancel), we have $\sum_{j=1}^{v} I^j = M$, where $M \equiv \sum_{j=1}^{v} M^j$ denotes the total quantities of money existing in the economy, so that it should be positive. Therefore, at least one of I^j is necessarily positive. Hence, we find that the conditions for the demand for each real commodity being homogeneous of degree zero in $p_1,..., p_n$ and the demand for cash balances being homogeneous of degree one in the same variables should be

$$\frac{\partial H^j}{\partial I^j} = 0 \quad \text{and} \quad p_b \frac{\partial B^j}{\partial I^j} = 1 \quad (j = 1,..., v). \tag{41}$$

Thus 'homogeneous' demand functions are obtained if all individuals devote their increased initial assets entirely to the acquisition of bonds.

In his paper Patinkin ([**2**], p. 50) arrived at the conclusion that the market demand for real commodities becomes homogeneous of degree zero in $p_1,..., p_n$, either if every individual has no initial stocks of money and bonds—an assumption that, as seen above, cannot hold for every consumer in the economy—or if the partial derivatives of each of the functions x_i with respect to the argument I are identically zero, i.e.

$$\frac{\partial x_i^j}{\partial I^j} = Z_i^j = 0 \quad (i = 1,..., n;\, j = 1,..., v) \tag{42}$$

—an assumption that was rejected by Patinkin because many economic studies show that the income effect is usually nonzero.

Assume, however, that goods $x_1,..., x_n$ are separable from money and bonds; then we have the relation (27). Hence the assumption (42) is reduced to (41) or

$$\frac{\partial x_i^j}{\partial E^j} = X_i^j = 0 \quad (i = 1,..., n;\, j = 1,..., v). \tag{43}$$

Assumption (43) is, of course, contradicted by many economic studies, but it seems to me that assumption (41) is not so far from reality as is the other assumption; it may approximately be satisfied in some cases.

According to Lange ([**1**], p. 22) a proportional rise of all current prices (except interest rates) results in no change in the real demand for cash balances when the elasticities of expectation are all unity; that is to say, if all elasticities of expectation are unity, then

$$\frac{\mathrm{d}H}{H} = \frac{\mathrm{d}p_i}{p_i} \quad (i = 1,..., n). \tag{44}$$

This analysis by Lange would be valid if we could say that

either I or Z_H (or both) are zero when all elasticities of expectation are unity (see (39)). But I is, of course, independent of elasticities of expectation and Z_H ($= \partial H/\partial I$) is not necessarily equal to zero, on the assumption that the elasticities of expectation are all unity or that the probability distribution of the future living standard is unchanged when $H, B, p_1,..., p_n$ are changed proportionally. Therefore, it is not a sufficient condition for (44) that all elasticities of expectation be unity.

5. Analysis of the Monetary Effect

In this section our attention is focused on the monetary effect which was first discussed by Lange ([**1**], pp. 15 ff). He treated it as a social phenomenon and left its individualistic analysis incomplete; but since the social monetary effect is to be derived as the sum of individual monetary effects, we must first analyse the individual monetary effects.

In a monetary economy any demand for a good implies a supply of money in exchange for the good, and any supply of a good implies a corresponding demand for money. Therefore, if we denote the stream of money into a consumer's budget during the present period by M_D and the stream of money offered by him during the same period by M_S, we have

$$M_D \equiv p_n y, \qquad M_S \equiv \sum_1^{n-1} p_i x_i + p_b(B - \bar{B}).$$

(These may be termed, respectively, the flow demand and flow supply of money during the period.) Since $y \equiv$ the supply of labour $= -x_n$, his excess demand for money is given as follows:

$$M_D - M_S \equiv -\sum_1^n p_i x_i - p_b(B - \bar{B}).$$

Taking into account the budget equation (1), we write this in the form

$$M_D - M_S \equiv H - M - \bar{B}.$$

If our consideration is restricted to a proportional change of all prices, we can define the real excess demand for money as

$$e \equiv (H - M - \bar{B})/P,$$

where P is a price index of goods in general, which is defined by

$$p_i = w_i P \qquad (w_i = \text{constant} > 0) \quad (i = 1,..., n).$$

Imitating Lange's definition of the monetary effect, we define the individual monetary effect as follows. From the viewpoint of a particular consumer, the monetary effect is positive when his real excess demand for money diminishes as all prices fall proportionally and increases as all prices rise proportionally. It is negative when the reverse is the case, and it is absent or zero when his real excess demand for money remains unchanged. Therefore, the sign of the monetary effect coincides with the sign of

$$\frac{\mathrm{d}e}{\mathrm{d}P} = \frac{(\mathrm{d}H/\mathrm{d}P)P-(H-M-\bar{B})}{P^2}.$$

Since $\mathrm{d}H/\mathrm{d}P = \sum_{i=1}^{n} (\partial H/\partial p_i)w_i$, it follows from (39) that

$$\frac{\mathrm{d}e}{\mathrm{d}P} = \frac{M}{P^2}\left(1-\frac{\partial H}{\partial I}\right)+\frac{\bar{B}}{P^2}\left[1-(1+p_b)\frac{\partial H}{\partial I}\right].$$

Therefore, putting $\alpha = \partial H/\partial I$ and $\beta = 1/(1+p_b)$, we obtain the signs of the monetary effect as the table below shows. As α is usually less than one, it is very likely that the monetary effect is positive.

	$\alpha < \beta$	$\beta < \alpha < 1$	$1 = \alpha$	$1 < \alpha$
$\bar{B} > 0$	+	?	—	—
$\bar{B} = 0$	+	+	0	—
$\bar{B} < 0$	?	+	+	?

Let us return to an exchange economy with v consumers and no firms. The total excess demand for money on the market is given by

$$\sum_{j=1}^{v} (M_D^j - M_S^j) = \sum_{j=1}^{v} (H^j - I^j),$$

and the sign of the social monetary effect coincides with the sign of

$$\frac{\mathrm{d}E^R}{\mathrm{d}P} = \sum_{j=1}^{v} \frac{\mathrm{d}e^j}{\mathrm{d}P} = \sum_{j=1}^{v} \frac{I^j\{1-(\partial H^j/\partial I^j)\}}{P^2},$$

where E^R represents the total real excess demand for money on the market. With the average of the $\partial H^j/\partial I^j$ $(j = 1,\ldots,v)$ defined as

$$A \equiv \frac{\sum_{j=1}^{v} I^j(\partial H^j/\partial I^j)}{\sum_j I^j},$$

the above equation can be written in the form

$$\frac{\mathrm{d}E^R}{\mathrm{d}P} = \frac{\sum_{j=1}^{v} I^j(1-A)}{P^2} = \frac{M(1-A)}{P^2},$$

where M is the total quantity of money (which is positive). Consequently, if the average of the $\partial H^j/\partial I^j$ is less than unity, the social monetary effect is positive, and if A is larger than unity it is negative. The social monetary effect is zero when $A = 1$.

In particular, if the $\partial H^j/\partial I^j$ are the same for all consumers, we find

$$\frac{\mathrm{d}E^R}{\mathrm{d}P} = \frac{M\{1-(\partial H^j/\partial I^j)\}}{P^2}.$$

In this case, the sign of the social monetary effect depends only on $\partial H^j/\partial I^j$ and is independent of the distribution of I^j. Since it is realistic to assume that $\partial H^j/\partial I^j$ is non-negative and less than 1,[7] it is very probable that the social monetary effect is positive.

6. The Effect of a Change in Interest Rate

In this section we shall examine the effects of a change in interest rate with constant prices. Differentiating (1) and (9) partially with respect to r and solving,

$$\frac{\partial x_i}{\partial r} = \frac{1}{r^2}(B-\bar{B})Z_i - \frac{1}{r^2}\lambda Z_{Bi} - \sum_{j=1}^{B} U^0_{j(r)}\, Z_{ji}, \tag{45}$$

$$\frac{\partial H}{\partial r} = \frac{1}{r^2}(B-\bar{B})Z_H - \frac{1}{r^2}\lambda Z_{BH} - \sum_{j=1}^{B} U^0_{j(r)}\, Z_{jH}, \tag{46}$$

$$\frac{\partial B}{\partial r} = \frac{1}{r^2}(B-\bar{B})Z_B - \frac{1}{r^2}\lambda Z_{BB} - \sum_{j=1}^{B} U^0_{j(r)}\, Z_{jB}, \tag{47}$$

where $U^0_{j(r)}$ denotes the value which $\partial U_j/\partial r$ takes on at the equilibrium point $(j = 1,\ldots, n, H, B)$.

[7] Evidently, this means that if the consumer's initial assets are increased by one unit of cash, less than the entire unit will be devoted to the acquisition of cash.

Now, substituting (27), (28), (29), (30) into (45), we obtain

$$\frac{\partial x_i}{\partial r} = \frac{1}{r^2}(B-\bar{B})X_i - \frac{1}{r^2}(B-\bar{B})(Z_H+p_b Z_B)X_i + $$
$$+\frac{1}{r^2}\lambda(Z_{BH}+p_b Z_{BB})X_i + \sum_{j=1}^{B} U^0_{j(r)}(Z_{jH}+p_b Z_{jB})X_i -$$
$$-\left(\frac{\partial U}{\partial \phi}\right)^{-1} \sum_{j=1}^{n} U^0_{j(r)} X_{ji}. \quad (48)$$

The last term of this equation vanishes, because in view of

$$\frac{\partial U_j}{\partial r} = \frac{\partial \phi}{\partial x_j}\frac{\partial^2 U}{\partial r \partial \phi} \quad (j = 1,\dots, n),$$

we have from (23) $\sum_{j=1}^{n} U^0_{j(r)} X_{ji} = 0.$

Consequently, together with (46) and (47), equation (48) leads to

$$\frac{\partial x_i}{\partial r} = -\left[\frac{\partial H}{\partial r} + p_b \frac{\partial B}{\partial r} - \frac{1}{r^2}(B-\bar{B})\right] X_i. \quad (49)$$

As $H+p_b(B-\bar{B})-M-\bar{B}$ is saving (denoted by S) and M and $\bar{B}$ are independent of r, the part in the brackets on the right-hand side of (49) is equal to $\partial S/\partial r$. Hence

$$\frac{\partial x_i}{\partial r} = -\frac{\partial S}{\partial r} X_i. \quad (50)$$

From (50) we have the following laws.

(a) If saving increases when the interest rate rises, the demand for a 'real' commodity decreases if it is a proper superior good and increases if it is a proper inferior good.

(b) If saving is unchanged in spite of a change in interest rate, the demand for any commodity is unchanged.

(c) If saving decreases when interest rate rises, the reverse of (a) is the case.

By a similar procedure, we can transform (46) and (47) into

$$\frac{\partial H}{\partial r} = \frac{\partial S}{\partial r}(p_b U^0_{HB} - U^0_{BB})/W + p_b(p_b U^0_{H(r)} - U^0_{B(r)} - p_b^2 \lambda)/W, \quad (51)$$

$$\frac{\partial B}{\partial r} = \frac{\partial S}{\partial r}(U^0_{BH} - p_b U^0_{HH})/W - (p_b U^0_{H(r)} - U^0_{B(r)} - p_b^2 \lambda)/W. \quad (52)$$

In each of (51) and (52), the first term represents the income effect that is obtained when a change in interest rate induces a change in the saving of the consumer, while the second term represents the substitution effect that arises when the equilibrium condition $U_H = U_B/p_b$ is disturbed by a change in interest rate.

Let us first ignore the substitution effect on cash and bonds. Since both $(p_b U^0_{HB} - U^0_{BB})/W$ and $(U^0_{BH} - p_b U^0_{HH})/W$ are assumed to be positive (see section 3), we can interpret the results as follows:

(i) if saving is increased by a rise in the interest rate, the demand for cash balances and the number of bonds held at the end of the period will be increased;

(ii) if saving is unchanged in spite of a change in the interest rate, they are constant;

(iii) if saving decreases when the interest rate rises, we obtain the reverse of (i).

Next we examine the substitution effect. We would lose little generality by assuming that the marginal rate of substitution of bonds for cash is increased when r is increased, that is

$$\frac{\partial}{\partial r}\left(\frac{U_B}{U_H}\right) > 0.$$

In fact, it would be reasonable enough to assume that if the rate of interest rises, the quantity of bonds that would just compensate the consumer for the loss of a marginal unit of cash will be decreased. We thus have

$$p_b U^0_{H(r)} - U^0_{B(r)} < 0$$

at the point $(H^0, B^0, p_1, ..., p_n, r)$. Therefore, we arrive at the conclusion that if we neglect the income effect, a rise in interest rate leads to a decrease in the demand for cash balances and to an increase in the number of bonds held at the end of the period.

Assuming that the utility function of the jth consumer is of the form $u^j(x^j_1, ..., x^j_n, B^j/rp, H^j/p)$ (where $p = \sum c_i p_i =$ the price index), Patinkin ([**2**], p. 49) has erroneously deduced that the individual demand functions can be written as

$$\left.\begin{aligned} x_i^j &= f_i^j\left(\frac{p_1}{p},\ldots,\frac{p_n}{p},r,\frac{I^j}{p}\right) \\ B^j &= pf_B^j\left(\frac{p_1}{p},\ldots,\frac{p_n}{p},r,\frac{I^j}{p}\right) \\ H^j &= \quad -\sum_1^n p_i x_i - \frac{B_j}{r} + I^j \end{aligned}\right\}, \tag{53}$$

where $I^j = (\bar{B}^j/r)+\bar{B}^j+M^j$. The correct versions can be obtained by writing $B^j/rp = x_{n+1}^j$ and $H^j/p = x_{n+2}^j$, and putting the budget constraint and the equilibrium conditions in the respective forms,

$$\sum_{i=1}^n \frac{p_i}{p} x_i^j + x_{n+1}^j + x_{n+2}^j = \frac{I^j}{p} \tag{54}$$

and

$$\frac{u_i^j(x_1^j,\ldots,x_{n+2}^j)}{u_k^j(x_1^j,\ldots,x_{n+2}^j)} = \frac{p_i}{p} \quad (i = 1,\ldots,n;\ k = n+1, n+2). \tag{55}$$

We then have from (54) and (55)

$$x_i^j = f_i^j\left(\frac{p_1}{p},\ldots,\frac{p_n}{p},\frac{I^j}{p}\right) \quad (i = 1,\ldots,n+2).$$

Therefore, the individual demand functions must be of the forms

$$\left.\begin{aligned} x_i^j &= f_i^j\left(\frac{p_1}{p},\ldots,\frac{p_n}{p},\frac{I^j}{p}\right) \qquad (i = 1,\ldots,n) \\ B^j &= prf_{n+1}^j\left(\frac{p_1}{p},\ldots,\frac{p_n}{p},\frac{I^j}{p}\right) \\ H^j &= pf_{n+2}^j\left(\frac{p_1}{p},\ldots,\frac{p_n}{p},\frac{I^j}{p}\right) \end{aligned}\right\}. \tag{56}$$

Now let us consider an exchange economy, where the partial derivative of each of the functions (56) with respect to its $(n+1)$th argument I^j/p is globally as well as locally the same for all consumers. Then, as the sum of $\bar{B}^j$ vanishes, the market demand functions are of the forms

$$\left.\begin{aligned} X_i &= F_i\left(\frac{p_1}{p},\dots,\frac{p_n}{p},\frac{M}{p}\right) \qquad (i = 1,\dots, n) \\ B &= prF_{n+1}\left(\frac{p_1}{p},\dots,\frac{p_n}{p},\frac{M}{p}\right) \\ H &= pF_{n+2}\left(\frac{p_1}{p},\dots,\frac{p_n}{p},\frac{M}{p}\right) \end{aligned}\right\}, \tag{57}$$

where $X_i = \sum_{j=1}^{v} x_i^j$, $B = \sum_{j=1}^{v} B^j$, $H = \sum_{j=1}^{v} H^j$, $M = \sum_{j=1}^{v} M^j$. Therefore, from the revised Patinkin functions (57) it follows that (a) the demand for each 'real' good, X_i, (b) saving, $H+p_b B-I$, and (c) the demand for cash balances, H, are all independent of the rate of interest. None of the monetary theories so far developed supports this conclusion. Moreover, in such an economy the rate of interest is indeterminate because each of the monetary equilibrium conditions $H = M$ and $B = 0$ (or $F_{n+1}(p_1/p,\dots,p_n/p, M/p) = 0$) is independent of the rate of interest; consequently we must reject Patinkin's model.

Patinkin assumed that the individual is concerned only with the real value of the bonds he holds and, therefore, his utility function is homogeneous of degree zero in B^j and r. However, when the consumer holds the amount B^j of bonds, he is, of course, paid B^j dollars per period; and when he holds the amount ϵB^j of bonds, he gains ϵB^j dollars per period. Hence, if $\epsilon > 1$, the situation $(x_1^j,\dots,x_n^j, H^j, \epsilon B^j, p, \epsilon r)$ is, clearly, preferred to the situation $(x_1^j,\dots,x_n^j, H^j, B^j, p, r)$, although in both situations the real value of bonds is the same. Consequently, we must conclude that the consumer's utility function is not homogeneous of degree zero in B^j and r.

If the utility function were of the form

$$u^j = U^j\left(x_1^j,\dots,x_n^j,\frac{B^j}{p},\frac{H^j}{p},r\right),$$

then the individual demand functions would not take the forms of (56) but those of (53).

IX. Veblen Effects and Portfolio Selection

M. G. ALLINGHAM *and* M. MORISHIMA

1. Introduction

A MAJOR problem in the theory of value is the introduction of money and financial assets, the main reason being the nature of money as a store of value as well as a medium of exchange, which implies a further role for prices and leads to their introduction into the utility function. This chapter examines the relation between apparently unconnected attempts to deal with the twin problems of the demand for money and prices in the utility function, and provides some extensions.

Section 2 introduces monetary goods, and thus prices, into the utility function, and uses Sono's proposition of separability to interpret the resulting generalized Slutsky equation,(1) so extending the analysis of Chapter VIII in this volume.

The third section considers an alternative reason for introducing prices into the utility function, the 'Veblen hypothesis', and examines Kalman's approach to the problem.(2) This is shown to be unsatisfactory, and some alternatives are suggested.

We then consider more explicitly some problems of portfolio selection. Section 4 examines this under the mean–variance restriction, and shows the relationship between the approach adopted here and the 'standard' approach, as used, for example, by Royama and Hamada [**1**]. The final section works in the more general expected utility framework, examining conditions for portfolio diversification and responses to changes in probabilities and 'risks'.

2. The Generalized Slutsky Equation

Morishima's paper [**2**] reproduced in Chapter VIII of this volume with minor revisions proposes a utility function which

(1) Sono [**1**]. (2) Kalman [**1**].

is in effect of the form

$$u[\phi(x_1,\ldots,x_n), \psi(H, B, p_1,\ldots,p_n, p_b)],$$

where x_i is the quantity of the ith real good with money price p_i ($i = 1,\ldots,n$), H is the amount of cash held (with money price identically unity), and B is the number of bonds held, each paying one unit of money per period, with price p_b. u, ϕ, ψ are real-valued differentiable functions, ϕ being the proper utility function defined on the real goods and ψ that on the monetary goods and prices. The function u is maximized subject to a budget constraint

$$\sum_{i=1}^{n} p_i x_i + H + p_b B = I,$$

where income I is fixed.

We summarize the results obtained by this approach in a more general environment. We now have a real-valued differentiable utility function defined on the quantities of commodities $x_1,\ldots,x_n$ and their prices $p_1,\ldots,p_n$, but we assume that the marginal rate of substitution between commodities i and j is independent of the amount of commodity k and of all prices, for all $i, j \leqq m$, $k > m$ where m is some index, $0 < m < n$. We also assume that commodities $x_{m+1},\ldots, x_n$ and prices $p_1,\ldots, p_n$ are separable from $x_1,\ldots, x_m$. As Sono [**1**] has shown, the utility function may then be written in the form

$$u[\phi(x_1,\ldots,x_m), \psi(x_{m+1},\ldots,x_n, p_1,\ldots,p_n)],$$

which we maximize subject to the budget constraint

$$\sum_{i=1}^{n} p_i x_i = I.$$

(Clearly we are faced with Morishima's money problem if we write our m, n, x_{m+1}, x_{m+2}, p_{m+1}, p_{m+2} as n, $n+2$, H, B, 1, p_b, respectively.) We may term the commodities $m+1,\ldots, n$, whose amounts are denoted by the subvector x^M, as monetary goods, and $1,\ldots, m$, denoted by x^N, as non-monetary goods, following the original phrasing of the problem; later we may interpret the first set as 'Veblen' and the second as 'non-Veblen' goods.

If we obtain the equilibrium conditions for this problem,

differentiate these with respect to p_k, and solve, we again obtain the generalized Slutsky equation

$$\frac{\partial x_i}{\partial p_k} = -x_k Z_i + \lambda Z_{ki} - \sum_{j=1}^{n} u_{j(k)} Z_{ji} \quad (i = 1,..., n), \tag{1}$$

where Z_i, Z_{ki} are now the ratios of the cofactors of p_i, u_{ki} in the determinant

$$\begin{vmatrix} 0 & p_1 & \cdot & \cdot & \cdot & p_n \\ p_1 & u_{11} & \cdot & \cdot & \cdot & u_{1n} \\ \cdot & \cdot & & & & \cdot \\ \cdot & \cdot & & & & \cdot \\ \cdot & \cdot & & & & \cdot \\ p_n & u_{n1} & \cdot & \cdot & \cdot & u_{nn} \end{vmatrix}$$

to the value of the determinant; $u_{j(k)} = \partial u_j / \partial p_k$, and λ is a Lagrangian Multiplier. We may consider the basic equation (1), taking the terms in order, as

price effect = income effect+substitution effect+ want pattern effect

(or Cournot term = Engel term+Slutsky term+Veblen term). The want pattern term, or Veblen effect, is the change in demand arising through a change in tastes (or in preference orderings over commodities) brought about by the change in prices.

This decomposition does not use our assumption of separability. Further decomposition of the terms in this equation does, however, depend on this assumption, and we now follow Sono [**1**] in analysing the effects on both categories of goods (x^N, x^M) of a change in the price of a good in each category under this assumption.

The composition of the terms in the generalized Slutsky equation depends on the relations between the bordered Hessians of the actual utility function of u and of the proper utility functions ϕ and ψ. We define X_i, X_{ki} and Y_i, Y_{ki} analogously to Z_i, Z_{ki}, but for the determinants

$$\begin{vmatrix} 0 & p_1 & \cdot & \cdot & \cdot & p_m \\ p_1 & \phi_{11} & \cdot & \cdot & \cdot & \phi_{1m} \\ \cdot & \cdot & & & & \cdot \\ \cdot & \cdot & & & & \cdot \\ \cdot & \cdot & & & & \cdot \\ p_m & \phi_{m1} & \cdot & \cdot & \cdot & \phi_{mm} \end{vmatrix}$$

and
$$\begin{vmatrix} 0 & p_{m+1} & \cdot & \cdot & \cdot & p_n \\ p_{m+1} & \psi_{m+1\,m+1} & \cdot & \cdot & \cdot & \psi_{m+1\,n} \\ \cdot & \cdot & & & & \cdot \\ \cdot & \cdot & & & & \cdot \\ \cdot & \cdot & & & & \cdot \\ p_n & \psi_{n\,m+1} & \cdot & \cdot & \cdot & \psi_{nn} \end{vmatrix},$$

respectively. The following results then follow from the Laplace determinant theorem in a way exactly analogous to that used by Morishima.

For $i = 1,\ldots, m$:

$$\left.\begin{aligned} Z_i &= X_i - X_i \sum_{j=m+1}^{n} p_j Z_j \\ Z_{ik} = Z_{ki} &= \frac{1}{u_\phi} X_{ki} - X_i \sum_{j=m+1}^{n} p_j Z_{kj} \quad (k \leqq m) \\ Z_{ik} = Z_{ki} &= -X_i \sum_{j=m+1}^{n} p_j Z_{kj} \quad (k > m) \end{aligned}\right\} \qquad (2)$$

and for $i = m+1,\ldots, n$:

$$\left.\begin{aligned} Z_i &= Y_i - Y_i \sum_{j=1}^{m} p_j Z_j \\ Z_{ik} = Z_{ki} &= -Y_i \sum_{j=1}^{m} p_j Z_{kj} \quad (k \leqq m) \\ Z_{ik} = Z_{ki} &= \frac{1}{u_\psi} Y_{ki} - Y_i \sum_{j=1}^{m} p_j Z_{kj} \quad (k > m). \end{aligned}\right\} \qquad (3)$$

We may now consider the composition of the effect of a change in the price of a non-monetary good, starting with the effect on x^N. Using (2) we may write the individual terms in (1) as, for $k \leqq m$, $i = 1,\ldots, m$,

$$-x_k Z_k = -x_k X_i - X_i\Big(-\sum_{j=m+1}^{n} p_j x_k Z_j\Big),$$

$$\lambda Z_{ki} = \lambda' X_{ki} - X_i\Big(\sum_{j=m+1}^{n} p_j \lambda Z_{kj}\Big),$$

$$-\sum_{j=1}^{n} u_{j(k)} Z_{ji} = 0 - X_i\Big(-\sum_{j=m+1}^{n} p_j \sum_{l=1}^{n} u_{l(k)} Z_{lj}\Big),$$

where $\lambda' = \lambda/u_\phi$, which we may consider as, respectively:

income effect = proper income effect + additional income effect via income effect on x^M, substitution effect = proper substitution effect+additional income effect via substitution effect on x^M,

want pattern effect = (zero proper want pattern effect)+ additional effect via want pattern effect on x^M.

The proper income effect is the effect of a change in income, the proper substitution effect that of an income-compensated change in prices, and the proper want pattern effect that of a change in the proper utility function, all with quantities of commodities in the separated group (here x^M) held constant; it is apparent that the proper want pattern effect is zero here as the proper utility function is independent of prices.

Since the price effect is the sum of its components we may combine these expressions in (1) to obtain

$$\frac{\partial x_i}{\partial p_k} = -x_k X_i + \lambda' X_{ki} - X_i \sum_{j=m+1}^{n} p_j \frac{\partial x_j}{\partial p_k}, \tag{4}$$

which we may consider as

price effect on x^N = proper income effect+proper substitution effect+additional income effect via price effect on x^M.

We may similarly decompose the effect on x^M, so we have the individual terms in (1) as, for $k \leqq m$, $i = m+1,\dots, n$,

$$-x_k Z_i = -x_k Y_i - Y_i\Big(-\sum_{j=1}^{m} p_j x_k Z_j\Big),$$

$$\lambda Z_{ki} = 0 - Y_i\Big(\sum_{j=1}^{m} p_j \lambda Z_{kj}\Big),$$

$$-\sum_{j=1}^{n} u_{j(k)} Z_{ji} = -\sum_{j=m+1}^{n} \psi_{j(k)} Y_{ji} - Y_i\Big(\sum_{j=1}^{m} p_j \sum_{l=1}^{n} u_{l(k)} Z_{lj}\Big),$$

which we may consider as

income effect = proper income effect+additional income effect via income effect on x^N,

substitution effect = (zero proper substitution effect)+ additional income effect via substitution effect on x^N, want pattern effect = proper want pattern effect+additional income effect via want pattern effect on x^N.

Combining these we similarly have

price effect on x^M = proper income effect+proper want pattern effect+additional income effect via price effect on x^N.

We next consider the composition of the effect of a change in the price of a monetary good, again starting with the effect on x^N. Now using (2) we may write the individual terms in (1) as, for $k > m$, $i = 1,\dots,m$,

$$-x_k Z_i = -x_k X_i - X_i\Big(-\sum_{j=m+1}^{n} p_j x_k Z_j\Big),$$

$$\lambda Z_{ki} = 0 - X_i\Big(\sum_{j=m+1}^{n} p_j \lambda Z_{kj}\Big),$$

$$-\sum_{j=1}^{n} u_{j(k)} Z_{ji} = 0 - X_i\Big(-\sum_{j=m+1}^{n} p_j \sum_{l=1}^{n} u_{l(k)} Z_{lj}\Big),$$

which we may consider as

income effect = proper income effect+additional income effect via income effect on x^M,

substitution effect = (zero proper substitution effect)+ additional income effect via substitution effect on x^M,

want pattern effect = (zero proper want pattern effect)+ additional income effect via want pattern effect on x^M.

Again, combining these expressions in (1) we obtain

$$\frac{\partial x_i}{\partial p_k} = -x_k X_i - X_i \sum_{j=m+1}^{n} p_j \frac{\partial x_j}{\partial p_k}, \tag{5}$$

which we may consider as

price effect on x^N = proper income effect+additional income effect via price effect on x^M.

We may similarly decompose the effect on x^M, so we have the individual terms in (1) as, for $k > m$, $i = m+1,\dots, n$,

$$-x_k Z_i = -x_k Y_i - Y_i\Big(-\sum_{j=1}^{m} p_j x_k Z_j\Big),$$

$$\lambda Z_{ki} = \lambda'' Y_{ki} - Y_i\Big(\sum_{j=1}^{m} p_j \lambda Z_{kj}\Big),$$

$$-\sum_{j=1}^{n} u_{j(k)} Z_{ji} = -\sum_{j=m+1}^{n} \psi_{j(k)} Y_{ji} - Y_i\Big(-\sum_{j=1}^{n} p_j \sum_{l=1}^{n} u_{l(k)} Z_{lj}\Big),$$

where $\lambda'' = \lambda/u_\psi$, which we may consider as

income effect = proper income effect + additional income effect via income effect on x^N,

substitution effect = proper substitution effect + additional income effect via substitution effect on x^N,

want pattern effect = proper want pattern effect + additional income effect via want pattern effect on x^N.

Combining these we again have

price effect on x^M = proper income effect + proper substitution effect + proper want pattern effect + additional income effect via price effect on x^N.

As we do not have definite qualitative comparative statical results in the simple case where prices do not enter the utility function, it is clear that we also lack these in our more general case. We may, however, obtain qualitative results in terms of the basic properties of the commodities, that is, properties displayed in the simple Slutsky equation; this is equivalent to showing the relationship between superior–inferior and substitute–complement properties in the simple Slutsky equation and their analogues in the modified Slutsky equation. This has been investigated by Morishima [**2**] for non-monetary commodities, so we merely summarize these results and extend them to monetary commodities.

A commodity, i, is said to be proper (or Hicksian) superior if, when some price is increased, the proper income effect in the generalized Slutsky equation for this commodity is negative (that is, if $X_i > 0$ for a non-monetary commodity, or if $Y_i > 0$ for a monetary commodity), and general superior if the (over-all) income effect is negative (that is, if $Z_i > 0$); the converse applies for inferiority. Using the relationship (2) Morishima shows that if some of an increase in income is spent on non-monetary goods, the proper superior non-monetary goods are general superior, and conversely. By the same reasoning, an analogous result applies for monetary goods, so that as long as x^N and x^M are both general superior in aggregate, all proper superior commodities are general superior and conversely.

Two commodities, i and j, both non-monetary or both monetary, are said to be proper (or Hicksian) substitutes if, when the price of i is increased, the proper substitution effect in the Slutsky equation for j is positive (that is, if $X_{ij} > 0$, or if $Y_{ij} > 0$), and general substitutes if the (over-all) substitution effect is positive (that is, if $Z_{ij} > 0$); the converse applies for complements. (Note that both relations are symmetric.) Here we have the result for non-monetary commodities that, if both commodities are (proper) superior or inferior, then proper complements are general complements and general substitutes are proper substitutes, while if one commodity is (proper) superior and the other inferior, then proper substitutes are general substitutes and general complements are proper complements; these implications are, however, not reversible. As a special case of this, the general self-substitution effect for any commodity is greater in absolute value than the corresponding proper effect. Again, the same reasoning may be used to apply these results to monetary goods.

We are then left with the qualitative effect of a change in price of a monetary good on the demand for a non-monetary (or of a non-monetary on that of a monetary). Here we take the income and substitution properties together: in the case where $i \leqq m$, $k > m$, we may write the generalized Slutsky equation

(1) as (5) or as

$$\frac{\partial x_i}{\partial p_k} = -X_i\left(x_k + \sum_{j=m+1}^{n} p_j \frac{\partial x_j}{\partial p_k}\right) = -X_i \frac{\partial M}{\partial p_k},$$

where M is the expenditure on all monetary goods. This gives the comparative statical result that if aggregate expenditure on monetary goods increases when one of their prices increases, the demand for a non-monetary good decreases if it is a proper superior good and increases if it is a proper inferior good. From the form of (3), an analogous result applies where $i > m$, $k \leqq m$.

3. Analysis of the Veblen Effect

We have so far considered the theory of consumer demand when prices enter into the utility function in connection with the demand for money. There are, however, alternative reasons why we may be interested in consumer behaviour under these conditions, particularly the well-known Veblen effect, or that quality may be judged by price; these are independent of the monetary effect, and may exist in a non-monetary economy. The more general problem then concerns a utility function of the form

$$u(x_1,\ldots, x_n, p_1,\ldots, p_n)$$

with the standard budget identity. As shown above, the generalized Slutsky equation resulting from this form is given by (1), which indicates the existence of the want pattern or Veblen term. The above section does not, however, examine the properties of this term, which is the problem we consider here. In the general case, we cannot sign any of the terms in this equation, except Z_{ii}, so we have no qualitative comparative statical results; to obtain these then it is necessary to consider restrictions on u.

This has been considered by Kalman [**1**], but in a way that is not completely satisfactory. We first examine the deficiencies in this existing approach, and then present our alternatives.

Kalman commences with the general utility function referred to above, assuming the usual ordinal utility axioms, and also that

$$u_i > 0, \quad u_{(i)} \geqq 0 \quad (i = 1,\ldots, n),$$

with strict inequality in the latter holding for at least one i, where $u_{(i)} = \partial u/\partial p_i$. The generalized Slutsky equation (1) is then derived in the usual way.

Kalman derives various comparative statical results under two alternative 'qualitative' restrictions on u. The first of these is that the marginal utility of commodity i is (locally) independent of the prices of all other commodities, that is

$$u_{i(j)} = 0 \quad (i \neq j).$$

This, however, is a cardinal requirement. Consider some arbitrary increasing monotonic transform of the utility function

$$u^* = F(u), \quad F' > 0, \quad F'' \neq 0;$$

then if utility is measurable only ordinally, we may equivalently write the above condition in terms of u^* as

$$u^*_{i(j)} = 0 \quad (i \neq j),$$

that is
$$F'u_{i(j)} + F''u_i u_{(j)} = 0,$$

requiring
$$u_i u_{(j)} = 0 \quad (i,j = 1,..., n, j \neq i),$$

and thus, as all $u_i > 0$,

$$u(j) = 0 \quad (j = 1,..., n),$$

contradicting the assumptions.

The second 'qualitative' restriction is that the change in the marginal utility of commodity i with respect to a change in the price of j is equal to the change in the marginal utility of i with respect to a change in the quantity of j multiplied by the price of j, that is

$$u_{i(j)} = p_j u_{ij}.$$

This, however, is not independent of the units of measurement of commodities. Measuring commodity j in new units β ($\beta \neq 1$) times the old, we have

$$\frac{1}{\beta} u_{i(j)} = \beta p_j \beta u_{ij},$$

which, with the original conditions, implies $\beta = 1$, contradicting our assumption.

It follows then that Kalman's two results are inappropriate even in his model. Perhaps more important, however, is the relevance of the model itself in this framework, for the assumption that all $u_{(i)} \geqq 0$ with strict equality for some i implies that inflation increases the level of utility, which in view of the arbitrariness of the scale of prices is untenable.

We now consider two alternatives to Kalman's approach: first, a simple case based on values, and then an interesting more general case.

If we assume that it is values rather than quantities which enter into the utility function, then u has the form

$$u\left(x_1\frac{p_1}{p_0},\ldots, x_n\frac{p_n}{p_0}\right),$$

where $p_0 = \sum_{i=1}^{n} a_i p_i$ represents the general price level, the a_i being some fixed weights, with $a_i \geqq 0$, $\sum a_i = 1$ (for example, the proportions of income *originally* spent on the commodities, or Laspeyre's index weights). This is a 'legitimate' assumption, the inflation problem being avoided by the introduction of p_0. Writing $v_i = x_i(p_i/p_0)$ we have the utility function as

$$u(v_1,\ldots, v_n)$$

and the budget constraint as

$$\sum_{i=1}^{m} v_i = I/p_0 \equiv Y.$$

If we treat this as a problem in the variables v_i, obtain the equilibrium conditions, differentiate with respect to p_k, and solve, we obtain the Slutsky equation equivalent

$$\frac{\partial v_i}{\partial p_k} = -\frac{a_k Y}{p_0} H_i,$$

where H_i is the ratio of the cofactor of the ith '1' in the determinant of the matrix

$$\begin{bmatrix} 0 & 1 \\ 1 & \dfrac{\partial^2 u}{\partial v_j \partial v_i} \end{bmatrix} = \begin{bmatrix} 1/p_0 & & & 0 \\ & p_0/p_1 & & \\ & & \ddots & \\ 0 & & & p_0/p_n \end{bmatrix} \begin{bmatrix} 0 & p_i \\ p_j & u_{ji} \end{bmatrix} \begin{bmatrix} 1/p_0 & & & 0 \\ & p_0/p_1 & & \\ & & \ddots & \\ 0 & & & p_0/p_n \end{bmatrix}$$

to the value of this determinant (writing $\partial^2 u/\partial x_i \partial x_j$ as u_{ij}). It follows then that

$$H_i = p_i Z_i$$

where Z_i is interpreted as before, so we have

$$\frac{\partial v_i}{\partial p_k} = -a_k Y \frac{p_i}{p_0} Z_i.$$

Thus, in value terms we have no substitution term, and the income effect is of the same sign as the proper income effect on x_i, $-x_k Z_i$. We may now immediately obtain our results in quantity terms, since

$$\frac{\partial v_i}{\partial p_k} = \frac{p_i}{p_0}\frac{\partial x_i}{\partial p_k} + x_i\left(\frac{\delta_{ik}}{p_0} - \frac{a_k p_i}{p_0^2}\right)$$

so we have

$$\frac{\partial x_i}{\partial p_k} = -\left(\frac{a_k Y}{x_k}\right) x_k Z_i + x_i\left(\frac{a_k}{p_0} - \frac{\delta_{ik}}{p_i}\right).$$

This is our new Slutsky equation, which we may interpret as

price effect = modified income effect+modified substitution effect.

The modified income effect is simply the original income effect modified by the factor $a_k Y/x_k$. Clearly, the modified and original effects will in general differ, but on average they will be the same. This is because the sum of the modified effects, weighted by prices, is

$$-\sum_k p_k a_k Y Z_i = -I Z_i$$

as $\sum a_k p_k = p_0$ and $p_0 Y = I$, which is the same as the weighted sum of original effects

$$-\sum_k p_k x_k Z_i = -I Z_i.$$

Thus, over- and under-modifications are compensating.

The modified substitution effect is a combination of the original substitution and want pattern effects plus the difference between the original and modified income effects; it is purely technical—that is, independent of the curvature of indifference curves. Because of its technical nature, we have definite qualitative information on this term. If $k \neq i$, it reduces to $x_i(a_k/p_0)$ which is clearly positive, while if $k = i$, it becomes $(x_i/p_0 p_i)(a_i p_i - p_0)$ which is negative since $a_i p_i < p_0$; the matrix of modified substitution effects is thus of the 'gross substitutes' form. We may compare the properties of this matrix with those of the matrix of proper or Hicksian substitution terms, X_{ij}. The latter has the following well-known properties: (i) negative diagonal, $X_{ii} < 0$; (ii) symmetry, $X_{ij} = X_{ji}$; (iii) zero weighted row sums, $\sum_j p_j X_{ij} = 0$; (iv) Hicksian stability, principal minors alternating in sign starting with $X_{ii} < 0$, and negative definiteness $\sum_i^{n-1} \sum_j^{n-1} \xi_i \xi_j X_{ij} < 0$. We have already shown that (i) holds for the modified terms; (ii), however, does not, since this would clearly require $x_i a_j = x_j a_i$, which, given the fixed nature of the as, cannot hold in general; (iii) continues to apply, since the modified weighted row sums are

$$\sum_j \frac{a_j p_j}{p_0} - \frac{p_i}{p_i}$$

which is zero since both terms are unity. Finally, in (iv) we have the property of principal minors alternating in sign from the gross substitutes form of the matrix and the zero row sum property, though we do not necessarily have negative (quasi) definiteness.

Finally we consider an interesting and less restrictive assumption, that the marginal rate of substitution between any pair of commodities is independent of the prices of all other commodities, that is

$$\partial\left(\frac{u_i}{u_j}\right) \Big/ \partial p_k = 0 \quad (i, j, k = 1, \ldots, n, k \neq i, j).$$

Again we may note that this assumption is independent of the scale of measurement of utility, quantities, or prices. Further, such an assumption is non-vacuous, for a sufficient condition for it is that the utility function should have the form

$$u = u[\phi(x_1, \ldots, x_n) + \phi^1(x_1, p_1) + \ldots + \phi^n(x_n, p_n), p_1, \ldots, p_n].$$

For example, this would imply that the marginal rate of substitution between diamonds and rubies was independent of the price (but not quantity) of sapphires, as well as the prices of non-Veblen goods, but may depend on the prices of diamonds and rubies.

We have then

$$\partial\left(\frac{u_i}{u_j}\right)\Big/\partial p_k = \frac{1}{u_j^2}(u_j u_{i(k)} - u_i u_{j(k)}) = 0,$$

so $$u_{i(k)}/u_i = u_{j(k)}/u_j \equiv \mu_k \quad (i = 1,\ldots,n, i \neq k).$$

We now write

$$\partial\left(\frac{u_k}{u_j}\right)\Big/\partial p_k = \frac{1}{u_j^2}(u_j u_{k(k)} - u_k u_{j(k)}) \equiv \epsilon_j > 0,$$

so $$u_{k(k)} = \epsilon_j u_j + \frac{u_k}{u_j} u_{j(k)} = \epsilon_j u_j + \mu_k u_k.$$

Now if we obtain the equilibrium conditions and partially differentiate these with respect to p_k, we obtain

$$\begin{bmatrix} 0 & p_i \\ p_j & u_{ji} \end{bmatrix}\begin{bmatrix} -\dfrac{\partial\lambda}{\partial p_k} \\ \dfrac{\partial x_i}{\partial p_k} \end{bmatrix} = \begin{bmatrix} -x_k \\ -u_{1(k)} \\ \vdots \\ -u_{k(k)} + \lambda \\ \vdots \\ -u_{n(k)} \end{bmatrix} = -\begin{bmatrix} 0 \\ \mu_k \lambda p_1 \\ \vdots \\ \mu_k \lambda p_k \\ \vdots \\ \mu_k \lambda p_n \end{bmatrix} + \begin{bmatrix} -x_k \\ 0 \\ \vdots \\ \lambda - \epsilon_j u_j \\ \vdots \\ 0 \end{bmatrix}$$

since $u_{i(k)} = \mu_k u_i = \mu_k \lambda p_i$ $(i \neq k)$ from the equilibrium conditions. We may write this system as

$$\begin{bmatrix} 0 & p_i \\ p_j & u_{ji} \end{bmatrix}\begin{bmatrix} -\dfrac{\partial\lambda}{\partial p_k} + \mu_k \lambda \\ \dfrac{\partial x_i}{\partial p_k} \end{bmatrix} = \begin{bmatrix} -x_k \\ 0 \\ \vdots \\ \lambda - \epsilon_j u_j \\ \vdots \\ 0 \end{bmatrix}$$

which when solved for $\partial x_i/\partial p_k$ gives the modified Slutsky equation

$$\frac{\partial x_i}{\partial p_k} = -x_k Z_i + \lambda Z_{ki} - \epsilon_j u_j Z_{ki},$$

that is

price effect = income effect + substitution effect + want pattern effect;

equivalently, we may write this as

$$\frac{\partial x_i}{\partial p_k} = -x_k Z_i + (\lambda - \epsilon_j u_j) Z_{ki},$$

or

price effect = income effect + modified substitution effect.

We now define the Veblen elasticity of k, ν_k, to be the elasticity of the marginal rate of substitution between the commodity k and *any* other commodity j with respect to the price of k, that is

$$\nu_k = \frac{\partial(u_k/u_j)}{\partial p_k} \frac{p_k}{u_k/u_j}.$$

From the equilibrium conditions $u_i = \lambda p_i$, so we may write this as

$$\nu_k = p_j \frac{\partial(u_k/u_j)}{\partial p_k} = p_j \epsilon_j = \frac{u_{k(k)}}{\lambda} - \frac{\mu_k u_k}{\lambda},$$

which makes clear its independence of the index j. It is then immediate from the *modified* Slutsky equation that if $\nu_k < 1$, substitutes are modified substitutes and conversely, while if $\nu_k > 1$, substitutes are modified complements and conversely. In the limiting case where $\nu_k = 1$, the modified substitution effect vanishes, and, of course, where $\nu_k = 0$, there is no modification in the substitution effect.

We have then the appealing result that under this assumption the introduction of prices into the utility function does not affect the income effect and maintains the direction of the substitution effect if the Veblen elasticity is less than unity, reversing it if this exceeds unity.

4. Portfolio Selection: The Mean–Variance Approach

The general subjective equilibrium approach to the demand for financial assets is now reviewed from the viewpoint of portfolio selection. Morishima [2] considered a two-period decision by the individual whose utility function is defined on his current consumption of commodities and the subjective probability distribution of his future living standard. In the current period he consumes commodities of the amounts $x = [x_1,..., x_n]$ and holds assets of $y = [y_1,..., y_m]$, their prices being $p = [p_1,..., p_n]$

and $q = [q_1,..., q_m]$, respectively. Throughout, we ignore borrowing, and assume that $y_i \geqq 0$ for all i.

If v_i is the real value of a unit of asset i, we may represent the individual's future living standards by the index

$$\xi = \sum_i v_i y_i. \tag{6}$$

The vs, however, are stochastic variables which we assume have the following subjective expected values and variance–covariances:

$$E(v_i) = \mu_i \quad (i = 1,..., m),$$

$$E[(v_i - \mu_i)(v_j - \mu_j)] = \sigma_{ij} \quad (i, j = 1,..., m).$$

We then have

$$\mu \equiv E(\xi) = \sum_i \mu_i y_i,$$

$$\sigma \equiv E(\xi - \mu)^2 = \sum_i \sum_j \sigma_{ij} y_i y_j.$$

We assume that present and future consumption decisions are separable, so we may write the individual's utility function as

$$U[\phi(x), \xi].$$

We also assume that the individual acts in accordance with the von Neumann–Morgenstern axioms so his chosen y maximizes the expected value of utility. In this section, we impose the further restriction that the individual believes that each v_i is normally distributed, or alternatively, that his utility function is quadratic in ξ. Under such a restriction, it is well known that we may write his expected utility function in the form(3)

$$u[\phi(x), f(\mu, \sigma)],$$

where ϕ and f are the proper utility functions defined on current consumption and future living standards, respectively. We assume that the partial derivatives u_ϕ, u_f, ϕ_{x_i} $(i = 1,..., n)$, f_μ are positive, and that f_σ is negative.

We may now note, from the final case of section 2, the effect on some asset y_k of a change in the current price of some asset,

(3) Such a form may be derived from the original Morishima function by assuming that the individual's subjective probability distribution of ξ may be represented by its first two moments μ and σ; for example, if this were normal.

q_r. We assume that a change in q_r induces a change in the expected real value of asset r, μ_r, all variances and covariances, σ_{ij} $(i, j = 1,..., m)$, as well as all the other expected real values μ_i, $i \neq r$, being unaffected. We then have

total effect on y_k = proper income effect+proper substitution effect+proper want pattern effect+ additional income effect via price effect on x.

These proper effects are all independent of x; we may investigate these by examining the maximization of

$$f\Big(\sum_i \mu_i y_i, \sum_i \sum_j \sigma_{ij} y_i y_j\Big)$$

subject to the constraint

$$\sum_i q_i y_i = I - \sum_i p_i x_i \equiv W.$$

The first-order conditions for this problem are

$$f_\mu \mu_i + 2f_\sigma \sum \sigma_{ij} y_j = \lambda q_i \quad (i = 1,..., m), \tag{7}$$

where λ is a Lagrangian multiplier. Differentiating these and the constraint with respect to q_r gives the system

$$\begin{bmatrix} 0 & q_i \\ q_j & g_{ji} \end{bmatrix} \begin{bmatrix} -\dfrac{\partial \lambda}{\partial q_r} \\ \dfrac{\partial y_j}{\partial q_r} \end{bmatrix} = \begin{bmatrix} -y_r \\ \lambda \delta_{jr} + g_j \end{bmatrix},$$

where

$$g_{ji} = f_{\mu\mu} \mu_j \mu_i + 2f_{\mu\sigma} \mu_j \sum_h \sigma_{ih} y_h + 2f_{\sigma\mu} \mu_i \sum_h \sigma_{jh} y_h + \\ + 2f_\sigma \sigma_{ji} + 4f_{\sigma\sigma} (\sum_h \sigma_{jh} y_h)(\sum_h \sigma_{ih} y_h)$$

and $$g_j = -\Big(f_\mu \delta_{jr} + f_{\mu\mu} \mu_j y_r + 2f_{\sigma\mu} y_r \sum_h \sigma_{jh} y_h\Big) \frac{\mathrm{d}\mu_r}{\mathrm{d}q_r},$$

δ_{jr} being the Kronecker delta. Solving this gives the proper 'price' effect

$$\frac{\partial y_k}{\partial q_r} = -y_r Y_k + \lambda Y_{rk} - [f_\mu Y_{rk} + f_{\mu\mu} y_r (\sum_j \mu_j Y_{jk}) + \\ + 2f_{\sigma\mu} y_r \sum_j (\sum_h \sigma_{jh} y_h) Y_{jk}] \frac{\mathrm{d}\mu_r}{\mathrm{d}q_r},$$

where Y_k, Y_{rk} are the ratios of the cofactors of q_k, g_{rk} in the determinant

$$\begin{vmatrix} 0 & q_1 & \cdot & \cdot & \cdot & q_m \\ q_1 & g_{11} & \cdot & \cdot & \cdot & g_{1m} \\ \cdot & \cdot & & & & \cdot \\ \cdot & \cdot & & & & \cdot \\ \cdot & \cdot & & & & \cdot \\ q_m & g_{m1} & \cdot & \cdot & \cdot & g_{mm} \end{vmatrix}$$

to the value of the determinant. Substituting for $\sum_h \sigma_{jh} y_h$ from (7) and noting that $\sum_j q_j Y_{jk} = 0$, we have

$$\frac{\partial y_k}{\partial q_r} = -y_r Y_k + \lambda Y_{rk} + f_\sigma \sum_j \left(R\delta_{jr} + \frac{\partial R}{\partial \mu} y_r \mu_j\right) \frac{d\mu_r}{dq_r} Y_{jk}, \tag{8}$$

where $R = -f_\mu / f_\sigma$, the marginal rate of substitution between μ and σ. On the right-hand side of this expression, the first term represents the proper income effect, the second the proper substitution effect, and the third the proper want pattern effect. Note that the part in the brackets on the right-hand side is simply $\partial R_j / \partial \mu_r$, where $R_j = -f_\mu \mu_j / f_\sigma$.

We may now show the relationship between this and the portfolio selection approach of Royama and Hamada [**1**], who assume a utility function of the form

$$U(\xi) = \xi - \tfrac{1}{2} a \xi^2,$$

where a is a sufficiently small positive constant, so that it may be assumed that $1/a > \xi > 0$. It then follows that their problem of maximizing the expected value of $U(\xi)$ subject to the constraint

$$\sum_i q_i y_i = W$$

is a special case of our above problem. In fact, in the Royama–Hamada problem we have effectively

$$E[U(\xi)] = f(\mu, \sigma) = \mu - \tfrac{1}{2} a \mu^2 - \tfrac{1}{2} a \sigma,$$

so

$$f_\mu = 1 - a\mu, \quad f_{\mu\mu} = -a, \quad f_\sigma = -\tfrac{1}{2} a, \quad f_{\sigma\sigma} = f_{\sigma\mu} = 0.$$

Further, they are concerned with effects on the ys of an autonomous change in the expected future value, or rate of return, of asset r (not a change of it induced by a change in the current price q_r), so that current prices are fixed at some values and consequently there are no proper income and substitution effects in their fundamental equations:

$$\frac{\partial y_k}{\partial \mu_r} = f_\sigma RY_{rk} + f_\sigma \frac{\partial R}{\partial \mu} y_r \sum \mu_j Y_{jk}. \tag{9}$$

They have shown that the second term can be interpreted as $y_r \left[\frac{\partial y_k}{\partial E(\xi)}\right]_{\mu_i\text{s constant}}$ and have identified the first and second terms as the substitution effect and the income effect, respectively. These, however, are no more than components of the want pattern effect.

A change in μ_r affects the individual's want pattern via two channels: through the change in the relativity of μ_r to other μ_is, and through the change in the absolute level of $\mu = \sum_i \mu_i y_i$. In order to obtain the pure effect on y_k of the former, we have to introduce an imaginary change in μ so as to leave the individual on the same level of μ as before. Such a compensated purely relative change in μ_r gives rise to a change in the y_is, since, as (7) shows, the marginal rates of substitution between the y_is depend on their relative expected real values. This effect, which we may call the relative want pattern effect, is represented by the first term in (9). On the other hand, the change in the absolute level of μ induced by the change in μ_r affects the marginal rate of substitution between μ and σ. If $\partial R/\partial \mu > 0$, then the individual will be prepared to bear more risk than before when the absolute level of μ is raised. Such a change in the individual's risk aversion brings about a change in the holding of assets, which is represented by the second term of (9) and may be called the absolute want pattern effect. Evidently, a similar analysis may be made if a change in a current price q_r induces a change in the variance of the real value of an asset or the covariance of the real values of some two assets.

5. Portfolio Selection: A More General Approach

We now consider the model of the previous section without making the mean–variance restriction. As before, the individual maximizes his expected utility

$$E\,U[\phi(x), \xi]$$

subject to his budget constraint

$$\sum p_i x_i + \sum q_i y_i = I,$$

so, if some q_i is changed, we have

total effect on y_k = proper income effect+proper substitution effect+proper want pattern effect+ additional income effect via price effect on x.

Now proper effects on y_k are effects with x held constant, so the three proper effects are obtained by maximizing

$$E\,U[\xi;\, \phi(x)] \equiv E\,\psi(\xi) \tag{10}$$

subject to

$$\sum q_i y_i = I - \sum p_i x_i \equiv I'. \tag{11}$$

We will assume that the individual considers there to be a finite number of states of the world, and that he attaches a subjective probability $\pi(s)$ to state s. Then as $\xi = \sum v_i y_i$, we may write his maximand $E\,\psi(\xi)$ as

$$\sum_{s \in S} \psi\Big[\sum_i v_i(s) y_i\Big]\pi(s),$$

where $v_i(s)$ is the value that v_i takes under state s (known with certainty), and S is the set of all states to which a non-zero probability is attached.

We first consider under what conditions the individual will diversify his portfolio, that is, hold non-zero amounts of more than one asset. Let us compare the ratios of the real values of assets in the next period in state s, $v_i(s)$, to their current prices, q_i. Those assets which have the largest ratio are called 'top' assets, and the set of the top assets in state s is denoted by T_s. Let the set of assets which are top in *all* states, that is, the intersection, $\bigcap_{s \in S} T_s$, be represented by T. The budget equation and the real value of wealth in the next period may be expressed as

$$q \cdot y = \sum_{i \in T} q_i y_i + \sum_{i \notin T} q_i y_i = I',$$

and $$v(s)y = \sum_{i \in T} v_i(s)y_i + \sum_{i \notin T} v_i(s)y_i = W(s),$$

respectively.

Now put $y_i = 0$ for $i \notin T$ and determine y_is for $i \in T$ such that they satisfy $\sum_{i \in T} q_i y_i = I'$. Let y^0 be a point which is determined in this way, then it is clear that $W(s)$ is maximized at y^0 subject to the budget equation. This is true for all s of S because the assets belonging to T are always top throughout all s of S. Thus, $v(s)y^0 \geqq v(s)y$ for all $s \in S$ for all y fulfilling the budget constraint, so that we obtain

$$\sum_s \psi[v(s)y^0]\pi(s) \geqq \sum_s \psi[v(s)y]\pi(s)$$

for all y fulfilling the budget equation. Hence, y^0 is an equilibrium point.

This general argument for non-diversification covers the following three special cases in which it is obvious that the individual chooses an undiversified portfolio. Firstly, when there is no uncertainty, S contains only one element, say a state s, and the set of top assets is not empty; i.e. $T = T_s$; the individual does not hold those assets which are non-top. Secondly, if the expectations of the *relative* real values of assets in the next period are certain, the $v(s)$s, $s \in S$, are proportional to each other. Then $T_s = T$ for all $s \in S$; the problem of maximizing $\sum_s \psi[v(s)y]\pi(s)$ subject to the budget equation is reduced to the problem of maximizing $v(s)y$ for any s in S under the same constraint. Thirdly, if it is certain that the ratio of the expected real value of a unit of asset i to its current price is higher than the similar ratios of all other assets, then i is the sole member of T and the individual spends his entire income on asset i.

However, the emptiness of the intersection T of the sets of the top assets is not sufficient for the diversification. This may be illustrated as follows. Let r and t be any two states with which positive probabilities are associated. Assume that there are only two assets, 1 and 2, and $v_1(r)/q_1 > v_2(r)/q_2$ and $v_1(t)/q_1 < v_2(t)/q_2$. Using the budget equation to eliminate $v_2 y_2$ from the equations of the real value of wealth in the next period in states r and t, we have

$$W(r) = k_{1r}q_1y_1 + k_{2r}(I' - q_1y_1)$$

and
$$W(t) = k_{1t}q_1y_1 + k_{2t}(I' - q_1y_1),$$

where $k_{is} = v_i(s)/q_i$ $(i = 1, 2;\ s = r, t)$. The expected utility may be written

$$\psi[k_{1r}q_1y_1 + k_{2r}(I' - q_1y_1)]\pi(r) + \psi[k_{1t}q_1y_1 + k_{2t}(I' - q_1y_1)]\pi(t),$$

which is maximized at $q_1 y_1 = I'$ when $\pi(t)$ is small enough and at $q_1 y_1 = 0$ when $\pi(r)$ is small enough. The expected utility is maximized at $q_1 y_1$ which is positive but less than I', if and only if neither $\pi(r)$ nor $\pi(t)$ is too small. For diversification, we require, in addition to the emptiness of T, that the probability distribution be more or less even; in fact, in the m asset case, complete diversification implies that 'similar' probabilities are attached to at least m states which have disjoint sets of top assets.

We now consider proper want pattern effects on $y_1,\ldots, y_m$ of a change in the probability distribution $\pi(s)$ $(s = 1,\ldots, s)$. Among all possible changes, the following two are of particular interest: (i) a change in $\pi(s)$ such that it gives rise to an increase in the expectation of the real value of a unit of asset i in the next period, with those of all other assets and the variance of the real value of wealth being constant; and (ii) a change in $\pi(s)$ such that it gives rise to an increase in the variance of the unit real value of asset i in the next period, with those of other assets and the covariances of the unit real values of any two assets as well as the expected values of the unit real values of all assets being constant. Their counterparts in our model may be produced by specifying changes in $\pi(s)$.

Let r be a state in which $v_i(r) > \alpha q_i$ and $v_j(r) = \alpha q_j$ for all j other than i, where α is a positive number and t another state in which $v_i(t) < \alpha q_i$ and $v_j(t) = \alpha q_j$ for all j other than i. Suppose the probability attached to r, $\pi(r)$, is increased with a compensating decrease in the probability attached to t, $\pi(t)$; that is to say,

$$\Delta\pi(r) > 0 \quad \text{and} \quad \Delta\pi(r) + \Delta\pi(t) = 0. \tag{12}$$

Such a change in the probability distribution implies that the expectation of the real value of a unit of asset i in the next period, μ_i, rises, while those of other assets are left unchanged, because

$$\mu_i^1 = \sum_s \pi^1(s)v_i(s) = \sum_s \pi^0(s)v_i(s)+\Delta\pi(r)v_i(r)+\Delta\pi(t)v_i(t)$$
$$= \sum_s \pi^0(s)v_i(s)+\Delta\pi(r)(v_i(r)-v_i(t)) > \sum_s \pi^0(s)v_i(s) = \mu_i^0, \quad (13)$$

and

$$\mu_j^1 = \sum_s \pi^1(s)v_j(s) = \sum_s \pi^0(s)v_j(s)+\Delta\pi(r)v_j(r)+\Delta\pi(t)v_j(t)$$
$$= \sum_s \pi^0(s)v_j(s) = \mu_j^0, \qquad \text{for all } j \neq i, \quad (14)$$

where $\pi^0(s)$ and $\pi^1(s)$ are the original and new probabilities of state s and μ_j^0 and μ_j^1 are the original and new expected values of the real value of a unit of asset j ($j = 1,\dots,m$). It also implies that the covariances of the unit real values of any two assets j and k ($j \neq i$ and $k \neq i$) do not change, as we have

$$\sigma_{jk}^1 = \sum_s \pi^1(s)(v_j(s)-\mu_j^1)(v_k(s)-\mu_k^1)$$
$$= \sum_s \pi^0(s)(v_j(s)-\mu_j^0)(v_k(s)-\mu_k^0)+$$
$$+\Delta\pi(r)[(v_j(r)-\mu_j^0)(v_k(r)-\mu_k^0)-(v_j(t)-\mu_j^0)(v_k(t)-\mu_k^0)]$$
$$= \sum_s \pi^0(s)(v_j(s)-\mu_j^0)(v_k(s)-\mu_k^0) = \sigma_{jk}^0, \quad (15)$$

because of (12), (14), $v_j(r) = v_j(t)$, and $v_k(r) = v_k(t)$. However, for asset i, we obtain

$$\sigma_{ij}^1 = \sum_s \pi^1(s)(v_i(s)-\mu_i^1)(v_j(s)-\mu_j^1)$$
$$= \sum_s \pi^0(s)(v_i(s)-\mu_i^0)(v_j(s)-\mu_j^0)+(\mu_i^1-\mu_i^0)(\mu_j^1-\mu_j^0)+$$
$$+\Delta\pi(r)[(v_i(r)-\mu_i^1)(v_j(r)-\mu_j^1)-(v_i(t)-\mu_i^1)(v_j(t)-\mu_j^1)]$$
$$= \sigma_{ij}^0+\theta_{ij}, \quad (16)$$

where

$$\theta_{ij} = (\mu_i^1-\mu_i^0)(\mu_j^1-\mu_j^0)+\Delta\pi(r)[(v_i(r)-\mu_i^1)(v_j(r)-\mu_j^1)-$$
$$-(v_i(t)-\mu_i^1)(v_j(t)-\mu_j^1)]$$
$$= \begin{cases} \Delta\pi(r)(v_i(r)-v_i(t))(v_j(r)-\mu_j^0), & \text{if } j \neq i, \\ \Delta\pi(r)(v_i(r)-v_i(t))(v_i(r)+v_i(t)-\mu_i^0-\mu_i^1), & \text{if } j = i. \end{cases}$$

Consequently, the covariance σ_{ij} becomes larger iff, in the state r whose probability increases, $v_j(r)$ is greater than the expected value μ_j^0; otherwise it is decreased or remains unchanged. It is also seen that the variance σ_{ii} becomes larger iff $v_i(r)+v_i(t) > \mu_i^0+\mu_i^1$, so that it increases only if $v_i(r)$ is larger than the new expected value μ_i^1, as $\mu_i^1 > \mu_i^0$; otherwise σ_{ii} decreases or remains unchanged. Thus, an increase in $\pi(r)$ in association with a compensating decrease in $\pi(t)$ may bring about a change in the variances and covariances. However, we may have an increase in σ_{ii} and/or σ_{ij} only in such favourable cases that, in the state r whose probability is increased, $v_i(r)$ and/or $v_j(r)$ are greater than their expected values. We may thus consider an increase in $\pi(r)$ compensated for by a decrease in $\pi(t)$ as an extension of the conventional idea of a solitary increase in the expected value of the returns of an asset; it cannot be accompanied by an increase in σ_{ii} and/or σ_{ij} except in the favourable cases mentioned above. (Markowitz [**1**] has proposed the idea of the 'semi-variance' to distinguish favourable and unfavourable increase in the variances and covariances, but their asymmetric effects on portfolios are completely ignored by the two-parameter approaches, such as that of Royama and Hamada [**1**]. It is not surprising to have, in the case of a compensating increase in $\pi(r)$ accompanied by a favourable increase (or decrease) in the variances and covariances, the same results as we have had in the conventional case of a solitary increase in the expected value of the returns of an asset.)

Next, let us assume that the expected values $\mu_1^0, \mu_2^0,\ldots, \mu_n^0$ are realized when a state r happens to occur, i.e. $v_i(r) = \mu_i^0$ $(i = 1,\ldots, m)$. Suppose that the probability attached to r is increased from $\pi^0(r)$ to $\pi^1(r)$ and the probabilities of all other states are diminished proportionately; $\pi^1(t) = (1+\beta)\pi^0(t)$, for all $t \neq r$, where $-1 < \beta < 0$. Since $\sum_s \pi^0(s) = \sum_s \pi^1(s) = 1$, we have

$$\Delta\pi(r) = \pi^1(r)-\pi^0(r) = -\sum_{s\neq r} \Delta\pi(s) = -\beta \sum_{s\neq r} \pi^0(s).$$

Therefore, we find that such a change in the probability distribution has no effects on the expected values of the unit real values of assets in the next period. In fact,

$$\mu_i^1 = \sum_s \pi^1(s)v_i(s) = \big(\pi^0(r) - \beta \sum_{s\neq r} \pi^0(s)\big)v_i(r) + \\ + \sum_{s\neq r} (1+\beta)\pi^0(s)v_i(s)$$
$$= \sum_s \pi^0(s)v_i(s) + \beta \sum_s \pi^0(s)v_i(s) - \beta\big(\sum_s \pi^0(s)\big)v_i(r)$$
$$= \sum_s \pi^0(s)v_i(s) = \mu_i^0 \qquad (17)$$

because $\sum_s \pi^0(s)v_i(s) = v_i(r)$ by assumption and $\sum_s \pi^0(s) = 1$. The change, however, gives rise to a decrease in the variances and positive covariances and an increase in negative covariances, because we have, for each pair of i and j,

$$\sigma_{ij}^1 = \sum_s \pi^1(s)\big(v_i(s) - \mu_i^1\big)\big(v_j(s) - \mu_j^1\big)$$
$$= \big(\pi^0(r) - \beta \sum_{s\neq r} \pi^0(s)\big)\big(v_i(r) - \mu_i^1\big)\big(v_j(r) - \mu_j^1\big) + \\ + \sum_{s\neq r} (1+\beta)\pi^0(s)\big(v_i(s) - \mu_i^1\big)\big(v_j(s) - \mu_j^1\big)$$
$$= \sum_s (1+\beta)\pi^0(s)\big(v_i(s) - \mu_i^0\big)\big(v_j(s) - \mu_j^0\big) = (1+\beta)\sigma_{ij}^0 \qquad (18)$$

(as $v_i(r) = \mu_i^0 = \mu_i^1$ $(i = 1, \ldots, m)$) which implies $\sigma_{ij}^0 > \sigma_{ij}^1$ if $\sigma_{ij}^0 > 0$, while $\sigma_{ij}^1 > \sigma_{ij}^0$ if $\sigma_{ij}^0 < 0$, since $-1 < \beta < 0$. Hence, in view of the fact that $\sum\sum \sigma_{ij}^0 y_i y_j > 0$ for all $y \geqq (\neq)\ 0$, we find that the variance of the real value of wealth in the next period diminishes, because

$$\sum_s \pi^1(s)\big(v(s)y - \sum_t \pi^1(t)v(t)y\big)^2 = \sum_i\sum_j \sigma_{ij}^1 y_i y_j$$
$$= (1+\beta) \sum_i\sum_j \sigma_{ij}^0 y_i y_j < \sum_s \pi^0(s)\big(v(s)y - \sum_t \pi^0(t)v(t)y\big)^2.$$

Therefore, the change in the probability distribution thus specified may be taken as an extension of the conventional case of the solitary increase in the variance of the returns of an asset.

With regard to these two changes in the probability distribution, we can derive some definite comparative statical laws.

We first examine the case of an increase in $\pi(r)$ being compensated by a decrease in $\pi(t)$. We extend the case slightly and assume that at state r

$$v_i(r) = \gamma q_i \quad \text{and} \quad v_j(r) = \alpha q_j, \quad \text{for all } j \neq i, \text{ with } \alpha < \gamma \tag{19}$$

and at state t

$$v_i(t) = \gamma' q_i \quad \text{and} \quad v_j(t) = \alpha' q_j, \quad \text{for all } j \neq i, \text{ with } \alpha' > \gamma'. \tag{20}$$

Our previous assumption, $\alpha = \alpha'$, is now unnecessary, so that α may be greater or less than α'. Before the shift of the probability distribution we have the equilibrium conditions (the first-order conditions for maximizing (10) subject to (11)):

$$\sum_s \psi'(v(s)y^0)\pi^0(s)v_k(s) \leqq \lambda^0 q_k \quad (k = 1,\ldots, m), \tag{21}$$

and after the shift:

$$\sum_s \psi'(v(s)y^1)\pi^0(s)v_k(s) + [\psi'(v(r)y^1)v_k(r) - \psi'(v(t)y^1)v_k(t)]\Delta\pi(r) \leqq \lambda^1 q_k \quad (k = 1,\ldots, m), \tag{22}$$

where y_k^0 or y_k^1 is zero if (21) or (22) holds with strict inequality, respectively. We assume first that (21) holds with equality for i and at least one other k. If we have

$$\frac{\psi'(v(r)y^1)v_k(r) - \psi'(v(t)y^1)v_k(t)}{q_k} = \frac{\psi'(v(r)y^1)v_i(r) - \psi'(v(t)y^1)v_i(t)}{q_i}, \tag{23}$$

for all k, then (22) can be written as

$$\sum_s \psi'(v(s)y^1)\pi^0(s)v_k(s) \leqq \lambda^* q_k \quad (k = 1,\ldots, m),$$

with λ^* determined appropriately, so that it is easily seen that the change in the probability distribution has no effects on y; it affects only the marginal expected utility of the individual's wealth (or income), λ. In view of (19) and (20), however, we find that (23) cannot be satisfied for any k. Hence, there must be a change in y.

As two distinct points, y^0 and y^1, give the maximum expected utilities before and after the change, respectively, we have

$$\sum_s \psi(v(s)y^0)\pi^0(s) > \sum_s \psi(v(s)y^1)\pi^0(s)$$

and

$$\sum_s \psi(v(s)y^1)\pi^1(s) > \sum_s \psi(v(s)y^0)\pi^1(s).$$

Therefore,

$$\sum_s [\psi(v(s)y^1)-\psi(v(s)y^0)][\pi^1(s)-\pi^0(s)] > 0,$$

which may be written

$$[\{\psi(v(r)y^1)-\psi(v(r)y^0)\}-\{\psi(v(t)y^1)-\psi(v(t)y^0)\}]\Delta\pi(r) > 0, \quad (24)$$

because $\Delta\pi(r) = -\Delta\pi(t)$ and $\Delta\pi(s) = 0$ for all other ss. As $\Delta\pi(r) > 0$, (24) requires either $v(r)y^1 > v(r)y^0$, or $v(t)y^1 < v(t)y^0$, or both. Subtracting the budget equation, $qy^1 = qy^0$, multiplied by α or α' from these inequalities, respectively, we have either $(\gamma-\alpha)v_i(r)(y_i^1-y_i^0) > 0$ or $(\gamma'-\alpha')v_i(t)(y_i^1-y_i^0) < 0$, or both, because of (19) and (20). As $\gamma > \alpha$ and $\gamma' < \alpha'$, we must have

$$y_i^1 > y_i^0; \quad (25)$$

that is to say, the demand for an asset i is increased when the following three things happen: (a) a state r where the real value of a unit of i in the next period is relatively higher than those of other assets becomes more probable, (b) a state t where the unit real value of i is relatively lower than those of other assets becomes less probable, and (c) the probabilities of all other states remain unchanged.

We have so far assumed that (21) holds with equality for i and at least one other k. If i is the only asset for which (21) holds with equality, (22) also holds with equality for i alone. We then find that $y_j = 0$ for all $j \neq i$ before and after the change. Hence, we have $y_i^1 = y_i^0 = I'/q_i$ from the budget equation. On the other hand, if (21) holds with equality only for some k other than i, (22) will hold with equality for the k only as long as $\Delta\pi(r)$ is small, so that $y_i^1 = y_i^0 = 0$. However, when $\Delta\pi(r)$ is big enough, (22) will hold with equality for i, so that y_i^1 takes on a positive value, and we have $y_i^1 > y_i^0 = 0$.

Now we turn to the second case where an increase in the probability distribution attached to a state r is associated with a proportional decrease in the probabilities attached to other states. We are concerned with a more general case than the one discussed previously, as we no longer assume

$$v_i(r) = \mu_i^0 \qquad (i = 1,\dots, m).$$

Since $\pi^1(s) = (1+\beta)\pi^0(s)$ for all $s \neq r$,

$$\pi^1(r) = 1-(1+\beta)\sum_{s\neq r}\pi^0(s) = \pi^0(r)-\beta\sum_{s\neq r}\pi^0(s),$$

we have

$$\sum_s \psi(v(s)y)\pi^1(s) = (1+\beta)\sum_s \psi(v(s)y)\pi^0(s)-\beta\psi(v(r)y). \tag{26}$$

Therefore, the subjective equilibrium conditions after the change may be written as

$$(1+\beta)\sum_s \psi'(v(s)y^1)v_k(s)\pi^0(s)-\beta\psi'(v(r)y^1)v_k(r) \leqq \lambda^1 q_k \qquad (k = 1,\dots,m). \tag{27}$$

We first consider the case of the unit real values of assets $v_k(r)$ $(k = 1,\dots,m)$ in state r being proportional to the current prices q_k $(k = 1,\dots,m)$. Then (27) is reduced to

$$\sum \psi'(v(s)y^1)v_k(s)\pi^0(s) \leqq \lambda^* q_k \quad (k = 1,\dots,m), \tag{27$'$}$$

with λ^* determined appropriately. Comparing (27′) with the original equilibrium conditions (21), we obtain $y^1 = y^0$; there are no effects on the demand for goods, though the marginal expected utility of the individual's wealth, λ, may be affected.

Next let us assume that

$$v_i(r) = \gamma q_i \quad \text{and} \quad v_j(r) = \alpha q_j, \quad \text{for all } j \neq i, \text{ with } \alpha < \gamma. \tag{28}$$

Also, assume that (21) holds with equality for at least one k $(\neq i)$ as well as i. In such a circumstance it can be easily shown that y^1 cannot be identical with y^0, provided $v(r) > 0$. We then have

$$\sum_s \psi(v(s)y^0)\pi^0(s) > \sum_s \psi(v(s)y^1)\pi^0(s) \tag{29}$$

before the change and

$$\sum_s \psi(v(s)y^1)\pi^1(s) > \sum_s \psi(v(s)y^0)\pi^1(s) \tag{30}$$

after the change. In view of (26), the latter may be written as

$$(1+\beta)\sum_s \psi(v(s)y^1)\pi^0(s)-\beta\psi(v(r)y^1) > (1+\beta)\sum_s \psi(v(s)y^0)\pi^0(s)-\beta\psi(v(r)y^0).$$

This, together with (29), implies

$$-\beta\psi(v(r)y^1) > -\beta\psi(v(r)y^0),$$

from which we obtain

$$v(r)y^1 > v(r)y^0,$$

because $\beta < 0$. Therefore, considering (28) and the budget equation $qy^1 = qy^0$, we obtain

$$(\gamma-\alpha)v_i(r)(y_i^1-y_i^0) > 0.$$

Hence

$$y_i^1 > y_i^0 \tag{31}$$

since $\gamma > \alpha$. Thus the holding of asset i is increased when (a) a state r where the ratio of $v_i(r)$ to q_i is higher than the similar ratios of other assets becomes more probable, and (b) the probabilities of all other states decrease proportionally. In this case, if it is furthermore assumed that each $v_j(r)$ is equal to the expected value of the real value of a unit of asset j in the next period, μ_j^0, then all the expected values remain constant (i.e. $\mu_j^0 = \mu_j^1$ for all j) and the variance of the real value of wealth $W = vy$ diminishes. Therefore, an increase in the holding of asset i obtained in (31) may be ascribed, in this case, to a decrease in 'risk'.

Finally, under (28) we consider the case of i being the sole index for which (21) holds with equality and the case of i being an index for which (21) holds with strict *in*equality. In the former case it can be shown that i is also the sole index for which (27) holds with equality. Therefore, we have $y_i^1 = y_i^0 = I'/q_i$. On the other hand, in the latter, we have $y_i^1 = y_i^0 = 0$ so long as β (< 0) is small in absolute value and $y_i^1 > y_i^0 = 0$ if it is big enough.

X. Optimal Transactions Demand for Money

M. MORISHIMA

1. Introduction

It has been discussed, notably by D. Patinkin [**1**], whether an individual will wish to hold cash if cash balance is not a variable of his utility function. A counter-example to his conclusion has later been presented by K. Brunner [**1**], who has derived a positive demand for money from a model in which the individual's utility function, depending on quantities of commodities and being independent of cash holding, is maximized subject to his budget equation and a certain additional restriction on the rate of utilization of given stocks of money. Unfortunately, his model is unsatisfactory, because he assumes that the velocity of circulation of money is positive, finite, and constant, whereas it should be an important unknown variable of the problem. Moreover, Brunner's approach, like Patinkin's, is static.

In this chapter, we are concerned with the same problem as Patinkin and Brunner, but we adopt a dynamic approach. We want to establish the simple, conventional view that cash may be demanded to transfer an excess of an individual's income over his consumption in one period to another period when he has deficits. We consider an economy where the individual can bridge two different points of time by two alternative means: cash and bonds, both of which do not enter the utility function. The problem is to find out the conditions under which the individual (who has a horizon extending over a multiplicity of marketing periods) chooses cash, rather than bonds, as the bridge. We shall show that his decision crucially depends on the relationship of the rate of interest of bonds to the transactions costs for buying, selling, or issuing them.

We have two important predecessors. First, J. Marschak [**2**] has been concerned with a similar model, to show that as soon as the individual needs to pay the transactions costs for buying commodities or as soon as he expects money prices of commodities to fall, he has a positive demand for money. But Marschak's model ignores lending and borrowing, so that the problem of substitution between cash and bonds is not discussed. Also, while Marschak has introduced uncertainty and market imperfections, we assume certainty and perfect markets for commodities, so that the prices are independent of the amounts of commodities the individual trades.

Secondly, J. Tobin [**1**] has analysed optimal average bond holding and cash holding, on the assumption that the streams of the receipts and the expenditures are given. It is obvious, however, that the expenditure plan should be simultaneously determined with the plan of cash and bond holdings. It is always possible for an individual to adjust his expenditure plan so that no cash and bond holdings are needed. We must ask why he chooses a plan that generates gaps in time between the receipts and expenditures.

Finally, a comment is desirable on the relationship of our model with the classical, multi-period consumption models by G. Tintner [**1**] and J. Hicks [**1**]. Their models assume, among other things, that (i) all commodities are perishable, (ii) there is no consideration concerning uncertainty and risk, and (iii) the gaps between the receipts and the expenditures are always filled by lending or borrowing, but not by cash. The first aspect is discussed in Chapter VI above, and the second in Chapters V, VIII, and IX. The present chapter frees their models from the unrealistic assumption (iii) concerning transaction balances.

2. The Subjective Equilibrium Conditions

We consider an individual in an economy where cash is the *sole* medium of exchange. There are bonds which bear an interest rate. The individual may hold transactions balances in cash or bonds; if he chooses the latter option, bonds have to be sold back for cash as he needs to make disbursements. To avoid complicated problems concerning uncertainty and risk, we assume that prices of commodities, the interest rate of bonds, and the transaction cost for selling or buying a unit of bond do not change over time.[1]

Suppose that the individual's preferences can be described by a utility function,

$$u = U[q(0), q(1),..., q(T)], \tag{1}$$

where $q(t)$ is an n-dimensional vector of consumption of goods at time t. He maximizes his utility subject to a number of constraints. First, the budget equations are written as

$$l(t-1)+m(t)+rw(t-1)+x(t)+z(t)$$
$$= p'q(t)+c_1 x(t)+(1+c_2)y(t)+c_3 z(t)+l(t) \quad (t = 0, 1,..., T), \tag{2}$$

where $l(t)$ denotes the amount of cash held at t, $m(t)$ the non-interest income at t, $w(t)$ the amount of bonds held at t, $x(t)$ bonds sold at t, $y(t)$ lending on bonds bought at t, $z(t)$ borrowing on bonds issued at t, r the rate of interest of bonds, p the n-dimensional price vector of commodities, and c_1, c_2, c_3 transaction costs for selling, buying, or issuing a bond. By assumption, r, p, and the cs are constant. The left-hand side of (2) represents the total amount of money available to the individual for spending at time t, and the right-hand side stands for his expenditure *plus* the amount of cash to be held at t.

Secondly, the increment of bonds held from $t-1$ to t equals the difference between bonds bought and bonds sold or issued; so we have

$$w(t) = w(t-1)+y(t)-x(t)-z(t) \quad (t = 0, 1,..., T). \tag{3}$$

Thirdly, the individual cannot sell more bonds than the amounts he has; so

$$\max(w(t-1), 0)-x(t) \geqq 0 \quad (t = 0, 1,.., T), \tag{4}$$

where $\max(a, b)$ means the larger of the numbers, a and b. It is noted that although $x(t)$, $y(t)$, and $z(t)$ are non-negative, $w(t)$ may be negative, since $x(t)$ plus $z(t)$ may exceed $y(t)$.

With given $m(t)$, $t = 0, 1,..., T$, $l(-1)$, $w(-1)$, and $w(T)$,

(1) However, our results are independent of the constancy of prices.

the individual maximizes (1) subject to the $3(T+1)$ conditions, (2), (3), and (4). Let $\lambda(t)$s be the Lagrange multipliers associated with (2), $\mu(t)$s with (3), and $\nu(t)$s with (4). The Lagrangian function is then written as

$$L = U + \sum_{t=0}^{T} \lambda(t)[l(t-1)+m(t)+rw(t-1)+ +(1-c_1)x(t)-(1+c_2)y(t)+(1-c_3)z(t)-p'q(t)-l(t)]+ + \sum_{t=0}^{T} \mu(t)[w(t-1)+y(t)-x(t)-z(t)-w(t)]+ + \sum_{t=0}^{T} \nu(t)[\max(w(t-1),0)-x(t)].$$

Considering that $q(t)$, $l(t)$, $x(t)$, $y(t)$, and $z(t)$ are all non-negative, we have the Kuhn–Tucker conditions:(2)

$$\frac{\partial U}{\partial q_i(t)} - \lambda(t)p_i \begin{cases} = 0 & \text{if } q_i(t) > 0, \\ \leqq 0 & \text{if } q_i(t) = 0, \end{cases} \tag{5}$$

$$\lambda(t)(1-c_1)-\mu(t)-\nu(t) \begin{cases} = 0 & \text{if } x(t) > 0, \\ \leqq 0 & \text{if } x(t) = 0, \end{cases} \tag{6}$$

$$\mu(t)-\lambda(t)(1+c_2) \begin{cases} = 0 & \text{if } y(t) > 0, \\ \leqq 0 & \text{if } y(t) = 0, \end{cases} \tag{7}$$

$$\lambda(t)(1-c_3)-\mu(t) \begin{cases} = 0 & \text{if } z(t) > 0, \\ \leqq 0 & \text{if } z(t) = 0, \end{cases} \tag{8}$$

$$\lambda(t+1)-\lambda(t) \begin{cases} = 0 & \text{if } l(t) > 0, \\ \leqq 0 & \text{if } l(t) = 0, \end{cases} \tag{9}$$

$$\lambda(t+1)r+\mu(t+1)-\mu(t)+\nu(t+1)\delta(t+1) = 0, \tag{10}$$

where $\delta(t+1)$ equals 1 if $w(t) > 0$ and 0 if $w(t) < 0$. It is noted that $\nu(t)$ vanishes if the constraint (4) is fulfilled with strict inequality and $\nu(t) \geqq 0$ otherwise; also, note that (5)–(9) hold for $t = 0, 1, \ldots, T$ and (10) for $t = 0, 1, \ldots, T-1$.

A further comment is required for affording a correct understanding of the equilibrium condition (10). It is seen that at $w(t) = 0$, the left-hand partial derivative of the Lagrangian

(2) See, for example, M. D. Intriligator [**1**].

function L with respect to $w(t)$, $\left(\frac{\partial L}{\partial w(t)}\right)_-$, is different from the right-hand one, $\left(\frac{\partial L}{\partial w(t)}\right)_+$. They are

$$\left(\frac{\partial L}{\partial w(t)}\right)_- = \lambda(t+1)r+\mu(t+1)-\mu(t)$$

and

$$\left(\frac{\partial L}{\partial w(t)}\right)_+ = \lambda(t+1)r+\mu(t+1)-\mu(t)+\nu(t+1);$$

clearly a point with $w(t) = 0$ could be an equilibrium point only if

$$\left(\frac{\partial L}{\partial w(t)}\right)_- \geqq 0 \quad \text{and} \quad \left(\frac{\partial L}{\partial w(t)}\right)_+ \leqq 0.$$

Hence, in view of $\nu(t+1) \geqq 0$, we have

$$\nu(t+1) = 0 \quad \text{and} \quad \lambda(t+1)r+\mu(t+1)-\mu(t) = 0, \qquad (10')$$

as necessary conditions for L to be a maximum at $w(t) = 0$.

Throughout the following we are concerned with the equilibrium points only, so that conditions (2)–(10) or (10′) are assumed to be satisfied, unless otherwise stated.

It is easy to compare our formulation with Tintner's and Hicks's and see that theirs are no more than an extreme case of ours. In the special case of no transaction costs of selling, buying, or issuing bonds (i.e. $c_1 = c_2 = c_3 = 0$), we have from (7) and (8)

$$\lambda(t) \leqq \mu(t) \leqq \lambda(t), \quad \text{for all } t.$$

Therefore,

$$\lambda(t) = \mu(t), \quad \text{for all } t. \qquad (11)$$

Hence (6) is reduced to

$$-\nu(t)\begin{cases} = 0 & \text{if } x(t) > 0, \\ \leqq 0 & \text{if } x(t) = 0. \end{cases} \qquad (6')$$

Now, let us suppose $\nu(t) > 0$ for some $t \geqq 1$; then $x(t) = 0$. Moreover $w(t-1)$ must be negative, because if it is zero, we have $\nu(t) = 0$, and if it is positive, (4) is fulfilled with strict inequality, so that $\nu(t) = 0$. We have a contradiction in any case. Therefore, we obtain $w(t-1) < 0$, which implies $\delta(t) = 0$. Thus, we have from (10)

$$\lambda(t)r+\mu(t)-\mu(t-1) = 0.$$

Of course, it is evident that we have the same equation when $\nu(t) = 0$. Thus, the term $\nu(t+1)\delta(t+1)$ disappears from (10) when $c_1 = c_2 = c_3 = 0$. Clearly, the revised equation (10) may be rewritten as

$$\lambda(t+1)(1+r) = \lambda(t) \tag{10''}$$

because of (11). As $r > 0$, (10″) implies $\lambda(t+1) < \lambda(t)$ for all t; so $l(t) = 0$, that is to say, there is no demand for cash balances. Furthermore, by virtue of (10″), the equilibrium conditions for commodities (5) may be put in the form

$$\frac{\partial U}{\partial q(t)} - \lambda(0)\pi(t)\begin{cases} = 0 & \text{if } q(t) > 0, \\ \leqq 0 & \text{if } q(t) = 0, \end{cases} \tag{5'}$$

where $\pi(t) = (1+r)^{-t}p$, the vector of discounted prices of commodities at time t. Evidently, (5′) is no more than the Tintner–Hicks subjective equilibrium conditions over time of the consumer which state that the marginal rate of substitution between two commodities, say i at time t and j at time s, must equal the ratio of their discounted prices.

On the other hand, it is seen that in the same extreme case of c_1, c_2, and c_3 being zero, (6), (7), and (8) are all reduced to the same condition (11), provided that $x(t) > 0$, because it implies $\nu(t) = 0$ by (6′). This means that $x(t)$, $y(t)$, and $z(t)$ may be lumped into a single variable

$$\xi(t) = y(t) - x(t) - z(t),$$

which implies that borrowing may be treated as negative lending. Since $l(t) = 0$ as has been seen above, we may write, in this case, the budget equations (2) and the equations of bond holding (3) in the following simple form:

$$m(t) + rw(t-1) = p'q(t) + \xi(t) \quad (t = 0, 1, \ldots, T), \tag{3'}$$

$$w(t-1) + \xi(t) = w(t) \quad (t = 0, 1, \ldots, T), \tag{4'}$$

respectively. Multiplying the equations (3′) by $(1+r)^{-t}$ with the corresponding t, adding them up, and considering (4′), then we have

$$\sum_{t=0}^{T}(1+r)^{-t}m(t) + r\sum_{t=0}^{T}(1+r)^{-t}w(-1)$$
$$= \sum_{t=0}^{T}\pi(t)'q(t) + (1+r)^{-T}\sum_{t=0}^{T}\xi(t). \tag{12}$$

It also follows from (4′) that

$$\sum_{t=0}^{T} \xi(t) = w(T) - w(-1).$$

In view of this, (12) can finally be put in the form

$$\sum_{t=0}^{T} (1+r)^{-t} m(t) + (1+r) w(-1) - (1+r)^{-T} w(T) = \sum_{t=0}^{T} \pi(t)' q(t). \tag{12'}$$

Thus, it is seen that the subjective equilibrium point determined by our Kuhn–Tucker conditions satisfies the budget equation over time (12′). It can also be seen easily that (5′) gives the maximum of the utility (1) subject to (12′). Thus, in the case of no transaction costs for selling, buying, or issuing bonds, our problem of finding the optimum consumption stream $q(t)$, $0 \leqq t \leqq T$ such that (1) is maximized subject to (2), (3), and (4) is identical with the Tintner–Hicks problem of finding $q(t)$ such that (1) is maximized subject to (12′) only. Their solution with no cash balances may be justified in this case, but in other cases it may happen that their solution is not feasible because of deficiency of transactions balances in some or all periods.

However, the Tintner–Hicks case can be extended into a case of the transaction costs being present. Let us assume that the individual must pay a cost whenever he sells, buys, or issues a bond, that is to say, c_1, c_2, and c_3 are all positive. To the individual, three options are available. First, he may hold an amount of money, say £1, in the form of cash, for a number of periods, say t periods; secondly, he may buy bonds of the value of £1 at time 0 and sell them back at t; or thirdly, he may buy bonds of £1 at time 0 and offset them by issuing bonds of the same amount at t. If he chooses the first option, he merely has £1 at t, while the second and the third option enable him to have the profits of the amounts $tr - c_1 - c_2$ and $tr - c_2 - c_3$, respectively, in addition to the original £1. If these profits are positive, it is not advantageous for the individual to hold cash balances over t periods; in particular, if

$$r - c_1 - c_2 > 0, \tag{13}$$

and

$$r - c_2 - c_3 > 0, \tag{14}$$

the individual will not hold his transaction balances in the form of cash (but in the form of bonds if at all), even for one period; that is to say, $l(t) = 0$ for all t.

This is confirmed in the following way. First consider the case of $\delta(t) = 1$. We have from (6), (7), and (10)

$$\lambda(t)r+\lambda(t)(1-c_1)-\lambda(t-1)(1+c_2) \leqq 0,$$

which contradicts $\lambda(t) = \lambda(t-1)$, because of (13). Hence $l(t) = 0$ by (9). Next consider the other case, $\delta(t) = 0$. We have from (7) and (8)

$$\mu(t-1) \leqq \lambda(t-1)(1+c_2) \quad \text{and} \quad \mu(t) \geqq \lambda(t)(1-c_3),$$

respectively. These, together with (10), result in

$$\lambda(t)r+\lambda(t)(1-c_3)-\lambda(t-1)(1+c_2) \leqq 0,$$

which again contradicts $\lambda(t) = \lambda(t-1)$ because of (14). Hence $l(t) = 0$. (Note that $\lambda(t) > 0$ because of (5).)

We have so far seen that conditions (13) and (14) are sufficient for $l(t) = 0$. This idea naturally leads to its counterpart. Suppose

$$Tr-c_1-c_2 < 0, \tag{15}$$

and

$$Tr-c_2-c_3 < 0. \tag{16}$$

They imply that the options of bond holding combined with selling bonds back into cash, or issuing new bonds, at the other end of the holding period are disadvantageous over the option of cash holding even if bonds are held throughout the entire T periods, so that the individual will never buy bonds, unless his initial holding of bonds is set to be less than the terminal holding, i.e. $y(t) = 0$ $(t = 0, 1, ..., T)$ unless $w(-1) < w(T)$.

A proof of this result is given as follows. Suppose the contrary, that is $y(t_0) > 0$ for some t_0 $(0 \leqq t_0 < T)$. Let $\bar{y}$ be a portion of $y(t_0)$ which is sold at time t_1 such that $t_0 < t_1 \leqq T$. It is clear that the individual can increase cash holding $l(t_0)$ by $\Delta l(t_0) = (1+c_2)\bar{y}$ by reducing the amount of bonds bought at t_0, $y(t_0)$, by $\bar{y}$. But this decrease in bond holding at t_0 gives rise to a decrease in interest income in the subsequent periods, amounting to $(t_1-t_0)r\bar{y}$ over the t_1-t_0 periods. In taking the decrease into account, the net increase in cash holding at t_1 amounts to

$$(1+c_2)\bar{y}-(t_1-t_0)r\bar{y},$$

which is compared with the value of money, $(1-c_1)\bar{y}$, that would be acquired by selling bonds of the amount $\bar{y}$ at t_1. Because of (15), the former is larger than the latter, so that the individual is benefited by increasing cash holding at t_0 instead of buying bonds. Therefore, $y(t_0)$ must be zero. In exactly the same way, $y(t_0) > 0$ is ruled out by (16) when bonds of the amount $\bar{y}$ are offset by issuing new bonds rather than selling them, at time t_1.

3. The Existence of Positive Transactions Demand for Cash

The remaining case of c_1 plus c_2 being between r and Tr is more plausible and interesting than the others. For investigating it, let us group individuals into two or three classes. First, an individual is called *thrifty* at time t if the total amount of money available to him at t before trade (i.e. his cash holding $l(t-1)$ plus his income $m(t)+rw(t-1)$) exceeds his consumption $p'q(t)$ at t, and *sumptuous* if the inequality is reversed. Thrifty people are further grouped into two subclasses. A person is said to be *strongly* thrifty at t if his income (including labour and interest incomes but excluding the cash balances left over from the previous period, of course) is greater than his consumption at t, or *weakly* thrifty if the former is not greater than the latter, but he is still thrifty in the wider sense.

We need the following lemmas.

LEMMA 1. *If $l(t) > 0$, then $y(t+1) = 0$.*

Proof. As $\lambda(t+1) > 0$ and $\nu(t+1)\delta(t+1) \geqq 0$, we have from (10)

$$\mu(t) > \mu(t+1).$$

On the other hand, we have from (7)

$$\mu(t) \leqq \lambda(t)(1+c_2), \qquad \mu(t+1) \leqq \lambda(t+1)(1+c_2),$$

and from (9) $$\lambda(t) = \lambda(t+1)$$

as $l(t) > 0$. Therefore, we obtain $\mu(t+1) < \lambda(t+1)(1+c_2)$, so that $y(t+1) = 0$ by (7).

LEMMA 2. *If* $l(t) > 0$, *then* $z(t) = 0$.

Proof. The proof is exactly the same as the one for Lemma 1.

LEMMA 3. *If* $l(t) > 0$, *then* $x(t) = 0$.

Proof. As $l(t) > 0$, we have $z(t) = 0$ from Lemma 2.

Suppose now the contrary, that is $x(t) > 0$. Then $y(t) = 0$ by Lemma 5 below. We also have $w(t-1) > 0$ from (4).

We now have from (3)

$$w(t) = w(t-1) - x(t),$$

which is non-negative because $w(t-1)$ is positive and $x(t)$ satisfies (4). First, examine the possibility of $w(t) > 0$. Then $\delta(t+1) = 1$; therefore, from (10) and (6)

$$\lambda(t+1)(r+1-c_1) \leqq \mu(t). \tag{17}$$

Also from (6) and (10), we have

$$\lambda(t)(r+1-c_1) = \mu(t-1), \tag{18}$$

because (6) holds with equality since $x(t) > 0$ and $\delta(t)$ is 1 since $w(t-1) > 0$. (17) and (18) imply $\lambda(t+1) < \lambda(t)$ because $\mu(t) < \mu(t-1)$. Hence $l(t) = 0$ by (9), a contradiction.

Next consider the case of $w(t) = 0$. In this case, we have $\nu(t+1) = 0$. We have (17) again from (6) and (10). Then exactly the same argument as above leads to a contradiction with $l(t) > 0$. Hence $x(t) = 0$.

LEMMA 4. *If* $y(t) > 0$, *then* $z(t) = 0$.

Proof. $y(t) > 0$ implies

$$\lambda(t)(1+c_2) = \mu(t). \tag{19}$$

As c_2 and c_3 are positive, this implies

$$\lambda(t)(1-c_3) < \mu(t).$$

Hence $z(t) = 0$ by (8).

LEMMA 5. *If* $y(t) > 0$, *then* $x(t) = 0$.

Proof. As $\nu(t) > 0$ and $c_1 > 0$, we have from (19)

$$\mu(t)+\nu(t) = \lambda(t)(1+c_2)+\nu(t) > \lambda(t)(1-c_1).$$

Hence $x(t) = 0$ by (6).

The lemmas are intuitively reasonable. Lemma 1 states that if the individual holds cash at time t, then he will not buy bonds at $t+1$. (It is more economic for him to buy bonds at t rather than at $t+1$, because he could receive interest on one more period; and he has money to do so.) Lemmas 2–5 state that if the individual holds cash or buys bonds, then he does not simultaneously issue or sell bonds.

The following corollaries may be derived from the lemmas. If the individual is sumptuous at time zero, then

$$l(-1)+m(0)+rw(-1)-p'q(0) < 0 \tag{20}$$

by definition, and the left-hand side of the inequality equals

$$-(1-c_1)x(0)+(1+c_2)y(0)-(1-c_3)z(0)+l(0)$$

by the budget equation (2). As $x(0)$, $y(0)$, $z(0)$, and $l(0)$ are all non-negative, (20) implies that either $x(0)$ or $z(0)$ or both should be positive. Therefore, by the contrapositions of Lemmas 2–5, we find that $y(0)$ and $l(0)$ must vanish. Similarly, if the individual is thrifty, $x(0) = 0$ and $z(0) = 0$ follow directly from the lemmas. Thus, there is no positive demand for cash balances from sumptuous persons and no borrowing by misers.

We now assume that the transaction cost for issuing a new bond, c_3, is higher than the cost for selling an existing bond, c_1. This assures the priority of selling bonds over borrowing. In fact, if the individual is sumptuous and his $x(0)$ is positive but less than $w(-1)$, then (4) is satisfied with strict inequality, so that $\nu(0) = 0$. Consequently, we have from (6)

$$\lambda(0)(1-c_1) = \mu(0),$$

which is compared with

$$\lambda(0)(1-c_3) \leqq \mu(0)$$

that follows from (8). As $c_1 < c_3$ by the assumption we have just introduced, we obtain

$$\lambda(0)(1-c_3) < \mu(0),$$

which implies $z(0) = 0$. Thus, the sumptuous person does not issue new bonds as long as he still owns some positive amount of bonds after subtracting from his initial holding, $w(-1)$, the amount, $x(0)$, which he wants to sell at time 0.

However, if his $x(0)$ reaches $w(-1)$, a positive borrowing, $z(0) > 0$, may be compatible with a positive sale of bonds, $x(0) > 0$. When $w(-1)$ is non-positive, a positive sale of bonds is impossible, and the sumptuous person must issue bonds.

Summarizing the above analysis, we find that there are three kinds of sumptuous persons: (i) those who have positive $w(-1)$ such that $w(-1) > x(0) > 0$, so that $z(0) = 0$; (ii) those who have positive $w(-1)$ such that $w(-1) = x(0)$, so that their $z(0) \geqq 0$; and (iii) those whose $w(-1) \leqq 0$, so that their $x(0) = 0$ and $z(0) > 0$. We can, therefore, conclude that borrowing is a monotonic decreasing function of $w(-1)$ under the additional, plausible assumption that $\dfrac{\partial x(0)}{\partial w(-1)} < 1$.

Let us turn to the analysis of the thrifty individual. Suppose the individual is thrifty (in the wider sense) at time 0 and strongly thrifty at time 1. Then it is clear that either $l(t)$ or $y(t)$ or both are positive, but both $x(t)$ and $z(t)$ are zero at $t = 0$ and 1. Also, by Lemma 1, $y(1) = 0$ if $l(0) > 0$. In view of the definition of strong thriftiness, we have at time 1

$$\begin{aligned} 0 &< m(1)+rw(0)-p'q(1) \\ &= -(1-c_1)x(1)+(1+c_2)y(1)-(1-c_3)z(1)+l(1)-l(0) \end{aligned}$$

on the right-hand side of which $x(1) = 0$, $z(1) = 0$, and $y(1) = 0$ (if $l(0) > 0$); therefore, $l(1) > l(0)$, if $l(0) > 0$.

If he is weakly thrifty or sumptuous at time 1 but still thrifty in the wider sense at 0, then we have either $l(0) > 0$, or $y(0) > 0$, or both. At time 1, $x(1) = z(1) = 0$ if he is weakly thrifty, or $l(1) = y(1) = 0$ if he is sumptuous. As before, $l(0) > 0$ implies $y(1) = 0$, and therefore,

$$0 > m(1)+rw(0)-p'q(1) = l(1)-l(0),$$

if the individual is weakly thrifty at time 1. Hence we may conclude that if $l(0) > 0$, then $l(0) > l(1) \geqq 0$ (or $= 0$) for the person being weakly thrifty (or sumptuous) at 1.

This final result may be strengthened to the effect that $l(0)$ is necessarily positive for the individual we are considering, i.e. a person who is thrifty in the wider sense at 0 and sumptuous or weakly thrifty at 1. To show this we assume the contrary, that is, $l(0) = 0$; then $y(0) > 0$ definitely. As the sumptuousness or weak thriftiness at time 1 implies

$$m(1)+rw(0)-p'q(1)$$
$$= -(1-c_1)x(1)+(1+c_2)y(1)-(1-c_3)z(1)+l(1)-l(0) < 0,$$

at least one of $x(1)$, $z(1)$, and $l(0)$ must be positive, because $y(1)$ and $l(1)$ cannot be negative. Since $l(0)$ is assumed to be zero, we have only two possibilities: either $x(1) > 0$ or $z(1) > 0$. We shall prove $l(0) > 0$ by showing that neither of them is compatible with $l(0) = 0$.

If $l(0) = 0$, the thriftiness at time 0 implies $y(0) > 0$. Suppose now $x(1) > 0$. It follows from (6) that

$$\lambda(1)(1-c_1) = \mu(1)+\nu(1). \tag{21}$$

It also follows from $w(0) \geqq x(1) > 0$ that $\delta(1)$ is 1, so that from (10) we get

$$\lambda(1)r+\mu(1)+\nu(1) = \mu(0).$$

This, together with (7) and (21), yields

$$\lambda(1)(r+1-c_1) = \lambda(0)(1+c_2)$$

as $y(0) > 0$. Therefore, $\lambda(0)(r+1-c_1) \geqq \lambda(0)(1+c_2)$ because of (9). But this is impossible as r is assumed to be less than c_1+c_2. Hence $x(1) = 0$.

Next we show that $z(1)$ should be zero if $l(0)$ is zero. Again we suppose the contrary, that is, $z(1) > 0$. We then have from (8)

$$\lambda(1)(1-c_3) = \mu(1).$$

Substituting this into (6), we have

$$\lambda(1)(c_3-c_1) \leqq \nu(1),$$

the left-hand side of which is positive because of $c_3 > c_1$; hence

$$\nu(1) > 0.$$

This implies that $w(0) \leqq 0$, because otherwise the inequality $w(0) > x(1) = 0$ would imply $\nu(1) = 0$, a contradiction. Hence $\delta(1) = 0$ in (10).

We have now from (10)

$$\lambda(1)r+\mu(1) = \mu(0). \tag{22}$$

On the other hand, the inequality $y(0) > 0$, which follows from the supposition $l(0) = 0$, implies

$$\mu(0) = \lambda(0)(1+c_2).$$

Also, we have

$$\mu(1) = \lambda(1)(1-c_3)$$

as $z(1) > 0$. Substituting these two into (22), we have

$$\lambda(1)(r+1-c_3) = \lambda(0)(1+c_2).$$

In view of (9), we obtain

$$\lambda(0)(r-c_2-c_3) \geqq 0,$$

which is impossible since $r < c_1+c_2 < c_2+c_3$. Hence $z(1) = 0$.

Thus, we obtain $x(1) = z(1) = 0$ if $l(0) = 0$ is assumed. This means that the individual cannot be sumptuous or weakly thrifty at time 1. This is a contradiction; hence, $l(0) > 0$.

The above argument may be generalized as follows. Assume

$$r < c_1+c_2 < Tr,$$

and $c_1 < c_3$, as before. Let t^* be defined as $(c_1+c_2)/r$. Then $1 < t^* < T$, t^* being not necessarily an integer. Suppose the individual is thrifty in the wider sense at time 0, his total income (the sum of labour and interest incomes) is equated with his consumption from $t = 1$ to $t = s-1$, and he is sumptuous or weakly thrifty at time s. Then we may find that if time s is before the critical point of time t^*, then the excess of the total income, $m(0)+rw(-1)$, plus the cash balances, $l(-1)$, over consumption $p'q(0)$, is kept in cash at time 0, i.e. $l(0) > 0$ and $y(0) = 0$, while if s is after t^*, then it is kept entirely in bonds, i.e. $l(0) = 0$ and $y(0) > 0$, as it is in the Tintner–Hicks model.

Finally, we have so far assumed that the individual can spend the money acquired by selling or issuing bonds in some period, on goods in the same period, so that money can change hands twice in a period. If it can change hands only once a period, his plan has to fulfil $T+1$ new constraints requiring expenditures on goods and bonds not to exceed the sum of the money income and cash balances in each period, as well as the other constraints. This consideration leads to a dynamic extension of the problem discussed by Clower [**1**].

Part V · Portfolio

XI. A Two-Parametric 'Revealed-Preference' Theory of Portfolio Selection

M. MORISHIMA

1. Introduction

In the theory of portfolio selection, we often consider an individual who determines his portfolio choice on the basis of his indifference map traced out in the plane measuring, along the two axes of coordinates, mean and variance of his subjective probability distribution of the returns from alternative possible holdings of assets. This two-parameter approach has recently been criticized by many authors for the reason that it requires some very restrictive assumptions for its validity.(1) None the less we derive a number of comparative statical laws of portfolio selection from a two-parameter model which is rationalized in the following way.

Let x_i be the amount of asset i to be held by the individual in the present period and m_i be the price of asset i which will be realized in the next period. In the present period m_is are merely expected, so that they are stochastic variables; the probability that $m_1, m_2, \ldots, m_n$ simultaneously take on definite values $m_1^0, m_2^0, \ldots, m_n^0$, respectively, is $\pi(m_1^0, \ldots, m_n^0)$ for m_i^0 such that $-\infty \leqq m_i^0 \leqq \infty$. The individual will enjoy the utility $u(W)$ when he has wealth of the amount $W = \sum_{i=1}^{n} m_i x_i$ in the next period with certainty. When $m_1, \ldots, m_n$ are stochastic variables distributed according to the probability density function $\pi(m_1, \ldots, m_n)$, he will enjoy the utility $v(\sum m_i x_i, \Pi)$ by holding $x_1, \ldots, x_n$, where Π represents the probability distribution of $(m_1, \ldots, m_n)$. $u(W)$ and $v(W, \Pi)$ are indicators of ordinal preference, so that $f(u)$ and $\phi(v)$ also serve as indicators of preference, where f and ϕ are arbitrary functions which increase

(1) See papers by K. Borch, M. S. Feldstein, and J. Tobin in *Review of Economic Studies*, Vol. 36, January 1969, pp. 1–14.

when u or v increases. Von Neumann and Morgenstern have shown that if the individual's behaviour under uncertainty satisfies a number of axioms, then there exist increasing functions ϕ and f, which establish[2]

$$\phi(v(\sum m_i x_i, \Pi)) = \int_{-\infty}^{\infty} \dots \int_{-\infty}^{\infty} f(u(\sum m_i x_i))\pi(m_1,\dots, m_n)\, dm_1 \dots dm_n.$$

Most of the axioms are reasonable but one of them which is called the strong independence axiom by Samuelson is not necessarily plausible.[3] Let $0 \leqq \alpha \leqq 1$ and $0 \leqq \beta \leqq 1$. The axiom states that if a probability combination of W_1 and W_2 with frequencies α and $1-\alpha$, respectively, is indifferent to holding W_3 with certainty, then a probability combination of W_1, W_2, and W_4 with frequencies $\beta\alpha$, $\beta(1-\alpha)$, and $1-\beta$ is indifferent to a probability combination of W_3 and W_4 with frequencies β and $1-\beta$, for any W_4 and β. There is no reason why an individual who considers that a 50–50 combination of $W_1 = £0$ and $W_2 = £10$ is indifferent to $W_3 = £4$ which is certain should be necessarily indifferent between a combination of £0, £10, and £5 with probabilities 0·25, 0·25, and 0·50 respectively and a 50–50 combination of £4 and £5. Once this axiom is not assumed, the von Neumann–Morgenstern result is no longer obtained; there remains room for an alternative specification of the preference function $v(W, \Pi)$.

The mean and variance of W are defined as

$$\mu_W = \int_{-\infty}^{\infty} \dots \int_{-\infty}^{\infty} (\sum m_i x_i)\pi(m_1,\dots, m_n)\, dm_1 \dots dm_n,$$

$$\sigma_W^2 = \int_{-\infty}^{\infty} \dots \int_{-\infty}^{\infty} (\sum m_i x_i - \mu_W)^2\pi(m_1,\dots, m_n)\, dm_1 \dots dm_n.$$

More generally, the kth moment about the mean is defined to be

$$\nu_W^k = \int_{-\infty}^{\infty} \dots \int_{-\infty}^{\infty} (\sum m_i x_i - \mu_W)^k\pi(m_1,\dots, m_n)\, dm_1 \dots dm_n \qquad (k = 1, 2, 3,\dots).$$

(2) J. von Neumann and O. Morgenstern [1], pp. 17–31.
(3) Samuelson [2], p. 672.

Evidently $\nu_W^1 = \mu_W$, and $\nu_W^2 = \sigma_W^2$. The distribution of W is characterized by these moments.

Let us now assume that in selecting an optimum portfolio, the individual takes not only the expected value of W, μ_W, but also the 'risk', σ_W^2, and other moments of higher order, $\nu_W^3, \nu_W^4, \ldots$, into account; then we have the preference function

$$f = F(\mu_W, \sigma_W^2, \nu_W^3, \nu_W^4, \ldots),$$

and the individual maximizes f subject to his budget equation

$$\sum_{i=1}^{n} p_i x_i = \overline{W},$$

where $\overline{W}$ is a given sum of wealth which the individual has at the beginning of the current period and p_i is the current price of asset i. The problem of portfolio selection thus formulated is usually discussed in a special case where F depends on μ_W positively (i.e. $\partial F/\partial \mu_W > 0$) and σ_W^2 negatively (i.e. $\partial F/\partial \sigma_W^2 < 0$) and is independent of other moments.(4)

As a first approximation to the reality, we are interested in the two-parameter approach thus rationalized, because it is rich in useful and interesting results. Our analysis is distinguished from the previous similar studies by Royama and Hamada [**1**] and by Bierwag and Grove [**1**] since we never use a preference function explicitly. Although we have to realize that there exists a two-parameter indifference map in the background, we do not use any technique of differential calculus for maximization and derivation of the equations of comparative statics. The only property which we assume is that if an individual chooses a portfolio which is not smaller in risk than a second portfolio, then the former has to give a greater expected return than the latter, and vice versa. In the same way that Samuelson established the basic law of demand on the basis of the weak axiom of revealed preference, we shall extract the same conclusions as those of Royama, Hamada, Bierwag, and

(4) The same interpretation of the two-parameter analysis is made by Hicks [**2**], pp. 103–6.

Grove, from the first principle of the mean–variance approach.[(5)] Such a refinement of logic will be useful in the theory of portfolio choice as it was also in the theory of consumer's demand. In this way we discuss the effects of a change in expected returns of asset in section 2, the effects of a change in risk in section 3, and the effects of a change in the current prices of assets in section 4.

2. A Change in Expected Returns

Let us consider an individual who has a given sum of money $\overline{W}$ available for distribution among n different assets. Let x be an n-dimensional *column* vector a typical component of which, x_i, is the amount of the ith asset to be held by him in the period we are concerned with. Let r be an n-dimensional *row* vector, its typical component r_i representing the rate of return of the ith asset in the same period. The returns accruing from holding x will amount to rx, so that his wealth will grow, during the period, from $\overline{W} = ex$ to $W = (e+r)x$, where e is the n-dimensional summation vector, i.e. the row vector consisting of n unities.

We assume that each r_i is a stochastic variable whose expected value is denoted by $\tilde{r}_i$. Let μ_i be $1+\tilde{r}_i$ and μ the n-dimensional row vector with components $\mu_1,\dots,\mu_n$. Then μx gives the expected value of W.

Let σ_{ij} be the covariance between r_i and r_j, and σ the $n\times n$ variance–covariance matrix with elements σ_{ij} $(i,j = 1,\dots,n)$. All assets are assumed risky, so that $\sigma_{ii} > 0$ for all i. For the sake of simplicity we write the quadratic form $x'\sigma x$ as $\sigma(x)$.

The following hypothesis is basic for the mean–variance analysis of portfolio choices. *If neither of the two inequalities* $\mu x > \mu x^*$ *and* $\sigma(x) < \sigma(x^*)$ *holds,* x *is not preferred to* x^*.

Consider now two circumstances, one with $\mu = \mu^0$ and $\sigma = \sigma^0$, and the other where μ is μ^1 which is different from μ^0 but σ

(5) P. A. Samuelson [**1**], pp. 107–17. It seems that there are some differences in interpretation of the results between Royama and Hamada on the one side and Bierwag and Grove and ourselves on the other. Although Royama and Hamada called the effects obtained income and substitution effects, they are no more than want pattern effects in the sense of the previous chapter, as the equations derived by Bierwag and Grove show.

takes on σ^0 as in the first circumstance. Suppose the individual chooses x^1 in the second circumstance which is different from x^0 chosen in the first. x^0 and x^1 satisfy the budget equation, so that $\overline{W} = ex^0 = ex^1$. Then it is evident from the basic hypothesis that we have the following two statements:

(i) either $\mu^0 x^0 > \mu^0 x^1$, or $\sigma(x^0) < \sigma(x^1)$, or both; and

(ii) either $\mu^1 x^1 > \mu^1 x^0$, or $\sigma(x^1) < \sigma(x^0)$, or both.

(Otherwise the individual would not prefer x^0 to x^1 in the first circumstance and x^1 to x^0 in the second circumstance.)

If $\sigma(x^0) > \sigma(x^1)$, we have, from (i), $\mu^0 x^0 > \mu^0 x^1$. If $\sigma(x^0) \leqq \sigma(x^1)$, we have, from (ii), $\mu^1 x^1 > \mu^1 x^0$. Therefore, we find that either $\mu^0 x^0 > \mu^0 x^1$ or $\mu^1 x^1 > \mu^1 x^0$. Or, in an alternative but equivalent way, we can state

(*) If $\mu^0 x^1 \geqq \mu^0 x^0$, then $\mu^1 x^1 > \mu^1 x^0$.

Obviously, there is an analogy between (*) and Samuelson's weak axiom of revealed preference (for the theory of consumer behaviour), although their corresponding inequalities have opposite senses.

The general effect of a change in μ on x is split up into two components: one due to a change in the general level of $\mu_1,\ldots, \mu_n$, and the other due to a change in their relativity. In order to isolate them from each other, we introduce a third situation with μ^2 which is proportional to μ^1 but whose absolute level is adjusted such that $\mu^2 x^0 = \mu^0 x^0$. In terms of μ^2, the levels of μ^0 and μ^1 may be defined as

$$\frac{\mu^0 x^0}{\mu^2 x^0} = 1 \quad \text{and} \quad \frac{\mu^1 x^0}{\mu^2 x^0} = \alpha,$$

respectively.

Let x^2 be an x which is chosen at μ^2 by the individual with given $\overline{W}$. Then the change in x from x^0 to x^1 can be regarded as the 'resultant' of the change from x^0 to x^2 and the further change from x^2 to x^1, which we call the Relative and the Absolute Expected Return Effects, respectively. This analysis of the total effect is visualized by the formula

$$x^1 - x^0 = (x^1 - x^2) + (x^2 - x^0) \tag{1}$$

and can be given the following explanation.

If the individual continued to choose the same portfolio x^0 as before in spite of an increase in the expected returns, he could expect a greater amount of wealth at the end of the period, without putting himself in a riskier position. Therefore, we could imagine the third circumstance where a relative increase in some elements of μ happened in combination with such a general decrease in μ as would result in the expectation of the same amount of wealth if the individual stuck to x^0 despite the change. A change from the original to the third circumstance would give rise to a change in the portfolio selected, which is given by the Relative Expected Return Effect. And a general increase in μ which compensates the general decline in μ imagined in the third circumstance gives the Absolute Expected Return Effect.

Let us now suppose μ_i to vary, other μs as well as $\overline{W}$ remaining unchanged. Per unit increase in μ_i we have the total effect on x_j as

$$\frac{x_j^1-x_j^0}{\mu_i^1-\mu_i^0} = \frac{x_j^1-x_j^2}{\mu_i^1-\mu_i^0}+\frac{x_j^2-x_j^0}{\mu_i^1-\mu_i^0}. \tag{2}$$

Writing $E^1 = \mu^1 x^0$ and $E^2 = \mu^2 x^0 = \mu^0 x^0$, we have

$$E^1-E^2 = x_i^0(\mu_i^1-\mu_i^0). \tag{3}$$

Therefore, (2) can be written as

$$\frac{x_j^1-x_j^0}{\mu_i^1-\mu_i^0} = x_i^0\frac{x_j^1-x_j^2}{E^1-E^2}+\frac{x_j^2-x_j^0}{\mu_i^1-\mu_i^0}. \tag{4}$$

In the limit of μ_i^1 tending to μ_i^0, it can be put in the form

$$\frac{\partial x_j}{\partial \mu_i} = x_i^0\frac{\partial x_j}{\partial E}+X_{ji}, \tag{4'}$$

where X_{ji} denotes the limiting Relative Expected Return Effect.

As is at once noticed, this equation is very similar to the Slutsky equation which Hicks called the 'fundamental equation of value theory', except that the latter has a minus sign before x_i^0 on the right-hand side. In analogy with the Slutsky equation, Royama and Hamada called the first and the second terms of (4′) the wealth and the substitution effects, respectively. However, (4′) is no more than the analysis of what I called the 'want pattern' effect in the previous chapter. It must be remembered that in the traditional theory of demand, prices appear in the budget equation but not in the utility function, while in the theory of portfolio choices, the expected rates of returns are not in the budget equation but affect the ranking of various portfolios.

In order to analyse the portfolio choice into a part which obeys a definite law of comparative statics and the residual, let us introduce a fourth circumstance in which there prevails μ^3 being proportional to μ^1 and inducing the individual to choose an x^3 such that

$$\mu^0 x^0 = \mu^0 x^3. \tag{5}$$

There is no necessity for the absolute level of μ^3 to equal that of μ^2 as the index number $\mu^3 x^0/\mu^0 x^0$ may be different from one, so that the change of x from x^0 to x^3 includes an absolute expected return effect in addition to the relative expected return effect. Inserting x^3 between x^1 and x^2, we have the following triple splitting of the total effect:

$$x^1 - x^0 = (x^1 - x^3) + (x^3 - x^2) + (x^2 - x^0). \tag{6}$$

As will be shown later, $x^3 - x^2$ is an infinitesimal of higher order than $\mu^1 - \mu^0$, when $\mu^1 - \mu^0$ is very small; we may, therefore, call $x^1 - x^3$ the quasi-absolute expected return effect and the sum of $x^3 - x^2$ and $x^2 - x^0$ the quasi-relative expected return effect. We can show that the latter is regulated by a law which is analogous to the fundamental law of consumer's demand established by Slutsky and Hicks.

Because of (5) we have $\mu^3 x^3 > \mu^3 x^0$ by virtue of (*). As μ^3 is proportional to μ^1, we may replace μ^3 of this inequality by μ^1 without any other change. Hence, in view of (5), we obtain the general law:

$$(\mu^1 - \mu^0)(x^3 - x^0) > 0. \tag{7}$$

In words, as far as the quasi-relative expected return effects are concerned, x and μ change in the 'same' direction, in the sense that the angle between vectors $\mu^1 - \mu^0$ and $x^3 - x^0$ is acute. In particular, if μ_i increases, other components of μ remaining constant, we have a quasi-relative effect on x_i which is positive.

Let us now write $E^3 = \mu^1 x^3$ and $E^2 = \mu^0 x^3 = \mu^0 x^0$. When only μ_i varies, we have

$$E^3 - E^2 = x_i^3(\mu_i^1 - \mu_i^0).$$

This, together with (6), gives us

$$\frac{x_j^1 - x_j^0}{\mu_i^1 - \mu_i^0} = x_i^3 \frac{x_j^1 - x_j^3}{E^3 - E^2} + \frac{x_j^3 - x_j^2}{\mu_i^1 - \mu_i^0} + \frac{x_j^2 - x_j^0}{\mu_i^1 - \mu_i^0}.$$

When $\mu_i^1 - \mu_i^0$ is infinitesimally small,

$$\frac{x_j^1 - x_j^0}{\mu_i^1 - \mu_i^0}, \quad \frac{x_j^1 - x_j^3}{E^3 - E^2}, \quad \frac{x_j^2 - x_j^0}{\mu_i^1 - \mu_i^0}, \quad \text{and} \quad x_i^3$$

tend to
$$\frac{\partial x_j}{\partial \mu_i}, \quad \frac{\partial x_j}{\partial E}, \quad X_{ij}, \quad \text{and} \quad x_i^0,$$

respectively. Therefore, taking (4′) into account, we obtain

$$\lim_{\mu_i^1 \to \mu_i^0} \frac{x_j^3 - x_j^2}{\mu_i^1 - \mu_i^0} = 0,$$

which establishes that $x_j^3 - x_j^2$ is an infinitesimal of higher order than $\mu_i^1 - \mu_i^0$. We can now write (7) in the limit as

$$\sum_{i=1}^{n} \sum_{j=1}^{n} X_{ij}\, \mathrm{d}p_i\, \mathrm{d}p_j \geqq 0,$$

which in turn implies $X_{ii} \geqq 0$ for all i.

3. A Change in Risk with Constant Expected Returns

In this section we are concerned with the effect of a change in the variance–covariance matrix (the expected rates of returns being held constant) upon the portfolio chosen. Let σ^0 and σ^1 be the previous and the current variance–covariance matrices respectively. The quadratic forms are simply denoted as

$$\sigma^0(x) = x'\sigma^0 x \quad \text{and} \quad \sigma^1(x) = x'\sigma^1 x.$$

μ is fixed at μ^0 in both circumstances. The individual chooses x^0 in the first circumstance and x^1 in the second.

By virtue of the basic hypothesis of the mean–variance theory it is clear that these choices imply

(iii) either $\mu^0 x^0 > \mu^0 x^1$ or $\sigma^0(x^0) < \sigma^0(x^1)$, or both; and
(iv) either $\mu^0 x^1 > \mu^0 x^0$ or $\sigma^1(x^1) < \sigma^1(x^0)$, or both.

Therefore, from (iii) it follows that if $\mu^0 x^0 < \mu^0 x^1$, then $\sigma^0(x^0) < \sigma^0(x^1)$; while from (iv), if $\mu^0 x^0 \geqq \mu^0 x^1$, then

$\sigma^1(x^1) < \sigma^1(x^0)$. Hence we obtain a proposition of fundamental importance which states:

(**) If $\sigma^0(x^1) \leqq \sigma^0(x^0)$, then $\sigma^1(x^1) < \sigma^1(x^0)$.

It is noted that although these inequalities have the same sense as those of Samuelson's weak axiom, they are different in the degree with respect to x; that is to say, $\sigma(x)$ is quadratic, while px of the weak axiom is linear, of course.

In order to educe the part of x which obeys a definite law of comparative statics, we introduce an imaginary μ, say μ^1, which is proportional to μ^0 and induces the individual to choose an x^2 such that

$$\mu^1 x^0 = \mu^1 x^2 \tag{8}$$

when σ^1 prevails. The effect of a change in σ on x is analysed into two parts, the first, $x^0 \to x^2$, being the effect of a change in σ (from σ^0 to σ^1) combined with a change in μ from μ^0 to μ^1, and the second, $x^2 \to x^1$, being the effect of a change in μ from the imaginary μ^1 to the original μ^0. The former is called the Pure Risk Effect, while the latter is called the Compensatory Expected-Wealth Effect.

This splitting can be rationalized in the following way. When there is a change in σ, the individual switches his portfolio from x^0 to x^1. They give different expected values of wealth, $\mu^0 x^0$ and $\mu^0 x^1$. Therefore, we make an adjustment in the expected wealth such that it eliminates the difference between $\mu^0 x^0$ and $\mu^0 x^1$, by introducing an imaginary change of μ from μ^0 to μ^1. When it happened in combination with the change of σ, then the individual would choose x^2, instead of x^1, which gives the same expected value of wealth as x^0 does, as we have

$$\mu^0 x^0 = \mu^0 x^2. \tag{9}$$

(This at once follows from (8) because μ^1 is proportional to μ^0.) Thus the Pure Risk Effect gives the pure effect of σ on x which is obtained when the resulting change of W is eliminated. The imaginary change in μ from μ^0 to μ^1 is offset by the counter-change from μ^1 to μ^0 which gives x the Compensatory Expected-Wealth Effect.

When μ^1 and σ^1 prevail, the individual chooses x^2 rather than

x^0, so that we must have either $\mu^1 x^2 > \mu^1 x^0$ or $\sigma^1(x^2) < \sigma^1(x^0)$ (or both). But the level of μ^1 is taken so as to make the individual choose x^2 fulfilling (8). Hence we obtain

$$\sigma^1(x^2) < \sigma^1(x^0). \tag{10}$$

On the other hand, when μ^0 and σ^0 prevail, he prefers x^0 to x^2. As we have (9), the same argument as above can be applied, which leads to the conclusion

$$\sigma^0(x^2) > \sigma^0(x^0). \tag{11}$$

Let us now write $\Delta\sigma = \sigma^1 - \sigma^0$ and $\Delta\sigma(x) = x'\Delta\sigma x$. Subtracting (11) from (10), we have

$$\Delta\sigma(x^2) < \Delta\sigma(x^0) \tag{12}$$

from which we can derive two laws concerning the Pure Risk Effect.

First, if σ_{ii} is the sole element which changes in the variance–covariance matrix, we have $\Delta\sigma_{ii}(x_i^2)^2 < \Delta\sigma_{ii}(x_i^0)^2$ from (12). Thus, as far as the Pure Risk Effect is concerned, an increase in the variance of the rate of returns of the ith asset has a negative effect on the holdings of it.

Second, if the covariance between r_i and r_j increases, we have from (12)

$$\Delta\sigma_{ij}\, x_i^2 x_j^2 < \Delta\sigma_{ij}\, x_i^0 x_j^0, \tag{13}$$

which implies that either x_i or x_j must decrease (possibly both will decrease).[6] If an increase in σ_{ij} gives rise to a decrease in x_i, we have from (13)

$$\left[\frac{x_i^0}{x_j^0}\frac{\Delta x_j}{\Delta x_i}\right] + \frac{\Delta x_j}{x_j^0} > -1, \tag{14}$$

where $\Delta x_k = x_k^2 - x_k^0$, $k = i, j$. When $\Delta\sigma_{ij}$ is infinitesimal, Δx_j is also infinitesimal. Consequently, (14) implies the following restriction on the elasticity:

$$\frac{x_i}{x_j}\frac{\mathrm{d}x_j}{\mathrm{d}x_i} > -1.$$

[6] In deriving (13) attention is invited to the fact that the variance–covariance matrices σ^0 and σ^1 (and hence their difference $\Delta\sigma$) are all symmetric.

4. A Change in Current Price

Finally, we deal with a problem which was discussed by Bierwag and Grove but not by Royama and Hamada, that is, the effect of a change in current price with constant wealth and constant expected returns. Let p be an n-dimensional row vector of current prices; the wealth constraint is written as

$$\overline{W} = px.$$

Consider two situations where different current prices p^0 and p^1 are prevailing and there is no difference in the initial holding of wealth, expected returns, and risk; so that $\overline{W}$, μ, and σ are common to these situations. The individual chooses x^0 at p^0 but x^1 at p^1:

$$\overline{W} = p^0x^0 = p^1x^1. \tag{15}$$

In examining the effect of a price change from p^0 to p^1 on x, from x^0 to x^1, we introduce an imaginary, third situation where $\overline{W}$ is adjusted so that a portfolio x^2 fulfilling

$$p^1x^2 = p^1x^0 \tag{16}$$

is chosen at p^1. Let us write the original $\overline{W}$ as $\overline{W}^1$ and the new $\overline{W}$ as $\overline{W}^2$. From (15) and (16)

$$\overline{W}^1 = p^0x^0 \quad \text{and} \quad \overline{W}^2 = p^1x^0. \tag{17}$$

Evidently, the individual could buy x^0 in the third situation but has preferred x^2 to x^0. Since there is no change in μ and σ, the same preference order of x as that in the third situation prevails in the first situation. Therefore, Samuelson's weak axiom of revealed preference holds exactly; namely, (16) implies that x^2 does not meet the wealth constraint in the first situation

$$p^0x^0 < p^0x^2. \tag{18}$$

Otherwise, the individual should have chosen x^2 in the first situation also, because he prefers x^2 to x^0.

A change in x from x^0 to x^1 can now be analysed into two components: a change from x^0 to x^2 and a further change from x^2 to x^1. Because of the weak axiom of revealed preference, the former obeys the familiar law of substitution effects. That is, from (16) and (18), we obtain

$$(p^1-p^0)(x^2-x^0) < 0 \tag{19}$$

for p^1 that is not proportional to p^0. In particular, in the case of only one price, say p_i, varying, (19) is reduced to

$$(p_i^1 - p_i^0)(x_i^2 - x_i^0) < 0,$$

so that as far as the substitution term is concerned, an increase in the current price of an asset i gives rise to a decrease in its holding.

In the same special case, we have from (17)

$$\overline{W}^1 - \overline{W}^2 = -(p_i^1 - p_i^0)x_i^0. \tag{20}$$

Therefore, dividing $x_j^1 - x_j^0 = (x_j^1 - x_j^2) + (x_j^2 - x_j^0)$ by $p_i^1 - p_i^0$ and taking (20) into account, we have

$$\frac{x_j^1 - x_j^0}{p_i^1 - p_i^0} = -x_i^0 \frac{x_j^1 - x_j^2}{\overline{W}^1 - \overline{W}^2} + \frac{x_j^2 - x_j^0}{p_i^1 - p_i^0},$$

or

$$\frac{\Delta x_j}{\Delta p_i} = -x_i^0 \frac{\Delta x_j}{\Delta \overline{W}} + \left[\frac{\Delta x_j}{\Delta p_i}\right], \tag{21}$$

where the term in the brackets represents the effect on the holding of asset j of a change in the current price of asset i combined with the compensating change in wealth. This term is distinguished by the brackets from the term on the left-hand side which represents the effect of a change in p_i on x_j with constant wealth. In the limit of p_i^1 tending to p_i^0, (21) can be written in the form

$$\frac{\partial x_j}{\partial p_i} = -x_i^0 \frac{\partial x_j}{\partial \overline{W}} + \left[\frac{\partial x_j}{\partial p_i}\right],$$

which is the Slutsky equation for assets. It must be noticed that the substitution effect of a change in the expected returns previously discussed is different from the present substitution effect $[\Delta x_j/\Delta p_i]$ or $[\partial x_j/\partial p_i]$, that is the effect on asset j of a wealth-compensated change in the current price of i.

The following laws are exactly parallel to those concerning the demand for consumption goods which have been established by Slutsky, Allen, Hicks, and others.

(i) From (15), (16), and (17), we have

$$\overline{W}^1 = p^1 x^1 \quad \text{and} \quad \overline{W}^2 = p^1 x^2;$$

therefore

$$p^1(x^1 - x^2) = \overline{W}^1 - \overline{W}^2.$$

Dividing this by $\overline{W}^1-\overline{W}^2$ and considering the definition of $\Delta x_j/\Delta\overline{W}$, we find the law concerning the income effects,

$$\sum_j p_j^1 \frac{\Delta x_j}{\Delta\overline{W}} = 1. \tag{22}$$

(ii) We have from (16)

$$p^1(x^2-x^0) = 0. \tag{23}$$

In the case of only one price p_i varying, this is divided by $p_i^1-p_i^0$. It is then seen, in view of the definition of $[\Delta x_j/\Delta p_i]$, that

$$\sum_j p_j^1 \left[\frac{\Delta x_j}{\Delta p_i}\right] = 0, \tag{24}$$

which represents Hicks's third rule of the substitution effects in the case of a finite change in price.

(iii) Let us next be concerned with a general change in prices. Between $p^0 = (p_1^0,\dots,p_n^0)$ and $p^1 = (p_1^1,\dots,p_n^1)$ we insert

$$p^{(1)} = (p_1^1, p_2^0,\dots,p_n^0),$$
$$p^{(2)} = (p_1^1, p_2^1, p_3^0,\dots,p_n^0),$$
$$\cdot \quad \cdot \quad \cdot \quad \cdot \quad \cdot \quad \cdot \quad \cdot$$
$$p^{(n-1)} = (p_1^1, p_2^1,\dots,p_{n-1}^1, p_n^0).$$

Let
$$\overline{W}^{(1)} = p^{(1)}x^0,$$

and let $x^{(1)}$ be the portfolio chosen by the individual with $\overline{W}^{(1)}$ at $p^{(1)}$. Similarly let $x^{(2)}$ be the portfolio chosen by the individual with $\overline{W}^{(2)} = p^{(2)}x^{(1)}$ at $p^{(2)}$, and so forth; finally, let $x^{(n-1)}$ be the portfolio chosen at $p^{(n-1)}$ when the individual's wealth amounts to $\overline{W}^{(n-1)} = p^{(n-1)}x^{(n-2)}$. We have the identity

$$x_j^2-x_j^0 = (x_j^{(1)}-x_j^0)+(x_j^{(2)}-x_j^{(1)})+\dots+(x_j^2-x_j^{(n-1)})$$

for all j. Therefore

$$x_j^2-x_j^0 = (p_1^1-p_1^0)\left[\frac{x_j^{(1)}-x_j^0}{p_1^1-p_1^0}\right]+(p_2^1-p_2^0)\left[\frac{x_j^{(2)}-x_j^{(1)}}{p_2^1-p_2^0}\right]+$$
$$+\dots+(p_n^1-p_n^0)\left[\frac{x_j^2-x_j^{(n-1)}}{p_n^1-p_n^0}\right]. \tag{25}$$

On the right-hand side the term within the first set of square brackets represents the substitution effect on x_j which we have when prices change from p^0 to $p^{(1)}$, in combination with a compensating change in wealth from $\overline{W}^0$ to $\overline{W}^{(1)}$; the term within the second set of square brackets represents the substitution effect due to a price change from $p^{(1)}$ to $p^{(2)}$ that is combined with a compensating change in wealth from $\overline{W}^{(1)}$ to $\overline{W}^{(2)}$, and so forth. Accordingly, (25) may be written as

$$x_j^2-x_j^0 = (p_1^1-p_1^0)\left[\frac{\Delta x_j}{\Delta p_1}\right]_{p^0}^{p^{(1)}} + (p_2^1-p_2^0)\left[\frac{\Delta x_j}{\Delta p_2}\right]_{p^{(1)}}^{p^{(2)}} + \\ +\dots+(p_n^1-p_n^0)\left[\frac{\Delta x_j}{\Delta p_n}\right]_{p^{(n-1)}}^{p^1},$$

where $\left[\frac{\Delta x_j}{\Delta p_i}\right]_{p^{(i-1)}}^{p^{(i)}}$ denotes the substitution effect due to a price change from $p^{(i-1)}$ to $p^{(i)}$. Substituting this into (19), we have

$$(p^1-p^0)(x^2-x^0) = \sum_i \sum_j \left[\frac{\Delta x_j}{\Delta p_i}\right]_{p^{(i-1)}}^{p^{(i)}} (p_i^1-p_i^0)(p_j^1-p_j^0) < 0, \tag{26}$$

where $p^{(0)} = p^0$ and $p^{(n)} = p^1$, provided that p^1 is not proportional to p^0. (26) is no more than a 'finite price-change' version of Hicks's fourth rule of the substitution effects. In the special case of $p^{(1)} = p^{(2)} = \dots = p^{(n-1)} = p^1$, (26) is reduced to

$$(p^1-p^0)(x^2-x^0) = \left[\frac{\Delta x_1}{\Delta p_1}\right]_{p^0}^{p^1}(p_1^1-p_1^0)(p_1^1-p_1^0) < 0.$$

This establishes $[\Delta x_i/\Delta p_i] < 0$ for all i, which corresponds to Hicks's first rule.

Finally, it is obvious that the formulae (22), (24), and (26) are reduced to the familiar ones when prices and wealth change infinitesimally:

(i) $\sum_j p_j \frac{\partial x_j}{\partial \overline{W}} = 1,$

(ii) $\sum_j p_j \left[\frac{\partial x_j}{\partial p_i}\right] = 0,$

(iii) $\sum_i \sum_j \left[\frac{\partial x_j}{\partial p_i}\right] \mathrm{d}p_i\, \mathrm{d}p_j < 0,$

for any non-vanishing $\mathrm{d}p$ which is not proportional to p^0.

XII. Portfolio Diversification as Optimal Precautionary Behaviour

M. R. GRAY *and* J. M. PARKIN

1. Introduction

WHY do we observe diversified portfolios of non-marketable, capital-value certain, financial assets? Such assets have interest yields which are not liable to short term fluctuation and are free from default risk. Why do we not observe zero holdings of all such assets except that with the highest yield?

This chapter constitutes an attempt to answer these questions in terms of optimal precautionary behaviour. The analysis is developed in terms of a choice model which views diversification as providing alternative sources for meeting cash requirements where each source has a different liquidation cost and different yield. Models in this same vein have been proposed before and all stem from Edgeworth [**1**]. We achieve a greater degree of generality than has been proposed before. Also, we produce predictions which are sufficiently strong to enable our model to be distinguished empirically from other models of asset choice.

Our motivation for tackling this problem has two aspects: theoretical and empirical. On the theoretical level, there is, apparently, no non-trivial model available which is capable of answering the questions posed at the beginning. It may be objected that models which stem from Friedman [**1**] can provide an answer. Such models postulate that assets give rise to an interest yield and a non-pecuniary service yield. The latter is usually attributed to risk reduction and convenience in transactions. Holdings of assets are selected to maximize some function of the interest income and non-pecuniary service yield, subject to a wealth constraint. Following conventional consumer theory, this produces a set of asset demand functions, the arguments of which are the interest rates on all assets and wealth.

We do not find this approach attractive. It does not explain why the non-pecuniary service yield of, say, a deposit with a non-bank financial intermediary should be different from a time deposit with a bank. *Post hoc* explanations can be given for the existence of such differences but they are not part of the theory. It is natural in rejecting the above approach to turn to that body of models which has sprung from reconsideration of Keynes's three motives for holding money. These are, of course, the transactions, the precautionary, and the speculative motives. The transactions motive ignores uncertainty and minimizes inventory costs by offsetting adjustment against holding costs. The precautionary motive explicitly considers the uncertainty surrounding the size of cash requirements, and seeks to minimize the expected cost of meeting these requirements. The speculative motive arises from an attempt to take account of price (or interest rate) uncertainty and typically maximizes an objective function involving the expected return and variance of return on asset holdings.(1)

As is well known, the speculative model is only capable of explaining diversification among assets whose yields are subject to unpredictable fluctuation. However, transactions and precautionary models are able to explain diversification among assets whose yields are not subject to short term fluctuation. Both focus on the problem of optimally allocating funds among a range of assets with different yields and liquidation costs. The transactions model treats cash requirements as being known with certainty, while the precautionary model treats such requirements as unpredictable. The transactions model explains the phenomena described above as a relatively trivial extension of the analysis presented by Feige and Parkin [**1**]. The precautionary motive solution, however, is less obvious and seems worth examining.

Several problems frequently arise in the empirical estimation of complete systems of asset demand functions. First, the number of assets involved, and the degree of multi-collinearity

(1) This analytic representation of the three motives is due to Arrow in Chapter 1 of Arrow, Karlin, and Scarf [**1**].

between the interest rates on them, make it difficult to obtain well-determined parameter estimates. Second, the length of time for which data runs are available is usually short, and degrees of freedom are scarce. Strong *a priori* theorizing can help to overcome both of these problems.

Models which derive from Friedman, as well as speculative models, help to some extent. They give rise to symmetry and aggregation restrictions, which reduce the number of parameters to be estimated.[2] The model presented here goes much further than these. It generates strong predictions about both the functional forms of asset demand systems and limitations on the number of interest rates to be included in each equation. The model is thus capable of refutation. If it turns out to be an adequate representation of the facts, it is also capable of yielding well-determined parameter estimates, even in the face of severe multi-collinearity.

We do not present this model as a replacement for the more usual speculative model, and as valid for all asset choices. Instead we present it as an explanation for the diversification of assets where the principal source of uncertainty surrounds the scale of cash requirements, rather than the yields on the assets, and where liquidation is costly at the margin.

In section 2 of this chapter we present our model, in section 3 we examine the implications for the demand functions of making alternative, specific assumptions about the form of the cash requirements probability distribution, and section 4 contains extensions and conclusions.

2. A Precautionary Model of Generalized Asset Diversification

2.1. *Abstractions and assumptions*

It is proposed that the decision-maker's situation be characterized by the following abstraction. A given stock of wealth may be held as a portfolio of n interest-bearing fixed capital value assets. The portfolio is reviewed at constant intervals. No attempt is made within the model to determine the optimal

(2) For examples of this see Parkin, Gray, and Barrett [1].

review period. For the purposes of the analysis, the period length is to be regarded as fixed. Adjustments in the portfolio carried out at the time of these reviews are costless. The rationale for this assumption is that such adjustments are foreseen and the portfolio is so structured that these costs will be insignificant. At a single time point before the next review date, a stochastic cash requirement occurs. In order to meet this cash requirement, asset holdings are run down. This stochastic cash requirement, which occurs at a time different from the portfolio review date, is assumed to lead to asset disposals which are costly. In particular we postulate that asset liquidation costs are linear homogeneous functions of the amount liquidated of each asset.

From this set of assumptions, we can define the profit accruing from a portfolio in a single period as

$$\pi = m'v + c'v^*, \tag{1}$$

where π is profit per decision period, m is an n-vector of interest rates per decision period, v is a non-negative n-vector of assets initially held, c is an n-vector of liquidation costs,[3] v^* is a non-positive n-vector of asset liquidations, and $'$ indicates vector transposition. Since we have assumed that the within-period cash requirements are stochastic, the liquidation cost c and the liquidations v^* and hence profit π will also be stochastic.

We assume that the objective of the decision-maker is the maximization of the expected value of π, written $\hat{\pi}$. We further assume that c_i and v_i^* are independently distributed for all assets, hence we may write

$$\hat{\pi} = m'v + \hat{c}'\hat{v}^*$$

as the objective function.

The maximization of $\hat{\pi}$ is performed subject to the constraint that the elements of v just exhaust total wealth, i.e.

$$i'v - w = 0$$

(3) Liquidation costs may be of two types; brokerage fees and forgone interest. The model is most readily interpreted as handling only the first of these. However, the c-vector can also be interpreted as including forgone interest given the additional assumption that the timing and size of liquidations are independent.

where i is the unit vector and w is the wealth at the start of the period. The formal maximization problem may now be stated thus.

Choose v and the conditional liquidations v^* such that

$$\hat{\pi} = m'v + \hat{c}'\hat{v}^* \tag{2}$$

is maximized subject to

$$i'v - w = 0. \tag{3}$$

We proceed to solve this problem in two stages. First we derive the optimal conditional liquidations, then, given these, we find the optimal v.

2.2. *The optimal liquidation strategy*

First, we order the elements in v, v^*, m, and c such that actual and expected liquidation costs are increasing as we move down the vectors, i.e. such that

$$\hat{c}_1 < \hat{c}_2 < \hat{c}_3 < \ldots < \hat{c}_n.$$

If any asset i exists such that

$$m_i < m_j$$

and
$$\hat{c}_i > \hat{c}_j,$$

that asset is dominated by j. Given the objective function (2), it is immediately clear that a zero holding for a dominated asset will always be optimal. Hence, we eliminate dominated assets from the choice set and interpret our n-vectors as referring only to assets which are not dominated.

It follows from this that not only are the elements of $\hat{c}$ ordered such that
$$\hat{c}_1 < \hat{c}_2 < \hat{c}_3 < \ldots < \hat{c}_n$$

but also
$$m_1 < m_2 < m_3 < \ldots < m_n.$$

Given these common orderings of assets on the basis of both expected liquidation costs and interest yields, we see that it will always be optimal, in the event of a stochastic cash requirement, to meet that requirement by liquidating assets starting with the first, and moving up the scale as far as necessary until the cash requirement is fully met. This strategy will be optimal regardless of the levels of the assets initially chosen. This is particularly important in simplifying the formulation of the problem of choosing the optimal elements of v.

We now go on to consider this problem.

2.3. *The choice of an optimal portfolio*

We proceed to solve the portfolio choice in two steps. First, we establish the relation between expected liquidations $\hat{v}^*$ and the assets initially chosen v. Then we go on to the choice of v. We assume that in each period the decision unit has a stochastic cash requirement of z, which has a probability function

$$\begin{aligned} \text{p.d.f. of } z &= f(z) \quad \text{for } \alpha \leq z \leq \beta, \\ &= 0 \qquad \text{otherwise.} \end{aligned} \tag{4}$$

We assume that $\beta \geq i'v$.[4] We specify the cumulative density function of z as $F(z)$ and require that $f(z) \neq 0$ for $\alpha \leq z \leq \beta$ so that $F(z)$ is monotonic increasing for $\alpha \leq z \leq \beta$. We denote the inverse of F by G which, given our assumptions, is also monotonic increasing. As we have already shown, assets are liquidated to meet the stochastic cash requirement in the order given by the magnitude of their liquidation costs, the cheapest (lowest $\hat{c}_i$) being disposed of first and the most costly last.

We can obtain the relation between asset disposals, asset levels, and the cash requirement by first specifying a set of mapping functions from z to v^* and then showing the relation between v^* and v. Define

$$v_i^* = g_i(z)$$

as the function which maps from z to the disposal of the ith asset. Recalling that the assets are ordered by liquidation costs this function is specified in detail as

$$g_i(z) = \begin{cases} 0 & \text{for } \alpha \leq z \leq V_{i-1}, & \text{(5 a)} \\ -(z - V_{i-1}) & \text{for } V_{i-1} < z \leq V_i, & \text{(5 b)} \\ -v_i & \text{for } V_i < z \leq \beta, & \text{(5 c)} \end{cases}$$

where $V_j = \sum_{i=1}^{j} v_i$.

[4] This assumption simplifies the analysis but its relaxation does not materially affect the conclusions.

The three parts of the mapping rule are simple to explain. (5 a) says that the ith asset is not disposed of if the stochastic cash requirement is negative or positive but less than the sum of the first $(i-1)$ assets. (5 b) says that if the stochastic cash requirement exceeds the sum of the first $(i-1)$ assets, but is less than the sum of the first i assets, then the ith asset will be partly disposed of. Finally, (5 c) states that if the stochastic cash requirement exceeds the sum of the first i assets, then the ith asset will be entirely liquidated. It will be noticed that, for $i = n$, (5 c) includes the case of bankruptcy.

Using the mapping rule (5) together with the p.d.f. of z, (4), we may write for the expectation of liquidation of the ith asset, $\hat{v}_i^*$,

$$\hat{v}_i^* = -\int_{V_{i-1}}^{V_i} zf(z)\,dz + \int_{V_{i-1}}^{V_i} V_{i-1}f(z)\,dz - \int_{V_i}^{\beta} v_i f(z)\,dz. \tag{6}$$

Multiplying the expected liquidations $\hat{v}_i^*$ by their expected liquidation costs $\hat{c}_i$ and summing over all n assets gives

$$\hat{c}'\hat{v}^* = \sum_{i=1}^{n} \hat{c}_i \left\{ -\int_{V_{i-1}}^{V_i} zf(z)\,dz + \int_{V_{i-1}}^{V_i} V_{i-1}f(z)\,dz - \int_{V_i}^{\beta} v_i f(z)\,dz \right\}. \tag{7}$$

Equation (7) now gives the expected liquidation cost, $\hat{c}'\hat{v}^*$, purely in terms of v. We may now go on to solve the problem of choosing the optimal v.

Defining $\hat{c}'\hat{v}^*$ in (7) as $h(v)$, we may write this problem thus. Choose v to maximize

$$\hat{\pi} = m'v + h(v)$$

subject to

$$i'v - w = 0.$$

Forming the Lagrangian

$$L = m'v + h(v) + \lambda(i'v - w) \tag{8}$$

and differentiating with respect to v and λ, we obtain the first order conditions:

$$\left.\begin{aligned} &\text{(a)}\ \frac{\partial L}{\partial v} = m + h_v + \lambda i = 0 \\ &\text{(b)}\ \frac{\partial L}{\partial \lambda} = i'v - w = 0 \end{aligned}\right\}, \tag{9}$$

where h_v is the vector of partial derivatives of $h(v)$ with respect to the elements of v.

We are interested in the solution of (9) for the asset vector v. Given the non-linearity of h_v we might proceed by considering the total differential of (9) and solve for the vector dv. However, it turns out, in this case, that the structure of h_v is such that we may obtain explicit solutions for v. In order to achieve this, it is necessary to examine in detail a typical element of h_v. Inspection of this will make it clear that the equations in (9 a) can be solved sequentially for the elements of v.

Let us first look at a typical element of (9 a). The only part of this which is not obvious is h_v. $h(v)$ is defined by equation (7), hence, to obtain a typical element of h_v we differentiate (7) with respect to a particular element of v, the kth. Thus, a typical element of h_v, h_{vk}, is

$$h_{v_k} = -\hat{c}_k \int_{V_k}^{\beta} f(z)\,dz + \sum_{i=k+1}^{n} \hat{c}_i \int_{V_{i-1}}^{V_i} f(z)\,dz. \tag{10}$$

In the form of equation (10) h_{v_k} is not very useful. It will be more convenient for the subsequent analysis to write it as

$$h_{v_k} = -\hat{c}_k\left\{\int_{\alpha}^{\beta} f(z)\,dz - \int_{\alpha}^{V_k} f(z)\,dz\right\} + \\ + \sum_{i=k+1}^{n} \hat{c}_i\left\{\int_{\alpha}^{V_i} f(z)\,dz - \int_{\alpha}^{V_{i-1}} f(z)\,dz\right\}$$

which, from the definition of the cumulative density function of z, $F(z)$, is

$$h_{v_k} = -\hat{c}_k[F(\beta)-F(V_k)] + \sum_{i=k+1}^{n} \hat{c}_i[F(V_i)-F(V_{i-1})]. \tag{11}$$

Incorporating this into (9) gives as a typical equation of the system of first order conditions:

$$m_k - \hat{c}_k[F(\beta)-F(V_k)] + \sum_{i=k+1}^{n} \hat{c}_i[F(V_i)-F(V_{i-1})] + \lambda = 0.$$

These equations may now be solved sequentially for the elements of v in the following manner.

Subtract the second equation from the first to obtain

$$m_1 - m_2 + (\hat{c}_2 - \hat{c}_1)F(\beta) - (\hat{c}_2 - \hat{c}_1)F(V_1) = 0. \tag{12}$$

Recalling that $V_1 = v_1$, $F(\beta) = 1$, and rearranging,

$$F(v_1) = \frac{m_1 - m_2 + \hat{c}_2 - \hat{c}_1}{\hat{c}_2 - \hat{c}_1} \tag{13}$$

which, given that G is the inverse function of F, yields

$$v_1 = G\left(\frac{(m_1 - m_2)}{(\hat{c}_2 - \hat{c}_1)} + 1\right). \tag{14}$$

We may, to solve the second equation in a similar way, take the third equation of (9 a) from the second to obtain

$$m_2 - m_3 + \hat{c}_3 - \hat{c}_2 - (\hat{c}_3 - \hat{c}_2)F(V_2) = 0. \tag{15}$$

Recalling that $V_2 = v_1 + v_2$ and rearranging,

$$F(v_1 + v_2) = \frac{(m_2 - m_3)}{(\hat{c}_3 - \hat{c}_2)} + 1. \tag{16}$$

Insert (14) into (16) and solve for v_2 as

$$v_2 = G\left(\frac{m_2 - m_3}{\hat{c}_3 - \hat{c}_2} + 1\right) - G\left(\frac{m_1 - m_2}{\hat{c}_2 - \hat{c}_1} + 1\right). \tag{17}$$

It will now be clear, or may be proven inductively, that the solution for a typical asset, v_k, may be written

$$v_k = G\left(\frac{m_k - m_{k+1}}{\hat{c}_{k+1} - \hat{c}_k} + 1\right) - G\left(\frac{m_{k-1} - m_k}{\hat{c}_k - \hat{c}_{k-1}} + 1\right). \tag{18}$$

Since there is no $(n+1)$th equation, this procedure is not available for solution for the nth asset. In this case we proceed as follows. From the constraint:

$$V_n - w = 0$$

or

$$V_{n-1} + v_n - w = 0,$$

by summing the solutions for assets 1 to $n-1$, and noting the sequential cancelling of terms, we obtain

$$G\left(\frac{m_{n-1} - m_n}{\hat{c}_n - \hat{c}_{n-1}} + 1\right) + v_n - w = 0$$

or

$$v_n = w - G\left(\frac{m_{n-1} - m_n}{\hat{c}_n - \hat{c}_{n-1}} + 1\right). \tag{19}$$

It will now be helpful to bring together the results just derived. We have obtained demand functions for the n assets given by equations (14), (18), and (19). The interior asset demand functions are given by (18) and the first and last assets by (14) and (19) respectively. These demand functions may be specified more compactly as

$$v = H(m, w), \tag{20}$$

where H is a non-linear vector-valued function.

The structure of these demand functions is very interesting. First, the demand for each interior asset is a function of only three interest rates, its own and the rates on the two adjacent assets. The demands are independent of wealth. The signs of the responses are unambiguous. Given the initial ordering of assets, all the own rate response coefficients are positive and all the adjacent rate coefficients are negative and symmetric. This implies that all assets are substitutes for their neighbours. The first and last assets are slightly different. The first asset demand is a function of only its own rate and the rate on the next asset. The last asset is a function of the last two rates and of wealth. All wealth increases go into the last asset.

In addition to these features, it is clear from the structure of the problem that Cournot and Engel aggregations are satisfied.

We now want to establish the conditions under which all the elements of v are positive. To establish these we need to consider the first asset, the interior assets, and the last asset separately.

For $v_1 > 0$ we require

$$G\left(\frac{m_1 - m_2}{\hat{c}_2 - \hat{c}_1} + 1\right) > 0.$$

Recalling that F is monotonic over the relevant range, we may write

$$F\left(G\left(\frac{m_1 - m_2}{\hat{c}_2 - \hat{c}_1} + 1\right)\right) > F(0).$$

Further, since $G = F^{-1}$, we have

$$\frac{m_1 - m_2}{\hat{c}_2 - \hat{c}_1} + 1 > F(0)$$

or

$$1 - F(0) > \frac{m_2 - m_1}{\hat{c}_2 - \hat{c}_1}. \tag{21}$$

For interior assets, i.e. for $v_k > 0$, $k = 2,\ldots, n-1$, we require

$$G\left(\frac{m_k - m_{k+1}}{\hat{c}_{k+1} - \hat{c}_k} + 1\right) - G\left(\frac{m_{k-1} - m_k}{\hat{c}_k - \hat{c}_{k-1}} + 1\right) > 0. \tag{22}$$

Using the monotonic property of G and rearranging we obtain

$$\frac{m_k - m_{k+1}}{\hat{c}_{k+1} - \hat{c}_k} > \frac{m_{k-1} - m_k}{\hat{c}_k - \hat{c}_{k-1}}.$$

Finally, for $v_n > 0$, we require

$$w - G\left(\frac{m_{n-1} - m_n}{\hat{c}_n - \hat{c}_{n-1}} + 1\right) > 0.$$

Operating on this in the same way as for v_1, we immediately obtain

$$\frac{m_n - m_{n-1}}{\hat{c}_n - \hat{c}_{n-1}} > 1 - F(w). \tag{23}$$

We may now bring together the conditions in equations (21), (22), and (23) for all n asset holdings to be positive. They are

$$1 - F(0) > \frac{m_2 - m_1}{\hat{c}_2 - \hat{c}_1} > \frac{m_3 - m_2}{\hat{c}_3 - \hat{c}_2} > \ldots >$$

$$> \frac{m_{n-1} - m_{n-2}}{\hat{c}_{n-1} - \hat{c}_{n-2}} > \frac{m_n - m_{n-1}}{\hat{c}_n - \hat{c}_{n-1}} > 1 - F(w). \tag{24}$$

The probability of some loss constitutes the upper bound and the probability of bankruptcy the lower, with ratios of interest rate differentials to cost differentials ordered between these. If for any asset the inequality contained in (24) is not satisfied, then the demand for that asset will be at the zero corner.

3. Asset Demand Functions for Particular Probability Distributions of Cash Requirements

It is illuminating to look at these demand functions for specific formulations of the probability density function of z, $f(z)$. We do this for three alternative forms: uniform, triangular, and exponential. The uniform distribution has the virtue of extreme simplicity and leads to demand functions which are linear in the interest rates and wealth. The triangular distribution is suggested by the work of Porter [**1**] and leads to demand functions which are a generalization of the familiar square root form. The exponential distribution was used in an attempt to get as close as possible to deriving logarithmic demand functions of the form which has been common in empirical demand studies. The equations from this form turn out to be mixed linear–logarithmic.

3.1. *Uniform distribution of cash requirements*

We specify

$$f(z) = \frac{1}{2\gamma} \quad \text{for } \hat{z}-\gamma \leq z \leq \hat{z}+\gamma, \tag{25}$$

$$= 0 \quad \text{otherwise,}$$

where $\hat{z}$ is the mean of z and 2γ the range. This gives for z in the range

$$y = F(z) = \frac{1}{2\gamma}z - \frac{1}{2\gamma}(\hat{z}-\gamma) \tag{26}$$

and

$$z = G(y) = 2\gamma y + \hat{z} - \gamma. \tag{27}$$

Using this with equations (14), (18), and (19) the demand functions become

$$\begin{bmatrix} v_1 \\ v_2 \\ v_3 \\ \vdots \\ \vdots \\ v_n \end{bmatrix} = 2\gamma \begin{bmatrix} a_1 & -a_1 & 0 & \cdots & & 0 \\ -a_1 & (a_1+a_2) & -a_2 & \ddots & & \vdots \\ 0 & -a_2 & \ddots & \ddots & \ddots & \vdots \\ \vdots & \ddots & \ddots & \ddots & \ddots & 0 \\ \vdots & & \ddots & -a_{n-2} & (a_{n-1}+a_{n-2}) & -a_{n-1} \\ 0 & \cdots & & 0 & -a_{n-1} & a_{n-1} \end{bmatrix} \begin{bmatrix} m_1 \\ m_2 \\ \vdots \\ \vdots \\ \vdots \\ m_n \end{bmatrix} + \begin{bmatrix} 0 \\ 0 \\ \vdots \\ \vdots \\ 0 \\ 1 \end{bmatrix} w + \begin{bmatrix} \hat{z}+\gamma \\ 0 \\ \vdots \\ \vdots \\ 0 \\ -(\hat{z}+\gamma) \end{bmatrix} \tag{28}$$

where $a_i = \dfrac{1}{\hat{c}_{i+1} - \hat{c}_i}$.

In this case the demands are linear functions of the interest rates where the coefficients depend on the liquidation cost parameters and the probability distribution range. This formulation, while based on an unlikely probability distribution, has the virtue of yielding empirical implications of great simplicity.

3.2. *Triangular distribution of cash requirements*

In this case, the probability distribution is specified as

$$f(z) = \frac{1}{2\beta^2}(\hat{z}+\beta-z) \quad \text{for } \hat{z}-\beta \leq z \leq \hat{z}+\beta \tag{29}$$

and

$$G(y) = \hat{z}+\beta-2\beta\sqrt{(1-y)}. \tag{30}$$

Using (30) with our demand functions (14), (18), and (19) gives

$$\begin{bmatrix} v_1 \\ v_2 \\ \vdots \\ v_{n-1} \\ v_n \end{bmatrix} = -\beta \begin{bmatrix} \frac{2}{\sqrt{(\hat{c}_2-\hat{c}_1)}} & 0 & \cdots & 0 \\ -\frac{2}{\sqrt{(\hat{c}_2-\hat{c}_1)}} & \frac{2}{\sqrt{(\hat{c}_3-\hat{c}_2)}} & \ddots & \vdots \\ 0 & \ddots & \ddots & 0 \\ \vdots & \ddots & \ddots & \frac{2}{\sqrt{(\hat{c}_n-\hat{c}_{n-1})}} \\ 0 & \cdots & 0 & -\frac{2}{\sqrt{(\hat{c}_n-\hat{c}_{n-1})}} \end{bmatrix} \begin{bmatrix} \sqrt{(m_2-m_1)} \\ \sqrt{(m_3-m_2)} \\ \vdots \\ \sqrt{(m_{n-1}-m_{n-2})} \\ \sqrt{(m_n-m_{n-1})} \end{bmatrix} + \begin{bmatrix} 0 \\ 0 \\ \vdots \\ 0 \\ 1 \end{bmatrix} w + \begin{bmatrix} \hat{z}+\beta \\ 0 \\ \vdots \\ 0 \\ -(\hat{z}+\beta) \end{bmatrix} \tag{31}$$

It will be noticed that the asset demands are square root functions of interest rate differences, with the coefficients depending only on the cost function parameters and the probability distribution parameter, β.

3.3. *Exponential distribution of cash requirements*[5]

In this case we specify

$$f(z) = \delta\eta e^{\delta(\alpha-z)} \quad \text{for } \alpha < z < \infty, \tag{32}$$

which gives

$$G(y) = \alpha+\frac{1}{\delta}\log\eta-\frac{1}{\delta}\log(1-y). \tag{33}$$

[5] This case was originally worked out by Ross Chapman and Leslie Robb in a University of Essex mimeograph.

Using (33) along with our demand relations (14), (18), and (19) gives

$$\begin{bmatrix} v_1 \\ v_2 \\ \vdots \\ \vdots \\ v_n \end{bmatrix} = -\frac{1}{\delta} \begin{bmatrix} 1 & 0 & \cdots & \cdots & 0 \\ -1 & 1 & \ddots & & \vdots \\ 0 & -1 & \ddots & \ddots & 0 \\ \vdots & \ddots & \ddots & \ddots & 1 \\ 0 & \cdots & 0 & & -1 \end{bmatrix} \begin{bmatrix} \log(m_2 - m_1) \\ \log(m_3 - m_2) \\ \vdots \\ \vdots \\ \log(m_n - m_{n-1}) \end{bmatrix} + \frac{1}{\delta} \begin{bmatrix} \log(\hat{c}_2 - \hat{c}_1) \\ \log \dfrac{\hat{c}_3 - \hat{c}_2}{\hat{c}_2 - \hat{c}_1} \\ \vdots \\ \vdots \\ \log \dfrac{1}{\hat{c}_n - \hat{c}_{n-1}} \end{bmatrix} + \begin{bmatrix} \alpha + \frac{1}{\delta}\log\eta \\ 0 \\ \vdots \\ 0 \\ w - \alpha - \frac{1}{\delta}\log\eta \end{bmatrix} \tag{34}$$

This set of demand functions is particularly interesting because the functions are close relations of the logarithmic functions fitted in asset demand function studies. It is particularly interesting that the coefficients on the logs of the interest rate differentials are all the same, while the intercepts only differ between equations.

4. Extensions and Conclusions

The model presented here makes restrictive assumptions about the nature of the objective function and the way in which uncertainty enters the problem. If we assume the liquidation costs c to be non-stochastic (but we continue to assume stochastic cash requirements), a generalization of the objective function can easily be achieved. We may adopt a von Neumann–Morgenstern utility function of the form $\int_{\alpha}^{\beta} u(m'v+cv^*)f(z)\,dz$ which is maximized subject to (3). The mapping (5) from z to v^* is unaffected by this change in the objective function (assuming c non-stochastic). The demand functions then become, in the same way as before,

$$\begin{aligned} v_1 &= D(p_1, k), \\ v_i &= D(p_i, k) - D(p_{i-1}, k) \quad (i = 2, \ldots, n-1), \\ v_n &= w - D(p_n, k) \end{aligned} \tag{35}$$

where $p_i = a_i(m_i - m_{i+1})$ and $k = m'v$. These, together with the definition of k, enable us to find the optimum value of k depends on all ms and cs. Thus, in this more general case, the demand for each asset is a function of its own and the adjacent interest rates and, through an 'income effect' (an effect via k) only, the rates on all assets. Compensated variations in 'income' yield substitution effects which have the same tri-diagonal structure as in the simpler model.

Even though it is easy to suggest modifications to the model presented here, which might make the envisaged choice problem look more 'realistic', it may still be worth examining the performance of our model in explaining observed behaviour. This is readily facilitated by virtue of the simplicity of the demand functions which we have derived. In addition, the existence of a number of restrictions on the form of these demand functions allows rigorous statistical test procedures to be applied to the model. Providing that care is taken in making aggregation assumptions, and in including any restrictions that may apply to particular institutions, our model can be readily estimated and tested, using standard restricted least squares estimation and hypothesis testing procedures.

It would be surprising if the model explained diversification among assets with a risky yield but it may well explain diversification among those with a known capital value and return but with non-zero marginal liquidation costs such as the deposit liabilities of banks and non-bank intermediaries. A complete explanation of asset choice can only be available when a model has been developed which incorporates a von Neumann–Morgenstern utility function and simultaneously allows for stochastic cash requirements, liquidation costs, and yields and also the more general transactions costs involved in planned portfolio reallocations.

Bibliography

PART I

ALLINGHAM, M. G., and M. MORISHIMA

[1] 'Some Extensions of the Gross Substitutes System', mimeograph, 1970.

ARCHIBALD, G. C.

[1] 'Chamberlin versus Chicago', *Review of Economic Studies*, 29 (1961), 2–28.

[2] 'Profit Maximising and Non-Price Competition', *Economica*, 31 (1964), 13–22.

[3] 'The Qualitative Content of Maximising Models', *Journal of Political Economy*, 73 (1965), 27–36. (Reprinted here.)

ARROW, K. J.

[1] *Social Choice and Individual Values*, 1951.

[2] 'Price Quantity Adjustments in Multiple Markets', *Mathematical Methods in the Social Sciences 1959*, ed. by K. J. Arrow, S. Karlin, and P. Suppes, 1960.

ARROW, K. J., and L. HURWICZ

[1] 'Stability of the Competitive Equilibrium I', *Econometrica*, 26 (1958), 522–52.

BASSETT, L. R.

[1] 'The "Correspondence Principle": An Evaluation', mimeograph, 1969.

BASSETT, L. R., H. HABIBAGAHI, and J. QUIRK

[1] 'Qualitative Economics and Morishima Matrices', *Econometrica*, 35 (1967), 221–33.

BASSETT, L. R., J. MAYBEE, and J. QUIRK

[1] 'Qualitative Economics and the Scope of the Correspondence Principle', *Econometrica*, 36 (1968), 544–63.

DEBREU, G., and I. N. HERSTEIN

[1] 'Nonnegative Square Matrices', *Econometrica*, 21 (1953), 597–607.

FISHER, M. E., and A. T. FULLER

[1] 'On the Stabilization of Matrices and the Convergence of Linear Iterative Processes', *Proceedings of the Cambridge Philosophical Society*, 1958.

FOLK, H. W., and J. N. WOLFE

[1] 'A Generalisation of the Hicks–Slutsky Theory with Some Applications to Consumer Behaviour as a Learning Process', *Econometrica*, 30 (1962), 589.

GANTMACHER, F. R.

[1] *The Theory of Matrices*, 2 vols., 1960.

GORMAN, W. M.

[1] 'More Scope for Qualitative Economics', *Review of Economic Studies*, 31 (1964), 65–8.

GREEN, H. A. J.

[1] 'Direct Additivity and Consumers' Behaviour', *Oxford Economic Papers*, 13 (1961), 132–6.

HABIBAGAHI, H.
[1] 'Qualitative Analysis of Dynamic Stability in General Equilibrium Theory', Ph.D. thesis, Purdue, 1966.

HABIBAGAHI, H., and J. QUIRK
[1] 'Hicksian Stability and Walras' Law', mimeograph, 1970.

HICKS, J. R.
[1] *Value and Capital*, 1946.
[2] *A Revision of Demand Theory*, 1956.

KARLIN, S.
[1] *Mathematical Methods and Theory in Games, Programming and Economics*, 1961.

KREIN, M. G., and M. A. RUTMAN
[1] 'Linear Operators Leaving Invariant a Cone in a Banach Space', *Uspekhi Matematicheskikh Nauk*, 1948.

LANCASTER, K.
[1] 'The Scope of Qualitative Economics', *Review of Economic Studies*, 29 (1962), 99–123.
[2] 'Partitionable System and Qualitative Economics', *Review of Economic Studies*, 31 (1964), 69–72.
[3] 'The Theory of Qualitative Linear Systems', *Econometrica*, 33 (1965), 395–408.
[4] 'The Solution of Qualitative Comparative Static Problems', *Quarterly Journal of Economics*, 80 (1966), 278–95.

LANCASTER, K., and R. G. LIPSEY
[1] 'McManus on Second Best', *Review of Economic Studies*, 26 (1959), 225–6.

LIPSEY, R. G., and K. J. LANCASTER
[1] 'The General Theory of the Second Best', *Review of Economic Studies*, 24 (1956–7), 11–32.

MAYBEE, J. S.
[1] 'Remarks on the Theory of Cycles in Matrices', mimeograph, 1966.

MAYBEE, J. S., and J. P. QUIRK
[1] 'Qualitative Problems in Matrix Theory', *SIAM Review*, 1969.

McKENZIE, L.
[1] 'The Matrix with Dominant Diagonal in Economic Theory', *Mathematical Methods in the Social Sciences 1959*, ed. by K. J. Arrow, S. Karlin, and P. Suppes, 1960.

McMANUS, M.
[1] 'Comments on the General Theory of Second Best', *Review of Economic Studies*, 26 (1959), 209–24.

MORISHIMA, M.
[1] 'On the Laws of Change of the Price System in an Economy which contains Complementary Commodities', *Osaka Economic Papers*, 1 (1952), 101–13.
[2] 'A Note on Definitions of Related Goods', *Review of Economic Studies*, 23 (1955–6), 132–4.
[3] *Equilibrium, Stability and Growth*, 1964.
[4] 'A Generalization of the Gross Substitute System', *Review of Economic Studies*, 37 (1970), 177–86.

MOSAK, J.
[1] *General Equilibrium Theory in International Trade*, 1944.
PAPANDREOU, ANDREAS G.
[1] 'Theory Construction and Empirical Meaning in Economics', *American Economic Review, Paper and Proceedings*, 53 (1963), 205–10.
QUIRK, J.
[1] 'Comparative Statics under Walras' Law: The Case of Strong Dependence', *Review of Economic Studies*, 35 (1968), 11–22.
[2] 'The Correspondence Principle: A Macroeconomic Application', *International Economic Review*, 9 (1968), 294–306.
[3] 'The Competitive Equilibrium—A Qualitative Analysis', *Economic Models, Estimation and Risk Programming*, ed. by M. Beckmann and H. Kunzi, 1969.
[4] 'Complementarity and Stability of Equilibrium', *American Economic Review*, 60 (1970), 358–63.
QUIRK, J., and R. RUPPERT
[1] 'Qualitative Economics and the Stability of Equilibrium', *Review of Economic Studies*, 32 (1965), 311–26.
[2] 'Global Stability and Phase Diagrams', mimeograph, 1967.
[3] 'Maximization and the Qualitative Calculus', *Papers in Quantitative Economics*, ed. by J. Quirk and A. Zarley, 1968.
QUIRK, J., and R. SAPOSNIK
[1] *Introduction to General Equilibrium Theory and Welfare Economics*, 1968.
SAMUELSON, P. A.
[1] *Foundations of Economic Analysis*, 1947.
WITTE, J. G.
[1] 'Walras' Law and the Patinkin Paradox: A Qualitative Calculus for Macroeconomics', *Journal of Political Economy*, 74 (1966), 72–6.

PART II

ALLEN, R. G. D.
[1] 'A Comparison between Different Definitions of Complementarity and Competitive Goods', *Econometrica*, 2 (1934), 168–75.
ARROW, K. J.
[1] 'Additive Logarithmic Demand Functions and the Slutsky Relations', *Review of Economic Studies*, 28 (1961), 176–81.
AYANIAN, R.
[1] 'A Comparison of Barten's Estimated Demand Elasticities with Those Obtained Using Frisch's Method', *Econometrica*, 37 (1969), 79–94.
BARTEN, A. P.
[1] 'Consumer Demand Functions under Conditions of Almost Additive Preferences', *Econometrica*, 32 (1964), 1–38.
[2] 'Maximum Likelihood Estimation of a Complete Set of Demand Equations', *European Economic Review*, 1 (1969), 7–73.
BARTEN, A. P., and S. J. TURNOVSKY
[1] 'Some Aspects of the Aggregation Problem for Composite Demand Equations', *International Economic Review*, 7 (1966), 231–54.

BERGSON (BURK), A.
[1] 'Real Income, Expenditure Proportionality, and Frisch's "New Methods of Measuring Marginal Utility"', *Review of Economic Studies*, 4 (1936), 33–52.

BLACKORBY, C., G. LADY, D. NISSEN, and R. RUSSELL
[1] 'Homothetic Separability and Consumer Budgetary', *Econometrica*, 38 (1970), 468–72.

BYRON, R. P.
[1] 'A Simple Method for Estimating Demand Systems under Separable Utility Assumptions', *Review of Economic Studies*, 37 (1970), 261–74.

DEBREU, G.
[1] 'Topological Methods in Cardinal Utility Theory', *Mathematical Methods in the Social Sciences 1959*, ed. K. J. Arrow, S. Karlin, and P. Suppes, 1960.

DIAMOND, P. A.
[1] 'Technical Change and the Measurement of Capital and Output', *Review of Economic Studies*, 32 (1965), 289–98.

FERGUSON, C.
[1] *The Neoclassical Theory of Production and Distribution*, 1969.

FISHBURN, P. C.
[1] 'Additivity in Utility with Denumerable Product Sets', *Econometrica*, 34 (1966), 500–3.
[2] 'A Study of Independence in Multivariate Utility Theory', *Econometrica*, 37 (1969), 107–21.
[3] *Utility Theory for Decision Making*, 1970.

FISHER, F. M.
[1] 'Embodied Technical Change and the Existence of an Aggregate Capital Stock', *Review of Economic Studies*, 32 (1965), 263–88.
[2] 'Embodied Technology and the Aggregation of Fixed and Movable Capital Goods', *Review of Economic Studies*, 35 (1968), 417–28.
[3] 'Embodied Technology and the Existence of Labour and Output Aggregates', *Review of Economic Studies*, 35 (1968), 391–411.
[4] 'Approximate Aggregation and the Leontief Conditions', *Econometrica*, 37 (1969), 457–69.
[5] 'The Existence of Aggregate Production Functions', *Econometrica*, 37 (1969), 553–77.

FRISCH, R.
[1] 'A Complete Scheme for Computing All Direct and Cross Demand Elasticities in a Model with Many Sectors', *Econometrica*, 27 (1959), 177–96.
[2] 'Dynamic Utility', *Econometrica*, 32 (1964), 418–24.

GOLDBERGER, A. S.
[1] 'Directly Additive Utility and Constant Marginal Budget Shares', *Review of Economic Studies*, 36 (1969), 251–3.
[2] 'Functional Form and Utility: A Review of Consumer Demand Theory', mimeograph, 1967.

GOLDMAN, S. M., and H. UZAWA
[1] 'A Note on Separability in Demand Analysis', *Econometrica*, 32 (1964), 387–98.

GORMAN, W. M.
[1] 'Klein Aggregates and Conventional Index Numbers', *Econometrica*, 22 (1954), 113–14 (abstract).
[2] 'Separable Utility and Aggregation', *Econometrica*, 27 (1959), 469–81.
[3] 'The Empirical Implications of a Utility Tree: A Further Comment', *Econometrica*, 27 (1959), 489.
[4] 'Additive Logarithmic Preferences: A Further Note', *Review of Economic Studies*, 30 (1963), 56–62.
[5] 'Conditions for Additive Separability', *Econometrica*, 36 (1968), 605–9.
[6] 'The Structure of Utility Functions', *Review of Economic Studies*, 35 (1968), 367–90.
[7] 'Capital Aggregation in Vintage Models', *Value, Capital and Growth: Essays in Honour of Sir John Hicks*, ed. J. N. Wolfe, 1969.
[8] 'Apologia for a Lemma', *Review of Economic Studies*, 38 (1971), 114.

GOSSEN, H.
[1] *Entwicklung der Gesetze des menschlichen Verkehrs, und der daraus fliessenden Regeln für menschliches Handelen*, 1854.

GRAAFF, J. DE V.
[1] 'Income Effects and the Theory of the Firm', *Review of Economic Studies*, 18 (1950–1), 79–86.

GREEN, H. A. J.
[1] *Aggregation in Economic Analysis: An Introductory Survey*, 1964.

HAKANSSON, N. H.
[1] 'Optimal Investment and Consumption Strategies under Risk for a Class of Utility Functions', *Econometrica*, 38 (1970), 587–607.

HALL, R. E.
[1] 'Technical Change and Capital from the Point of View of the Dual', *Review of Economic Studies*, 35 (1968), 35–46.

HICKS, J. R.
[1] *Value and Capital* (2nd ed.), 1946.
[2] *A Revision of Demand Theory*, 1956.
[3] 'The Inter-Relations of Shifts in Demand', *Review of Economic Studies*, 12 (1944), 71–8.
[4] 'A Comment on Mr. Ichimura's Definition', *Review of Economic Studies*, 18 (1950–1), 184–7.
[5] 'Direct and Indirect Additivity', *Econometrica*, 37 (1969), 353–4.

HOUTHAKKER, H. S.
[1] 'Additive Preferences', *Econometrica*, 28 (1960), 244–56.

ICHIMURA, S.
[1] 'A Critical Note on the Definition of Related Goods', *Review of Economic Studies*, 18 (1950–1), 180.

JEVONS, W. S.
[1] *The Theory of Political Economy* (4th ed.), 1924.

JOHANSEN, L.
[1] *Memorandum of University Institute of Economics*, Oslo, 24 March, 1958.

KLEIN, L. R.
[1] 'Macroeconomics and the Theory of Rational Behaviour', *Econometrica*, 14 (1946), 93–108.
[2] 'Remarks on the Theory of Aggregation', *Econometrica*, 14 (1946), 303–12.
KOOPMANS, T. C.
[1] 'Stationary Ordinal Utility and Impatience', *Econometrica*, 28 (1960), 287–309.
KOOPMANS, T. C., P. A. DIAMOND, and R. E. WILLIAMSON
[1] 'Stationary Utility and Time Perspective', *Econometrica*, 32 (1964), 82–100.
LANGE, O.
[1] 'Complementarity and Inter-Relations of Shifts in Demand', *Review of Economic Studies*, 8 (1940), 58–60.
[2] 'The Inter-Relations of Shifts in Demand', *Review of Economic Studies*, 12 (1944), 71–8.
LANCASTER, K.
[1] 'A New Approach to Consumer Theory', *Journal of Political Economy*, 74 (1966), 132–57.
LAU, L. J.
[1] 'Duality and the Structure of Utility Functions', *Journal of Economic Theory*, 1 (1970), 374–96.
LEONTIEF, W. W.
[1] 'A Note on the Interrelation of Subsets of Independent Variables of a Continuous Function with Continuous First Derivatives', *Bulletin of the American Mathematical Society*, 53 (1947), 343–50.
[2] 'Introduction to a Theory of the Internal Structure of Functional Relationships', *Econometrica*, 15 (1947), 361–73.
MAKOWER, H., and W. J. BAUMOL
[1] 'The Analogy Between Producer and Consumer Equilibrium Analysis', *Economica*, 17 (1950), 63–80.
MARSHALL, A.
[1] *Principle of Economics* (8th ed.), 1926.
MORISHIMA, M.
[1] 'Consumer's Behaviour and Liquidity Preference', *Econometrica*, 20 (1952), 223–46. (Reprinted here.)
[2] 'A Note on Definitions of Related Goods', *Review of Economic Studies*, 23 (1955–6), 132–4.
[3] 'The Problem of Intrinsic Complementarity and Separability of Goods', *Metroeconomica*, 11 (1959), 188–202. (Revised here.)
[4] 'Should Dynamic Utility be Cardinal?', *Econometrica*, 33 (1965), 869–71.
MUTH, R. F.
[1] 'Household Production and Consumer Demand Functions', *Econometrica*, 34 (1966), 699–708.
NATAF, A.
[1] 'Sur la Possibilité de la Construction de Certains Macromodèles', *Econometrica*, 16 (1948), 232–44.
[2] 'Possibilités d'Aggrégation de Fonctions de Production à Variables Capital et Main d'Œuvre', *Review of Economic Studies*, 34 (1967), 219–20.

NEGISHI, T.
[1] 'Conditions for Neutral Money', *Review of Economic Studies*, 31 (1964), 147–8.

VON NEUMANN, J., and O. MORGENSTERN
[1] *Theory of Games and Economic Behavior* (2nd ed.), 1947.

OKAMOTO, T., and M. MORISHIMA
[1] 'Shohin-gun no Riron to Kigyo-gun no Riron (Theory of Group of Commodities and Group of Firms)', *Riron Keizaigaku*, 4 (1950).

PARKS, R. W.
[1] 'Systems of Demand Equations: An Empirical Comparison of Alternative Functional Forms', *Econometrica*, 37 (1969), 629–50.

PATINKIN, D.
[1] *Money, Interest and Prices* (2nd ed.), 1965.

PEARCE, I. F.
[1] 'An Exact Method of Consumer Demand Analysis', *Econometrica*, 29 (1961), 499–516.
[2] 'A Method of Consumer Demand Analysis Illustrated', *Economica*, 28 (1961), 371–94.
[3] *A Contribution to Demand Analysis*, 1964.

POKROPP, F.
[1] 'A Note on the Problem of Aggregation', *Review of Economic Studies*, 39 (1972), 221–30.

POLLAK, R. A.
[1] 'Dynamic Utility: A Comment', *Econometrica*, 33 (1965), 872–7.
[2] 'Additive Utility Functions and Linear Engel Curves', Department of Economics, University of Pennsylvania, discussion paper No. 53, June 1967.

POWELL, A.
[1] 'A Complete System of Consumer Demand Equations for the Australian Economy Fitted by Model of Additive Preferences', *Econometrica*, 34 (1966), 661–75.

RAJAOJA, V.
[1] 'A Study in the Theory of Demand Functions and Price Indexes', *Societas Scientarum Fennica: Commentationes Physico-Mathematicae* XXI, Helsinki, 1958.

RAMSAY, F. P.
[1] 'A Mathematical Theory of Saving', *Economic Journal*, 38 (1928), 543–59.

SAMUELSON, P. A.
[1] *Foundations of Economic Analysis*, 1947.
[2] 'Using Full Duality to Show that Simultaneously Additive Direct and Indirect Utilities Implies Unitary Price Elasticity of Demand', *Econometrica*, 33 (1965), 781–96.
[3] 'Corrected Formulation of Direct and Indirect Additivity', *Econometrica*, 37 (1969), 355–9.

SATO, K.
[1] 'On Japan's Household Utility Function and Consumer Demand', *Keizai Kenkyu*, 21 (1970).

SHEPHARD, R. W.
[1] *Cost and Production Functions*, 1953.

SOLOW, R. M.
[1] 'The Production Function and the Theory of Capital', *Review of Economic Studies*, 23 (1955–6), 101–8.

SONO, M.
[1] 'The Effect of Price Changes on the Demand and Supply of Separable Goods', *International Economic Review*, 2 (1961), 239–71.

STIGUM, B. P.
[1] 'On Certain Problems of Aggregation', *International Economic Review*, 8 (1967), 349–67.
[2] 'On a Property of Concave Functions', *Review of Economic Studies*, 35 (1968), 413–16.

STONE, R.
[1] 'Linear Expenditure Systems and Demand Analysis: An Application to the Pattern of British Demand', *Economic Journal*, 64 (1954), 511–27.

STROTZ, R. H.
[1] 'Myopia and Inconsistency in Dynamic Utility Maximisation', *Review of Economic Studies*, 23 (1955–6), 165–80.
[2] 'The Empirical Implications of a Utility Tree', *Econometrica*, 25 (1957), 264–80.
[3] 'The Utility Tree: A Correction and Further Appraisal', *Econometrica*, 27 (1959), 482–9.

TANAKA, O.
[1] 'Noka Keizai Katsudo no Bunseki' (An Analysis of Economic Behaviour of a Farm), *Nogyo-Keizai Kenkyu*, 22 (1951), 1–22.

THEIL, H.
[1] 'The Information Approach to Demand Analysis', *Econometrica*, 33 (1965), 67–87.
[2] *Economics and Information Theory*, 1967.
[3] 'Introduction to Demand and Index Number Theory', mimeograph, 1971.

THOMPSON, E. A.
[1] 'Intertemporal Utility Functions and the Long-Run Consumption Function', *Econometrica*, 35 (1967), 356–61.

VIND, K.
[1] 'Note on "The Structure of Utility Functions"', *Review of Economic Studies*, 38 (1971), 113–16.

WALRAS, L.
[1] *Elements of Pure Economics* (Jaffe translation), 1954.

WHITAKER, J. K.
[1] 'Capital Aggregation and Optimality Conditions', *Review of Economic Studies*, 35 (1968), 429–42.

WOLD, H.
[1] 'A Comment on Gorman's "Klein Aggregates and Conventional Index Numbers"', *Econometrica*, 22 (1954), 114.

YAARI, M.
[1] 'On the Consumer's Lifetime Allocation Process', *International Economic Review*, 5 (1964), 304–18.

YASUI, T.

[1] 'Relation between Homogeneity Postulate and Separability Notion in Slutsky Theory', *Keizai oyobi Keizaigaku no Saishuppatsu* (1944), 189–206.

YOSHIHARA, K.

[1] 'Demand Functions: An Application to the Japanese Expenditure Pattern', *Econometrica*, 37 (1969), 257–74.

PARTS III–V

ARROW, K. J., S. KARLIN, and H. SCARF

[1] *Studies in the Mathematical Theory of Inventory and Production*, 1958.

BARTEN, A. P.

[1] 'Consumer Demand Functions under Conditions of Almost Additive Preferences', *Econometrica*, 32 (1964), 1–38.

BIERWAG, G. O., and M. A. GROVE

[1] 'Slutsky Equations for Assets', *Journal of Political Economy*, 76 (1968), 114–27.

BRUNNER, K.

[1] 'Inconsistency and Indeterminacy in Classical Economics', *Econometrica*, 19 (1951), 152–73.

CHOW, GREGORY C.

[1] *Demand for Automobiles in the United States*, 1957.

CLOWER, R. W.

[1] 'A Reconsideration of the Microfoundations of Monetary Theory', *Western Economic Journal*, 1 (1967), 1–8.

CRAMER, J. S.

[1] 'A Dynamic Approach to the Theory of Consumer Demand', *Review of Economic Studies*, 24 (1957), 73–86.

EDGEWORTH, F. Y.

[1] 'The Mathematical Theory of Banking', *Journal of the Royal Statistical Society*, 51 (1888), 113–27.

FEIGE, E. L., and J. M. PARKIN

[1] 'The Optimal Quantity of Money, Bonds, Commodity Inventories and Capital', *American Economic Review*, 61 (1971).

FRIEDMAN, M.

[1] 'The Quantity Theory of Money—A Restatement', *Studies in the Quantity Theory of Money*, ed. by M. Friedman, 1956.

HARBERGER, A. C. (ed.)

[1] *The Demand for Durable Goods*, 1960.

HICKS, J. R.

[1] *Value and Capital* (2nd ed.), 1946.

[2] *Critical Essays in Monetary Theory*, 1967.

INTRILIGATOR, M. D.

[1] *Mathematical Optimization and Economic Theory*, 1971.

KALMAN, P. J.

[1] 'Theory of Consumer Behaviour When Prices Enter the Utility Function', *Econometrica*, 36 (1968), 497–510.

LANGE, O.
[1] *Price Flexibility and Employment*, 1944.
LESER, C. E. VON
[1] 'The Consumer's Demand for Money', *Econometrica*, 11 (1943), 123–40.
LEWIS, E. E.
[1] 'Intercommodity Relationship in Stable Demand', *Econometrica*, 6 (1938), 130–42.
MARKOWITZ, H. M.
[1] *Portfolio Selection*, 1959.
MARSCHAK, JACOB
[1] 'Rational Behaviour, Uncertain Prospects, and Measurable Utility', *Econometrica*, 18 (1950), 111–41.
[2] 'The Rationale of the Demand for Money and of "Money Illusion"', *Metroeconomica*, 2 (1950), 71–100.
MORISHIMA, M.
[1] *Theory of Economic Growth*, 1969.
[2] 'Consumer's Behaviour and Liquidity Preference', *Econometrica*, 20 (1952), 223–46.
[3] 'Notes on the Theory of Stability of Multiple Exchange', *Review of Economic Studies*, 24 (1957), 203–8.
VON NEUMANN, J., and O. MORGENSTERN
[1] *Theory of Games and Economic Behavior* (2nd ed.), 1947.
PARKIN, J. M., M. R. GRAY, AND R. J. BARRETT
[1] 'The Portfolio Behaviour of Commercial Banks', *The Econometric Study of the United Kingdom*, ed. by Hilton and Heathfield, 1970.
PATINKIN, DON
[1] 'Relative Prices, Say's Law, and the Demand for Money', *Econometrica*, 16 (1948), 135–54.
[2] 'A Reconsideration of the General Equilibrium Theory of Money', *Review of Economic Studies*, 18 (1949–50), 44–61.
PORTER, R. C.
[1] 'A Model of Bank Portfolio Selection', *Financial Markets and Economic Activity*, ed. by D. D. Hester and J. Tobin, 1967.
ROYAMA, S., and K. HAMADA
[1] 'Substitution and Complementarity in the Choice of Risky Assets', *Risk Aversion and Portfolio Choice*, ed. by D. D. Hester and J. Tobin, 1967.
SAMUELSON, P. A.
[1] *Foundations of Economic Analysis*, 1947.
[2] 'Probability, Utility, and the Independence Axiom', *Econometrica*, 20 (1952), 670–8.
SHIBUYA, Y.
[1] 'A Study of Demand Functions for Durable Goods (I)', *The Economic Studies Quarterly*, 18 (1967), 18–26.
SONO, M.
[1] 'The Effect of Price Changes on the Demand and Supply of Separable Goods', *International Economic Review*, 2 (1961), 239–71.

STONE, R., and D. A. ROWE

[1] 'The Market Demand for Durable Goods', *Econometrica*, 25 (1957), 423–43.

[2] 'The Durability of Consumers' Durable Goods', *Econometrica*, 28 (1960), 407–16.

TINTNER, G.

[1] 'The Theoretical Derivation of Dynamic Demand Curves', *Econometrica*, 6 (1938), 375–80.

TOBIN, J.

[1] 'The Interest-Elasticity of Transactions Demand for Cash', *Review of Economics and Statistics*, 38 (1956), 241–7.

YAARI, M.

[1] 'On the Consumer's Lifetime Allocation Process', *International Economic Review*, 5 (1964), 304–18.

YASUI, T.

[1] 'Slutsky-Riron ni okeru Bunri-kano no Shiso to Dojisei no Katei' (Relation between Homogeneity Postulate and Separability Notion in Slutsky Theory), in *Keizai oyobi Keizaigaku no Sai-shuppatsu*, 1944.

Index